AF574036

HOW TO GET A JOB IN DALLAS/FORT WORTH

HOW TO GET A JOB IN DALLAS/FORT WORTH

THE INSIDER'S GUIDE

Thomas M. Camden
Nancy Bishop

SURREY BOOKS
500 N. Michigan Avenue, Suite 1940
Chicago, IL 60611 (312) 661-0050

HOW TO GET A JOB IN DALLAS/FORT WORTH—The Insider's Guide is published by Surrey Books, Inc., 500 N. Michigan Ave., Suite 1940, Chicago, IL 60611, (312) 661-0050.
Copyright © 1987 by Surrey Books, Inc. All rights reserved, including the right to reproduce this book or portions thereof in any form, including any information storage and retrieval system, except for the inclusion of brief quotations in a review.
This book is manufactured in the United States of America.
2nd edition.
1 2 3 4 5
Library of Congress Cataloging in Publication Data:
Camden, Thomas M., 1938–
How to get a job in Dallas, Fort Worth.

Bibliography: p.
1. Job hunting—Texas—Dallas—Dictionaries.
2. Job hunting—Texas—Fort Worth—Dictionaries.
3. Dallas (Tex.)—Industries—Directories. I. Bishop, Nancy, 1949– . II. Title.
HF5382.75.U6C353 1987 650.1'4'097642812 86-30123
ISBN 0-9609516-9-5

AVAILABLE TITLES IN THIS SERIES
How to Get a Job in Chicago © 1986
How to Get a Job in Dallas/Fort Worth © 1987
How to Get a Job in Los Angeles © 1985
How to Get a Job in New York © 1986

Single copies may be ordered directly from Surrey Books at the above address. Send check or money order for $16.95 (includes postage and handling) for each book. For quantity discounts, please contact the publisher.

Design by Joan Sommers Design, Chicago
Cover design by Cynthia Hoffman Design, Chicago

ACKNOWLEDGMENTS

The authors would like to thank the following people for their help:

Barbara Camden and Mitch Lobrovich for their loyal support; executive editor Susan Schwartz; editorial assistants Patricia Dillingham, Julie Pellinger, Wendy Rains, Kathy Dawson, and Jill Cossetti; and copy editors Sara Steinberg and Carla Babrick.

CONTENTS

How to Get the Most from This Book

So you want to get a job in the Dallas/Fort Worth area? Well, you've picked up the right book. Whether you're a recent graduate, new in town, or an old hand at the great Texas Job Search; whether or not you're currently employed; even if you're not fully convinced that you *are* employable—this book is crammed with helpful information.

It contains the combined wisdom of two top professionals: Tom Camden, a personnel professional who currently heads the nationally known consulting firm of Camden and Associates; and Nancy Bishop, a Dallas-based freelancer who specializes in writing about the employment market.

Tom contributes expert advice on both basic and advanced job search techniques, from how to write a resume to suggestions for racking up extra points in an employment interview.

Nancy combines her knowledge of the Dallas/Fort Worth working world with an impressive network of contacts developed while living in Dallas, Fort Worth, Arlington, and other suburban cities. Whether you're looking for a job in the city or the suburbs, her extensive listings will save you hours of research time.

Dozens of other Dallas/Fort Worth insiders have contributed tips, warnings, jokes, and observations in candid, behind-the-scenes interviews. All of which is to say that we have done our level best to pack more useful information between these covers than you'll find anywhere else.

We would love to guarantee that this book is the only resource you will need to find the job of your dreams, but we are not miracle workers. This is a handbook, not a Bible. There's just no getting around the fact that finding work *takes* work. *You* are the only person who can land the job you want.

What we *can* do—and, we certainly hope, have done—is to make the work of job-hunting in Dallas/Fort Worth easier and more enjoyable for you. We have racked our brains, and those of many others, to provide you with the most extensive collection of local resources in print.

To get the most from this book, first browse through the table of contents. Acquaint yourself with each chapter's major features, see what appeals to you, and turn to the sections that interest you the most.

It may not be necessary or useful for you to read this book from cover to cover. If you're currently employed, for example, you can probably skip Chapter 8—What to Do If Money Really Gets Tight. If you have no interest in using a professional employment service, you'll only need to browse through Chapter 6.

There are certain parts of this book, however, that no one should overlook. One of them is Chapter 4—Researching the Dallas/Fort Worth Job Market. Unless you're a professional librarian, we'd bet money that you won't be able to read this chapter without discovering at least a few resources that you never knew existed. We've tried to make it as easy as possible for you to get the inside information that can put you over the top in an employment interview.

Chapter 5 is another Don't Miss—especially our unique listing of organizations that you should know about to develop your network of professional contacts. We strongly suggest that you read Chapter 7, even if you think you already know all about how to handle an interview. And then, of course, there's Chapter 11—listings of the Dallas/Fort Worth area's top 1,300 employers of white-collar workers.

There's another thing you should know about in order to

get the most from this book. Every chapter, even the ones you don't think you need to read, contains at least one helpful hint or insider interview that is set off from the main text. Take some time to browse through them. They contain valuable nuggets of information and many tips that have never before appeared in print.

Keep in mind that no one book can do it all for you. While we've touched on the basic tasks of any job search—self-analysis, developing a resume, researching the job market, figuring out a strategy, generating leads, interviewing, and selecting the right job—we don't have space to go into great detail on each and every one of them. What we *have* done is to supply suggestions for further reading. Smart users of this book will follow those suggestions when they need to know more about a particular subject.

Dallas/Fort Worth in the '80s and '90s

What's the economic outlook for the metropolitan area over the next decade? We would love to be able to look into our crystal ball and tell you exactly what jobs have the most promising future, but it's not that easy.

Area analysts prefer to discuss general job market trends. Being more specific is risky because there are so many changes and unforeseen factors that can affect employment.

Looking at the broad picture, we see that the area follows the rest of the U.S. in the rise of the service industry, says Nic Santangelo, chief of economic analysis for the Southwest Regional office of the U.S. Bureau of Labor Statistics. That's particularly true for health and business services, including those that provide computer, legal, and accounting assistance.

The area continues to attract high-tech firms, although the success of these companies depends on many factors, including foreign competition and government contracts.

Manufacturing continues to decline slightly in Dallas and Fort Worth. Most of the job losses have been in the oil and electronic sectors, Santangelo says.

Construction-related businesses will continue to suffer, he predicts, because of the overbuilding of offices and single-family homes.

Some of the area's strongest industries will continue to do well. "There are new jobs being created in several areas, not the least of which are in insurance, real estate, and the financial industry. These have been Dallas' strong points in the past and will continue to do well in the future," Santangelo says.

The rapid migration of workers and creation of new jobs that occurred from the mid-1970s to the mid-1980s have

Need help finding your way around Dallas/ Fort Worth?

Keep in mind that most Dallas/Fort Worth residents depend on their cars to get around the 1,748-square-mile metropolitan area. And there's a good reason why. Public transportation is available and has improved, but in some areas, especially the suburbs, service is slow and limited.

If you plan to be in the area for several days, your best bet is to rent a car. Automobile rental companies are available in and around the Dallas/Fort Worth International Airport and Love Field.

Dallas has beefed up its DART bus service in recent years. If you're downtown, however, don't think you've been out in the Texas heat too long if a pink bus painted to look like a bunny pulls up. It's one of the Hop-A-Buses that makes frequent runs around major hotels and businesses.

Call (214) 934-DART to find out when and where the bus is scheduled to run, because the timetable varies during weekdays and weekends. You'll have a much easier time catching a bus during peak weekday business hours than on weekends or in the evening. And be sure to allow plenty of time to get from one destination to another.

For Fort Worth-area bus service, call The T, (817) 870-6200, which operates from 6 a.m. to 9:15 p.m. Monday through Saturday and 8 a.m. to 6 p.m. Sunday.

The Link buses provide transportation from D/FW Airport to major hotels from 8 a.m. to 6:25 p.m. Call metro (817) 481-6100 to check on schedules or use one of The Link telephones in the airport's terminals.

Other shuttle services that are available from the airport include The Airport Shuttle (214) 438-7213, Airport Limousine Service (214) 243-7434, and Airport International Limousine Service (214) 458-7433.

Major taxi companies include Taxi Dallas (214) 631-8588, State Taxicab Co. (214) 823-2161, Terminal Cab Co. (214)

350-4445, Republic Taxi (214) 631-5544, Yellow Checker Cab (817) 332-3137, Mid-Cities Taxi (817) 261-7551, Plano Cab Co. (214) 423-4229, Richardson Cab Company (214) 235-3500, American Cab Co. (817) 332-1919, and Yellow Cab (817) 335-3333.■

slowed down, notes Don Johnstone, regional labor market analyst for the Texas Employment Commission. Not as many new jobs will be created in the future as the economy continues to be sluggish, and Dallas/Fort Worth's higher cost of living doesn't make the area as competitive as it once was.

Considering all of the Metroplex's assets, however, Johnstone says he's optimistic about the future for the job market. Growth will continue to be slower but steadier. The Dallas/Fort Worth area should be in much better shape than many major cities in the country, he says.

By not depending too heavily on any one industry, the area won't suffer as greatly during recessions. This fact was proven during the oil decline of the mid-'80s, when Dallas/Fort Worth's unemployment rate remained lower than Houston's and many other major Texas cities.

Johnstone says other factors contribute to a more stable labor market.

"Business leaders are optimistic and encourage growth," he says. "When a company considers relocating here, people work to get the necessary information together. The area is also home for several of the country's largest real estate developers, who help stimulate business activity."

Want to learn more about the area?

Most major chambers of commerce have published material that is especially helpful to newcomers or anyone who wants to be better informed about a community. These brochures and maps are available for free or a nominal charge and provide much of what you want to know about area businesses, city services, transportation, public schools, utilities, and entertainment.

Whenever you have a question that's not answered in one of the publications, ask one of the chamber representatives. The two largest chambers in the area are:

Dallas Chamber of Commerce
1507 Pacific St., 3rd Fl.
Dallas, TX 75201
(214) 954-1480
Anyone moving to Dallas can greatly benefit from the newcomer's packet. It includes free material and maps that can be picked up downtown at the main information desk or mailed for a $5 fee that covers postage and handling. The chamber also assists aspiring business owners by providing a free booklet called "How to Start a Business." Anyone who wants information about the business community should contact the Information Services Department. The chamber publishes many informative booklets that cover everything from the top 100 companies to the high-tech firms in the Dallas/Fort Worth area. This information is sold at the chamber or it can be ordered by mail.

Fort Worth Chamber of Commerce
700 Throckmorton St.
Fort Worth, TX 76102
(817) 336-2491
Ask for the free newcomer's guide, which includes a booklet and map to help you get oriented to Fort Worth. You can pick up this information at the downtown office or request that it be mailed to you free of charge. If you want information about starting a business or have questions about

existing companies, check with the Economic Development Department. The chamber's information department publishes many worthwhile booklets and guides, including the top 100 Tarrant County employers, major manufacturers, and a list of area clubs, organizations, and associations.

The following chambers can provide information about other area cities:

Arlington Chamber of Commerce: Metro (817) 265-1911
Azle Chamber of Commerce: (817) 444-1112
Balch Springs Chamber of Commerce: (214) 557-0988
Cedar Hill Chamber of Commerce: (214) 291-4624
Colleyville Area Chamber of Commerce: (817) 281-7131
Crowley Chamber of Commerce: (817) 297-4211
Dallas Black Chamber of Commerce: (214) 421-5200
Dallas Hispanic Chamber of Commerce: (214) 637-2420
DeSoto Chamber of Commerce: (214) 224-3565
Duncanville Chamber of Commerce: (214) 298-6128
East Dallas Chamber of Commerce: (214) 321-6446
Fort Worth Hispanic Chamber of Commerce: (817) 334-2588
Fort Worth Metropolitan Black Chamber of Commerce: (817) 531-8510
French American Chamber of Commerce: (214) 821-7475
Garland Chamber of Commerce: (214) 272-7551
Grand Prairie Chamber of Commerce: (214) 264-1558
Grapevine Chamber of Commerce: Metro (817) 481-1522

Haltom-Richland Chamber of Commerce: (817) 281-9376
Hurst-Euless-Bedford Chamber of Commerce: (817) 283-1521
Irving Chamber of Commerce: (214) 252-8484
Keller Chamber of Commerce: (817) 431-2169
Lake Worth Area Chamber of Commerce: (817) 237-1071
Lancaster Chamber of Commerce: (214) 227-2579
Mansfield Chamber of Commerce: (817) 477-3331
Mesquite Chamber of Commerce: (214) 285-0211
Metrocrest Chamber of Commerce: (214) 245-0444
North Dallas Chamber of Commerce: (214) 368-6485
Oak Cliff Chamber of Commerce: (214) 948-2233
Plano Chamber of Commerce: (214) 424-7547
Richardson Chamber of Commerce: (214) 235-3593
Saginaw Chamber of Commerce: (817) 232-0500
Seagoville Chamber of Commerce: (214) 287-5184
Southeast Dallas Chamber of Commerce: (214) 381-1803
Southlake Chamber of Commerce: Metro (817) 481-8200
White Settlement Chamber of Commerce: (817) 246-1121■

What if your company transfers you?

Imagine how lost and confused most people feel when their company first transfers them to the Dallas/Fort Worth area. They take a look at the two major cities and dozens of suburbs and wonder: Where's the best place to live? Where should I enroll my kids in school? And what about job prospects for my spouse?

Larry Powers takes the guesswork out of getting settled through services offered by The Relocation Center, which he founded in May 1985. Any newcomer who has been transferred by his or her company is eligible to make an appointment to visit the center, located in the Las Colinas area of Irving.

Primarily, the independent relocation service is used by companies that seek help in transferring employees or new hires to the area. For instance, when the Kimberly-Clark Corporation moved its world headquarters from Neenah, Wis. to Las Colinas, The Relocation Center coordinated weekend group orientation trips and met with individual families to assist with housing and "human needs."

These "human needs" include many questions about where to find certain services and resources. Counselors who meet individually with newcomers provide some leads.

For example, when spouses of transferred employees want to know where to begin looking for a job, they are directed to the career center. They can browse through employment guides and watch a videotape produced by Karli and Associates on how to conduct a successful job hunt.

The Relocation Center also offers more in-depth career counseling. For a $75-per-hour fee, Mary Holdcroft helps individuals develop a job-hunting strategy, set up a network of contacts, and get job leads from recruiters and other sources. About a third of the spouses she sees are men whose wives have been transferred to the area.

Other families want to know more about school districts and day-care facilities. They may want to find out, for example, where their child can continue with a special computer course and also perform in a high school orchestra. For a $75 fee, a survey is done to determine which school districts offer these special programs.

Similar surveys are done for clients seeking day-care centers. Parents pay $50 for a list of day care centers that have been pre-screened.

Newcomers take a tour around the modern center to see real estate company displays of available housing and apartments. They can also drop by a large magazine rack to pick up free publications and newcomers' guides.

Even children get a packet with their own change of address cards, things to do during a move, and coloring book with Dallas/Fort Worth landmarks.

As newcomers leave the center, Powers says he often hears a common remark: "Why didn't I come here first? I sure could have saved a lot of wasted time."

To make an appointment for the free service, call Stacey Dyer at (214) 869-3131. She will schedule a visit to the center located in The Central Tower at Williams Square at 5215 N. O'Connor Blvd., Suite 1750.■

Establishing an Objective: Do You Know What You Want to Do?

One of the most common mistakes job-seekers make is not establishing an *objective* before beginning the job search. Practically everyone wants a job that provides personal satisfaction, growth, good salary and benefits, prestige, and a desirable location. But unless you have a more specific idea of the kind of work you want to do and are qualified to do, the chances are high that your job search will be less than satisfactory.

Many of our readers already have a clear objective in mind. You may want a job as a systems analyst, paralegal, production assistant, sales manager, or any one of the thousands of other occupations at which Texans work. That's all well and good—in fact, *establishing an objective is a necessary first step in any successful job search.*

But anyone who's looking for work, or thinking about

changing jobs or careers, can benefit from a thorough self-appraisal. What follows is a list of highly personal questions designed to provide you with insights you may never have considered, and to help you answer the Big Question, "What do I want to do?"

To get the most from this exercise, write out your answers. This will take some time, but it will help to ensure that you give each question careful thought. The more effort you put into this exercise, the better prepared you'll be to answer the tough questions that are bound to come up in any job interview. The exercise also will serve as the foundation for constructing a decent resume—a subject we'll discuss in more detail in the next chapter.

When you've completed the exercise, consider sharing your answers with a trusted friend or relative. Self-analysis is a difficult task. Although we think we know ourselves, we seldom have the objectivity to see ourselves clearly, to outline our personal and professional strengths and weaknesses, to evaluate our needs, and to set realistic objectives. Someone who knows you well can help.

Questions About Me

1. Taking as much time as necessary—and understanding the purpose of this appraisal—honestly describe the kind of person you are. Here are some questions to get you started. Are you outgoing or are you more of a loner? How well disciplined are you? Are you quick-tempered? Easygoing? Are you a leader or a follower? Do you tend to take a conventional, practical approach to problems? Or are you more imaginative and experimental? How sensitive are you to others?
2. Describe the kind of person others think you are.
3. What do you want to accomplish with your life?
4. What role does your job play in that goal?
5. What impact do you have on other people?
6. What are your accomplishments to date? Are you satisfied with them?
7. What role does money play in your standard of values?
8. Is your career the center of your life or just a part of it? Which should it be?
9. What are your main interests?
10. What do you enjoy most?
11. What displeases you most?

Insider's tips

Many of the same job-hunting principles apply no matter if you're looking for a job in Dallas/Fort Worth, Los Angeles or New York.

But to really stand out in the local job market, here are some tips from career counselors. These will be especially helpful as you begin your job marketing campaign, particularly if you're a newcomer.

Don Delaney, Career Connection: "People here are more willing to offer assistance, which helps in networking and obtaining information for the job search. More people will answer questions by telephone here than in any city I've ever visited.

"It's important to obtain sufficient information to determine whether or not there is a match between you and the employer and whether you share the same values. Talk to people who do business with the employer to find out more about him or her."

Peggy Davis, Personal Resources Group: "While people here are friendly and outgoing, that can be misleading to people from other places. They think we are not as serious or business-minded. That's not the case. Just as in any other place, a person should go into a job interview and get down to the business at hand of clearly discussing what skills he or she has to offer.

"A lot of people fail to remember there are many small businesses here. Eighty percent of the businesses have fewer than 20 people. These are often overlooked because larger businesses are better known."

Taunee Besson, Career Dimensions: "People who come here and want to find work quickly locate the pivotal individuals in their fields. I've known people who have come to Dallas and in an afternoon get the whole place scoped out. Dallas has some well-established networks, and if you can plug into one of the networks, you can piggyback on it and get around to people you need to talk to.

"People who have similar interests

enjoy helping each other out. Look up the local branch of a fraternal organization, sorority, or alumni club, or get involved in church. The fastest way to get plugged in is to get together with people of like minds. Those who are good at networking are going to be more successful."

Dr. Helen Harkness, Career Design Associates: "It helps to project an image of being in charge and having a sense of direction because Dallas sees itself as a positive town. People in the area look for others who share this belief and have an air of confidence and self-assurance."

Dr. Richard Citrin, Career Clinic: "Make sure you're prepared. Be very clear on what skills you have to offer and about your job values, and what you are looking for in the job market.

"You can get a map of the Dallas/Fort Worth area and determine how far you want to work from your home. We're fortunate to live in an area with two major metropolitan cities."

Dr. Herbert Hemmila: "Job-hunting is a full-time occupation. You should personally research the prospective company's background. Otherwise, you may not be prepared for the job interview and will be caught flat-footed."

Robert Boudreaux, Rehabilitation Services Associates: "A lot of people don't know how to shop for a job. They go into a job interview like this is the first date and the next step is marriage. It doesn't work that way. You should recognize when you aren't going to be happy and look for something else. You need to be open to what you can do and realize that the market and job titles change. Consider what you can do to become more marketable."■

Questions About My Job

1. Beginning with your most recent employment and then working back toward school graduation, describe *in detail* each job you had. Include your title, company, responsibilities, salary, achievements and successes, failures, and reason for leaving.
2. How would you change anything in your job history if you could?
3. In your career thus far, what responsibilities have you enjoyed most? Why?
4. What kind of job do you think would be a perfect match for your talents and interests?
5. What responsibilities do you want to avoid?
6. How hard are you really prepared to work?
7. If you want the top job in your field, are you prepared to pay the price?
8. What have your subordinates thought about you as a boss? As a person?
9. What have your superiors thought about you as an employee? As a person?
10. Can your work make you happier? Should it?
11. If you have been fired from any job, what was the reason?
12. How long do you want to work before retirement?

Your answers to these highly personal questions should help you to see more clearly who you are, what you want, what your gifts are, and what you realistically have to offer. They should also reveal what you *don't* want and what you *can't* do. It's important to evaluate any objective you're considering in light of your answers to these questions.

People who are entering the job market for the first time, those who have been working for one company for many years, and those who are considering a career change need more help in determining their objectives. Vocational analysis, also known as career planning or life planning, is much too broad a subject to try to cover here. But we can refer you to some excellent books.

Allen, Jeffrey. *How to Turn an Interview into a Job Offer.* New York: Simon & Schuster, 1983.

Applegath, John. *Working Free: Practical Alternatives to the 9 to 5 Job.* New York: AMACOM, 1984.

Blackledge, Walter L., et al. *The Job You Want—How to Get It.* New York: SW Publishers, 1984.

Bly, Robert W., and Gary Blake. *Dream Jobs: A Selective Guide to Tomorrow's Top Careers.* New York: John Wiley and Sons, 1983.

Bolin, Robert. *Finding a Job in the Eighties.* New York: Fireside Publishers, 1983.

How to Get a Job

Bolles, Richard N. *The Three Boxes Of Life and How to Get Out Of Them.* Berkeley, Calif.: Ten Speed Press, 1983.

Bolles, Richard N. *What Color Is Your Parachute?* Berkeley, Calif.: Ten Speed Press, 1986. The Bible for job-hunters and career-changers, this book is revised every year and is widely regarded as the most useful and creative manual available. Try it! We think you'll like it.

Camden, Thomas M. *Get That Job! How to Succeed in a Job Search.* Hinsdale, Ill.: Camden & Associates, 1981.

Camden, Thomas M. *The Job Hunter's Final Exam.* Chicago: Surrey Books, 1984.

Clawson, James G., et al. *Self Assessment and Career Development.* Englewood Cliffs, N.J.: Prentice-Hall, 1975.

Figler, Howard. *The Complete Job-Search Handbook.* New York: Holt, Rinehart, and Winston, 1980.

Fink, Edward J. *Building a Career in the Business World.* New York: Vantage Press, 1984.

Gates, Anita. *Nine Highest Paying Careers for the Eighties.* New York: Monarch Press, 1984.

Haldane, Bernard. *Career Satisfaction and Success: A Guide to Job Freedom.* New York: AMACOM, 1982.

Hillstrom, J.K. *Steps to Professional Employment—With Special Advice for Liberal Arts Students.* Woodbury, N.Y.: Barron's Educational Series, 1982.

Kisiel, Marie. *Design for Change—A Guide to New Careers.* New York: Franklin Watts, 1982.

Lee, Patricia. *The Complete Guide to Job Sharing.* New York: Walker, 1983.

Mazzei, George. *Moving Up: Digging In, Taking Charge, Playing the Power Game and Learning to Like It.* New York: Poseidon Press, 1984.

Miller, Arthur F. and Ralph T. Mattson. *The TRUTH About You: Discover What You Should Be Doing With Your Life.* Old Tappan, N.J.: Fleming H. Revell Co., 1977.

Scheele, Adele. *Making College Pay Off.* New York: Ballantine, 1983.

Wood, Orrin G. *Your Hidden Assets—The Key to Getting Executive Jobs.* Homewood, Ill.: Dow Jones-Irwin, 1984. Written by the co-founder of a job-changing workshop developed for Harvard Business School alumni; an upscale book.

For those of you involved in a **mid-life career change,** here are some books that might prove helpful:

Hecklinger, Fred J., and Bernadette M. Curtin. *Training for Life: A Practical Guide to Career and Life Planning.* Kendall-Hunt, 1984.

Matthews, Kathy. *On Your Own: 99 Alternatives to a 9-to-5 Job.* New York: Vintage Books, 1977.

Robbins, Paula. *Successful Midlife Career Change: Self-understanding and Strategies for Action.* New York: AMACOM, 1980.

For workers who are **nearing retirement age** or have already reached it, here are some books that might be useful:

DeCrow, Roger. *Older Americans: New Uses of Mature Ability.* Washington, D.C.: American Association of Community and Junior Colleges, 1978. Identifies and discusses programs run by community colleges to return older people to the work force through senior employment centers.

Jackson, Beverly. *Young Programs for Older Workers.* New York: Van Nostrand Reinhold, 1980. Describes 69 company personnel policies affecting older workers.

Myers, Albert, and Christopher P. Anderson. *Success Over Sixty.* New York: Summit Books, 1984.

And for **handicapped** job-seekers, this title could prove helpful:

Lewis, Adele and Edith Marks. *Job Hunting for the Disabled.* Woodbury, N.Y.: Barrons, 1983.

For **women** in the work force, these titles will be of interest:

Catalyst Staff. *What to Do With the Rest of Your Life: The Catalyst Career Guide for Women in the '80s.* New York: Simon & Schuster, 1980.

Josefowitz, Natasha. *Paths to Power: A Working Woman's Guide from First Job to Top Executive.* Reading, Mass.: Addison Wesley, 1980.

Morrow, Jodie B., and Myrna Lebov. *Not Just a Secretary: Using the Job to Get Ahead.* New York: Wiley Press, 1984.

Nivens, Beatrice. *The Black Woman's Career Guide.* New York: Anchor Books, 1982.

Senter, Dr. Sylvia, Marguerite Howe, and Dr. Donald Saco. *Women at Work: A Psychologist's Secret to Getting Ahead in Business.* New York: Coward, McCann & Geoghegan, 1982.

Wyse, Lois. *The Six-Figure Woman (and How to Be One).* New York: Linden Press, 1984. How to break into top corporate management.

Professional Vocational Analysis

It would be great if there were some psychological test that would confirm without a doubt who you are and precisely what job, career, or field best suits you. Unfortunately, there isn't. Professionals in vocational planning have literally dozens of tests at their disposal designed to assess personality and aptitude for particular careers.

The test most commonly used is probably the Strong-Campbell Interest Inventory (SCII). This multiple-choice test takes about an hour to administer and is scored by machine. The SCII has been around since 1933. The most recent revision, in 1981, made a serious and generally successful attempt to eliminate sex bias.

The SCII offers information about an individual's interests on three different levels. First, the test provides a general statement about the test-taker's interest patterns. These patterns suggest not only promising occupations but also characteristics of the most compatible work environments and personality traits affecting work. Second, the test reports how interested a person is in a specific work activity compared with other men and women. Finally, the occupational scales compare the test-taker with satisfied workers in some 90 different occupations. If you think you'd enjoy being a librarian, for example, you can compare yourself with other librarians

Tips for women

The motto of the **Women's Center of Tarrant County** is: "Everyone is Employable." No matter what the circumstances, women from all walks of life—from Ph.Ds to those who are uneducated and speak little English—are assisted through the center's comprehensive program.

The first step in preparing a woman for the job-search is often to help raise her self-esteem. "When people feel good about themselves, it's easier to confront the job search," believes Daphne Macke Myles, director of the employment program.

Following individual counseling sessions, participants join the Job Hunt Club. It helps women acquire job-hunting skills that will lead to finding employment in a fairly short time. Anyone participating in the program can use the job bank, which contains an average of 1,000 openings.

Many extra-help features are available, such as the Models and Mentors program, which offers women an opportunity to receive advice from someone in their field. The 50 mentors who volunteer for the program include fast-food managers, attorneys, construction workers, and hairdressers.

Project Second Chance helps battered women and displaced homemakers come to grips with their personal problems in order to get ready for work. The Senior Employment Services help persons over the age of 60 to confront the barriers of age discrimination and find full-time and part-time jobs.

This well-established program is offered to anyone in the area; even out-of-state residents have used it. Thanks to contributions and government contracts, the service continues to be provided free of charge. For more information, call the Women's Center employment hotline at (817) 338-1185.

The center is located at 1203 Lake St., Suite 208 in Fort Worth. Other services for women include:

The Everywoman Program
Richland College
Crockett Hall, First Fl.
12800 Abrams Rd.
Dallas, TX 75243-2199
(214) 238-6034
Special personal and employment counseling provided free of charge to single parents— men and women— earning less than $20,000 per year. Referrals are made to special courses and programs at the community college.

Woman's Center in Richardson
532 Lockwood Dr.
Richardson, TX 75080
(214) 238-9516
Variety of free programs, including Pathways to Achievement, Women-In-Transition, and Befrienders programs. Resource center and informal network help women locate employment. When requested in advance, child care is provided. (For more information, see listing in social service section.)

Women's Center of Dallas
3220 Lemmon Ave., Suite 210
Dallas, TX 75204
(214) 521-9606
Employment Chairperson:
Marilyn Casey
Mainly an advocacy program that sponsors special programs throughout the year on employment-related topics.

YWCA Women's Resource Center
Headquarters
4621 Ross Ave.
Dallas, TX 75204
(214) 827-5600
Employment services available at the YWCA's headquarters at 4621 Ross Ave. and seven branches in Dallas County. Services include individual career counseling, testing, support groups, and quarterly YWCA Breakfast with networking opportunities and guest speakers. Pathways I 12-hour program prepares women for the job search. Pathways II nine-hour program helps women become even more successful once they are employed.■

and see how similar your likes and dislikes are. The occupational scales indicate the degree of probability, confirmed by extensive research, that you'll be satisfied with the choice of a particular occupation.

Personality/vocational tests come in a variety of formats. Many are multiple choice; some require you to finish incomplete sentences; others are autobiographical questionnaires. No single test should ever be used as an absolute. Personality tests are more important for generating discussion and for providing data that can be used in making judgments.

In the Dallas/Fort Worth area, vocational guidance and testing are available from a variety of sources. The most comprehensive service is generally provided by private career counselors and career consultants. Their approaches and specialties vary greatly. Some primarily provide testing while others also offer long-term programs that include counseling, resume-writing, preparing for the job interview, and developing a job marketing campaign. Fees usually range from $50 to several thousand dollars.

It's best to find a professional who specializes in the type of vocational help you need. You don't want to spend hundreds of dollars on a lengthy job search when you only need several counseling sessions and tests. The list at the end of this section gives you some idea of what counselors and consultants offer. Telephone these professionals to find out whether their services fit your needs.

Although the terms are often used synonymously, there is a difference between a career counselor and consultant.

Who's good? Who's not?

It pays to check out any service, says Ron Berry, president of the **Better Business Bureau of Metropolitan Dallas.**

You can call the BBB to ask if any complaints have been filed against the company. If they have, summaries of reports are read over the telephone. Or, you can write and ask someone to mail the information to you.

Berry advises talking to several people who have recently used the service to find out if they were satisfied. "If you don't know someone, ask the company for several references and call them," he suggests.

Be especially wary of employment services that sell lists of job openings, adds Deborah Veryzer, director of the BBB's information services department. When the unemployment rate increases, she sees a rise in the number of companies that exploit out-of-work people by charging up to $350 for photocopied lists of job openings that in many cases were copied from newspaper want-ad sections.

Many of these unscrupulous companies open and close in a matter of months after doing very little to help their clients, she says. That's why it's important to read employment service and vocational guidance service contracts very carefully to make sure you know what you're getting for your money, Veryzer adds.

Once you think you have a good job prospect, call the Better Business Bureau to check on the company. The time to find out about customer complaints or law enforcement action is before you go to work there, not after you have accepted the position.

Here are addresses for the two area BBB offices. It's also a good idea to check with the City of Dallas Action Center or City of Fort Worth Consumer Affairs Department to find out if any complaints have been filed there. You can call, write, or drop by those offices for information.

Better Business Bureau of Metropolitan Dallas
2001 Bryan Tower, Suite 850
Dallas, TX 75201
(214) 220-2000

Better Business Bureau of Tarrant County
709 Sinclair Bldg.
Fort Worth, TX 76102
(817) 332-7585

Action Center
City of Dallas
1500 Marilla St.
Dallas, TX 75201
(214) 670-4014

Consumer Affairs Office: Housing & Human Services Dept.
City of Fort Worth
Public Health Center
1800 University Dr.
Fort Worth, TX 76107
(817) 870-7570■

Most professionals use the title *counselor* if they have fulfilled educational and professional requirements determined by the State of Texas to become a Licensed Professional Counselor. In Texas, you can provide career counseling and testing without a license. Professionals who aren't licensed often call themselves career consultants. This field attracts people from a wide variety of backgrounds, education, and levels of competency. That's why it's important to talk to people who have used the service you are considering, and check with the Better Business Bureau to make sure you are getting the best possible help.

Because career counseling and consulting firms are private, for-profit businesses with high overhead costs, they usually charge more for testing than local community colleges or social service agencies. A fuller discussion of services offered by career consultants is provided in Chapter 6. Also in Chapter 6 is a list of social service agencies, some of which offer vocational testing.

Career Counselors and Consultants Offering Vocational Testing and Guidance

A Comprehensive Audit
8080 N. Central Expwy., Suite 286
Dallas, TX 75206
(214) 891-8153
Contact: Dr. Gary Holmgren
Clients take detailed test and receive comprehensive report on intellectual capabilities, interpersonal characteristics, and careers that are likely to "fit" and be most satisfying. Also receive advice on how to develop strengths and avoid problem areas. Fee: $950 for executive vocational testing, $650 for students, and $50 for mini-audit.

Aptitude Inventory Measurement Service
2506 McKinney Ave.
Dallas, TX 75201
(214) 741-2430
Non-profit research organization offering battery of tests to determine what career will be most satisfying according to aptitude. Works with all age groups, including high school and college students, to help determine long-term career goals. Fee: $450 for three, half-day sessions that include counseling and evaluation.

Awareness, Inc.
9441 LBJ Frwy., Suite 620
Dallas, TX 75243
(214) 690-0626
Contact: Dr. Alan Griffin
Administers tests to evaluate personality, interests, and skills. Comprehensive report discussed during consultation. Fee: $265.

Dr. Douglas Bellamy
13601 Preston Rd., Suite 614W
Dallas, TX 75240
(214) 458-1263
Individualized program that includes testing to assess work values, interests, and personality. Work alternatives explored during counseling sessions. Also provides job-search strategies and resume-writing. Fee: $80 an hour.

Career Clinic
2516 Oakland Blvd., Suite 6
Fort Worth, TX 76103
(817) 535-1555
Contact: Dr. Richard Citrin or Christine Combs
Counselors use testing, skill assessment, and job values to determine type of work that will be most enjoyable. Marketing plan developed for the job hunt. Counselors available afterwards for consultations. Fee: Varies.

Career Connection
5956 Sherry Ln., Suite 1000
Dallas, TX 75225
(214) 692-1525
Contact: Don Delaney
Assists individuals in finding career niche and making successful employment connection through resume preparation, career/psychological testing and evaluation, individual workshops, and job-hunt skills training. Fee: Varies.

Career Consultations
620 Haggard St., Suite 608
Plano, TX 75074
(214) 578-1859
Contact: Ruth Glover or Carol Kepner
Comprehensive career service offering counseling, testing, interviewing tips with videotaping, resume writing and practical information about the job market. Clients learn how to focus skills into effective marketing campaign. Special help provided for relocation assistance, spouse re-employment, and career-changers. Also works directly with companies in outplacement and conducting special career development seminars. Fee: Varies.

Career Design Associates, Inc.
2818 Country Club Rd.
Garland, TX 75043
(214) 278-4701
Contact: Dr. Helen Harkness
Comprehensive program that lasts six months to a year. Begins with assessing career profile and targets areas of special needs. Provides special help for career-changers and those whose careers have reached a plateau. Fee: Ranges from $1,000 to $4,000.

Career Dimensions
11520 N. Central Expwy., Suite 229
Dallas, TX 75243
(214) 349-0573
Contact: Taunee Besson or Sue Ann Hoster
Full-service career and life-planning program that includes a self-directed job search with emphasis on self-assessment, resume-writing, job-interviewing, researching job market, and salary negotiation. Offers special help to newcomers, women returning to work force, career-changers, and spouse re-employment through the Catalyst Career Network. Publishes free Dimensions Associates newsletter. Fee: $30 for exploratory session, $75 per hour for counseling, and $485 for 20-hour program.

C.L. Carter Jr. & Associates, Inc.
811 S. Central Expwy., Suite 434
Richardson, TX 75080
(214) 234-3296
Program includes evaluation, assessment, and guidance. Fee: $75 an hour.

Center for Counseling & Developmental Services, Inc.
7525 John C. White Rd.
Fort Worth, TX 76112
Metro (817) 429-5050
Combines aptitude with vocational testing. Surveys area employment opportunities. Fee: Average cost is $150 and can vary according to needs.

College & Career Counseling
5646 Milton St.
411 Meadows Bldg.
Dallas, TX 75206
(214) 361-0554
Contact: Dr. Cliff Jones or Dr. Peggy Ladenberger
Primarily a testing service. Fee: $400 for full battery of tests, preliminary conference, and follow-up discussion.

Creative Career Counseling
Richardson, TX
(214) 235-4689
Contact: Joan Youngblood
(Telephone inquiries only)
Customized counseling process that covers many facets of the job search, including self-marketing, negotiation techniques, skill transfers, and initiating job search through an eight-step plan. Special assistance for re-entry employment, career change, midlife assessment, first-job guidance, and redefinition of present employment. Fee: Varies.

Carol Duncan Enterprises, Inc.
North Dallas Bank Tower
12900 Preston Rd., Suite 500
Dallas, TX 75230
(214) 385-1130
Provides individual assessment, explores work opportunities, and offers follow-up support. Newcomers assisted through The Relocation Group. Fee: $50 an hour.

Executive Advancement, Inc.
14900 Landmark Blvd., Suite 400
Dallas, TX 75240
(214) 490-1088
Year-long job search program for senior-level executives earning a minimum of $50,000 annually. Testing and counseling targeted to meet individual needs. Marketing service uncovers job leads.
Fee: Varies.

Future Solutions, Inc.
5501 LBJ Frwy., Suite 500
Dallas, TX 75240
(214) 960-6903
Part of national chain of marketing consulting firms that teaches professionals and managers how to market themselves to companies. Helps clients evaluate skills and job opportunities on a practical level. Has data base with employment information. Group sessions are available. Fee: First visit is free. Costs of other services vary.

A. Phillip Gerard Associates, Inc.
Three NorthPark East, Suite 330
Dallas, TX 75231
(214) 373-9902
Personalized counseling and testing program for the professional that includes assessment of skills and abilities. Helps develop networking and interviewing skills. Consultation for spouses also available. Fee: Varies.

Dr. Steven E. Greer
235 NE Loop 820, Suite 401
Hurst, TX 76053
Metro (817) 589-0788
Works mainly with Texas Rehabilitation referrals, young adults, middle management, and midlife crisis transitions. Fee: $200 for battery of tests, $80 an hour for counseling.

Weldon Hall
12790 Merit Dr., Suite 708
Dallas, TX 75251
(214) 770-4120
Marketing firm for executives earning a minimum of $25,000 a year. Provides testing, training sessions, and arranges interviews. Clients have unlimited contract until job is found. Fee: Varies.

Dr. Herbert Hemmila
1221 Abrams Rd., Suite 107
Dallas, TX 75081
(214) 234-1400
Offers vocational tests and helps clients prepare for job hunt by reviewing resume and preparing for job interview through role-playing. Discusses area job opportunities. Fee: Averages $210 for tests and counseling.

Dr. Diane Holloway
8210 Walnut Hill Ln., Suite 619
Dallas, TX 75231
(214) 750-6030
Job dilemma counseling, career evaluation with vocational testing, and guidance counseling. Fee: Averages $85 per session plus charge for test processing.

Jameson Associates
4099 McEwen, The Centre
Dallas, TX 75244
(214) 386-7755
National organization that assists executives earning a minimum of $30,000 a year who have three years of management experience. Provides testing, resume-writing, and arranges interviews with major U.S. corporations. Fee: Varies.

Johnson O'Connor Research Foundation
4950 N. O'Connor Blvd., Suite 250
Irving, TX 75062
Metro (214) 256-1169
National non-profit educational organization that tests aptitude during three sessions. Interpretation of results helps clients make vocational and educational decisions. Fee: $405.

Karli & Associates
5710 L B J Frwy., Suite 405
Dallas, TX 75240
(214) 788-1950
Comprehensive testing and targeting jobs for executives earning a minimum of $40,000 a year. Fee: $4,000 to $15,000. Seminars conducted using "The Successful Job Hunter" or "You're Hired!: The Nuts and Bolts of Job Hunting" video-based programs with workbooks that were developed by Karli & Associates. Teaches individuals to conduct a self-directed job search. Fee varies for special help programs.

Lake Highlands Counseling Center
7475 Skillman St., Suite 103A
Dallas, TX 75231
(214) 348-4536
Short-term structured counseling and testing primarily for adolescents, young adults, women, and recent college graduates. Deals with career development and personal growth. Fee: $90 per hour. Some sliding scale fees available.

Personal Resources Group
9111 Dusti Dr.
Dallas, TX 75243
(214) 553-9632
Contact: Peggy Davis
Helps individuals in self-assessment and testing to find right job match. Includes counseling, tests, computer scoring, and interpretation. Fee: $175 for career assessment program or $50 per session.

Rehabilitation Services Associates, Inc.
Dallas/Fort Worth Regional Office
4607 Fairmount St.
Dallas, TX 75219
(214) 638-2586 or Metro (817) 261-3098
Contact: Robert Boudreaux or Carol Bennett
Assists the general public in addition to providing special help for disabled individuals who seek vocational rehabilitation. Comprehensive program includes analyzing work history, helping clients brush up on job-hunting skills, preparing resumes, and assisting with the employment search. Fee: $50 an hour.

James C. Warren Associates
North Central Plaza II, Suite 901
12770 Coit Rd.
Dallas, TX 75251
(214) 991-2227
Comprehensive year-long program designed for executives who earn a minimum of $30,000 annually. Consultation and testing prepares candidates for identifying skills, establishing objectives and direction, preparing materials for the job hunt and marketing campaign, and negotiating for the job and benefits. Fee: Minimum of $2,500. Amount determined by special needs.

Yellow Brick Road
3017 Lubbock Ave.
Fort Worth, TX 76109
(817) 926-8691
Career and personal counseling for groups and individuals. Conducts workshops on sharpening job-hunting skills. Fee: $40 to $75 per hour for testing and counseling.

Colleges Offering Vocational Testing and Guidance

Even students don't always realize how much help is available through college and university career and placement centers. And at several area community colleges, non-students can benefit as well.

Several of the Dallas County Community College District campuses have extended services to assist everyone, no matter whether or not they are enrolled. The extent of assistance varies from campus to campus; however, all seven schools offer some services, such as a computerized job bank with listings of employment openings.

Several of the colleges provide counseling and testing for non-students. Fees vary, but the cost is often considerably less than what is charged by professionals in private practice.

Many of the major colleges and universities offer non-credit and credit courses, as well as special lectures and seminars to help individuals prepare for the job hunt and explore

What to expect from a career counselor

What kind of help can you expect from a career counselor that you can't find on your own?

For one thing, counselors offer an objective viewpoint, says Dr. Diane Holloway. You may not be able to discuss everything with family, friends, and especially co-workers if you happen still to be working. A trained professional can serve as a sounding board and offer strategies and information that you can't get elsewhere.

"We can essentially help a person become more resourceful," says the licensed professional career counselor.

Dr. Holloway says she usually spends four sessions with individuals who want to establish a sense of direction for their careers. Here's what sessions cover:

- Exploring problems that have blocked progress, and considering solutions.
- Establishing career objectives and determining strengths and areas to work on.
- Writing a career plan that outlines a strategy to achieve goals.
- Preparing an ongoing, self-directed plan to explore career goals.

"A counselor should help people develop methods and a framework from which to base continual exploration about what they want from a career, even after they are employed," Dr. Holloway says.

All too often people look for "quick fixes" in order to get back to work, she says. In haste, they may not take time to reflect on where their career is going, to make sure they look for a job that will be challenging and satisfying.■

options in the work world. In recent years, schools have also offered more practical courses that are designed to help individuals acquire job skills or brush up on ones they already have.

Current or prospective students should check on what's available to help them plan their courses and future careers. Counselors say that too many students waste time in school taking the wrong subjects because they aren't sure what they want to do with their lives.

Once students graduate, many colleges and universities continue to work with alumni, especially through the placement office, where former students can check on job openings.

It's best to check with each school to find out what's available and who is eligible for assistance. Here's a rundown of the basic services:

Bishop College
3837 Simpson-Stuart Rd.
Dallas, TX 75241
(214) 372-8744
Free counseling, testing, and placement for students and alumni offered by Career Planning and Placement Office. Area companies publicize job openings to recruit current and former students.

Brookhaven Community College
3939 Valley View Ln.
Farmers Branch, TX 75244
(214) 620-4830
Free counseling and testing for students. Computer job bank available to students and non-students in placement office. Credit and non-credit courses and seminars assist individuals in many phases of career education. Special programs for single parents entering non-traditional jobs.

Cedar Valley Community College
3030 N. Dallas Ave.
Lancaster, TX 75134
(214) 372-8280
Free counseling, testing, and job bank for students and non-students. Job listings posted on bulletin board. Human development credit courses assist individuals making career choices.

Eastfield Community College
3737 Motley Dr.
Mesquite, TX 75150
(214) 324-7039
Career and Placement Center offers free counseling, testing, and placement for students. Non-students pay $15 for vocational tests. Job fair scheduled every April along with employment seminars and other special programs.

El Centro Community College
Main and Lamar Streets
Dallas, TX 75202-3604
(214) 746-2415
Free career testing and counseling for students. Non-students pay fees for tests ranging from $5 to $25. Employment openings listed in computer job bank and on the bulletin board in the career center. Numerous references and books available in the Career Resource Center. Human Development courses offered on career planning and exploration.

Mountain View Community College
4849 W. Illinois Ave.
Dallas, TX 75211
(214) 333-8606
Free testing for students and prospective students, $40 for non-students. Counseling and the Career Center's job bank are free and available to everyone.

North Lake Community College
5001 N. MacArthur Blvd.
Irving, TX 75062
(214) 659-5218
Free counseling and testing for students and non-students at Career Planning and Placement Center. Weekly brown-bag luncheons open to the public, especially for women returning to school. Women's Center at (214) 659-5373 provides additional support and information about careers.

Richland Community College
12800 Abrams Rd.
Dallas, TX 75243
(214) 238-6020
Free career counseling and testing for students. Non-students pay $30 per session for counseling and $10 for vocational tests. (Two counseling sessions required when tests are taken.) Computer job bank and employment listings available to everyone. Special help provided in Everywoman Program offered free to men and women who are single parents and earn less than $20,000.

Southern Methodist University
P.O. Box 256
Dallas, TX 75275
(214) 692-2266
Services offered free to students and to alumni during first year after graduation. Other alumni pay $25 charge for six-month counseling and testing service. Computerized self-assessment program prepares person to explore career options. Career Center offers individual and group counseling, referrals to testing center, and information about job openings. MBA placement program prepares graduates for entering the job market.

What's available at community colleges

Adults often have trouble asking for vocational help. Many assume they are supposed to be self-sufficient and that they can steer their careers in the right direction.

But people often hit career snags, and when they do, Richland College Counseling Director Peggy Davis says she's frequently asked, "Is it normal for me to be asking these questions?"

She assures them it is and tells them what Richland College offers the community—meaning non-students as well as students—in the way of assistance.

A community college is one of the few places where individuals can receive professional career counseling for a lower charge. At Richland, fees are $30 per session plus a one-time $10 fee for tests.

In some cases, individuals may not only want career counseling but should consider personal counseling to release "emotional baggage" that weighs them down. This service is provided on a sliding scale basis.

Richland has an Adult Resource Center for anyone who needs vocational help. As the name implies, the center encourages older students—usually those over the age of 25—and anyone from the community to use its services without feeling out of place.

This center is a good place for people to explore their options, says counselor Patsy Shockley. They may end up attending a workshop, enrolling in a course, browsing through the resource library, getting a referral, or using the placement office's computerized job bank. Any such assistance helps clients get pointed in the right direction, she says.

Another specialized service in Richland's Adult Resource Center is the Everywoman Program for displaced homemakers and single parents who earn less than $20,000 a year. Although more women than men have used the program since it started nine years ago, men who have custody of children also seek out the free service.

Through short-term career counseling, seminars, and workshops, these people are helped to get through a difficult period of their lives. Many who sign up for the Everywoman Program are going through such personal anguish that it's difficult for them to identify marketable job skills.

For information about Richland's Community Counseling service, call (214) 238-6020. The phone number for the Everywoman Program is (214) 238-6034.■

Tarrant County Junior College-Northeast Campus
828 Harwood Rd.
Hurst, TX 76053
(817) 656-6661
Free career counseling, testing, and placement for students and former students. Non-students assisted through community college courses.

Tarrant County Junior College-Northwest Campus
4801 Marine Creek Pkwy.
Fort Worth, TX 76179
(817) 232-7788
Counseling and Career Placement Center offers free standard vocational tests and counseling for students and alumni. Also assists in helping locate part-time, seasonal, and full-time work. Special services provided for the handicapped. Students meet with professionals in their field through the Rotary Club Career Counseling Program.

Tarrant County Junior College-South Campus
5301 Campus Dr.
Fort Worth, TX 76119-5998
(817) 534-4861 ext. 347
Counseling and testing offered to students. Job placement service available to students and former students. Non-students assisted through non-credit courses.

Texas Christian University
2800 S. University Dr.
Fort Worth, TX 76129
(817) 921-7860
The Career Planning and Placement Center offers a full range of free testing, counseling and placement services. Special programs include videotaping mock job interviews, career fairs, and summer job fairs as well as more than 40 workshops on all aspects of employment. Assistance in self-assessment and decision-making provided by a computerized program. Job listings for students and alumni are published weekly in The Career Connection bulletin. Subscribers pay a minimal fee for postage.

Texas Wesleyan College
1201 Wesleyan Dr.
P.O. Box 50010
Fort Worth, TX 76105
Metro (817) 429-8224 or (817) 531-4432
Counseling and testing center provides free services to students and alumni. Special help offered to those who are undecided about a major, going through a career change, or want to pursue additional graduate studies. Placement office regularly updates job listings on bulletin board, sponsors job fairs, and sets up interviews with employers for graduating seniors. One-time fee of $10 is charged for setting up a job placement file for seniors.

The University of Texas at Arlington
800 S. Cooper St.
Arlington, TX 76019
(817) 273-3671
Counseling, Testing and Career Placement Office assists students and UTA graduates in many phases of career guidance. Entrance exams for all types of programs administered by department. Older students receive help in re-entering school. Student Employment Service offers counseling and placement for students and their spouses. For $3 fee, UTA graduates receive The Jobs Hotline weekly publication that lists more than 100 job openings in the Dallas/Fort Worth area.

University of Texas at Dallas
2601 Floyd Rd.
Richardson, TX 75080
(214) 690-2943
Office of Career Planning and Placement offers testing, counseling, and placement for students and alumni. Nominal fee charged for registration and vocational tests. Special services include career development library, special seminars, and information about internships. Students and non-students encouraged to bring resumes and attend job fairs during fall and spring semesters.

▶ Thinking of starting your own small business?

Many basic questions about starting your own small company can be answered by the **U.S. Small Business Administration.** Free information will be mailed on a variety of topics, including loan programs, tax preparation, government contracts, and management problems.

Although simple questions can be answered by telephone, you'll learn more by dropping by one of the main offices to meet with staff members or volunteers from SCORE (Service Corps of Retired Executives). You will be matched up with a retired professional in your field who can share information that will help you get started. In addition, members of ACE (Active Corps of Executives), a volunteer group of working professionals, are on hand to offer assistance.

These volunteers conduct free seminars covering major topics of interest to new business owners. Programs are scheduled regularly at the main offices; others are held at community colleges and elsewhere in the community.

The chambers of commerce in Arlington, Plano, and Richardson provide some SBA information. The full range of services are available at the following offices:

Dallas District Office
1100 Commerce St., Room 3C36
Dallas, TX 75242
(214) 767-0605

Fort Worth Office
819 Taylor St.
Fort Worth, TX 76102
(817) 334-3613 ■

3

Writing a Resume That Works

Volumes have been written about how to write a resume. That's because, in our opinion, generations of job-seekers have attached great importance to the creation and perfection of their resumes. Keep in mind that *no one ever secured a job offer on the basis of a resume alone.* The way to land a good position is to succeed in the employment interview. *You have to convince a potential employer that you're the best person for the job. No piece of paper will do that for you.*

The resume also goes by the name of *curriculum vita* ("the course of one's life"), or *vita* ("life") for short. These terms are a little misleading, however. A resume cannot possibly tell the story of your life, especially since, as a rule, it shouldn't be more than two pages long. The French word *resume* means "a summing up." In the American job market, a resume is a concise, written summary of your work experience, education, accomplishments, and personal background – the essentials an employer needs to evaluate your qualifications.

A resume is nothing more or less than a simple marketing tool, a print ad for yourself. It is sometimes useful in generating interviews. But it is most effective when kept in reserve until after you've met an employer in person. Sending a follow-up letter after the interview, along with your resume, reminds the interviewer of that wonderful person he or she met last Thursday.

The Basics of a Good Resume

The resume is nothing for you to agonize over. But since almost every employer will ask you for one at some point in the hiring process, make sure that yours is a good one.

What do we mean by a good resume? First, *be sure it's up to date and comprehensive.* At a minimum it should include your name, address, and phone number; a complete summary of your work experience, and an education profile. (College grads need not include their high school backgrounds.)

In general, your work experience should include the name, location, and dates of employment of every job you've held since leaving school, plus a summary of your responsibilities and, most important, your accomplishments on each job. If you're a recent graduate, or have held several jobs, you can present your experience chronologically. Begin with your present position and work backward to your first job. If you haven't had that many jobs, organize your resume to emphasize the skills you've acquired through experience.

A second rule of resume-writing is to *keep the resume concise.* Most employers don't want to read more than two pages, and one page is preferable. In most cases your resume will be scanned, not read in detail. Describe your experience in short, pithy phrases. Avoid large blocks of copy. Your resume should read more like a chart than a short story.

There are no hard and fast rules on what to include in your resume besides work experience and education. A statement of your objective and a personal section containing date of birth, marital status, and so on are optional. An employer wants to know these things about you, but it's up to you whether to include them in your resume or bring them up during the interview. If you have served in the military, you ought to mention that in your resume. Your salary history and references, however, should not be included in your resume; these should be discussed in person during the interview.

Keep in mind that a resume is a sales tool. Make sure

More than just a resume service

The "extras" that resume preparers offer run the gamut from writing cover letters to providing career counseling. One of the most unique services that we ran across is Eleanor Baldwin's Hour Savers program.

She wasn't in the business for six months before she began providing more than just resumes. "A lot of people simply don't know how to get jobs," she says, so she began offering suggestions based on what she observes about individuals.

As she talks to clients, she asks pointed questions and listens very carefully. She observes their body language, handwriting, and basic demeanor.

"There are really obvious things I look for," she says, "such as people's ability to sit still. I'll ask questions like, 'Do you delegate well or do you want to do a job yourself to make sure it's done right?' I pick up if a person is under stress."

Using a combination of indicators, she assesses a person's work style, aptitude, and what will help make them more marketable. All of this information helps her write the resume and guide her clients in their job search.

Baldwin says she prefers to do resumes for professionals who know what type of position they want. "If they don't know yet whether they want to be a ballerina or a train engineer," she recommends one of the many courses she teaches at area community colleges or one of the Fun/Ed educational classes.

Her courses are as witty and down-to-earth as she is. You get an inkling of this by one of the titles—"Resurrecting Your Dinosaur Degree."

It's important to take a creative approach to job-hunting, Baldwin says, because "even Dallas can be a tough market to crack."■

that it illustrates your unique strengths in a style and format *you* can be comfortable with. Indicate any unusual responsibilities you've been given, or examples of how you've saved the company money or helped it grow. Include any special recognition of your ability. For example, if your salary increased substantially within a year or two, you might state the increase in terms of a percentage.

Third, *keep your resume honest.* Never lie, exaggerate, embellish, or deceive. Tell the truth about your education, accomplishments, and work history. You needn't account for every single work day that elapsed between jobs, however. If you left one position on June 15 and began the next on August 1, you can minimize gaps by simply listing years worked, instead of months.

Fourth, *your resume should have a professional look.* If you type it yourself or have it typed professionally, use a high-quality office typewriter with a plastic ribbon (sometimes called a "carbon" ribbon). Do *not* use a household or office typewriter with a cloth ribbon.

If your budget permits, consider having your resume typeset professionally or typed on a good quality word processor. In either case you have a choice of type faces, such as bold face, italics, and small caps. You can also request that the margins be justified (lined up evenly on the right and left sides, like the margins of a book).

No matter what method you use to prepare your resume, be sure to *proofread* it before sending it to the printer. A misspelled word or typing error reflects badly on you, even if it's not your fault. Read every word out loud, letter for letter and comma for comma. Get a friend to help you.

Do *not* make copies of your resume on a photocopy machine. Have it printed professionally by a top-quality offset printer. The resume you leave behind after an interview or send ahead to obtain an interview may be photocopied several times, and copies of copies can be very hard to read. You should also avoid such gimmicks as using colored paper (unless it's very light cream or light grey), or using a paper size other than 8½ × 11.

Our purpose here is not to tell you how to write the ideal resume (there *is* no such thing), but rather to provide some general guidelines. The following books are full of all the how-to information you'll need to prepare an effective resume, and are available from bookstores or your local library.

Bostwick, Burdette. *Resume Writing.* New York: John Wiley and Sons, 1985.
Corwin, Leonard. *Your Resume: Key to a Better Job.* New York: Arco, 1984.
Foxman, Loretta D. and Walter L. Polsky. *Resumes That Work: How to Sell Yourself On Paper.* New York: John Wiley and Sons, 1984.
Jackson, Tom. *The Perfect Resume.* New York: Anchor/Doubleday, 1981.
Lewis, Adele. *How to Write a Better Resume.* Woodbury, N.Y.: Barron's Educational Series, 1983.

Parker, Yana. *Damn Good Resume Guidelines.* Berkeley: Ten Speed Press, 1983.

Should You Hire Someone Else to Write Your Resume?

In general, if you have reasonable writing skills, it's better to prepare your own resume than to ask someone else to do it. If you write your own job history, you'll be better prepared to talk about it in the interview. "Boiler plate" resumes also tend to look and sound alike.

On the other hand, a professional resume writer can be objective about your background and serve as a sounding board on what you should and shouldn't include. You might also consider a professional if you have trouble writing in the condensed style that a good resume calls for.

Here is a list of Metroplex-area firms that will assist you in preparing your resume. Remember that a listing in this book does not constitute an endorsement. Before engaging a professional writer, ask for a recommendation from someone whose judgment you trust—a personnel director, college placement officer, or a knowledgeable friend. Check with the Better Business Bureau and other consumer advocates listed in Chapter 2 to see if there have been any complaints made about the resume service you are considering.

Professional Resume Preparers

Action Business Services
4600 Greenville Ave., Suite 150
Dallas, TX 75206
(214) 368-7251
Fee: $10 and up per page depending on needs. Also has placement service.

Advision Business Services, Inc.
500 Grapevine Hwy.
Hurst, TX 76054
Metro (817) 498-0600
Fee: $25 to $55 depending on needs.
Contact: Val Waters

American Resume Service
1907 Elm St., Suite 1108
Dallas, TX 75201
(214) 641-0267
Fee: $9 to $395 depending on needs. Includes writing and printing of resumes and cover letters.

BJ's Professional Secretarial Service
1401 W. Pioneer Pkwy.
Arlington, TX 76013
(817) 277-7643
Fee: $17.50 for one page, $7.50 each additional page depending on services required.
Contact: B. J. Tchobanian

Creative Resumes
4099 McEwen St., Suite 120
Dallas, TX 75234
(214) 680-9722
Fee: $45 for consultation and critique of existing resume, $75 for one-page resume, and $200 for two-page resume. Also provides career counseling and job campaign service.
Contact: George Hunter

▶ How to choose a professional

Before engaging a professional to help you write your resume, run through the following checklist of questions.

■ **What will it cost?** Some firms charge a set fee. Others charge by the hour. Though many firms will not quote an exact price until they know the details of your situation, you should obtain minimum and maximum costs before you go ahead.

■ **What does the price include?** Does the fee cover only writing? Or does it include typesetting? Most firms will charge extra for printing.

■ **What happens if you're not satisfied?** Will the writer make changes you request? Will changes or corrections cost extra?

■ **How do this writer's fees and experience stack up against others?** It's wise to shop around before you buy writing services, just as you would when purchasing any other service.■

Effective Resumes
4912 Westlake Dr.
Fort Worth, TX 76132
(817) 292-3307
Fee: Minimum of $8, usually averages $50 for resume composition and printing.
Contact: Lewis Ellis or Jim White

Hour Savers
6440 N. Central Expwy., Suite 100
Dallas, TX 75206
(214) 363-3453 or (214) 349-2992
Fee: $75 for graduating seniors, $95 plus age for everyone under 30, $75 plus age for everyone over 30, which includes resume counseling, preparation, and printing. Also conducts seminars and does corporate outplacement.
Contact: Eleanor Baldwin

Keystone Park/A Better Answer
401 Keystone Park
Dallas, TX 75243
(214) 231-0842
Fee: $12 per page for resume preparation.
Contact: Marilyn Monske

Marshall Career Service, Inc.
6421 Camp Bowie Blvd.
Fort Worth, TX 76116
(817) 737-2645
Fee: $58.95 for typing, editing, and printing 25 copies.
Contact: Dana Marshall

Plaza Resume & Thesis Service
8560 Park Ln., Suite 22
Dallas, TX 75231
(214) 363-6567
Fee: $85 for consultation and writing two-page resume.
Contact: Bettina Kruger

Professional Resume Service
100 N. University Dr.
Fort Worth, TX 76107
(817) 335-4464
Fee: $9 to $190 for basic resume. Includes consultation, composition, and printing.
Contact: Sandra Olshefski

Professional Resume & Writing Service
1106 N. Hwy. 360
Grand Prairie, TX 75050
Metro (817) 647-8568
Fee: Varies from $9 to $250 for resume composition, editing, and printing depending on needs.
Contact: Suzanne Ancy

Resume Specialist of Arlington
4201 W. Green Oaks Blvd.
Arlington, TX 76016
(817) 483-6100
Fee: Typing fees begin at $15. Full service begins at $65 for resume counseling, composition, typing, printing, and marketing.

Resumes International
Richardson, TX 75080
(214) 231-9366
(Telephone inquiries only.)
Fee: Up to $500 for consultations and business writing.
Contact: Mrs. H. D. Johnson

Resumes Plus
1201 W. Airport Frwy.
Euless, TX 76040
(817) 283-2849
Fee: $25 for one-page resume with 25 copies. Also provides cover letters.

Resumes That Win
845 E. Arapaho Rd.
Richardson, TX 75081
(214) 234-2274
Fee: Varies according to needs for composition and printing of resumes and cover letters.

Top O' The Stack
2917 Belt Line Rd.
Garland, TX 75042
(214) 530-3334
Fee: $12 and up for resume preparation and typing.

The Word Factory
4208 College Ave.
Fort Worth, TX 76115
(817) 924-4517
Fee: $10 for one page, $5 for each additional page for resume composition, typing, and printing. Lifetime storage on computer disc.

What NOT to do with Your resume once you have it printed

Do not change your resume except to correct an obvious error. Everyone to whom you show the resume will have some suggestion for improving it: "Why didn't you tell 'em that you had a scholarship?" or "Wouldn't this look better in italics?" The time to consider those kinds of questions is *before* you go to the typesetter. Afterward, the only thing to keep in mind is that there is no such thing as a perfect resume, except typographically.

A second point to remember: Do NOT send out a mass

The power of verbs

Gary J. has been an engineer in Dallas for 20 years. During those years he has changed jobs seven times, enhancing his career with each move. Gary realized early that using powerful active verbs to describe his accomplishments made his resume stand out. Here are some sample verbs that job-seekers in various career areas might use to help build a more effective resume.

Management
Controlled
Headed
Implemented

Methods and Controls
Restructured
Catalogued
Verified
Systematized

Public Relations/ Human Relations
Monitored
Handled
Sponsored
Integrated

Creative
Devised
Effected
Originated
Conceived

Advertising/ Promotion
Generated
Recruited
Tailored
Sparked

Communications
Facilitated
Edited
Consulted
Disseminated

Resourcefulness
Rectified
Pioneered
Achieved

Negotiations
Engineered
Mediated
Proposed
Negotiated ■

mailing. If you send letters to 700 company presidents, you can expect a response of from 1 to 2 percent—and 95 percent of the responses will be negative. The shotgun approach is expensive; it takes time and costs money for postage and printing. You'll get much better results if you are selective about where you send your resume. We'll discuss this at greater length in Chapter 5. The important thing is to concentrate on known hiring authorities in whom you are interested.

This brings us to a third important "don't": Do NOT send your resume without a cover letter. Whether you are answering a want ad or following up an inquiry call or interview, you should always include a letter with your resume. If at all possible, the letter should be addressed to a specific person—the one who's doing the hiring—and not "To Whom It May Concern." A good cover letter, like a good resume, is brief—usually not more than three or four paragraphs. No paragraph should be longer than three or four sentences. If you've already spoken to the contact person by phone, remind him or her of your conversation in the first paragraph. If you and the person to whom you are writing know someone in common, the first paragraph is the place to mention it. You should also include a hard-hitting sentence about why you're well qualified for the job in question.

In the next paragraph or two, you should specify what you could contribute to the company in terms that indicate you've done your homework on the firm and the industry.

Finally, either request an interview or tell the reader that you will follow up with a phone call within a week to arrange a mutually convenient meeting.

Here are some sample resumes and cover letters to help you with your own. The books listed earlier in this chapter will supply many more examples than we have room for here.

SAMPLE/CHRONOLOGICAL RESUME

Stephanie Gardner
715 Woodlawn Avenue
Dallas, TX 75208
(214) 946-0010

BUSINESS EXPERIENCE

1983–
Present LEISURE PRODUCTIONS, INC. Dallas, Texas.

Nationwide renters of party and corporate special events tents.

Director, Market Research: Responsible for developing a feasibility study to determine the potential of a national program for the marketing of LEISURE services. The study, completed ahead of schedule, resulted in a program that doubled LEISURE's sales in two years.

1980–
1983 HOME INN—FT. WORTH Fort Worth, Texas

Flagship hotel for HOME INN in the convention/meeting market. Opened December, 1981.

Sales manager: Formulated the marketing plan prior to opening, which included defining key market areas and implementing the sales program.

—Contacted major corporations and associations throughout the Southwest, which resulted in over $600,000 new business in the first eleven months.

—Supervised three account executives.

1976–
1980 DC HOTELS/RESORTS Dallas, Texas

1979–
1980 Regional Director of Sales—Southwest: Reported to the Vice President of Sales. Responsible for the overall marketing, sales and new business development in the Southwest.

—Maintained liaison with each of the individual properties to plan and coordinate their short-and long-range sales effort.

—Assisted the Vice President of Sales in future marketing plans.

1977–
1979 Sales Manager: Responsible for the development of business with the major corporations and associations in the Southwest.

1976–
1977 Sales Representative: Initial responsibilities involved the development of new business by calling all Texas associations not previously contacted.

EDUCATION

Tulane University, New Orleans, Louisiana

Bachelor of Arts degree, June, 1976

REFERENCES

Furnished upon request.

SAMPLE/SKILLS RESUME

Henry M. Phillips
4652 Melody Lane
Dallas, Texas 75231
(214) 368-7520

OBJECTIVE

Management Assistant

In an Operations Center, in Planning or in Sales and Marketing representing the organization in the introduction and distribution of products/ services to users.

SUMMARY OF BACKGROUND

Self-starter with demonstrated success in planning and directing projects/operations. Innovative—continually looking for better ways to accomplish tasks. Excellent record for "selling" new concepts and introducing plans. Have been exposed to relatively complex plans and operations. Work well under pressure and with short-notice demands to negotiate commitments or analyze and resolve management bottlenecks. Reputation for excellence in interpersonal relationships. Have represented top management in important undertakings (briefings, negotiations, and conferences).

EMPLOYMENT HISTORY

1967–1987 UNITED STATES AIR FORCE

Officer. Enlisted 1967. Commissioned through Navigator Training Program 1969. Navigator 1971–76. Pilot training 1977. Pilot and Squadron Flight Commander 1977–81. Airfield Manager 1981–82. Pilot, Flight Commander, Operations Officer and Executive Officer 1982–83. Operations Staff Officer 1983–present.

Some Details

Planning

Wrote USAF plan to test capability of the U.S. Army computerized air defense missile system. Test provided data for large multinational compact decision makers. Wrote plan to conduct complex training missions. The plan was the first of its kind to permit executive evaluation of realistic aircrew training for all USAF fighter forces west of the Mississippi. Portions of the plan have been adopted for other exercises, and the concept has set the tone for USAF tactical aircrew training. Regularly review plans and plan for USAF commitments.

Innovation

Developed procedure to distribute job responsibilities in an equitable manner. The procedure gave a precise, understandable explanation of each individual's commitment. The efficiency, flexibility, and morale of the organization improved. Submitted study to reduce personnel required for the management of an airport. Over 730 annual man-days were saved. Submitted suggestion to redistribute aircraft assets during unit change of aircraft type. Implementation of idea resulted in more efficient allocation of men and aircraft.

Communication

Experienced in briefing management on complex plans and operations. Successful negotiator—can sense mood of individuals and establish and maintain rapport, creating a climate conducive to productive dialogue. Considerable experience in handling human resources: counseling, training, developing, and evaluating. Excellent record representing top management. Involved in planning and implementing social functions.

Problem Solving

Sent to headquarters to analyze cost estimates and operational requirements and then recommend most desirable option; involved an expenditure of $140,000. Solved a complex air traffic flow bottleneck during a USAF exercise. Drawing on experience in dealing with FAA Air Traffic System, managed to avert many FAA/USAF problems and was credited with doing much to enhance FAA/USAF relations.

EDUCATION

B.S. in Business Management, University of Texas at Dallas, 1981, Cum Laude.

PERSONAL

Married, three children. Excellent health. Born April 18, 1947.

SAMPLE/CHRONOLOGICAL RESUME

Ned S. Schwartz
5741 S. Maple Ave.
Grand Prairie, Texas 75050
(214) 647-8568

OBJECTIVE

Entry-level management work in sales or marketing department which would lead eventually to an executive position.

WORK EXPERIENCE

1986
Summer SALES REPRESENTATIVE, Champion Parts Rebuilders, Ft. Worth, Texas. Responsible for developing and carrying out plan to introduce Dallas/Fort Worth area GM dealers to new diesel fuel pump program. Called on parts managers, explained program and Champion's policies, and followed up with request for order.

June, 1984– August, 1985 RECORDING SUPERVISOR, Recording for the Blind, Dallas. Responsible for scheduling and technical aspects of recording sessions.

WAITER, Costa's Restaurant, Grand Prairie.

GUARD, Kane Security Service, Dallas.

1983 Summer SALES ASSISTANT, Big Four Automotive. Assisted salesmen on local calls to jobbers. Checked stock, picked orders, and helped with record keeping and deliveries.

1982 Summer WAREHOUSE CLERK, Champion Parts Rebuilders, Fort Worth, Texas. Picked and boxed orders.

EDUCATION

B.A., University of Michigan, Ann Arbor, 1987

INTERESTS

Painting and sculpture, movies, bicycling, rock music

SAMPLE/COVER LETTER

3420 Rosedale Ave.
Dallas, Texas 75205
June 26, 1988

Ms. Jacqueline Doe
Wide World Publishing Company
1400 Walnut Hill Lane, Suite 250
Dallas, Texas 75231

Dear Ms. Doe:

As an honors graduate of Galveston College with two years of copy editing and feature writing experience with the Galveston *Weekly Herald*, I am confident that I would make a successful editorial assistant with Wide World.

Besides my strong editorial background, I offer considerable business experience. I have held summer jobs in an insurance company, a law firm, and a data processing company. My familiarity with word processing should prove particularly useful to Wide World now that you're about to become fully automated.

I would like to interview with you as soon as possible and would be happy to check in with your office about an appointment. If you prefer, your office can contact me between the hours of 11 a.m. and 3 p.m. at (214) 935-6886.

Sincerely,

Valerie Jones

SAMPLE/COVER LETTER

2239 Forest Park Boulevard
Fort Worth, TX 76110
March 31, 1988

Advertiser
Box 1826
The Dallas Morning News
Communications Center
Dallas, TX 75265

Dear Employer:

Your advertisement in the March 13 issue of the *Morning News* for an entry-level bookkeeper seems perfect for someone with my background. I am about to graduate from Smith High School in a business preparatory course that includes two semesters of accounting.

As you can see from my resume, my work experience consists mainly of miscellaneous summer employment and part-time jobs while in school. But I hope to offset my lack of experience with hard work, enthusiasm, and a desire to succeed.

My activities with Junior Achievement should give you an idea of my aptitude for business. I would appreciate the opportunity of an interview at your convenience.

Sincerely,

Jim Clark
(817) 555-4414

SAMPLE/COVER LETTER

228 S. Meadowlark Lane
Fort Worth, TX 76116
December 1, 1988

Dear Mike:

Just when everything seemed to be going so well at my job, the company gave us a Christmas present that nobody wanted—management announced that half the department will be laid off before the end of the year. Nobody knows yet just which heads are going to roll. But whether or not my name is on the list, I am definitely back in the job market.

I have already lined up a couple of interviews. But knowing how uncertain job-hunting can be, I can use all the contacts I can get.

You know my record—both from when we worked together at 3-Q and since then. But in case you've forgotten the details, I've enclosed my resume.

I know that you often hear of job openings as you wend your way about Dallas and Fort Worth. I'd certainly appreciate your passing along any leads you think might be worthwhile.

My best to you and Fran for the holidays.

Cordially,

Emily Noir

Seven ways to ruin a cover letter

1. Spell the name of the firm incorrectly.

2. Don't bother to find out the name of the hiring authority. Just send the letter to the president or chairman of the board.

3. If the firm is headed by a woman, be sure to begin your letter, "Dear Sir." Otherwise, just address it, "To Whom It May Concern."

4. Make sure the letter includes a couple of typos and sloppy erasures. Better yet, spill coffee on it first, then mail it.

5. Be sure to provide a phone number that has been disconnected, or one at which nobody is ever home.

6. Tell the firm you'll call to set up an appointment in a few days; then don't bother.

7. Call the firm at least three times the day after you mail the letter. Get very angry when they say they haven't heard of you.■

Researching the Dallas/ Fort Worth Job Market

To a large extent, the success of your job search will depend on how well you do your homework. Once you've figured out what kind of job you want, you need to find out as much as you can about which specific companies might employ you. Your network of personal contacts can be a highly worthwhile source of information about what jobs are available where. But networking can't do it all; at some point, you'll have to do some reading. This chapter fills you in on the directories, newspapers, and magazines you'll need in your search, and notes the libraries where you can find them.

Libraries

Public libraries are an invaluable source of career information—everything from books on resume-writing to Standard and Poor's *Register of Corporations, Directors, and Executives* can usually be found in the business and economics sections.

Save time by checking with reference librarians on what is available and where to find it. These staff members will be especially cooperative if you first ask them when their "slow" periods are. These are the times when they can give you their undivided attention.

Dallas Public Library: The most extensive collection of job-hunting books and reference material can be found in the modern eight-floor downtown library located at 1515 Young St. The 18 branch libraries carry many of the most frequently used guides and directories. Any book that isn't available in one library can be requested through the interlibrary loan system.

At the main library, most of the major business directories, magazines, and books can be found in the business and technology section on the fifth floor. Few signs are posted, so ask at the main desk for directions on where to find what you're looking for and advice on where else to look for information.

Time invested in finding out as much as possible about a company before a job interview can pay off. For example, if you want to find out about a major business's financial outlook, check the annual report. Hundreds of annual reports, including those for most major Dallas companies, are on microfilm.

U.S. Securities and Exchange Commission reports on the sixth floor offer additional information about businesses. You may find even more revealing information than what is contained in annual reports, such as the profitability of different divisions within a company.

The sixth floor also includes many government documents, including U.S. Labor Department employment outlooks. You may wonder, for example, about the future for computer programmers during the next decade. Government publications can offer some predictions.

The first and eighth floors have stacks with general career books, such as *What Color Is Your Parachute?* and other popular guides. Information about government jobs and samples of tests are kept on the eighth floor.

The library regularly schedules free lectures on a variety of topics of interest to job-hunters. Many are part of a brown-bag lecture series that encourages people to bring a sack lunch and find out about everything from changing careers to setting up a business at home. Call (214) 749-4100 to find out the date and time of the next career course.

Inquirers should be encouraged by the success stories—the people who say they landed their jobs thanks to the help they received from the Dallas Public Library, says Gail Tomlinson, the library's public information representative.

She recalls how years ago a man read a trade journal in the library about the popularity of the Belgian waffle stand at the Seattle World's Fair. If it was popular at that event, he wondered, why couldn't it work at the State Fair of Texas in Dallas? He tried it and the stand has been one of the fair's most popular attractions.

Another man dropped in to read books on microcomputers and use the library's computer equipment for patrons. This research and hands-on experience helped him find a job, Tomlinson says.

"Lots of people tell us how helpful the library was in helping them find a job," Tomlinson adds. "For one thing, it's one of the few resources that's free. And that can be a big help to someone who is out of work."

Here's a list of the Dallas branch libraries:

Audelia Road
10045 Audelia Rd.
(214) 348-6160

Casa View
10355 Ferguson Rd.
(214) 328-4113

Dallas West
2332 Singleton Blvd.
(214) 637-1204

Forest Green
9015 Forest Ln.
(214) 231-0991

Fretz Park
6990 Belt Line Rd.
(214) 233-8262

Hampton-Illinois
2210 W. Illinois Ave.
(214) 337-4796

Highland Hills
3624 Simpson Stuart Rd.
(214) 225-7321

Lakewood
6121 Worth St.
(214) 821-5128

Lancaster-Kiest
3039 S. Lancaster Rd.
(214) 371-3446

Martin Luther King Library-Learning Center
2922 Martin Luther King Jr. Blvd.
(214) 421-4171

North Oak Cliff
302 W. 10th St.
(214) 946-8104

Oak Lawn
4100 Cedar Springs Rd.
(214) 528-6269

Park Forest
3421 Forest Ln.
(214) 241-1434

Pleasant Grove
1125 S. Buckner Blvd.
(214) 398-6625

Polk-Wisdom
7151 Library Ln.
(214) 224-5586

Preston Royal
5626 Royal Ln.
(214) 363-5479

Skyline
6006 Everglade Rd.
(214) 381-1149

Walnut Hill
9495 Marsh Ln.
(214) 357-8434

Fort Worth Public Library: The downtown Fort Worth Public Library and nine branches prove to be an invaluable resource for job-hunters. Many library staff members go out of their way to help people who are looking for work.

The largest collection of material can be found in the business and technology section in the lower level of the downtown library at 300 Taylor St. Many of the annual and 10K reports of major corporations, government study guides, and self-help material are available. A list of City of Fort Worth job openings can be found here.

Limited information is provided by calling the business and technology section at (817) 870-7727. You'll gather much more from dropping by one of the libraries.

When you do, be sure to ask for a librarian's help. It's common for people to flounder if they aren't familiar with what's available in the library, says Harold Ard, manager of the business, science, and technology section. That's why he likes to help point people in the right direction, so they can make the best use of the resources.

The main library and several of the branches have Adult Learning Centers that can be very useful to people who want to upgrade skills, prepare for taking the GED exam, or get help when English is their second language. The program, coordinated by the Fort Worth Independent School District, assists adults in getting the extra boost they need to find better jobs.

You can also find job-hunting information at the following Fort Worth branch libraries:

East Berry
4300 E. Berry St.
(817) 536-1945

Meadowbrook
5651 E. Lancaster Ave.
(817) 451-0916

North Side
601 Park St.
(817) 626-8241

Ridglea
3628 Bernie Anderson Ave.
(817) 737-6619

Riverside
2913 Yucca Ave.
(817) 838-6931

Seminary South
501 E. Bolt St.
(817) 926-0215

Shamblee
959 E. Rosedale Ave.
(817) 870-1330

Southwest Regional Library
Library Lane
(To open in 1987)

Wedgwood
3816 Kimberly Ln.
(817) 292-3368

Major **suburban libraries** have many valuable books and references. The main libraries include:

Arlington
101 E. Abram St.
(817) 275-2763

Balch Springs
4301 Pioneer Rd.
(214) 286-8856

Bedford
2000 Forest Ridge Dr.
(817) 283-4651

Burleson
216 SW Johnson Ave.
(817) 295-6131

Carrollton
2001 Jackson Rd.
(214) 323-5014

Cedar Hill
502 Cedar Hill Rd.
(214) 291-4216

DeSoto
300 Lion St.
(214) 223-8406

Duncanville
103 Wheatland Rd.
(214) 298-5400

Euless
201 Ector Dr.
(817) 283-5151

Farmers Branch
13613 Webb Chapel Rd.
(214) 247-3131

Garland
625 Austin St.
(214) 494-7187

Grand Prairie
901 Conover Dr.
(214) 264-1571

Haltom City
3201 Friendly Ln.
(817) 834-7341

Highland Park
4700 Drexel Dr.
(214) 521-4150

Hurst
901 Precinct Line Rd.
(817) 284-5931

Hutchins-Atwell
300 N. Denton St.
(817) 225-4711

Irving
915 N. O'Connor Rd.
(214) 253-2606

Lake Worth
4000 Merrett Rd.
(817) 237-9681

Lancaster
220 W. Main St.
(214) 227-1080

Mansfield
103 W. Broad St.
(817) 473-4391

Mesquite
300 W. Grubb Cir.
(817) 285-6369

North Richland Hills
7301 NE Loop 820
(817) 281-0041

Richardson
900 Civic Center
(214) 952-9700

Richland Hills
3201 Diana Dr.
(817) 284-4991

River Oaks
4900 River Oaks Blvd.
(817) 626-5421

Rowlett
Main St. at Skyline Dr.
(214) 475-3010

Sachse
3033 6th St.
(214) 495-1212

Saginaw
404 Saginaw Blvd.
(817) 232-2100

Seagoville
702 N. Hwy. 175
(214) 287-1022

Sunnyvale
Belt Line Rd. at Town East Blvd.
(214) 226-4491

White Settlement
214 Meadow Park Rd.
(817) 246-4971

Wilmer
205 E. Belt Line Rd.
(214) 225-6620

Directories

When you're beginning your homework, whether you're researching an entire industry or a specific company, there are four major sources of information with which you should become familiar.

Standard and Poor's **Register of Corporations, Directors, and Executives** (Standard and Poor's Publishing Co., 25 Broadway, New York, NY 10004) is billed as the "foremost guide to the business community and the executives who run it." This three-volume directory lists more than 38,000 corporations and 70,000 officers, directors, trustees, and other bigwigs.

Each business is assigned a four-digit number called a Standard Industrial Classification (S.I.C.) number, which tells you what product or service the company provides. Listings are indexed by geographical area and also by S.I.C. number, so that it's easy to find all the companies in Dallas that produce, say, industrial inorganic chemicals. You can also look up a *particular* company to verify its correct address and phone number, its chief officers (that is, the people you might want to contact for an interview), its products and, in many cases, its annual sales and number of employees. If you have an appointment with the president of XYZ Corporation, you can consult Standard and Poor's *Register* to find out where he or she was born and went to college—information that's sure to come in handy in an employment interview. Supplements are published in April, July, and October.

The **Thomas Register of American Manufacturers** and the **Thomas Register Catalog File** (Thomas Publishing Co., One Penn Plaza, New York, NY 10119) are published annually. This 16-volume publication is another gold mine of information. You can look up a particular product or service and find every company that provides it. (Since this is a national publication, you'll have to weed out companies that are not in the Dallas/Fort Worth area, but that's easy.) You can also look up a particular company to find out about branch offices, capital ratings, company officials, names, addresses, phone numbers, and more. The *Thomas Register* even contains five volumes of company catalogs. Before your appointment with XYZ Corporation, you can bone up on its product line using the *Thomas Register.*

Moody's manuals (Moody's Investor Service, 99 Church St., New York, NY 10007) give you the equivalent of an encyclopedia entry on more than 20,000 corporations. This is the resource to use when you want really detailed information on a particular company. Moody's can tell you about a company's history—when it was founded, what name changes it has undergone, and so on. It provides a fairly lengthy description of a company's business and properties, what subsidiaries it owns, and lots of detailed financial information. Like the directories above, Moody's lists officers and directors of companies. It can also tell you the date of the annual meeting and the number of stockholders and employees. Every year Moody's publishes a manual on each of the following: industrial corporations, over-the-counter industrials, transportation, banking (including insurance companies), public utilities, and municipalities. Use Moody's *Complete Corporate Index* to find out which manual your company is in.

▶ **Double-check names and numbers**

Printed directories, even those that are regularly and conscientiously revised, go out of date as soon as someone listed in them gets promoted or changes companies. Always double-check a contact whose name you get from a directory or other printed resource, including this one, to make sure he or she is still in the same job. If necessary, call the company's switchboard to confirm the name and title of the person who heads the division or department you're interested in. You can always tell the operator that you're working on updating the directory where you found the name in the first place.■

The **Million Dollar Directory** (Dun & Bradstreet, Inc., 1211 22nd St., Oak Brook, IL 60521) is a three-volume listing of approximately 120,000 U.S. businesses with a net worth of more than half a million dollars. Listings appear alphabetically, geographically, and by product classification, and include key personnel. Professional and consulting organizations such as hospitals, engineering services, credit agencies, and financial institutions other than banks and trust companies are not generally included.

So much for the Big Four directories. The following list contains dozens of additional directories and guides that may come in handy during your job search.

Accounting Firms and Practitioners
(American Institute of Certified Public Accountants, 1211 Avenue of the Americas, New York, NY 10036.) Covers about 25,000 certified public accounting firms belonging to the institute, as well as member accountants with independent practices.

Advertising Research Foundation Yearbook
(Advertising Research Foundation, 3 E. 54th St., New York, NY 10022.) Lists 375 member advertising agencies, research organizations, trade associations, advertisers, academic institutions, and broadcasting and publishing firms.

Apparel Trades Book
(Dun & Bradstreet, 99 Church St., New York, NY 10007.) Lists apparel retailers and wholesalers.

Associations' Publications in Print
(R.R. Bowker Co., 1180 Avenue of the Americas, New York, NY 10036.) Lists 13,000 associations with acronym cross-references, 82,000 publications, and audio-video materials.

Ayer Directory of Publications
(IMS Press, 426 Pennsylvania Ave., Fort Washington, PA 10036.) Lists national, local, and trade magazines alphabetically and by state.

Bacon's Publicity Checker
(Bacon's Publishing Company, 332 S. Michigan Ave., Chicago, IL 60604.) Covers over 4,800 trade and consumer magazines, 1,700 daily newspapers, and 8,000 weekly newspapers in the United States and Canada.

Billion Dollar Directory: America's Corporate Families
(Dun and Bradstreet, Inc., 99 Church St., New York, NY 10007.) Lists 2,600 U.S. parent companies and their 24,000 domestic subsidiaries. Organized alphabetically by name of parent company.

College Placement Annual
(College Placement Council, 62 Highland Ave., Bethlehem, PA 18017, $10.) Directory of the occupational needs of over 1,200 corporations and government employers. Lists names and titles of recruitment representatives.

Consultants and Consulting Organizations Directory
(Gale Research Co., Book Tower, Detroit, MI 48226, $85.) Contains descriptions of 6,000 firms and individuals involved in consulting; indexed geographically.

Consumer Assistance Directory
(Federal Executive Board, 1100 Commerce St., Room 13E1, Dallas, TX 75242.) Directory of services available to the public from private, federal, state, and local agencies.

Contacts Influential: Dallas
(Contacts Influential of Texas, 1200 Corporate Dr. West, Arlington, TX 76011, annual rental fee varies.) Lists companies alphabetically by name, and includes officers, number of employees, branch or headquarters designation, and SIC number.

Contacts Influential: Fort Worth
Same categories as *Contacts Influential: Dallas.*

DFW Metroplex Commercial Directory with Fact Finder
(GTE Directories Corp., 4300 N. Belt Line Rd., Irving, TX 75062.) Alphabetical list of businesses in four-county area, classified section, restaurants and lodging guide, zip codes, and fact finder.

Using the Dallas Public Library's on-line information service

Let's say you have an interview with the sales director of XYZ Corporation, a company that has the perfect job opportunity. You've done your homework by searching through the directories listed at the beginning of this chapter, you've familiarized yourself with the appropriate trade magazines, and you have an information file with the XYZ Corporation's annual report and product brochures.

You know where the sales director went to college and even what sorority she joined. But you need more up-to-date information on what has happened to the company during the past six months.

One quick way to find out is through the Dallas Public Library's on-line search service available in the information and reference section at (214) 749-4321. All reference questions are funneled through this department in the central library located at 1515 Young St.

The library has access to more than 200 data bases, including DIALOG, Dun & Bradstreet, and Dow Jones. A computer search on XYZ Corporation will go through these data bases and print out a bibliography of recent articles that have been written about that company.

The cost for the service is determined by the number of sources and time involved in doing the search. You tell the librarian the maximum amount of money you can spend on the search. The public isn't charged for the librarian's time, making this offering one of the best values in town■

Dallas Buyer's Guide and Membership Directory
(Dallas Chamber of Commerce, 1507 Pacific Ave., Dallas, TX 75201, $5.) Chamber of Commerce members listed alphabetically and according to products and services.

Dallas County Business Guide
(Executive Services Companies, P.O. Box 2407, Richardson, TX 75080.) Major Dallas-area businesses listed alphabetically and according to business category.

Dallas/Fort Worth Metroplex Handbook for Careers
(Mid-America Handbooks, 9302 W. 87 Terr., Suite C, Overland Park, KS 66212.) Annual reference guide to training, educational opportunities for job market, higher education, and secondary careers.

Dallas/Fort Worth Metropolitan Area Manufacturers
(Dallas Chamber of Commerce, Business Development Group, 1507 Pacific Ave., Dallas, TX 75201, $25.) Manufacturers in a nine-county area indexed alphabetically and according to the SIC number. Includes product description, decision makers, sales dollars, and total employment.

Data Sources: Hardware-Data Communications Directory and **Data Sources: Software Directory**
(Ziff-Davis Publishing Co., New York, NY 10020.) Two-volume guide to most products, companies, services, and personnel in the nationwide computer industry.

Dictionary of Occupational Titles
(U.S. Dept. of Labor, Washington, DC 20210.) Occupational information on job duties and requirements; describes almost every conceivable job.

Directory of Agencies
(National Association of Social Workers, Publications Sales, 1425 H. St., NW, Washington, DC 20005, $5.) Provides information on over 300 U.S. and international voluntary intergovernmental agencies involved in social work.

Directory of Community Resources for Fort Worth and Tarrant County
(United Way of Metropolitan Tarrant County, 210 E. 9th St., Fort Worth, TX 76102, $5.50.) Major social service agencies in Tarrant County listed alphabetically.

Directory of Computer Facilities in the Southwest
(Industrial Economics Research Division, Texas Engineering Experiment Station, Texas A&M University, P.O. Box 83, College Station, TX 77843, $22.50.) Computer facilities listed alphabetically and according to location and equipment.

Directory of Construction Associations
(Metadata, Inc., 441 Lexington Ave., New York, NY 10017.) Lists about 3,000 local, regional, and national professional societies, technical associations, trade groups, manufacturer bureaus, government agencies, labor unions, and other construction information sources. Arranged by topic.

The Directory of Directories
(Gale Research Co., Book Tower, Detroit, MI 48226.) Contains detailed descriptions of all published directories: what they list, who uses them, and who publishes them.

Directory of Foreign-Owned Companies and Organizations in the Dallas/Fort Worth Area
(North Texas Commission, International Marketing Dept., P.O. Box 61246, D/FW Airport, TX 75261.) Foreign-owned companies listed by country.

Directory of High Technology Firms
(Dallas Chamber of Commerce, 1507 Pacific Ave., Dallas, TX 75201, $10.) Listing of high technology firms in the Dallas/Fort Worth area.

Directory of Human Resources in Health, Physical Education and Recreation
(ERIC Clearing House on Teacher Education, 1 DuPont Circle, Suite 616, Washington, DC 20036, $3.50.) Covers information centers in the U.S. and Canada concerned with health, physical education, and recreation. Geographical index.

Directory of Human Services & Resources for the North Texas Area
(Junior League of Wichita Falls.) Alphabetical listing of North Texas employment services, housing, food and nutrition, transportation, health, social, and senior citizens programs.

Directory of Services
(Community Council of Greater Dallas, 2121 Main St., Suite 500, Dallas, TX 75201-4321, $5.) Lists 400 agencies and services for residents of Dallas and Collin counties and the Lewisville Independent School District.

Directory of Texas Manufacturers
(Bureau of Business Research, The University of Texas, P.O. Box 7459, Austin, TX 78712-7459.) Texas manufacturers listed alphabetically and according to SIC number and major product.

Directory of Women-Owned Businesses
(National Association of Women Business Owners, 2000 P St., Suite 511, Washington, DC 20036, free.) Lists women-owned businesses by state; describes products and services.

Electronic News Financial Fact Book and Directory
(Fairchild Publications, Inc., 7 E. 12th St., New York, NY 10003.) Background and financial information about leading companies in the electronics industry.

Employment Opportunities Directory
(Dun's Marketing Services, 1 Penn Plaza, New York, NY 10119.) Designed for those beginning a career; describes job prospects at hundreds of companies.

Encyclopedia of Associations
(Gale Research Co., Book Tower, Detroit, MI 48226.) Lists 14,000 local and national associations, professional clubs, and civic organizations by categories; includes key personnel. Indexed geographically.

Encyclopedia of Business Information Sources
(Gale Research Co., Book Tower, Detroit, MI 48226.) Lists each industry's encyclopedias, handbooks, indexes, almanacs, yearbooks, trade associations, periodicals, directories, computer data bases, research centers, and statistical sources.

Everybody's Business
(Harper & Row, 10 E. 53rd St., New York, NY 10022, available at bookstores for $10.) Candid profiles of 300 American manufacturers of well-known brand name products.

Fairchild's Financial Manual of Retail Stores
(Fairchild Books, Fairchild Publications, Inc., 7 E. 12th St., New York, NY 10003.) Lists 500 publicly held companies in the U.S. and Canada that deal partly or exclusively in retail sales. Arranged alphabetically.

Fairchild's Textile and Apparel Financial Directory
(Fairchild Books, Fairchild Publications, Inc., 7 E. 12th St., New York, NY 10003.) Lists 275 publicly owned textile and apparel corporations. Arranged alphabetically.

Fort Worth Chamber of Commerce Membership Directory & Buyer's Guide
(Fort Worth Chamber of Commerce, 700 Throckmorton St., Fort Worth, TX 76102.) Membership roster, classified listings, and business index.

Fortune Double 500 Directory
(Time, Inc., 1271 Avenue of the Americas, New York, NY 10020.) Lists the 500 largest and the 500 second largest industrial corporations, as well as the 500 largest commercial banks, utilities, life insurance companies, diversified-financial companies, retailers, transportation companies, and diversified service companies. Arranged by annual sales.

Graphics Pages
(Graphics Publishers, Inc., Dallas, TX.) Information about 1,000 graphic, film, and advertising companies in the Dallas/Fort Worth area.

▶ Using the Dallas Public Library's community information data base

You have hundreds of resources at your fingertips through the Dallas Public Library's community information data base called APL/CAT.

Say you want to find out the names of major professional organizations in your field of interest. Go to a computer terminal at any one of the Dallas city libraries and use the on-line information service to find more than 300 listings under this heading. You also will be given cross-reference listings for more sources.

APL/CAT can be especially useful to job-seekers who may want to know about social services or employment agencies, women's programs, day care centers for child care, and organizations that provide food and clothing for the unemployed. Dozens of other major categories are listed in the information service that contains more than 4,000 single entries.

Print-outs of some of the categories are available through the Urban Information Center on the sixth floor of the main library at 1515 Young St. The cost ranges from $10 to $35, depending on the number of listings. Call in advance to order the category you want.

Ask any librarian to help you learn to use APL/CAT. You can call the main reference desk at (214) 749-4321 to ask a librarian for information you need from the data base.

New listings are continuously added to APL/CAT. Most of the data is for the City of Dallas, although some entries are listed for Dallas County suburbs.■

Guide to American Directories
(B. Klein Publications, P.O. Box 8503, Coral Springs, FL 33065.) Lists 1,500 national directories and 500 that are no longer published.

Guide to Dallas-Area Industrial Districts
(Dallas Chamber of Commerce, 1507 Pacific Ave., Dallas, TX 75201, $8.40.) Directory of current and planned districts in a six-county area.

Guide to Special Issues and Indexes of Periodicals
(Special Libraries Association, 235 Park Ave. S., New York, NY 10003.) Alphabetical listing of consumer, trade, and technical periodicals.

Hotel and Motel Management—Buyer's Directory
(Harcourt Brace Jovanovich, Inc., 757 3rd Ave., New York, NY 10017.) Lists about 2,100 companies that supply goods and services to the lodging market; includes separate sections for hotel chains, related associations, manufacturers' representatives, franchise and referral organizations, consulting firms, personnel agencies, publishers, and schools.

The 1986 IMS Directory of Publications
(IMS Press, 426 Pennsylvania Ave., Ft. Washington, PA 19034.) Reference guide of print media published in the U.S., Canada, and Puerto Rico.

International Advertising Association—Membership Directory
(IAA, 475 5th Ave., New York, NY 10017.) Covers 2,700 member advertisers, advertising agencies, media, and other firms involved in advertising. Arranged geographically and by function or service.

International Association for Personnel Women—Membership Roster
(IAPW, 211 E. 43rd St., New York, NY 10017.) Lists 1,500 members-at-large and members of affiliated chapters.

International Television Almanac
(Quigley Publishing Company, Inc., 159 W. 53rd St., New York, NY 10019, $42.) Lists television networks, major program producers, major group station owners, cable television companies, distributors, firms serving the industry, equipment manufacturers, casting agencies, literary agencies, advertising and publicity representatives, and television stations.

Job Openings
(Publication #510K, Consumer Information Center, Dept. G, Pueblo, CO 81009, free.) This 80-page booklet is revised monthly. Formerly called *Occupations in Demand*, it highlights occupations with large numbers of openings and indicates where they are located.

Metroplex Mediaguide
(Bob Lawler Public Relations, P.O. Box 7597, Dallas, TX 75209, $200.) Guide to 11-county newspaper, television, radio, city sources, and seating charts for major public facilities.

National Directory of Newsletters and Reporting Services
(Gale Research Co., Book Tower, Detroit, MI 48226.) Reference guide to national and international information and financial services, association bulletins, and training and educational services.

National Minority Purchasing Council Data Bank—Minority Vendor Information Service
(National Minority Purchasing Council, 1500 Broadway, Suite 3001, New York, NY 10036.) Not a published directory but a computerized data bank with information concerning more than 10,000 minority firms nationwide. Data available by geographical region or by product or service capability.

National Trade and Professional Associations
(Columbia Books, Inc., 734 15th St., N.W., Washington, DC 20005, $30.) Lists all associations and labor unions in the U.S. and Canada; indexed geographically and by key words.

The Newsletter Yearbook/Directory
(The Newsletter Clearing House, 44 W. Market St., Rhinebeck, NY 12572, $35.) Company newsletters indexed alphabetically, including the company address and frequency of publication.

Occupational Outlook Handbook
(U.S. Dept. of Labor, Washington, DC 20210.) Describes in clear language what people do in their jobs, the training and education they need, earnings, working conditions, and employment outlook.

O'Dwyer's Directory of Public Relations Firms
(J.R. O'Dwyer & Co., 271 Madison Ave., New York, NY 10016.) Describes 900 public relations firms in the U.S., their key personnel, local offices, and accounts; indexed geographically.

Open Dallas
(Dallas Public Library, 1515 Young St., Dallas, TX 75201, $11.95.) Collection of community resources in the Dallas County area, including human services, educational opportunities, and community organizations.

Peterson's Annual Guide to Careers and Employment for Engineers, Computer Scientists and Physical Scientists
(Peterson's Guides, Inc., 228 Alexander St., Princeton, NJ 08540, $13.25.) Describes 800 government agencies, technical firms, and manufacturers that hire engineers, computer scientists, and physical scientists.

Reference Book of Corporate Management
(Dun & Bradstreet, Inc., 1211 W. 22nd St., Oak Brook, IL 60521.) National directory of 2,400 companies with at least $20 million in sales; listed by name. Also lists biographies of key personnel and directors, including schools attended and past jobs.

Rotan-Mosle Guide
(Scholl Communications, Inc., P.O. Box 560, Deerfield, IL 60015, $23.50.) Directory of major publicly held corporations and financial institutions headquartered in Texas and Oklahoma.

The Sibbald Guide to the Texas Top Two-Fifty
(The Sibbald Guide, 5725 E. River Rd., Suite 575, Chicago, IL 60631.) Profile of the state's leading public companies and financial institutions.

Standard Directory of Advertising Agencies
(National Register Publishing Co., 5201 Old Orchard Rd., Skokie, IL 60077.) The Red Book of 4,000 advertising agencies and their 60,000 accounts.

Starting & Operating a Business in Texas
(Michael P. Jenkins & Donald L. Sexton, Oasis Press, 1287 Lawrence Station Rd., Sunnyvale, CA 94086.) Guide to deciding whether to go into business, legal information, license requirements, taxes, etc.

Tarrant County Business Guide
(Executive Services Companies, P.O. Box 2407, Richardson, TX 75080.) Lists major businesses alphabetically and according to business category.

Texas Banking Red Book
(Bankers Digest, Inc., 6440 N. Central Expwy., Suite 215, Dallas, TX 75206, $15.75.) Lists banks, federal deposit insurance corporations, holding companies, and other banking institutions.

Texas Trade and Professional Associations
(Bureau of Business Research, The University of Texas at Austin.) Lists trade and professional associations.

Woman's Guide to Career Preparation: Scholarships, Grants and Loans
(Anchor Press, Doubleday Publishing Company, 245 Park Ave., New York, NY 10017, $5.95.) Lists organizations that provide counseling, scholarships, and other assistance to older women and minority women who are returning to work or seeking a career change.

Yearbook of International Organizations
(Union of International Associations and International Chamber of Commerce, 1 rue aux Laines, B-1000, Brussels, Belgium.) Lists 14,000 worldwide organizations indexed by name, address, and description.

Newspapers

Answering want ads is one of several tasks to be done in any job search, and generally among the least productive. According to *Forbes* magazine, only about 10 percent of professional and technical people find their jobs through want ads. Like any other long shot, however, answering want ads sometimes pays off. Be sure to check not only the classified listings but also the larger display ads that appear in the

Sunday business sections of the major papers. These ads are usually for upper-level jobs.

Help-wanted listings generally come in two varieties: open advertisements and blind ads. An open ad is one in which the company identifies itself and lists an address. Your best bet is *not* to send a resume to a company that prints an open ad. Instead, you should try to identify the hiring authority (see Chapter 5) and pull every string you can think of to arrange an interview directly. The personnel department is in business to screen out applicants. Of the several hundred resumes that an open ad in a major newspaper is likely to attract, the personnel department will probably forward only a handful to the people who are actually doing the hiring. It's better for you to go to those people directly than to try to reach them by sending a piece of paper (your resume) to the personnel department.

Blind ads are run by companies that do not identify themselves because they do not want to acknowledge receipt of resumes. This is among the longest of long shots and usually pays off only if your qualifications are exactly suited to the position that's being advertised. Just remember that if you depend solely on ad responses, you're essentially conducting a passive search, waiting for the mail to arrive or the phone to ring. Passive searchers usually are unemployed a long time.

Newspaper business sections are useful not only for their want ads but also as sources of local business news and news about personnel changes. Learn to read between the lines. If an article announces that Big Bucks, Inc. has just acquired a new vice-president, chances are that he or she will be looking for staffers. If the new veep came to Big Bucks from another local company, obviously that company may have at least one vacancy, and possibly several.

Major Newspaper Resources

The Dallas Morning News
Communications Center
Dallas, TX 75265
(214) 977-8222
In one of the few remaining major cities with two viable daily newspapers, *The News* leads in circulation and carries the area's largest Sunday classified section. The first edition hits the newstands at 2 p.m. Saturday. Business news continues to be expanded in scope and depth, especially in the Sunday and "Business Tuesday" sections.

Dallas Times Herald
1101 Pacific Ave.
Dallas, TX 75202
(214) 720-6111
An early edition of the Sunday *Times Herald* with an extensive want-ad section is available at major newstands and convenience stores after noon Saturday. Business news, including Monday's "Dallas Inc." tabloid section, continues to be one of the newspaper's major assets.

Fort Worth Star-Telegram
400 W. 7th St.
Fort Worth, TX 76102
(817) 336-9271
The *Star-Telegram* often competes head-on with the two Dallas newspapers, which accounts for its increase in circulation and quality coverage. A large staff stays on top of business news and pays close attention to what's happening in the Mid-Cities area. The hefty Sunday newspaper contains an extensive want-ad section.

National Business Employment Weekly
Box 300
Princeton, NJ 08540
(212) 285-5000
The *Weekly* is published every Sunday by *The Wall Street Journal*. It includes the want-ad sections of the *Journal's* four regional editions, as well as articles and editorials about the business community.

The Wall Street Journal
1233 Regal Row
Dallas, TX 75247
(214) 631-7250
The nation's leading weekday business publication carries the Southwest edition, which is published locally. Its classified section usually carries ads for mid- to upper-level management positions. The *Journal* only covers news about the business community—everything from the economy to personnel changes in the country's major corporations. If you really want to do your homework on the business community, the *Journal* is the place to start.

Suburban and Community Newspapers

Addison-North Dallas Register
4950 Keller Springs Rd., Suite 160
Addison, TX 75248
(214) 385-3547
Published on Thursday.

An alternative to want ads

JOBSearch offers an alternative to scanning newspaper want ads.

This magazine-style publication lists job openings for professionals who earn at least $20,000 a year.

Co-publisher Michael Shea says, "I'm the type of guy who was always looking for a job when I had a job. I knew there were other people like myself who wanted a job but didn't want to go through the newspaper. There are a lot of people in this area who are trying to better themselves and make more money. We created a magazine that makes it more convenient."

As a result, the magazine isn't strictly targeted toward the unemployed. It's also for people who have jobs and want to find something better.

The bimonthly magazine also includes employment articles geared toward the positive aspects of the local job market. "I don't think people need to hear only the negative aspects. There are plenty of jobs in Dallas. It's a matter of knowing where to look for them and whom to talk to. We're in the business of helping people look and showing them the statistics on the job situation," Shea says.

JOBSearch is available at 7-Eleven stores and major newstands. Future plans call for publishing JOBSearch in other metropolitan areas across the country.■

Addison-North Dallas Today
1712 Belt Line Rd.
Carrollton, TX 75006
(214) 446-0303
Published on Wednesday.

Arlington Citizen-Journal
1111 W. Abram St.
Arlington, TX 76012
(817) 277-4131
Wednesday and Sunday publications inserted in the Arlington edition of the Fort Worth Star-Telegram.

Arlington Daily News
1000 Ave. H East
Arlington, TX 76001
Metro (817) 640-0146
Published every day except Saturday by the Dallas/Fort Worth Suburban Newspapers.

Carrollton Chronicle
1712 Belt Line Rd.
Carrollton, TX 75006
(214) 446-0303
Published Wednesday, Friday, and Sunday.

Cedar Hill Chronicle
109 S. Main St.
Cedar Hill, TX 75104
(214) 291-4223
Published on Thursday.

The Colony Courier
5201 S. Colony Blvd., Suite 695
The Colony, TX 75056
(214) 370-1529
Published on Thursday.

Coppell Gazette
1712 Belt Line Rd.
Carrollton, TX 75006
(214) 446-0303
Published on Wednesday.

Coppell News Weekly
120 S. Denton Tap Rd., Suite 210A
Coppell, TX 75019
(214) 393-1371
Published on Thursday.

Dallas Downtown News
3600 Commerce St., Suite B
Dallas, TX 75226
(214) 826-7661
Published on Monday for the Central Business District, Oak Lawn, Fair Park, North Oak Cliff, East Dallas, and Market Center.

Dallas Post Tribune
2726 S. Beckley Ave.
Dallas, TX 75224
(214) 946-7678
Published on Thursday for the black community.

The Dallas Weekly
3101 Martin Luther King Jr. Blvd.
Dallas, TX 75215
(214) 428-8958
Published on Thursday for the black business and consumer market.

El Sol De Texas
4255 LBJ Frwy., Suite 105
Dallas, TX 75234
Metro (214) 263-3645
Spanish language newspaper published on Tuesday and Friday with news about Dallas, Fort Worth, and Latin countries.

Farmers Branch Times
1712 Belt Line Rd.
Carrollton, TX 75006
(214) 446-0303
Published on Wednesday, Friday, and Sunday.

Fort Worth News-Tribune
212 S. Main St.
Fort Worth, TX 76104
(817) 338-1055
Fort Worth government and business news published on Friday.

Garland Daily News
613 State St.
Garland, TX 75040
(214) 272-6591
Published every day except Saturday by the Dallas/Fort Worth Suburban Newspapers.

Grand Prairie Daily News
1000 Ave. H East
Arlington, TX 76011
Metro (214) 640-0146
Published every day except Saturday by the Dallas/Fort Worth Suburban Newspapers.

Grapevine Sun
332 Main St.
Grapevine, TX 76051
(817) 488-8561
Published Thursday and Sunday.

Irving Daily News
1000 Ave. H East
Arlington, TX 76011
Metro (817) 640 0140
Published every day except Saturday by the Dallas/Fort Worth Suburban Newspapers.

The Journal
3501 MacArthur Blvd., Suite 300
Irving, TX 75062
(214) 257-1055
Published on Monday for Las Colinas and D/FW Airport.

Lancaster News
Towne Square
Lancaster, TX 75146
(214) 227-6033
Published on Thursday.

Lewisville Daily Leader
591 W. Main St.
Lewisville, TX 75067
(214) 436-3566
Published Tuesday through Friday and on Sunday.

Lewisville News
131 W. Main St.
Lewisville, TX 75067
(214) 436-5551
Published Wednesday, Friday, and Sunday.

Mesquite Daily News
303 N. Galloway Ave.
Mesquite, TX 75149
(214) 285-6301
Published Sunday through Wednesday and Friday.

Metrocrest News
1430 Valwood Pkwy., Suite 125
Carrollton, TX 75006
(214) 243-0194
Published on Thursday for Carrollton, Farmers Branch, Addison, and Coppell.

Mid-Cities Daily News
1000 Ave. H East
Arlington, TX 76011
Metro (817) 640-0146
Published every day except Saturday for Hurst, Euless, and Bedford by the Dallas/Fort Worth Suburban Newspapers.

Oak Cliff Tribune
322 W. Jefferson Blvd.
Dallas, TX 75208
(214) 339-3111
Published on Thursday.

Oak Lawn Today
4009 N. Hall St.
Dallas, TX 75219
(214) 528-4954
Published on Thursday.

Park Cities News
6060 N. Central Expwy., Suite 134
Dallas, TX 75206
(214) 369-7570
Published on Thursday for Highland Park and University Park.

Park Cities People
236 Expressway Tower
Dallas, TX 75206
(214) 739-2244
Published on Thursday for Highland Park and University Park.

Plano Daily Star-Courier
1301 19th St.
Plano, TX 75074
(214) 424-6565
Published every day except Saturday.

The Pleasant Grove News
303 N. Galloway St.
Mesquite, TX 75149
(214) 285-6301
Published on Friday.

Richardson Daily News
210 Campbell Rd.
Richardson, TX 75080
(214) 234-1131
Published every day except Saturday by the Dallas/Fort Worth Suburban Newspapers.

Seagoville Suburbia News
115-A Hall Rd.
Seagoville, TX 75159
(214) 287-3277
Published on Wednesday for Balch Springs, Combine, Crandall, and Seagoville.

Suburban Tribune
8017 Lake June Rd., Suite B
Dallas, TX 75217
(214) 398-1456
Published on Friday for the Southeast Dallas area.

The White Rocker News
1350 N. Buckner Blvd.
Dallas, TX 75218
(214) 327-9335
Published on Friday for the White Rock area.

General Business Magazines

The smart job-seeker will want to keep abreast of changing trends in the economy. These periodicals will help you keep up with the national business scene.

Business Week
1221 Avenue of the Americas
New York, NY 10020
(212) 997-1221
Weekly.

Forbes
60 5th Ave.
New York, NY 10011
(212) 620-2200
Bi-weekly.

Fortune
1271 Avenue of the Americas
New York, NY 10020
(212) 586-1212
Published 26 times per year.

Money
Time Life Building
1271 Avenue of the Americas
New York, NY 10020
(212) 586-1212
Monthly.

Newsweek
444 Madison Ave.
New York, NY 10022
(212) 350-4000
Weekly.

Savvy
111 8th Ave.
New York, NY 10011
(212) 255-0990
Monthly.

Time Magazine
1271 Avenue of the Americas
New York, NY 10022
(212) 586-1212
Weekly.

Venture
35 W. 45th St.
New York, NY 10036
(212) 840-8850
Monthly.

Working Woman
342 Madison Ave.
New York, NY 10173
(212) 599-2080
Monthly.

Trade and Special Interest Magazines

Almost every industry or service business has a trade magazine that covers specialized topics not found in general interest publications. You can approach a job interview better prepared by reading up on the latest developments in your field. Also, some magazines carry help-wanted sections and announcements of employee transfers and promotions, indicating potential job openings.

Trade magazines are usually expensive and available by subscription only. Many of the magazines listed below are available in Dallas/Fort Worth area public libraries. For publications not found there, call the magazine's editorial or sales office and ask if you can look at the latest issue.

The following magazines have editorial offices in the Dallas/Fort Worth area. In some industries, knowing about inside news as it happens can make the difference in a job interview. For other listings of the trade press, consult the Ayer *Directory of Publications* and the "Business Publications" volume of *Standard Rate and Data.*

Accessory Merchandising
170 World Trade Center
Dallas, TX 75258
(214) 747-4274
Quarterly furniture accessories publication.

Adweek/Southwest
2909 Cole Ave., Suite 115
Dallas, TX 75204
(214) 871-9550
Weekly advertising and marketing publication.

Bankers Digest
6440 N. Central Expwy., Suite 215
Dallas, TX 75206
(214) 373-4544
Weekly Texas banking publication.

Black Tennis
P.O. Box 210767
Dallas, TX 75211
(214) 339-7370
Bimonthly publication for tennis players and clubs.

Cotton Gin and Oil Mill Press
2626 Valley View Ln., Suite 1
Dallas, TX 75234
(214) 243-3509
Biweekly cotton industry publication.

Drilling-The Wellsite Publication
10300 N. Central Expwy., Suite 580
Dallas, TX 75231
(214) 691-3911
Monthly petroleum industry publication.

Farm Journal
811 S. Central Expwy., Suite 525
Richardson, TX 75080
(214) 231-6033
Regional editorial office for monthly farm industry publication.

Gift Digest
170 World Trade Center
Dallas, TX 75258
(214) 747-4274
Published five times a year for store owners and buyers.

Greenhouse Manager
120 St. Louis Ave.
Fort Worth, TX 76104
(817) 332-8236
Monthly worldwide publication for greenhouse managers.

Impressions
15400 Knoll Trail Dr., Suite 112
Dallas, TX 75248
(214) 239-3060
Monthly publication for the imprinted sportswear and textile screen printing industries.

Industry Trader
2110 Panoramic Cir.
Dallas, TX 75212
Metro (214) 263-3747
Monthly state publication for industrial executives.

The Insurance Record
2730 Stemmons Frwy., Suite 507
Dallas, TX 75207
(214) 630-0687
Biweekly insurance trade publication.

Nursery Manager
120 St. Louis Ave.
Fort Worth, TX 76104
(817) 332-8236
Monthly worldwide publication for nursery industry.

Oil & Gas Journal
4849 Greenville Ave., Suite 318
Dallas, TX 75206
(214) 739-3338
Monthly petroleum industry publication.

Performance
1020 Currie St.
Fort Worth, TX 76107
(817) 338-9444
Weekly international touring talent magazine.

Petroleum Engineer International
10300 N. Central Expwy., Suite 580
Dallas, TX 75231
(214) 691-3911
Monthly petroleum engineers publication.

Pipeline & Gas Journal
10300 N. Central Expwy., Suite 580
Dallas, TX 75231
(214) 691-3911
Monthly petroleum industry publication.

SAF–Society of American Florists
120 St. Louis Ave.
Fort Worth, TX 76104
(817) 332-8236
Monthly florist industry publication.

Southwest Real Estate News
18601 LBJ Frwy.
Dallas, TX 75150
(214) 270-6651
Monthly real estate publication.

Texas Contractor
2510 National Dr.
Garland, TX 75041
(214) 271-2693
Weekly contracting and related industries publication.

Local Feature Magazines and Newspapers

In your job search you'll find it helpful to know as much about the Dallas/Fort Worth area as possible. The following periodicals do not necessarily cover local business news, but they are valuable sources of information about the community. Reading these publications will help you become better informed.

Baptist Standard
2343 Lone Star Dr.
Dallas, TX 75212
(214) 630-4571
Weekly publication for Southern Baptists.

Buddy Magazine
2506 Swiss Ave.
Dallas, TX 75201
(214) 826-8742
Monthly music magazine with a special edition for the Dallas/Fort Worth area that includes entertainment listings.

D Magazine
3988 N. Central Expwy., Suite 1200
Dallas, TX 75204
(214) 827-5000
Monthly magazine that explores trends in area politics, business, education, lifestyle, entertainment, and dining.

Daily Commercial Record
706 Main St.
Dallas, TX 75202
(214) 741-6366
Dallas County legal news published Monday through Friday.

Dallas Cowboys Weekly
Dallas Cowboys Football Club
Cowboys Center
1 Cowboys Pkwy.
Irving, TX 75063
(214) 556-9972
Dallas Cowboys publication distributed weekly during football season and monthly during off-season.

Dallas/Fort Worth Business Journal
12200 Park Central Dr., Suite 470
Dallas, TX 75251
Metro (214) 263-0449
Weekly business publication.

Dallas Magazine
1507 Pacific Ave.
Dallas, TX 75201
(214) 954-1390
Monthly Dallas Chamber of Commerce magazine.

Dallas Observer
2330 Butler St.
Dallas, TX 75235
(214) 637-2072
Weekly entertainment, lifestyles, and current events publication.

Dallas/Fort Worth Home & Garden
2930 Turtle Creek Plaza, Suite 114
Dallas, TX 75219
(214) 522-1320
Monthly magazine featuring area homes, gardens, food, entertaining, arts, and travel.

Dallas/Fort Worth Living
5757 Alpha Rd., Suite 400
Dallas, TX 75240
(214) 239-2399
Bimonthly real estate and entertainment publication.

Fort Worth Magazine
700 Throckmorton St.
Fort Worth, TX 76102
(817) 336-2491
Monthly Fort Worth Chamber of Commerce publication.

The Intowner
2714 W. Kingsley Rd., Suite G5
Garland, TX 75041
(214) 864-1586
Monthly direct mail publications for Garland, Plano, and McKinney.

Key Magazine
3726 N. Hall St., Suite 406
Dallas, TX 75219
(214) 528-5070
Weekly entertainment guide to restaurants, nightclubs, and special events.

Las Colinas Now
5215 N. O'Connor Blvd.
Las Colinas Urban Center
Irving, TX 75261
(214) 556-3750
Monthly magazine reporting on Las Colinas business, lifestyle, and leisure activities.

Living Magazine
5757 Alpha Rd., Suite 400
Dallas, TX 75240
(214) 239-2399
Monthly real estate, entertainment, and lifestyles magazine.

National Christian Reporter
2520 W. Commerce St.
Dallas, TX 75212
(214) 630-6495
Weekly publication for Christian faith.

Texas Business
5757 Alpha Rd., Suite 400
Dallas, TX 75240
(214) 239-4481
Monthly business magazine.

The Texas Catholic Newspaper
3915 Lemmon Ave.
Dallas, TX 75219
(214) 528-8792
Weekly publication with local and international news for Catholics.

Texas Homes Magazine
3988 N. Central Expwy., Suite 1200
Dallas, TX 75204
(214) 827-5000
Monthly magazine featuring homes, entertaining, wine guides, food, and collectibles.

Texas Jewish Post
11333 N. Central Expwy., Suite 213
Dallas, TX 75243
(214) 692-7283
Weekly publication with local and international news for the Jewish faith.

The Texas Woman's News
15790 Dooley Rd., Suite 101
Dallas, TX 75244
(214) 960-NEWS
Monthly magazine with news and features about women.

Travelhost Magazine
6116 N. Central Expwy., Suite 1020
Dallas, TX 75206
(214) 691-1163
Weekly travel magazine with features on real estate, entertainment, and dining available at area hotels.

United Methodist Reporter
2520 W. Commerce St.
Dallas, TX 75212
(214) 630-6495
Weekly publication for Methodists.

▶ Only a phone call away: local job banks

Here's a way to find out about job openings by "letting your fingers do the walking." Just dial any one of the numerous telephone job banks and listen to the taped recordings that describe available positions and how to apply. There is no charge for most of these job hot lines other than what you might spend at a pay telephone or on a long-distance telephone call.

The one exception is the Communicator's Job Bank, a joint service project between the local International Association of Business Communicators and the Public Relations Society of America. Each week, job bank coordinator Cami Hardee updates a 6-minute recording that relays information about openings in public relations, advertising, marketing, design, and related fields. She describes the job, qualifications, and salary range, but no company name is disclosed.

To apply for the openings, you request that your resumes be sent to the job listings of your choice. To register with the job bank, you pay a small charge that covers mailing your resumes to an unlimited number of employers during a three-month period. IABC and PRSA members pay $5 and non-members are charged $10.

The success rate has been outstanding for matching up applicants with positions. An average of 30 jobs are usually on file each week. Ms. Hardee, who volunteers her time for the project, can testify to its benefits. She found her own job through the service.

Area job information lines include:

City of Dallas
(214) 670-5908
City of Fort Worth
(817) 870-7760
Communicators' Job Bank
(214) 744-6056
Dallas County Community College District (214) 746-2438
Dallas Times Herald
(214) 720-6696
Environmental Protection Agency
(214) 767-2994
Federal Job Information Line
(214) 767-8035
Health and Human Services
(214) 767-3528
Southern Methodist University
(214) 692-2157
Tarrant County Junior College
(817) 877-9277
Texas Christian University
(817) 921-7791

Texas Instruments, Inc.
(214) 995-6666
University of Texas at Arlington
Metro (817) 273-3455 ■

Developing a Strategy: The ABC's of Networking

The successful job search doesn't happen by accident. It's the result of careful planning. Before you rush out to set up your first interview, it's important to establish a strategy—that is, to develop a plan for researching the job market and contacting potential employers.

This chapter and Chapter 7 will cover specific techniques and tools that you'll find useful in your search. But before we get to them, a few words are in order about your overall approach.

It's Going to Take Some Time

Looking for a new job is no easy task. It's as difficult and time-consuming for a bright young woman with a brand-new MBA as it is for a fifty-year-old executive with years of front-line experience. Every once in a while someone lucks out. One of Tom's clients established a record at Camden and Associates by finding a new position in four days. But most people should plan on two to six months of full-time job-hunting before they find a position they'll really be happy with.

According to *Forbes* magazine, the older you are and the more you earn, the longer it will take to find what you're looking for—in fact, up to six months for people over 40 earning more than $40,000. People under 40 in the $20,000–$40,000 bracket average two to four months.

Your line of work will also affect the length of your search. Usually, the easier it is to demonstrate tangible, bottom-line results, the faster you can line up a job. Lawyers, public relations people, and advertising executives are harder to place than accountants and salespeople, according to one top personnel specialist.

Be Good to Yourself

Whether or not you're currently employed, it's important to nurture your ego when you're looking for a new job. Rejection rears its ugly head more often in a job search than at most other times, and self-doubt can be deadly.

Make sure you get regular exercise during your job search to relieve stress. You'll sleep better, feel better, and perhaps even lose a few pounds.

Take care of your diet and watch what you drink. Many people who start to feel sorry for themselves tend to overindulge in food or alcohol. Valium and other such drugs are not as helpful as sharing your progress with your family or a couple of close friends.

Beef up your wardrobe so that you look and feel good during your employment interviews. There's no need to buy an expensive new suit, especially if you're on an austerity budget, but a new shirt, blouse, tie, pair of shoes, or hairstyle may be in order.

Maintain a positive outlook. Unemployment is not the end of the world; few people complete a career without losing a job at least once. Keep a sense of humor, too. Every job search has its funny moments. It's OK to joke about your situation and share your sense of humor with your friends and family.

Life goes on despite your job search. Your spouse and kids still need your attention. Try not to take out your anxieties, frustrations, and fears on those close to you. At the very time you need support and affirmation, your friends may prefer to stay at arm's length. You can relieve their embarrassment by being straightforward about your situation and by telling them how they can help you.

Put Yourself on a Schedule

Looking for work is a job in itself. Establish a schedule for your job search and stick to it. If you're unemployed, work at getting a new job full-time—from 8:30 a.m. to 5:30 p.m. five days a week, and from 9 a.m. to noon on Saturdays. During a job search, there is a temptation to use "extra" time for recreation or to catch up on household tasks. Arranging two or three exploratory interviews will prove a lot more useful to you than washing the car or cleaning out the garage. You can do such tasks at night or on Sundays, just as you would if you were working.

Don't take a vacation during your search. Do it after you accept an offer and before you begin a new job. You might be tempted to "sort things out on the beach." But taking a vacation when you're unemployed isn't as restful as it sounds. You'll spend most of your time worrying about what will happen when the trip is over.

Even if you're currently employed, it's important to establish regular hours for your job search. If you're scheduling interviews, try to arrange several for one day so that you don't have to take too much time away from your job. You might also arrange interviews for your lunch hour. You can make phone calls during lunch or on your break time. You'd also be surprised at how many people you can reach before and after regular working hours.

Watch Your Expenses

Spend what you have to spend for such basic needs as food, transportation, and housing. But watch major expenditures that could be delayed or not made at all. The kids will still need new shoes, but a $200 dinner party at a fancy place could just as well be changed to sandwiches and beer at home.

Keep track of all expenses that you incur in your job search, such as telephone and printing bills, postage, newspapers, parking, transportation, tolls, and meals purchased during the course of interviewing. These are all tax deductible.

Networking Is the Key to a Successful Job Search

The basic tasks of a job search are fairly simple. Once you've figured out what kind of work you want to do, you need to know which companies might have such jobs and then make contact with the hiring authority. These tasks are

▶ Tax-deductible job hunting expenses

Remember that many job-hunting expenses are tax deductible, says Bill Barron, a Dallas Certified Public Accountant who owns a company called Your Controller, Inc.

To qualify, you must look for a job in the same trade or business. You can't be compensated for the cost of switching careers. For example, a public school teacher couldn't deduct fees for getting a real estate license and looking for a job in that profession.

Anyone seeking the same type of work is eligible to take off costs for preparing, printing, and mailing resumes; vocational guidance counseling/testing, and the standard government reimbursement for miles driven to and from job interviews. Long-distance and pay phone calls, postage for correspondence with employers, and newspapers purchased to check want ads are also deductible. Even the cost of purchasing this book can be taken off because it assists you in the job search.

If you go out of town to find employment, additional write-offs are allowed for transportation, food, and lodging. An important factor is determining whether the trip was primarily related to seeking new employment or for personal activities. Only when most of the time during the trip was spent in pursuit of a job can travel expenses be deducted. Record the travel and local transportation expenses on the Income Tax Statement of Employee Business Expenses form and itemize the rest of the costs on Schedule A of Form 1040.

Even if you don't find a job after all of this work, you can take the deductions for allowable expenses. Unfortunately, first-time job-hunters aren't eligible for any write-offs.

Barron reminds people that the expenses must be "ordinary and necessary" and must be "reasonable" in amount to fulfill IRS requirements. Keep in mind that tax laws are subject to change, and you should check with your CPA or tax consultant if you have any questions.■

also known as researching the job market and generating leads and interviews. Networking, or developing your personal contacts, is a great technique for finding out about market and industrial trends, and is unsurpassed as a way to generate leads and interviews.

Networking is nothing more than asking the people you already know to help you find out about the job market and meet the people who are actually doing the hiring. Each adult you know has access to at least 300 people you do not know. Of course, a lot of them will not be able to do much in the way of helping you find a job. But if you start with, say, 20 or 30 people, and each of them tells you about three other people who may be able to help you, you've built a network of 60 to 90 contacts.

Mark S. Granovetter, a Harvard sociologist, reported to *Forbes* magazine that "informal contacts" account for almost 75 percent of all successful job searches. Agencies find about 9 percent of new jobs for professional and technical people, and ads yield another 10 percent or so.

How to Start

To begin the networking process, draw up a list of all the possible contacts who can help you gain access to someone who can hire you for the job you want. Naturally, the first sources, the ones at the top of your list, will be people you know personally: friends, colleagues, former clients, relatives, acquaintances, customers, and club and church members. Just about everyone you know, whether or not he or she is employed, can generate contacts for you. Don't forget to talk with your banker, lawyer, insurance agent, dentist, and other people who provide you with services. It is the nature of their business to know a lot of people who might help you in your search. Leave no stone unturned in your search for contacts. Go through your Christmas card list, alumni club list, and any other list you can think of.

On the average, it may take 10 to 15 contacts to generate one formal interview. It may take five or 10 of these formal interviews to generate one solid offer. And it may take five offers before you uncover the exact job situation you've been seeking. You may have to talk to a minimum of 250 people before you get the job you want. The maximum may be several hundred more.

Don't balk at talking to friends, acquaintances, and neighbors about your job search. In reality, you're asking for advice, not charity. Most of the people you'll contact will be willing to help you, if only you tell them *how*.

The Exploratory Interview

If I introduce you to my friend George at a major Dallas bank, he will get together with you as a favor to me. When you have your meeting with him, you will make a presentation about what you've done in your work, and what you want to do, and you will ask for his advice, ideas, and opinions. That is an exploratory interview. As is true of any employment interview, you must make a successful sales presentation to get what you want. You must convince George that you are a winner and that you deserve his help in your search.

▶ You've already got a lot of contacts!

Networking paid off for Liz, a young woman eager to make her way in the banking industry. She told us why she's glad she took the time to talk with her friends and neighbors about her job search. "While walking the dog, I ran into my neighbor, a stockbroker, and told him about my job search," says Liz. "During the conversation, he mentioned a banker friend he thought might be hiring. As it turned out, the friend didn't have a job for me, but he suggested I come in, meet with him, and discuss some other possibilities. He put me in touch with an independent marketing firm servicing the banking industry. The owner of the firm was looking for someone with my exact qualifications. One thing led to another, and pretty soon I had landed the position I wanted."■

The help the interviewer provides is usually in the form of suggestions to meet new people or contact certain companies. I introduced you to George. Following your successful meeting, he introduces you to Tom, Dick, and Mary. Each of them provides additional leads. In this way, you spend most of your time interviewing, not staying at home waiting for the phone to ring or the mail to arrive.

A job doesn't have to be vacant in order for you to have a successful meeting with a hiring authority. If you convince an employer that you would make a good addition to his or her staff, the employer might create a job for you where none existed before. In this way, networking taps the "hidden job market."

To make the most of the networking technique, continually brush up on your interviewing skills (we've provided a refresher course in Chapter 7). Remember, even when you're talking with an old friend, you are still conducting an exploratory interview. Don't treat it as a casual conversation.

Developing Professional Contacts

Friends and acquaintances are the obvious first choice when you're drawing up a list of contacts. But don't forget professional and trade organizations, clubs, and societies—they are valuable sources of contacts, leads, and information. In certain cases, it isn't necessary for you to belong in order to attend a meeting or an annual or monthly lunch, dinner, or cocktail party. Many such groups also publish newsletters, another valuable source of information on the job market and industry trends. Some professional associations offer placement services to members, in which case it may be worth your while to join officially. At the end of this chapter, we've provided a list of selected organizations that might prove useful for networking purposes.

▶ Executive networking

The higher your rung on the corporate ladder, the greater the chances that networking with executives outside your own field will pay off. If you're looking for a top spot in electronics, don't pass up a chance to discuss your credentials and employment needs with the recruiting executive of an advertising firm. He or she just might have the hidden connection that could land you a great job.

One hiring exec from a large corporation reports: "I network with recruiters from more industries than most people would think, both industries that are related to ours and those that are not. It helps to find out what talent is available. If one of my contacts has someone in a file he doesn't need and I do, he's happy to tell me about that person. And I work the same way."■

Keeping Yourself Organized

The most difficult part of any job search is getting started. A pocket calendar or engagement diary that divides each work day into hourly segments will come in handy.

You will also want to keep a personal log of calls and contacts. You may want to develop a format that's different from the one shown here. Fine. The point is to keep a written record of every person you contact in your job search and the results of each contact.

Your log (it can be a notebook from the dime store) will help keep you from getting confused and losing track of the details of your search. If you call someone who's out of town until Tuesday, your log can flag this call so it won't fall between the cracks. Your log may also come in handy for future job searches.

Your log's "disposition" column can act as a reminder of additional sources of help you'll want to investigate. You'll also have a means of timing the correspondence that should follow any interview.

Calls and Contacts

Date	*Name & Title*	*Company*	*Phone*	*Disposition*
2/10	Chas. Junior, VP sales	Top Parts	(214) 277-5500	Interview 2/15
2/10	E. Franklin Sls.mgr.	Frameco	446-0303	out of town until 2/17
2/10	L. Duffy Dir. marketing	Vassar, Inc.	826-6112	out of office call in aft.
2/10	P. Lamm Sls. dir.	Golfco. Ent.	386-9100	busy to 2/28 call then
2/10	E. Waixel, VP Mktg. & sales	Half 'n' Half Foods, Inc.	(817) 338-1055	call after 2

If you're unemployed and hunting full-time for a job, schedule yourself for three exploratory interviews a day for the first week. Each of these meetings should result in at least three subsequent leads. Leave the second week open for the appointments you generated during the first. Maintain this pattern as you go along in your search.

We can't emphasize too strongly the importance of putting yourself on a job-searching schedule, whether or not you're currently employed. A schedule shouldn't function as a straitjacket, but it ought to serve as a way of organizing your efforts for greatest efficiency. Much of your job-hunting time will be devoted to developing your network of contacts. But you should also set aside a certain portion of each week for doing your homework on companies that interest you (see Chapter 4), and for pursuing other means of contacting employers (we'll get to these in a minute).

As you go through your contacts and begin to research the job market, you'll begin to identify certain employers in which you're interested. Keep a list of them. For each one that looks particularly promising, begin a file that contains articles about the company, its annual report, product brochures, personnel policy, and the like. Every so often, check your "potential employer" list against your log to make sure that you're contacting the companies that interest you most.

Go for the Hiring Authority

The object of your job search is to convince the person who has the power to hire you that you ought to be working for him or her. The person you want to talk to is not necessarily the president of the company. It's the person who heads the department that could use your expertise. If you're a salesperson, you probably want to talk with the vice-president of sales or marketing. If you're in data processing, the vice-president of operations is the person you need to see.

How do you find the hiring authority? If you're lucky, someone you know personally will tell you whom to see and introduce you. Otherwise, you'll have to do some homework. Some of the directories listed in Chapter 4 will name department heads for major companies in the Dallas/Fort Worth area. If you cannot otherwise find out who heads the exact department that interests you, call the company and ask the operator. (It's a good idea to do this anyway, since directories go out of date as soon as a department head leaves a job.)

Use an introduction wherever possible when first approaching a company—that's what networking is all about. For those companies that you must approach "cold," use the phone to arrange a meeting with the hiring authority beforehand. Don't assume you can drop in and see a busy executive without an appointment. And don't assume you can get to the hiring authority through the personnel department. If at all possible, you don't want to fill out any personnel forms until you have had a serious interview. The same goes for sending resumes (see Chapter 3). In general, resumes are better left behind, *after* an interview, than sent ahead to generate a meeting.

Other Tactics for Contacting Employers

Direct contact with the hiring authority—either through a third-party introduction (networking) or by calling for an appointment directly—is far and away the most effective job-hunting method. Your strategy and schedule should reflect that fact, and most of your energy should be devoted to direct contact. It's human nature, however, not to put all your eggs in one basket. You may want to explore other methods of contacting potential employers, but these should take up no more than a quarter of your job-hunting time.

Calling or writing to personnel offices may occasionally

▶ Meetings are for meeting people

Laid off during a real estate slump, one enterprising 32-year-old escrow officer decided he would build up his finances by doing something he enjoyed—carpentry. After a few phone calls to friends and former business associates, his newly formed Home Carpentry Service was launched.

At the same time, he attended every possible escrow association meeting, dinner, and other professional event. "I set a goal," he recalls, "to contact at least three escrow company owners at each meeting, to let them know I was looking and available. Then I'd write a letter to give them my phone number in case they wanted to get in touch right away."

About four months after his first dinner meeting, an officer from one of the larger title companies called him for an interview. "He couldn't get me working on that desk fast enough," he remembers. "The $15 I'd spent on that dinner ticket was the best investment I ever made."■

be productive, especially when you know that a company is looking for someone with your particular skills. But personnel people, by the nature of their responsibility, tend to screen out rather than welcome newcomers to the company fold. You're always better off going directly to the hiring authority.

Consider the case of a company that runs an ad in *The Wall Street Journal.* The ad may bring as many as 600 responses. The head of personnel asks one of the secretaries to separate the resumes into three piles according to age: "under 30," "over 30," and "I don't know." The personnel chief automatically eliminates two of the three stacks. He or she then flips through the third and eliminates all but, say, eight resumes. The personnel specialist will call the eight applicants, screen them over the phone, and invite three for a preliminary interview. Of those three, two will be sent to the hiring authority for interviews. That means that 598 applicants never even got a chance to make their case.

Statistically, fewer than one out of four job-hunters succeed by going to personnel departments, responding to ads (either open or blind, as described in Chapter 4), or using various employment services. Some do find meaningful work this way, however. We repeat, if you decide to use a method other than networking or direct contact, don't spend more than 25 percent of your job-hunting time on it.

As you might expect, many books have been written on job-hunting strategy and techniques. Here is a list of selected resources.

Selected Books on Job-Hunting Strategy

Baker, Nancy C. *The Mid-Career Job Change and How to Make It.* New York: Vanguard Press, 1985.

Bolles, Richard N. *The Three Boxes of Life and How to Get Out of Them.* Berkeley, Calif.: Ten Speed Press, 1983.

Bolles, Richard N. *What Color Is Your Parachute?* Berkeley, Calif.: Ten Speed Press, 1986.

Camden, Thomas M. *Get That Job—How to Succeed in a Job Search.* Hinsdale, Ill.: Camden and Associates, 1978.

Camden, Thomas M. *The Job Hunter's Final Exam.* Chicago: Surrey Books, 1984.

Cowle, Jerry. *How to Survive Getting Fired and Win.* New York: Warner Books, 1980.

Figler, Howard. *The Complete Job Search Handbook.* New York: Holt, Rinehart & Winston, 1980.

Gerberg, Robert Jameson. *The Professional Job Changing System.* New York: Performance Dynamics, Inc., 1984.

Hart, Lois Borland. *Moving Up—Women and Leadership.* New York: AMACOM, 1980.

Higginson, Margaret V., and Thomas L. Quick. *The Ambitious Woman's Guide to a Successful Career.* New York: AMACOM, 1980.

Jackson, Tom, and Davidyne Mayleas. *The Hidden Job Market for the 80's.* New York: Times Books, 1981.

Kennedy, Marilyn Moats. *Career Knockouts: How to Battle Back.* New York: Warner Books, 1982.

Kennedy, Marilyn Moats. *Salary Strategies.* New York: Rawson Associates, 1982.

Kleiman, Carol. *Women's Networks.* New York: Ballantine, 1981.

La Rouche, Janice, and Regina Ryan. *Janice La Rouche's Strategies for Women at Work.* New York: Avon, 1984.

Lussier, Donald E. *The Homemaker's Guide to Entering the Job Market.* Englewood Cliffs, N.J.: Prentice Hall, 1984.

Moses, Bruce E. *How To Market Yourself... Yourself.* New York: Pro-Search, Inc., 1979.

Pettus, Theodore. *One On One—Win the Interview, Win the Job.* New York: Random House, 1981.

▶ Here's an example of a networking letter

B ox 7457
Texas Christian University
2800 S. University Dr.
Fort Worth, TX 76109

April 11, 1987

Dr. Norman Hartman
President
Combined Opinion Research
1400 Forest Square, Suite 300
Dallas, Texas, 75231

Dear Dr. Hartman:

Dr. Obrigon Partito, with whom I have studied these past two years, suggested that you might be able to advise me of opportunities in the field of social and political research in the Dallas area.

I am about to graduate from Texas Christian University with a B.A. in American History, and am a member of Phi Beta Kappa. For two of the last three summers, I have worked in the public sector as an intern with Citizens for a Better Government in Dallas and with Senator Claghorn in Washington. Last summer I worked as a desk assistant at Newsweek Magazine's Dallas office.

I am eager to begin to work, and would appreciate a few minutes of your time to discuss employment possibilities in the field of social and political research. I will be finished with exams on May 24, and would like to arrange a meeting with you shortly thereafter.

I look forward to hearing from you, and in any case will be in touch with your office next week.

Sincerely,

Debra Black ■

Selected Dallas/Fort Worth professional organizations, networks, clubs, and societies

Administrative Management Society
Dallas Chapter
P.O. Box 215183
Dallas, TX 75221
(214) 720-2109
President: Doyle Maricle
Professional society for office managers, personnel professionals, and field operations managers. Publishes a newsletter and conducts monthly meetings.

Administrative Management Society
Fort Worth Chapter
300 Oil & Gas Bldg.
Fort Worth, TX 76102
(817) 336-3382
Membership Vice President: Linda Gosdin
Same as Dallas chapter.

Administrative Women in Education
201 N. Bailey Ave.
Fort Worth, TX 76107
(817) 626-0321
President: Ruth McCreath
Organization for women in educational administrative positions. Awards scholarships.

Advertising Club of Fort Worth
601 Penn St.
Fort Worth, TX 76102
(817) 877-4707
Contact: Grace Collins
Organization for professionals in the advertising business. Sponsors educational programs and publishes a newsletter with job openings.

American Association for Respiratory Therapy
1720 Regal Row, Suite 112
Dallas, TX 75235
(214) 630-3540
Executive Director: Sam Giordano
National headquarters for respiratory therapists. Organization publishes two magazines with job listings.

American Association of Medical Transcription
Fort Worth Chapter
c/o St. Joseph Medical Records Dept.
1401 S. Main St.
Fort Worth, TX 76104
(817) 336-9371 ext. 5587
Membership: Lorraine Keating
National organization for medical transcribers. Conducts continuing education workshops and publishes a newsletter with job information.

American Association of Petroleum Landmen
777 Main St., Suite 1470
Fort Worth, TX 76102
(817) 335-2275
Executive Vice President: Harry Sprinkle
Conducts monthly educational meetings and publishes a magazine.

American Association of University Women
Organization of college graduates who promote education. Contacts and phone numbers for area branches include:
Arlington: Diane Feldman (817) 461-2096
Dallas: Florence Mason (214) 241-0964
Farmers Branch-Carrollton: Sheila Gaiser (214) 620-7060
Fort Worth: Dr. Ann Sewell (817) 735-9834
Garland: Marty Anderson (214) 864-8277
Grand Prairie: Gwen Zimmerman (214) 264-2827
Hurst-Euless-Bedford: Rosemary Jobe (817) 283-8552
Irving: Barbara Pickhard (214) 255-7698
Mesquite: Len McCurdy (214) 288-5991
Plano: Gail Simpler (214) 596-2665
Richardson: Betsy Balaze (214) 348-4165
Tarrant County: Marsha West (817) 738-4987

American Business Women's Association
Organization for professional business women. Awards scholarships and conducts regular educational meetings.
Big D Chapter: Opal Martin (214) 423-4500
Big Tex Chapter: Jane Wirick (214) 234-6179
Camaraderie Chapter: Edna Griffith (214) 348-0394
Carelico Chapter: Sue Ann Whitehead (214) 247-3202
Celebrity Chapter: Jackie Trahan (817) 267-8444
Charisma Chapter: Sara Crawford (214) 464-0440
Cinco Chapter: Georgia Davis (817) 293-1532
DeSoto Chapter: Elizabeth Taylor (214) 223-3237
Fort Worth Chapter: Charlene Durham (817) 924-7505
Garland Chapter: Charlotte Harper (214) 272-7668
Irving Laurel Chapter: Emmy Perdue (214) 790-6972
Pathlight Chapter: Betty Cordell (214) 942-7459
Skyline Chapter: Virginia Payne (817) 332-7001
Tourmaline Chapter: Lynn Downing (817) 336-0778
Trinity Chapter: Melba Livingston (817) 465-2030
Vanguard Chapter: Martha Jean Hadley (214) 327-0822

American Fashion Association
P.O. Box 586454
Dallas, TX 75258
(214) 631-0821
Contact: Betty Hamilton
Organization of sales representatives, apparel, and accessory manufacturers. List of manufacturers seeking sales representatives available to AFA members only.

American Guild of Organists
Fort Worth Chapter
6701 John Dr.
Fort Worth, TX 76118
(817) 589-0258
Contact: Marialice Parish
Provides placement service for substitute and occasional full-time church organist positions.

American Institute of Architects
Dallas Chapter
2811 McKinney Ave., Suite 218
Dallas, TX 75204
(214) 871-2788
Executive Director: Loretta Thomas
Professional organization of licensed architects, affiliates, and associates in related fields. Conducts monthly meetings and publishes a newsletter. Keeps resumes on file, has job referral service, offers state and national networking opportunities.

American Institute of Architects
Fort Worth Chapter
4388 W. Vickery Blvd.
Fort Worth, TX 76107
(817) 763-0242
Executive Secretary: Suzie Adams
Same membership requirements as Dallas Chapter. Conducts monthly meetings and publishes a newsletter.

American Institute of Chemical Engineers
Dallas/Fort Worth Section
100 N. Central Expwy., Suite 910
Richardson, TX 75080
(214) 234-8567
Chairman: Debbie Fusselman
Monthly educational meetings, national job fairs, job ads in newsletter, informal referral service, and support groups.

American Institute of Industrial Engineers
12833 Pennystone Dr.
Farmers Branch, TX 75234
(214) 620-AIIE
President: Gary Gollhofer
International organization that provides full range of services and publications. Members and non-members assisted by unemployment council. Networking and employment-related topics discussed at regular meetings.

American Management Association
P.O. Box 466
Princeton, TX 75077
(214) 736-2455
Executive Director: Jim Junsch
International organization that provides training for all levels of management. A division of the organization publishes management books, including several on how to get a job.

American Orthodontics Society
9550 Forest Ln., Suite 215
Dallas, TX 75243
(214) 343-0805
Executive Administrator: Murray Forsvall
National educational organization for dentists, pedodontists, and orthodontists. Conducts more than 40 educational meetings a year throughout the country.

American Petroleum Institute
211 N. Ervay St., Suite 1700
Dallas, TX 75201
(214) 741-6791
Trade association of producers, refiners, marketers, and transporters of petroleum and natural gas.

American Planning Association
North Central Texas Section
P.O. Box 358
Plano, TX 75074
(214) 578-7151
Director: Frank Turner
Organization of city planners. Publishes a bimonthly newsletter with job openings.

American Society for Training and Development
P.O. Box 50951
Dallas, TX 75250
(214) 651-8157
National association for trainers, developers, and human resource managers. Networking opportunities at monthly meetings. Publishes a monthly newsletter and offers job referrals to members.

American Society of Heating, Refrigeration, and Air-Conditioning Engineers
c/o Hydro-Air, Inc.
707 N. Freeway, Suite 118
Fort Worth, TX 76102
(817) 335-4900
President: Marcella Wilemon
International organization of consulting engineers, mechanical contractors, and vendors. Monthly meetings and informal job referrals. National organization publishes newsletter, yearly handbook, and other publications.

American Society of Interior Designers
World Trade Center, Suite 117-1
Dallas, TX 75258
(214) 748-1541
President: Wes Byrd
Meets monthly and publishes a newsletter. Job openings are posted on bulletin board and resumes are kept on file.

American Society of Landscape Architects
8506 Eustis Ave.
Dallas, TX 75218
(214) 871-9220
State Treasurer: Mike Chapman
Association conducts monthly meetings and publishes a newsletter. National association's newsletter advertises job openings.

American Society of Magazine Photographers
2700 Commerce St.
Dallas, TX 75226
(214) 939-0550
President: Michael Haynes
Conducts monthly meetings, publishes a newsletter, and provides informal job referrals. Provides speakers to colleges and universities. Helps graduates make transition from school to full-time work.

The American Society of Mechanical Engineers
Southern Regional Office
13773 N. Central Expwy., Suite 1251
Dallas, TX 75243
(214) 690-0810
Regional Director: David Cook
Professional organization with more than 1,500 members in North Texas Section, which includes Dallas and Tarrant Counties. Each section has monthly meetings and publishes a newsletter. Provides informal job referrals.

American Society of Safety Engineers
Southwest Chapter
P.O. Box 47831
Dallas, TX 75247
(214) 688-2250
President: Jim Presswood
Placement coordinator assists job-hunters. Conducts monthly meetings and publishes a newsletter.

American Society of Women Accountants
Dallas Chapter
5644 Richard Ave.
Dallas, TX 75206
(214) 521-2357
President: Nancy Phillips
Professional association for accountants and educators. Holds monthly educational meetings.

American Society of Women Accountants
Fort Worth Chapter
4417 Ridgeton Rd.
Fort Worth, TX 76116
(817) 732-8032
President: Sandra Tye
Same as Dallas Chapter.

American Subcontractors Association
North Texas Chapter
9400 N. Central Expwy., Suite 901
Dallas, TX 75231
(214) 363-1331
Executive Director: Nicole Kuhnell
Professional association of building subcontractors. Resumes kept on file.

Analytical Psychology Association of Dallas
10118 Medlock Dr.
Dallas, TX 75218
(214) 526-7799
President: Martha Wolf
Monthly meetings and lectures open to the public. Publishes a newsletter.

▶ How to distinguish yourself

A senior employment relations representative for a large firm headquartered in Dallas offers the following tip for standing out in a crowd of interviewees.

"Almost everybody will show up well dressed, with a neatly typed resume and as professional a manner as he or she can muster. You have to show an employer that you're someone special. Try bringing a **backup book** with you to every interview, one that contains examples of your work. If you're a secretary, bring some samples of your most beautiful typing. If you're a research chemist, perhaps you've published something that you can show, or maybe articles have appeared about your work, or you can bring along a product that utilizes your research. It all depends on what you do for a living, of course, but use your imagination."■

Apartment Association of Greater Dallas
9221 LBJ Frwy., Suite 214
Dallas, TX 75243
(214) 437-0177
Executive Vice President: Dick Covert
Organization for apartment managers. Conducts monthly educational meetings, publishes a newsletter, and has a job bank.

Associated General Contractors
11111 Stemmons Frwy.
Dallas, TX 75229
(214) 247-9962
Executive Vice President: Raleigh Roussell
Schedules regular meetings, maintains a resume file, and publishes a newsletter.

Association for Information and Image Management
Dallas/Fort Worth Chapter
2 Forest Plaza
12201 Merit Dr., Suite 250
Dallas, TX 75251
(214) 239-1881
President: Jim Torbert
Professional association for micrographics and records management. Conducts monthly meetings, publishes newsletter with job openings, and makes informal job referrals.

Association for Systems Management
P.O. Box 474
Dallas, TX 75221
(214) 939-0821
President: Larry Gist
Professional organization of systems managers. Conducts monthly meetings to share technical information. International organization provides job listings for members.

Association of American Dentists
10511 Wyatt St.
Dallas, TX 75218
(214) 327-6662
Contact: Melvin Munn
Organization of practicing dentists. Sponsors study groups for research.

Association of Executive Saleswomen
700 N. Pearl Expwy.
Lock Box 368
Dallas, TX 75201
(214) 969-7326
President: Jolene Campbell
Conducts monthly networking and educational luncheons.

Association of Information Systems Professionals
Dallas Chapter
P.O. Box 2652
Dallas, TX 75221-2652
(214) 987-7977
President: Donna Newsom
Organization for people who design, manage, and use information systems. Conducts monthly meetings and publishes newsletter with job openings. Bimonthly international magazine also lists employment opportunities.

Association of Information Systems Professionals
Fort Worth Chapter
610 S. Jennings Ave.
Fort Worth, TX 76104
(817) 332-4070
President: Shirley Owens
Conducts monthly meetings and publishes a newsletter.

Association of Records Managers and Administrators
P.O. Box 2428
Dallas, TX 75221
(214) 746-7112
Contact: Marilyn Suggs
Conducts monthly meetings and publishes a newsletter. Coordinates local job clearinghouse with resume file and employment openings.

Association of Women Entrepreneurs of Dallas, Inc.
P.O. Box 835232
Richardson, TX 75083
(214) 980-1007
President: Carol Hammond
Provides education and support for women business owners. Holds monthly meetings and publishes a newsletter.

Association of Women Entrepreneurs of Tarrant County
P.O. Box 14247
Arlington, TX 76094-1247
(817) 461-6488
President: Pat Fowler
Same as Dallas Chapter.

Beau Monde League
2670 Belknap Ave.
Dallas, TX 75216
(214) 948-7066
Contact: Louise Richardson
Association of cosmetologists. Awards scholarships and keeps a resume file.

Builders Association of Fort Worth-Tarrant County
6464 Brentwood Stair Rd.
Fort Worth, TX 76112
(817) 429-3472
Executive Vice President: Rene Adams
Trade organization for builders and associated personnel. Meets monthly, sponsors seminars and workshops, and publishes a newsletter.

Building Owners and Managers Association of Fort Worth
P.O. Box 7002
Fort Worth, TX 76111
(817) 834-5251
President: Natalie Shelton
Surveys changes in commercial building industry, publishes a newsletter, conducts monthly meetings, and provides informal job referrals.

Business and Professional Women's Clubs
Dallas District
3241 Cassidy Dr.
Plano, TX 75023
(214) 960-1220
District Director: Fay Griffith
Network of clubs. District office and local clubs make informal job referrals. Clubs located in Carrollton, Dallas, downtown Dallas, Garland, Grand Prairie, Lancaster, Las Colinas, Oak Cliff, Plano, Richardson, South Dallas, Town North, and White Rock.

Business and Professional Women's Clubs
Fort Worth District
509 N. Elm St., Suite 2
Arlington, TX 76011
(817) 461-2674
District Director: Genevieve Ramer
Same as Dallas district with the following clubs: Arlington, Cross Timbers, Crowley, Fort Worth, Hurst, La Hispana, Lone Star, Meadowbrook, Metropolitan, Northeast Ridglea, River Oaks, and South Fort Worth.

Certified Public Accountants
Dallas Chapter
12222 Merit Dr., Suite 300
Dallas, TX 75251-2217
(214) 960-8311
Executive Director: Margaret Cartwright
Promotes professional education and publishes a newsletter with job advertisements. Keeps resumes on file.

Certified Public Accountants
Fort Worth Chapter
520 Fort Worth Club Bldg.
Fort Worth, TX 76102
(817) 335-5055
Executive Director: Sherrie Marshall
Same as Dallas Chapter.

Christian Medical Society
National Administrative Office
1616 Gateway Blvd.
Richardson, TX 75080
(214) 783-8384
Controller: Brenda McFarlane
Organization for Christian medical students, physicians, and dentists. Promotes spiritual growth and evangelism.

Classroom Teachers of Dallas
3816 San Jacinto St.
Dallas, TX 75204
(214) 821-2061
President: Pauline Dixon
Largest teachers' organization. Affiliated with Texas State Teachers Association. Promotes professional education and publishes a newsletter.

Council of Petroleum Accountants Societies
2104 Roosevelt Dr.
Arlington, TX 76013
Metro (817) 265-7971
Executive Director: John Jolly
Representatives for 23 petroleum accounting societies in North America. Publishes manuals.

CPS Association of North Central Texas
10312 Garwood Dr.
Dallas, TX 75238
(214) 348-4447
President: Karen Donawho
Organization for Certified Professional Secretaries. Two educational meetings per year. Publishes quarterly newsletter. Provides informal job referrals.

Dallas Advertising League
5757 Alpha Rd., Suite 400
Dallas, TX 75240
(214) 386-8767
Executive Director: Joan Organ
Trade association for professionals in the advertising business. Publishes a newsletter with a want-ad section.

Dallas American Institute of Banking
750 Fidelity Union Life Building
Dallas, TX 75201
(214) 954-0515
Contact: Jennifer Tittle
Training organization for financial service industry.

Dallas Association for Childhood Education
P.O. Box 116
Dallas, TX 75204
(214) 224-8588
President: Annie Bell
Organization of teachers, parents, nursery school helpers, and elementary school principals. Conducts workshops for elementary and early childhood education. Holds monthly meetings.

Dallas Association of Black Women Attorneys
P.O. Box 50633
Dallas, TX 75250
(214) 361-7971
President: Rhonda Hunter
Has job bank and makes informal employment referrals. Participates in community projects.

Dallas Association of Counselors
3700 Ross Ave.
Dallas, TX 75202
(214) 824-1620
Professional organization of career, special education, and elementary counselors employed by the Dallas Independent School District.

Dallas Association of Investment Analysts
P.O. Box 8300
Dallas, TX 75283
(214) 880-9000
Secretary-Treasurer: Perry Rushing
Association of primarily portfolio managers and security analysts. Conducts bimonthly luncheon meetings. Has a placement committee that keeps a resume file and assists job-hunters.

Dallas Association of Law Librarians
P.O. Box 50183
Dallas, TX 75250
(214) 969-4824
President: Frank Lee
Coordinates job bank, holds monthly meetings, and conducts two workshops each year.

Dallas Association of Legal Assistants
P.O. Box 2938
Dallas, TX 75221
(214) 269-2037
Professional organization of paralegals. Has a job bank and newsletter with employment notices.

Dallas Association of Legal Secretaries
1700 Mercantile Dallas Building
Dallas, TX 75201
(214) 745-5345
Vice President: Betty Willmon
Organization for paralegals and legal secretaries. Job bank available to members. Conducts monthly meetings and publishes a newsletter.

Dallas Association of Life Underwriters, Inc.
Allied Bank Plaza
Lock Box 52
12655 N. Central Expwy., Suite 808
Dallas, TX 75243
(214) 991-2364
Executive Director: Faye Woodard
Conducts monthly educational programs and publishes a magazine.

Dallas Association of Speech Pathologists and Audiologists
8820 Southwestern Blvd., Suite 303
Dallas, TX 75206
(214) 373-0766
President: Mary Ann Lonergan
Informal job referrals, conducts educational bimonthly meetings, and publishes a newsletter.

Dallas Association of Texas Professional Educators
3700 Ross Ave.
Dallas, TX 75204
(214) 328-3869
President: Richard Campbell
Professional organization for administrators, counselors, librarians, teachers, and clerks. State organization publishes magazine with employment information.

Dallas Association of Young Lawyers
2101 Ross Ave.
Dallas, TX 75201
(214) 741-1001
President: Mark Shank
Organization for lawyers under the age of 36.

Dallas Bar Association
2101 Ross Ave.
Dallas, TX 75201
(214) 969-7066
Executive Director: JoAnna Morelan
Organization for attorneys. Provides continuing education and publishes a newsletter.

Dallas Beauticians Association
2617 Martin Luther King Blvd.
Dallas, TX 75215
(214) 946-8947
Executive Director: J. L. Boykin
Organization of beauticians who seek to maintain professional standards.

Dallas Building Owners and Managers Association
1700 Pacific Ave.
1260 First City Center
Dallas, TX 75201
(214) 953-1170
Executive Director: W. D. Hill
Trade association for commercial property managers. Job referrals for members only.

Dallas Business League
13422 Montfort Dr., Suite 1002
Dallas, TX 75240
(214) 980-4294
Contact: Virginia Altman
Association of business workers, primarily in banking, law, and sales. Schedules monthly luncheon meetings.

Dallas Cable Club
12750 Merit Dr.
Dallas, TX 75251
(214) 387-8557
President: Jane Ketcham
Organization of communications and cable educators who meet regularly.

Dallas Communications Council
6300 N. O'Connor Rd., Suite N29
Irving, TX 75039
(214) 869-7674
Executive Director: Becky Shaw
Association of professionals in film, tape, talent, recording, and other communications industries. Promotes the local communications industry, schedules monthly meetings, raises funds, and publishes a monthly newsletter.

Dallas County Chiropractic Society
2407 W. 12th St.
Dallas, TX 75211
(214) 339-2020
Contact: Cliff Nearpass
Sponsors educational programs and keeps a resume file.

Dallas County Dental Society
4100 McEwen Rd., Suite 141
Dallas, TX 75244
(214) 386-5741
Executive Director: Linda Hill
Sponsors continuing education courses and publishes a newsletter.

Dallas County Federation of Teachers
3626 N. Hall St., Suite 608
Dallas, TX 75219
(214) 522-8455
Organization of teachers and non-supervisory teaching professionals. Represents teachers in grievances and provides legislative information. Sponsors workshops and distributes publications.

Dallas County Funeral Directors Association
P.O. Box 31000
Dallas, TX 75231
(214) 238-7111
President: J. A. Hutchinson
Provides informal job referrals.

Dallas County Library Association
1515 Young St.
Dallas, TX 75201
(214) 749-4182
President: Joan Dobson
Association for librarians or those interested in the field. Publishes a quarterly newsletter with job listings and makes informal referrals.

Dallas County Medical Society
P.O. Box 4680
Dallas, TX 75208
(214) 948-3622
Contact: Robert Heath
Professional organization of medical doctors. Provides continuing education and publishes a medical journal.

Dallas County Podiatric Medical Society
P.O. Box 508-303
Dallas, TX 75248
(214) 521-9221
Schedules monthly meetings and publishes a newsletter.

Dallas County Rental Association
4401 N. Belt Line Rd.
Mesquite, TX 75150
(214) 226-7017
President: Jim Reagan, Jr.
Organization of general rental store managers. Schedules monthly meetings and has local and national newsletters.

Dallas County Sheriffs Association
3300 W. Mockingbird Ln., Suite 609
Dallas, TX 75235
(214) 351-3599
President: Lt. Jack Watson
Organization for all members of Dallas County Sheriffs department. Schedules monthly meetings and publishes a newsletter.

Dallas County Veterinary Medical Association
P.O. Box 210675
Dallas, TX 75211
(214) 467-3106
Contact: Elizabeth Heineken
Professional association of veterinarians. Promotes continuing education and publishes a monthly newsletter with employment notices.

Dallas Credit Management Association
P.O. Box 64728
Dallas, TX 75206
(214) 699-6000
Professional organization of credit and collection employees.

Dallas Dental Hygienists Society
10931 Stone Canyon Place, Suite 124
Dallas, TX 75230
(214) 696-9935
President: Bonny McInosh
Employment committee provides information about temporary and permanent job opportunities.

Dallas Dietetic Association
10525 Mapleridge Dr.
Dallas, TX 75238
(214) 348-8841
President: Hazel Cattlett
Professional organization for registered/licensed dietitians and those in related fields. Career guidance committee assists job-hunters.

Dallas Educational Secretaries Association
3700 Ross Ave.
Dallas, TX 75204
(214) 824-1620
President: Phyllis Weghorst
Organization of secretaries, clerks, and data processors who work for the Dallas Independent School District.

Dallas Fire Fighters Association
P.O. Box 26099
Dallas, TX 75226
(214) 941-1354
President: Don Howard
Professional association that lobbies for training, education, and safety.

Dallas/Fort Worth Association of Black Communicators
c/o The Dallas Morning News
Communication Center
Dallas, TX 75265
(214) 977-6294
Contact: Kevin Merida
Professional organization for journalists working in TV, radio, magazines, and newspapers. Conducts monthly meetings, awards an annual scholarship, and maintains a job bank.

Dallas/Fort Worth Association of Metroplex Personnel Consultants
5520 LBJ Frwy., Suite 204
Dallas, TX 75240
(214) 788-1804
Executive Director: Henry Wright
Trade association of account executives of personnel service companies. No services available for members, but the organization does assist people who are looking for help with the job search. Individuals should call (214) 969-0505 for referrals to job fairs, employment seminars, and agencies that specialize in their field.

Dallas/Fort Worth Organizational Psychologists
8210 Walnut Hill Ln., Suite 619
Dallas, TX 75231
(214) 750-6031
Consulting Firm Liaison: Dr. Diane Holloway
Organization of counselors, management consultants, and psychologists. Schedules monthly meetings and publishes a newsletter.

Dallas Freelance Network
P.O. Box 1653
Dallas, TX 75221
(214) 522-7544
Executive Board Director: Earl Fisher
Network of freelance writers, photographers, graphic artists, and film/tape professionals. Conducts monthly meeting, publishes a newsletter and directory. Refers contract work to members.

Dallas Geological Society
4925 Greenville Ave., Suite 100
Dallas, TX 75206
(214) 890-5742
President: Edward Dowd
Conducts continuing education programs and has an employment committee that keeps a resume file.

Dallas Group Psychotherapy Society, Inc.
2505 Wycliff Ave.
Dallas, TX 75219
(214) 528-9240
Dean of Training: Juanita Kirby
Professional organization that provides training for members and non-members.

Dallas Metropolitan Black Nurses Association
P.O. Box 4104
Dallas, TX 75208
(214) 375-6276
President: Fayrene Tolbert
International organization of black nurses who support racial equality. Newsletter lists job-wanted ads.

Dallas Metropolitan Home Economists in Homemaking
2213 Creekview Dr.
Carrollton, TX 75006
(214) 245-4048
President: Carol Sprawls
Professional Opportunity Board helps members find jobs. Monthly meetings conducted from September through May.

Dallas Music Teachers Association
P.O. Box 12034
Dallas, TX 75225
(214) 341-4495
President: Karen Austin
Organization of professional music teachers.

Dallas Personnel Association
P.O. Box 2727
Dallas, TX 75221
(214) 351-3975
President: Neil Thomas
Meets regularly, has an annual conference, and maintains a resume file.

Dallas Police Association
2108 Jackson St.
Dallas, TX 75201
(214) 747-6839
President: James Ramsey
Support organization for Dallas police officers.

Dallas Producers Association
1110 Ave. H East, Suite 200
Arlington, TX 76011
(817) 640-9955
President: Joe Wilson
Organization of corporate and commercial film/video producers. Holds monthly meetings and publishes a newsletter.

Dallas Professional Photographers Association
2323 N. Belt Line Rd.
Mesquite, TX 75150
(214) 289-1851
President: Hulda Neve
Professional organization for photographers. Publishes a newsletter with employment information.

Dallas Psychological Association
P.O. Box 190584
Dallas, TX 75219
(214) 386-4362
Employment Chairperson: Karen Schultheis
Organization of psychologists, psychological associates, and students. Provides state-wide employment information.

Dallas Restaurant Association
6124 Sherry Ln., Suite 175
Dallas, TX 75225
(214) 240-2388
President: Alexandra Fincher
Organization for the food and beverage industry. Provides information about the restaurant industry during monthly meetings, publishes a newsletter and magazine, and awards scholarships.

Dallas School Administrators Association
3700 Ross Ave.
Dallas, TX 75204
(214) 943-1196
President: Dr. Joseph Granado
Supports professional development and sponsors seminars.

Dallas Security Dealers Association
P.O. Box 50065
Dallas, TX 75250
(214) 747-0321
President: Merrill Lankford
Conducts educational meetings.

Dallas Society of Accounting Librarians
1400 First City Center
Dallas, TX 75201
(214) 922-8040
Contact: Karleen Smith
Provides professional development opportunities at bimonthly meetings.

Dallas Society of Illustrators
c/o D–Art
2917 Swiss Ave.
Dallas, TX 75204
(214) 821-2522
President: Rusty Jones
Organization for graphic and commercial artists who meet each month and provide informal job referrals.

Dallas Society of the Institute of Certified Financial Planners
9400 N. Central Expwy., Suite 510
Dallas, TX 75231
(214) 661-9331
President: Hal Rachel
Holds monthly meetings.

Dallas Society of Visual Communication
3530 High Mesa Dr.
Dallas, TX 75234
(214) 241-2017
Executive Director: Sue Reynolds
Organization of advertising's creative staff members. Conducts monthly meetings and provides employment referral service.

Dallas Southwest Osteopathic Physicians, Inc.
2929 S. Hampton Rd.
Dallas, TX 75224
(214) 330-4611 ext. 300
Executive Director: Don Hicks
Charitable organization that makes donations to non-profit organizations.

Dallas Women Lawyers Association
2101 Ross Ave.
Dallas, TX 75201
(214) 969-7066
Holds monthly meetings and publishes a newsletter.

Dallas Women's Network
8131 LBJ Frwy., Suite 170
Dallas, TX 75251
(214) 437-5077
President: Phil Hartung
Organization for women in the business field, including secretaries, clerks, and office support personnel. Sponsors several career fairs each year and has monthly meetings.

Data Processing Managers Association
8200 Walnut Hill Ln.
Dallas, TX 75231
(214) 696-8527
Contact: Bill Gaston
Organization of data processors, system analysts, consultants, and vendors. Conducts monthly meetings and publicizes job openings in newsletter and on bulletin board.

Desk and Derrick Club of Dallas
2600 Thanksgiving Tower
Dallas, TX 75201
(214) 880-7077
President: Pamela Aquino
Organization of women employed in petroleum and allied industries. Has an employment committee that assists members only.

Desk and Derrick Club of Fort Worth
1100 Everman Rd.
Fort Worth, TX 76140
(817) 551-4140
President: Suzanne Darnell
Same as Dallas Chapter.

Direct Marketing Association of North Texas
P.O. Box 612368
D/FW Airport, TX 75261
Metro (817) 263-3989
Organization for list brokers, printers, catalogers, and others in direct marketing industry. Conducts monthly meetings.

Downtown Network of Career Women
3818 N. Hall St., Suite 124
Dallas, TX 75219
(214) 658-3166
President: Karen Nixon
Provides networking opportunities for professional women from all fields. Meets during monthly luncheons.

Educational Secretaries Association of Grand Prairie
2205 S.E. 4th St.
Grand Prairie, TX 75051
(214) 264-8651
President: Judy Siddall
Organization of para-professionals in Grand Prairie School District. Conducts monthly meetings.

Executive Women International
7000 Camp Bowie Blvd.
Fort Worth, TX 76116
(817) 731-8666
President: Joan Hlavaty
Representatives selected by major companies to join this exclusive organization.

Executive Women of Dallas
109 N. Akard St., Suite 1010
Dallas, TX 75201
(214) 747-8988
President: Marsha Williams
Organization of women executives and business owners.

Fort Worth Area Medical Records Association
812 E. Mustang Dr.
Crowley, TX 76036
(817) 336-5521
Contact: Kathy Earl
Holds monthly meetings, continuing education courses, and workshops. State organization publishes newsletter with employment section.

Fort Worth Area Medical Staff Services Association
6808 Park Place Dr.
Fort Worth, TX 76118
(817) 921-3431 ext. 1230
Contact: Joy Sanders
Organization of medical secretaries. Meets regularly to discuss medical information and award scholarships.

Fort Worth Art Education Association
4137 Middlebrook Rd.
Fort Worth, TX 76116
(817) 731-0669
President: Georgia Blaydes
Organization for Fort Worth art educators.

Fort Worth Association for the Education of Young Children
4108 Toledo Ave.
Fort Worth, TX 76133
(817) 294-1758
President: Minerva Serrano
Conducts bimonthly education meetings for people who work with children under the age of nine.

Fort Worth Association of Petroleum Landmen
P.O. Box 2546
Fort Worth, TX 76113
(817) 390-6981
President: Frank Lawson
Conducts monthly meetings.

Fort Worth Classroom Teachers Association
6021 Westcreek Dr.
Fort Worth, TX 76133
(817) 294-2282
President: Dotti Rosson
Professional teachers organization.

Fort Worth District Dental Society
3301 Hamilton Ave., Suite 108
Fort Worth, TX 76107
(817) 336-3693
Executive Secretary: Liz Lucas
Professional organization of dentists, dental students, dental assistants, and hygienists. Schedules monthly meetings from September through May and publishes a newsletter.

Fort Worth Federation of Teachers
2804 Race St., Suite 11
Fort Worth, TX 76111
(817) 877-3130
Organization of teachers and non-supervising teaching professionals. Represents members in grievances and provides legislative information. Sponsors workshops and distributes publications.

Fort Worth Librarians Association
P.O. Box 8661
Fort Worth, TX 76124
(817) 735-4085
Contact: Alice Terrell
Professional organization of librarians employed by the City of Fort Worth.

Fort Worth Professional Women's Organization
Rec. Box 44,002
Texas American Bank Building
Fort Worth, TX 76102
(817) 338-8291
President: Pam Roach
Network for business women in managerial positions.

Fort Worth/Tarrant County Young Lawyers Association
2015 Texas Building
200 W. 7th St.
Fort Worth, TX 76102
(817) 338-4092
President: Brad Rice
Professional organization for young lawyers under the age of 36. Publishes newsletter with job-opening information and has resume file and job bank.

Garland Board of Realtors
911 Main St.
Garland, TX 75040
(214) 276-1139
Executive Officer: Joy Saunders
Trade association for realtors. Publishes a newsletter and conducts educational seminars.

Grand Prairie Board of Realtors
214 SW 4th St.
Grand Prairie, TX 75051
(214) 262-7747
President: Jan Moon
Trade association for realtors.

Greater Dallas Board of Realtors
2989 N. Stemmons Frwy.
Dallas, TX 75247
(214) 637-6660
Executive Vice President: Benny McMahan
Trade association for realtors. Keeps a resume file.

Greater Fort Worth Dental Hygienists Society
2914 Kathleen Ln.
Euless, TX 76039
(817) 283-5376
Contact: Cindy Bollom, R.D.H.
Professional organization for licensed dental hygienists. Job referrals made by employment chairman. Conducts monthly meetings and publishes a newsletter.

Home & Apartment Builders Association of Metropolitan Dallas
8730 King George Dr.
Dallas, TX 75235
(214) 631-4840
Executive Vice President: Simon McHugh
Trade association for residential builders and developers. Publishes newsletter with employment ads and keeps resumes on file.

Home Economists in Business
North Texas Chapter
SMU
P.O. Box 372
Dallas, TX 75275
(214) 692-2367
Hot Line Chairman: Carol Taylor
Job hot line assists companies and members. Monthly meetings scheduled from September through May. Publishes a newsletter.

Hotel & Motel Association of Greater Dallas
1507 Pacific Ave., 3rd Fl.
Dallas, TX 75201
(214) 954-1468
Executive Vice President: Alex Seymour
Sponsors continuing education programs and provides job referrals.

Illuminating Engineering Society
P.O. Box 17101
Fort Worth, TX 76102
(817) 877-0515
Board of Directors: Harvey Blankenship
Organization of lighting designers.

Independent Insurance Agents of Dallas
2 Turtle Creek Village, Suite 1424
Dallas, TX 75219
(214) 559-4555
Executive Director: Edwin Butcher
Schedules seminars and educational meetings.

Institute of Business Designers
North Texas Chapter
P.O. Box 58047
Dallas, TX 75258
(214) 742-4250
Chapter Administrator: Jan Weinschenk
Association for designers, architects, and facilities management personnel. Conducts monthly meetings, has job bank, and publishes newsletter and annual membership roster.

Insurance Women of Dallas, Inc.
4023 Oak Lawn Ave.
Dallas, TX 75219
(214) 526-8701
Contact: B. J. Ellis
Employment committee assists insurance professionals to locate jobs. Has monthly meetings and publishes a newsletter.

Insurance Women of Fort Worth, Inc.
1515 Frontier Dr.
Arlington, TX 76012
(817) 737-4000
President: Marilyn McEnrowe
Keeps resumes on file.

International Association of Business Communicators
Dallas Chapter
P.O. Box 2681
Dallas, TX 75221
(214) 550-5460
President: Sharon Larkin
Meets regularly for continuing education programs. Co-sponsors telephone job bank. Call (214) 744-6056 to hear recording of job openings.

International Association of Business Communicators
Fort Worth Chapter
P.O. Box 17033
Fort Worth, TX 76102
Metro (817) 429-7290
President: Karen Rayl
Same as Dallas Chapter.

Irving Association of Educational Office Personnel
2016 Vickie Dr.
Irving, TX 75060
(214) 790-2505
President: Cleon Crossland
Organization for all Irving Independent School District office personnel. Conducts meetings from September through May.

Irving Bar Association
P.O. Box 153325
Irving, TX 75015
(214) 986-1508
Professional organization for attorneys.

Irving Music Teachers Association
1701 Live Oak Dr.
Irving, TX 75061
(214) 254-1033
Contact: Virginia Jenkins
Association of professional music teachers.

League of Women Voters of Dallas
2727 Inwood Rd.
Dallas, TX 75235
(214) 351-4125
Non-partisan political organization of women and men who provide information on candidates, elections, and governmental issues.

League of Women Voters of Tarrant County
512 W. 4th St.
Fort Worth, TX 76102
(817) 336-1333
President: Tom Gooch
Same as Dallas Chapter.

Licensed Vocational Nurses Association
Dallas Chapter
2663 Moffatt Ave.
Dallas, TX 75216
(214) 637-8550
President: Bernice Shelton
Promotes continuing education and helps members find employment.

Licensed Vocational Nurses Association
Fort Worth Chapter
5800 Maceo Ln.
Fort Worth, TX 76112
(817) 429-3004
President: Survesterlean Gowen
Same as Dallas Chapter.

Mechanical Contractors Association of Dallas, Inc.
2720 Stemmons Frwy., Suite 201 South
Dallas, TX 75207
(214) 630-8991
Director: Anne Copeland
Trade association that helps members find employment through informal referrals.

Mesquite Area Music Teachers Association
1038 Tranquilla St.
Dallas, TX 75218
(214) 321-5308
Program Coordinator: Carol Wilcoxson
Schedules semi-monthly meetings. Provides referral service for students seeking instruction.

Mesquite Bar Association
P.O. Box 1601
Mesquite, TX 75149
(214) 750-4747
President: Steven C. Crane
Professional association for attorneys.

Mesquite Education Association
P.O. Box 634
Mesquite, TX 75149
(214) 288-6411
President: Melanie Packwood
Organization for Mesquite Independent School District employees. Meets regularly and publishes a newsletter.

Mesquite Fire Fighters Association
P.O. Box 1291
Mesquite, TX 75149
(214) 289-7310
Contact: Gary Ward
Organization of firefighters and paramedics. Conducts quarterly meetings.

Metroplex Retail Bakers Association
6029 Luther Ln.
Dallas, TX 75225
(214) 368-6425
President: Richard Aston
Provides informal job referrals. Schedules bimonthly meetings. National organization publishes a magazine.

National Association of Accountants
2001 Ross Ave., Suite 2800
Dallas, TX 75201
(214) 979-1700
President: Bonnie Kennedy
Provides employment service, conducts biweekly meetings, and publishes a newsletter.

National Association of Bank Women
Dallas Chapter
Promenade National Bank
P.O. Box 835010
Richardson, TX 75083
(214) 238-8261
President: Reva Bartlett
Professional organization for women executives in the banking industry. Provides informal job referrals, schedules educational programs, and awards scholarships.

National Association of Bank Women
Greater Fort Worth Chapter
Texas American Bank
P.O. Box 7676
Fort Worth, TX 76111
(817) 834-2881
Contact: Pat Ralstin
Same as Dallas Chapter.

National Association of Female Executives
14375 Haymeadow Cir.
Dallas, TX 75240
(214) 386-6475
Coordinator: Anita Scott
Networking group provides job referrals. Helps newcomers find housing.

National Association of Theatre Owners of Texas
6060 N. Central Expwy., Suite 450
Dallas, TX 75206
(214) 369-3295
Executive Director: Bill Slaughter
Provides information about news and legislation that affects theater industry. Publishes a newsletter.

National Association of Women Business Owners
P.O. Box 791804
Dallas, TX 75379
(214) 239-9022
President: Valarie Freeman
Conducts monthly meetings. Information about organization published in Texas Woman's News.

National Association of Women in Construction
Dallas Chapter
1318 Crestridge Dr.
Mesquite, TX 75149
(214) 827-9260
President: Teresa Kinney
Organization conducts educational meetings, awards scholarships, and maintains a job bank through a referral committee.

National Association of Women in Construction
Fort Worth Chapter
P.O. Box 1379
Fort Worth, TX 76101
(817) 332-5181
President: Glenda Mitchell
Same as Dallas Chapter.

National Council of Jewish Women
219 Preston Royal Village, Suite 9
Dallas, TX 75230
(214) 368-4405
President: Brenda Brand
Sponsors integrated program of education, service, and social activities. Schedules study groups and promotes community involvement and fund-raising projects.

National Electrical Contractors Association
Northeast Texas Chapter
12201 Merit Dr., Suite 390
Dallas, TX 75251-2212
(214) 239-3412
Executive Director: Ray Emmons
Trade association of electrical contractors.

National Home Fashions League, Inc.
107 World Trade Center
P.O. Box 58045
Dallas, TX 75258
(214) 747-2406
Executive Director: Marilyn Miller
Association for executive women in interior design and furnishing. Publishes educational booklets about the industry.

National Organization for Women
Dallas County Chapter
10442 Brockbank Dr.
Dallas, TX 75229
(214) 352-6112
President: Janie Bush
Organization of women and men who work to achieve equality between the sexes. Sponsors seminars and has a job bank.

National Organization for Women
D/FW Mid-Cities Chapter
P.O. Box 1850
Arlington, TX 76004-1850
(817) 265-1219
President: Jeannie Brubaker
Same as Dallas County Chapter.

National Organization for Women
North Dallas Chapter
P.O. Box 820397
Dallas, TX 75382-0397
(214) 235-6914
President: Linda Varunich
Same as Dallas County Chapter.

National Organization for Women
Southwest Dallas County Chapter
734 N. Merrill Rd., Suite 234
Duncanville, TX 75116
(214) 296-0122
President: Polly Austin
Same as Dallas County Chapter.

National Organization for Women
Tarrant County Chapter
P.O. Box 1811
Fort Worth, TX 76101
Metro (817) 735-4073
President: Carolyn Utberg-Hood
Same as Dallas County Chapter.

National Society of Fund Raising Executives
Dallas Chapter
P.O. Box 271189
Dallas, TX 75227
(214) 321-4544
President: Dwaine Wheatley
Organization of volunteers who are associated with major charitable organizations. Conducts monthly meetings and publishes a quarterly newsletter.

National Society of Fund Raising Executives
Fort Worth Chapter
Huguley Memorial Hospital
P.O. Box 6337
Fort Worth, TX 76115
(817) 293-9110
President: Sheree Parris Nudd
Same as Dallas Chapter.

National Society of Real Estate Appraisers
109 N. Akard St., Suite 1008
Dallas, TX 75201
(214) 742-3404
Executive Director: Norah Crow
Job-wanted notices published in local newsletter. Conducts monthly professional development meetings.

Network for Executive Women
P.O. Box 2567
Fort Worth, TX 76113
(817) 485-5172
Executive Secretary: Dr. Mimi Ayars
Career-oriented women meet weekly in Fort Worth, Arlington, and Mid-Cities area. Job openings are announced and employment-related topics are discussed at meetings.

Network of Hispanic Communicators
P.O. Box 222313
Dallas, TX 75222
(214) 324-5220
Contact: Jesse Chairez
Organization for journalists, advertising, and public relations professionals. Schedules monthly meetings, publishes newsletter with ads, and awards scholarships.

New Car Dealers of Metropolitan Dallas
2777 N. Stemmons Frwy., Suite 1161
Dallas, TX 75207
(214) 637-0531
President: Drew Campbell
Trade association promoting new car dealers by sponsoring car shows. Job referrals made.

Newspaper Advertising Sales Association
333 W. Campbell Rd., Suite 370
Richardson, TX 75080
(214) 699-0766
President: Robert Collins
National organization of advertising salespeople. Offers informal employment network and schedules monthly meetings.

North Central Texas Registry of Interpreters for the Deaf
2309 Riverway Dr.
Dallas, TX 75227-2099
(214) 388-1170
President: Diane Boles
Conducts meetings and workshops to improve skills. Has informal job referral network.

Don't overlook the watering holes

You can't beat weekday happy hours at local bars as an informal way of making contacts.

In Dallas, journalists long ago adopted Joe Miller's (3531 McKinney Ave.) as the place to congregate and pick up leads for stories from **lawyers, politicians,** and **public relations** execs. The **artists** hang out at the Prophet Bar (2713 Commerce St.) among other places in Deep Ellum.

Many downtown professionals, especially **bankers, lawyers,** and **computer professionals,** opt for Dick's Last Resort (1701 N. Market St.). Studio C (6311 N. O'Connor) serves as an oasis in the middle of Las Colinas for **film, video,** and **audio** types.

In Fort Worth, **attorneys, legal secretaries** and **bankers** tip oversize drinks during happy hour at Billy Miner's Saloon (150 W. 3rd St.). **Creative types**—artists, writers, and musicians—have adopted J&J Blues Bar (937 Woodward) with the unforgettable telephone number 870-BEER.

Doctors, nurses and others from the health field favor Mable's Summit Club (555 S. Summit Ave.).

J.R. Ewings of the **oil** business prefer the downtown Petroleum Club (777 Main St.). The uppercrust take turns cooking breakfast for each other every Saturday morning at The Carriage House (5136 Camp Bowie Blvd.).

Up-and-coming **bank executives** and rising young **realtors** can be found at the Ice House (4600 Dexter) along with women who hope to meet the same.■

North Dallas Bar Association
5757 Alpha Rd.
Dallas, TX 75240
(214) 661-5114
Contact: Samantha Arthur
Attorneys' organization that schedules monthly meetings.

North Dallas Network of Career Women
4309 Hyer St.
Dallas, TX 75205
(214) 559-2048
Forum for women in corporate and professional positions to give and seek help with their careers. Meets biweekly.

North Fort Worth Business Association
131 E. Exchange Ave.
Fort Worth, TX 76106
(817) 626-7921
Business Manager: Carol Becker
Organization of North Fort Worth business professionals. Meets monthly, publishes a newsletter, and sponsors the annual Pioneer Days celebration.

North Texas Optometric Society
2016 Promenade Center
Richardson, TX 75080
(214) 669-9229
President: Arnold M. Stockol
Organization of optometrists. Publishes local newsletter. State journal lists job openings.

North Texas Speakers Association
6526 Chevy Chase St.
Dallas, TX 75225
(214) 386-0907
President: Bob Handley
Association of professional and aspiring speakers. Meets monthly and publishes a newsletter.

North Texas State Juvenile Officers Association
3500 Hwy. 67E
Mesquite, TX 75150
(214) 291-7131
Contact: Randy Coffey
Conducts monthly meetings and publishes a newsletter.

Nurses Association
Texas District 4
515 Texas American Bank
Dallas, TX 75235
(214) 357-6227
President: Sarah Moody
Professional organization of licensed RNs. Meets monthly and publishes a newsletter with employment notices.

Official Professional Nursing Bureau, Inc.
515 Texas American Bank Building
Dallas, TX 75235
(214) 357-9247
Contact: Director
Cooperative organization that assists members in marketing job skills in hospitals, clinics, and for private duty assignments. Two general membership meetings per year. Publishes a newsletter.

PBX Telecommunicators of Dallas
1732 Culberson Dr.
Mesquite, TX 75150
(214) 279-3796
President: Louise Mason
Sponsors workshops and fund-raising projects.

PBX Telecommunicators of Fort Worth
2012 Bluebonnet Dr.
Fort Worth, TX 76111
(817) 834-3907
President: Lela Johnston
Same as Dallas Chapter.

Press Club of Dallas
400 S. Houston St.
Dallas, TX 75202
(214) 748-3329
Executive Director: Mary Jane Hewes
Sponsors fund-raising projects and social events, publishes a newsletter, and provides informal job referrals.

Printing Industries Association of Texas
8585 Stemmons Frwy., Suite 1112
Dallas, TX 75247
(214) 630-8871
Executive Director: Nolan Moore
Regular meetings promote continuing education. Free employment service for members and non-members.

Professional Secretaries International
Big D Chapter
1506 Overlook Dr.
Grapevine, TX 75051
(214) 880-0990
President: Linda Cook, C.P.S.
Provides job referrals for members. Meets monthly, conducts seminars, and publishes a bulletin.

Professional Secretaries International
Garland Chapter
1229 Delores Dr.
Garland, TX 75040
(214) 495-4918
President: Elaine Jones, C.P.S.
Same as Dallas Chapter.

Professional Secretaries International
Trinity Chapter
P.O. Box 1128
Fort Worth, TX 76109
(817) 926-3346
President: Janice Whisenand
Same as Dallas Chapter.

Pro-Musica
3137 Caruth Blvd.
Dallas, TX 75225
(214) 363-4782
President: Susan Hamman Carlisle
Organization of professional women musicians. Schedules regular meetings and awards scholarships.

Public Relations Society of America
North Texas Chapter
P.O. Box 12033
Dallas, TX 75225
(214) 327-4889
Chapter Administrator: Layne Lauck
Organization for practicing public relations professionals in the Dallas/Fort Worth area. Conducts monthly professional development meetings and seminars. Publishes a newsletter. Co-sponsors telephone job bank. Dial (214) 744-6056 to hear recorded message about employment opportunities.

Registered Nurses of Arlington
1413 Roanoke St.
Arlington, TX 76014
(817) 465-1336
President: Jeanne Spoon
Sponsors continuing education programs and awards scholarships.

Retail Marketing Professionals of Tarrant County
3200 Hilldale Rd.
Fort Worth, TX 76116
(817) 737-2177
President: Julie Lydon
Organization of shopping center marketing, advertising, and promotions/special events directors. Meets monthly and publishes newsletter with want ads.

Richardson Bar Association
P.O. Box 73
Richardson, TX 75080
(214) 235-8365
President: Charles Hitt
Professional association of attorneys.

Richardson Music Teachers Association
7710 La Sobrina Dr.
Dallas, TX 75248
(214) 233-8014
President: Carole Rollins
Conducts monthly meetings. Makes job referrals.

Rotary Club of Dallas
400 S. Houston St., Suite 390
Dallas, TX 75202
(214) 742-5451
Executive Director: Jan Sargent
Business and professional men's service organization that conducts weekly meetings.

Sales and Marketing Executives of Fort Worth
P.O. Box 7002
Fort Worth, TX 76111
(817) 834-5381
Executive Director: Natalie Shelton
Professional organization for sales and marketing professionals and students.

Salesmanship Club of Dallas
400 S. Houston St., Suite 350
Dallas, TX 75202
(214) 742-3896
Contact: Janie Hebert
Men's civic organization that meets weekly. Sponsors fund-raising projects for emotionally disturbed children.

Sierra Club
P.O. Box 215
Dallas, TX 75221
(214) 369-5543
Non-profit organization promoting conservation and outdoor recreation. Organizes group trips, publishes monthly newsletter, and raises funds.

The Society for Marketing Professional Services
P.O. Box 214336
Dallas, TX 75221
(703) 549-6117
Job hot line for members only. Meets bimonthly and distributes several publications.

Society for Theatrical Artists Guidance and Enhancement
P.O. Box 214820
Dallas, TX 75221
(214) 559-3917
Executive Director: Robin Stanton
Support group that promotes the performing arts in the Dallas/Fort Worth area. Maintains resume file. Conducts annual membership meeting.

Society of Consumer Affairs Professionals in Business
c/o Zoecon Industries, Inc.
12005 Ford Rd., Suite 800
Dallas, TX 75234
(817) 355-2131
Contact: E. M. Dieringer
Education and issue-oriented organization that meets bimonthly and publishes a newsletter.

Society of Diagnostic Medical Sonographers
10300 N. Central Expwy.
Bldg. 1, Suite 276
Dallas, TX 75231
(214) 369-4332
Executive Director: Gwen Grim
Organization of professionals who work with medical diagnostic ultrasound. Schedules two meetings each year, has national job listings, and publishes a newsletter.

Society of Hispanic Professional Engineers
P.O. Box 59614
Dallas, TX 75229
(214) 350-9976
Public Relations Director: Fernando Laclette
Human Resource Committee makes job referrals. Publishes a newsletter.

Society of Industrial and Office Realtors
North Texas Chapter
8235 Douglas Ave., Suite 1225
Dallas, TX 75225
(214) 750-1377
President: Thomas E. Clarke
Provides educational courses for commercial/industrial realtors.

Society of Petroleum Engineers
P.O. Box 833836
Richardson, TX 75083-3836
(214) 669-3377
Executive Director: Dan Adamson
Publishes several publications with employment sections.

Society of Professional Journalists, Sigma Delta Chi
Dallas Chapter
P.O. Box 50163
Dallas, TX 75250
(214) 871-1390
President: Stan Matthews
Schedules monthly meetings, awards scholarships, and provides informal job referrals.

Society of Professional Journalists, Sigma Delta Chi
Fort Worth Chapter
P.O. Box 2001
Fort Worth, TX 76113
(817) 332-6130
Executive Secretary: Delbert Bailey
Same as Dallas Chapter. Also awards scholarships from proceeds of annual Texas Gridiron show.

Society of Women Engineers
Dallas/Fort Worth Section
4555 Rose Tree Ct.
Fort Worth, TX 76137
(817) 656-5411
President: Karla Seidel
Professional organization that encourages women to enter and excel in engineering. Meets monthly from September through May. Publishes job information in newsletter.

Southwest Council of Optometry
P.O. Box 8482
Dallas, TX 75205
(214) 871-3032
Contact: Pierce Almond
Regional organization for Doctors of Optometry in five states. Conducts annual meeting.

Southwestern Association of Advertising Agencies
8700 Stemmons Frwy., Suite 303
Dallas, TX 75247
(214) 637-4442
Executive Director: Robert Burke
Association of advertising agency owners and managers. Publishes membership directory and monthly newsletter. Sponsors professional workshops and educational seminars.

Southwestern Booksellers Association
P.O. Box 8362
Dallas, TX 75205
(214) 692-2436
Contact: Marvin Steakley
Trade organization of booksellers, writers, librarians, publishers, and agents. Publishes newsletter with job advertisements.

Southwestern Meat Packers Association
1333 Corporate Dr., Suite 213
Irving, TX 75038
(214) 550-1838
Executive Director: Leon Kothmann
Trade organization representing meat packers and suppliers in Texas and surrounding states. Occasional job openings published in newsletter.

Tarrant County Bar Association
2015 Texas Building
Fort Worth, TX 76102
(817) 338-4092
President: Cynthia Leeper
Professional association of lawyers.

Tarrant County Veterinary Medical Association
13055 Rendon Rd.
Burleson, TX 76028
(817) 478-1515
President: Dr. Barry Brier
Organization of veterinarians. Conducts continuing education programs and publishes a newsletter with job listings.

Tarrant County Women's Bar Association
P.O. Box 17676
Fort Worth, TX 76102
(817) 870-7600
President: Sarah Grace
Professional organization for women lawyers. Maintains job bank.

Texas Association of Film & Tape Professionals
3023 Routh St., Suite 208
Dallas, TX 75201
(214) 871-2701
Office Manager: Jane Sibley
Association of film and video freelancers who promote the motion picture, video, and commercial production industry. Publishes the annual Texas Film/Tape Directory, sponsors meetings and seminars.

Texas Association of Nurse Anesthetists, Inc.
8408 Old Moss Rd.
Dallas, TX 75231
(214) 348-7599
Contact: Susan Jaros
Professional organization that promotes continuing education. National group publishes two magazines with job ads.

Texas Association of Teachers of Dancing
402 Park Forest Shopping Center
Dallas, TX 75234
(214) 827-1934
Examination Chairman: Jackie Troup Miller
Organization of members from five-state area who pass an examination to qualify for membership. Supplies informal job referrals, sponsors meetings, and publishes a newsletter.

Texas Economic and Demographic Association
1000 Throckmorton St.
Fort Worth, TX 76102
Metro (817) 429-1090 ext. 1879
President: Judi Cole
Education and information-oriented organization that meets quarterly. Publishes a newsletter and membership directory.

Texas Electronics Association
6016 Belt Line Rd.
Dallas, TX 75240
(214) 385-1185
President: Michael Goodman
Organization for professionals in radio, TV, and video. Publishes monthly newsletter.

Texas Environmental Health Association
P.O. Box 349
Longview, TX 75606
(214) 236-7086
Executive Secretary: Dick Minnick
Organization of sanitary engineers and inspectors. Six regional chapters meet regularly. Employment opportunities listed in local and state newsletters.

Texas Federation of Teachers
Regional Office
1201 N. Watson Rd., Suite 190
Arlington, TX 76006
Metro (817) 640-9019
State Representative: Nicki Thomas

▶ What professional organizations can do for you

"To begin networking with professional organizations, all it takes is a few phone calls to the president and a couple of other members," says Gary Gollhofer, president of the Dallas chapter of the American Institute of Industrial Engineers.

"These people often have their fingers on the pulse of the job market," says Gollhofer, who says his organization has helped quite a few jobless people.

Because of the fluctuations in the job market, Gollhofer says, his organization has been sensitive to employment issues. The AIIE regularly schedules meetings on career change, job-hunting skills, and other topics that help people who are out of work.

During board meetings, members often discuss who's looking for work and what's available. Gollhofer is often personally contacted by unemployed engineers along with headhunters who ask for freak recommendations.

He recalls how an engineer sent him a very impressive resume. But Gollhofer had trouble convincing the manager of another company that he should talk to the engineer. The manager said he didn't have any openings. Gollhofer urged the manager to at least meet with the engineer, adding, "You shouldn't let this guy get away."

Sure enough, he didn't. Once the manager talked to the engineer, he offered to create a job for him.■

Texas Hairdressers and Cosmetologists Association
P.O. Box 9802-235
Austin, TX 78766
(817) 283-4753
President: Faye McDonald
Promotes continuing education.

Texas International Business Association
P.O. Box 780412
Dallas, TX 75378
(214) 934-1234
Executive Director: Ann Lukesh
Organization to promote Texas business involvement in international business market. Conducts monthly meetings and publishes a newsletter.

Texas Music Association
Dallas Chapter
P.O. Box 31819
Dallas, TX 75231
(214) 869-1742
Contact: Barbara Daniels Rice
Organization of musicians, agents, managers, and others who promote the Texas music industry. Conducts monthly meetings and publishes a state newsletter.

Texas Nurses Association
District 4
515 Texas American Bank Building
Dallas, TX 75235
(214) 357-6227
Professional organization for registered nurses. Holds monthly meetings and publishes newsletter with occasional job listings.

Texas Professional Photographers Association, Inc.
P.O. Drawer 828
Temple, TX 76503
(817) 771-3781
Executive Director: Walt Hawkins
Offers education, fellowship, and competition for professional photographers.

Texas Recreation & Park Society
P.O. Box 905
Arlington, TX 76010
Metro (817) 261-0876
Executive Director: Susan Eaves
Professional organization for municipal park and recreation personnel.

Texas Society of Medical Assistants
Dallas Chapter
7777 Forest Ln., Suite B420
Dallas, TX 75230
(214) 788-6444
President: Geneva Straughn
Continuing education and certification program. Informal job referrals.

Texas Society of Medical Assistants
Tarrant County Chapter
4712 Marsalis St.
Fort Worth, TX 76117
(817) 923-7393
President: Jane Harvey
Same as Dallas Chapter.

Texas Society of Professional Engineers
Dallas Chapter
P.O. Box 814128
Dallas, TX 75381
(214) 243-3509
Executive Secretary: Don Swanson
Conducts monthly meetings. Involved in local, state, and national legislative issues.

Texas Society of Professional Engineers
Fort Worth Chapter
P.O. Box 17355
Fort Worth, TX 76102
Metro (817) 429-7560
President: Ted Everage
Professional organization for engineers in all fields.

Third Coast Screenwriters Forum
P.O. Box 28
Bedford, TX 76021
Metro (817) 267-4514
President: Done Robinson
Assists screenwriters to find work, market themselves, and improve through monthly professional development programs. Acts as clearinghouse for producers who ask for referrals.

United Teachers of Dallas
6220 Gaston Ave., Suite 601
Dallas, TX 75214
(214) 824-1745
President: Harley Hiscox
Organization of DISD teachers. Represents teachers who are involved in disputes.

Urban Management Assistants of North Texas
c/o North Central Texas Council of Governments
P.O. Drawer C.O.G.
Arlington, TX 76005
(817) 640-3300
Organization of individuals in entry-level and mid-management positions in local governments. Conducts regular meetings and publishes newsletter with job openings.

Woman's Traffic Club of Fort Worth
P.O. Box 2373
Fort Worth, TX 76101
(817) 481-2801
President: Bernice Eakin
Organization of women in transportation. Schedules monthly meetings, has job placement committee, and publishes newsletter.

Women in Communications, Inc.
Dallas Professional Chapter
P.O. Box 740022
Dallas, TX 75374
(214) 691-4888
President: Marilyn Pippin
Professional organization for men and women in all fields of communication. Has a career advisory committee that keeps resume file and solicits jobs for members. Schedules monthly meetings and publishes a newsletter.

Women in Communications, Inc.
Fort Worth Professional Chapter
P.O. Box 9858
Fort Worth, TX 76107
(817) 731-8681
President: Verlie Edwards
Same as Dallas Chapter. Also provides a job bank for members and non-members.

Women in Computing, Inc.
P.O. Box 741174
Dallas, TX 75374-1174
(214) 954-8663
Professional organization for women in computing and data processing. Awards scholarships, publishes a newsletter with job advertisements, and sponsors regular professional development meetings.

Women in Management
Edwin L. Cox School of Business
SMU Station
Dallas, TX 75275
(214) 692-2776
Contact: Claire Cunningham
Mainly a student organization for women in business school.

Women of the Motion Picture Industry
5603 Bell St.
Dallas, TX 75206
(214) 828-4190
Contact: Claudia Patterson
Service organization for women in the motion picture industry.

▶ Turning volunteer work into a job

After spending many years working as a volunteer for various organizations, Marian Simon recalls, her daughters advised her to "stop giving it away." She decided to look for paying employment. But because she had never held a paying job, Simon was not sure how to begin her job search.

"As a woman in my middle years, I wondered where in the world I would go," says Marian. "I had a good education and a great deal of volunteer experience. I had planned and orchestrated large benefits and had done an inordinate amount of fund-raising over the years. I also had done community work in Fort Worth.

"I talked to some people at a local college. They told me I was well qualified and that I should just go out and look for a job. But I didn't know where 'out' was. Later, career counselors at another local college helped me put together a resume. Then I began to talk to people I knew. I was offered various jobs, none of which thrilled me.

"Then I happened to mention my job search to the president of a hospital where I had done a great deal of volunteer work," says Marian. "He asked me not to take a job until I had talked to him. Later, he hired me as his special assistant, with the charge to 'humanize' the hospital. Over a period of time, I developed a patient representative department.

"When I began the job 11 years ago, I was a one-person operation. As time went on, I added staff. I currently supervise a staff of nine, plus about 25 volunteers. In fact, the job of patient representative is now a full-fledged profession. Many women in the field began as volunteers. They knew a lot about the hospital where they were volunteering, and thus made the transition into a paid position more easily."

We asked Marian what advice she has for volunteers who want to move into the paid work force. "Go to the career counseling departments of some of the small colleges. Ask them to review your background and tell you what kinds of jobs you may be qualified for. If they suggest that you need additional training, get it. But before you go back to school, investigate the kinds of jobs available in your chosen field. Think about how you can use your volunteer experience in a paid position. Take what you've done and build from it."■

Women's Association of Allied Beverage Industries
9208 Seagrove Dr.
Dallas, TX 75243
(214) 341-6907
President: Patricia Deere
Service-oriented organization of employees in the alcoholic beverage industry. Schedules monthly meetings, makes informal job referrals, and publishes a newsletter.

Women's Council of Realtors/National Association of Realtors
6757 Arapaho Rd., Suite 751
Dallas, TX 75248
(214) 458-9300
Contact: Clarice Langran
Professional organization for women in real estate.

Women's Transportation Club of Dallas
P.O. Box 10691
Dallas, TX 75207
(214) 840-5304
President: Sherry Boyd
Organization of women who work for transportation companies or in a transportation department. Sponsors monthly educational meetings and publishes a newsletter with job openings.

6

Using Professional Employment Services

Conducting a job search is no easy task. When the pressure is on, many a job-seeker's first instinct is to turn to professional employment services for relief. "After all," he or she reasons, "everyone knows that professional services have all the job listings." Wrong!

It's smart to use every available resource to generate leads and interviews. But professional employment services vary from agencies that specialize in temporary clerical help to executive recruiters who deal primarily with top-management types. Employment agencies, career consultants, and executive recruitment firms differ greatly in the kinds of services they offer and in how—and by whom—they get paid. You can save yourself a lot of time, effort, and perhaps even money and anguish by informing yourself about the advantages and disadvantages of the various kinds of professional employment services. One handbook that might prove useful is the *Directory of Approved Counseling Services* (American Personnel and Guidance Association, 5201 Leesburg Pike 400, Falls Church, VA 22041).

Employment Agencies

The thousands of employment agencies that have succeeded through the years have done so by acting as intermediaries in the job market between buyers (companies with jobs open) and sellers (people who want jobs). An employment agency obtains a fee when a person it refers to a company is hired by that company. The fee may be paid by the company, but in some cases it is paid by the worker. Agencies that specialize in restaurant and domestic help, for example, often charge the worker a fee. Usually the placement fee amounts to a certain percentage of the worker's annual salary.

Seldom will an employment agency place a candidate in a job that pays more than $30,000 a year. Most employment agencies concentrate on support jobs. Supervisory openings also may be listed, but employment agencies usually don't handle middle or upper management positions. In the computer field, for example, computer operators, programmers, and perhaps systems analysts could find work through an agency. But directors of data processing or MIS (management information systems) would go to an executive search firm or would job-hunt on their own.

A company that's looking for a secretary gains certain advantages by going to a reputable agency. It doesn't have to advertise or screen the hundreds of resumes that would probably pour in from even a small want ad in the Sunday *Morning News.* A good employment agency will send over only qualified applicants for interviews. Referrals are made quickly, and there is no cost to the company until it hires the secretary. For many companies, it's worth it to pay an agency fee to avoid the hassle of prescreening dozens, if not hundreds, of applicants.

The advantage to the agency of a successful placement (besides the fee) is repeat business. After two or three referrals work out well, an employment agency can generally count on receiving future listings of company vacancies.

The value to the job-seeker of using an employment agency depends on a number of factors, including the quality of the agency, the kind of work you're looking for, how much experience you have, and how broad your network of personal and business contacts is.

In general, an agency's loyalty will be to its source of income. Agencies are more interested in making placements

▶ **Who's good? Who's not?**

A listing in this book does not constitute an endorsement of an employment agency or career consultant. In Texas, employment agencies and career consultants that charge individuals a fee for finding them a job must be licensed by the Texas Department of Labor. No license is required if the employer pays the total cost. If you want to find out whether or not a firm has been licensed, call the Labor License and Enforcement Division of the Texas Department of Labor at (512) 463-5520. Before engaging these professional services, check with the Better Business Bureau and other resources listed in Chapter 2.■

than in seeing to it that applicants land in jobs that are really fulfilling. An agency is likely to put pressure on its applicants to accept jobs that they don't really want, just so it can collect its fee. With certain exceptions, unless you're just starting out, new in town, or switching to a field in which you have no experience, an agency probably can't do much more for you than you could do for yourself in an imaginative and energetic job search. If a company has to pay a fee to hire you, you're at a disadvantage compared with applicants who are "free." Also, giving an employment agency your resume could be a serious mistake if you're trying to conduct a confidential job search.

On the other hand, a good agency can help its candidates develop a strategy and prepare for employment interviews. This training can be very valuable to people who are inexperienced in job-hunting techniques. Agency pros know the market, screen well, and provide sound advice. A secretary who tries to investigate the Metroplex job market on his or her own will take up to six times longer to get the "right" job than someone who uses a quality agency.

Historically, certain employment agencies engaged in practices that can only be called questionable at best, and the field as a whole is trying to polish up a somewhat tarnished image. In Texas, all employment agencies that charge individuals a fee for finding a job must be licensed by the state. There are many highly respected and successful employment agencies able and willing to help qualified job-seekers. But as in any profession, there are also crooks. It's still a practice in some agencies to advertise nonexistent openings to attract applicants for other, less desirable positions.

So much for the pros and cons of employment agencies.

If you decide to try one, be sure it's a reputable firm. Ask people in your field to recommend a quality agency, and consult the Better Business Bureau and other resources listed in Chapter 2 to see if there have been any complaints about the agency you're considering. Most important, *be sure to read the contract thoroughly, including all the fine print, before you sign it.*

If you have any questions, or if there's something you don't understand, don't be afraid to ask. It's your right. Make sure you know who is responsible for paying the fee, and what the fee is. Remember that *in some cases, an agency's application form is also the contract.*

Here, then, is a selective listing of Dallas/Fort Worth-area employment agencies.

Major Employment Agencies

Account Abilities
2001 Ross Ave.
360 LTV Center
Dallas, TX 75201
(214) 979-9001
Accounting.

Accounting Reserve Personnel
3301 Airport Frwy.
Bedford, TX 76021
Metro (817) 267-5757
Accounting and data processing.

ADIA Personnel Services
4100 Spring Valley Rd., Suite 103
Dallas, TX 75243
(214) 661-1356
Administrative, accounting, legal, and word processing.

American Metroplex Consultants
12900 Preston Rd., Suite 500
Dallas, TX 75230
(214) 385-7738
Mortgage/banking and finance.

Aware Personnel Service, Inc.
901 Summit Ave.
Fort Worth, TX 76102
(817) 870-2590
EDP, technical, and mortgage.

Babich & Associates
6060 N. Central Expwy., Suite 544
Dallas, TX 75206
(214) 361-5735
Sales, administrative, and technical.

Browne & Keene
8150 N. Central Expwy., Suite 701
Dallas, TX 75206
(214) 750-4420
Administrative support.

Carrollton Employment Services
1925 Belt Line Rd., Suite 409
Carrollton, TX 75006
(214) 242-2176
Secretaries, word processing, and sales.

Computer Consultants
4101 McEwen Rd., Suite 350
Farmers Branch, TX 75244
(214) 980-4090
Data processing.

Datapro Personnel Consultants
12720 Hillcrest Rd., Suite 520
Dallas, TX 75230
(214) 661-8600
Data processing.

Dr. Personnel
3505 Turtle Creek Blvd., Suite 105
Dallas, TX 75219
(214) 559-3201
Health care.

FirstWord
2121 San Jacinto St., Suite 202
Dallas, TX 75201
(214) 880-0231
Administrative assistants, data processors, and receptionists.

General Employment Enterprises
8350 N. Central Expwy., Suite 690
Dallas, TX 75206
(214) 788-4462
Data processing, engineering, and general office.

Robert Half, Inc.
1701 River Run
Fort Worth, TX 76107
(817) 870-1200
Accounting, financial, and data processing.

Marshall Career Service
6421 Camp Bowie Blvd., Suite 400
Fort Worth, TX 76116
Metro (817) 654-0067
Professional positions.

Peggy Miller Personnel Consultants
15770 Dallas Pkwy., Suite 600
Dallas, TX 75248
(214) 960-9995
Administrative support.

Office Mates 5
5720 LBJ Frwy., Suite 101
Dallas, TX 75240
(214) 233-3633
Sales.

Opportunity Unlimited Professional Placement, Inc.
2720 W. Mockingbird Ln.
Dallas, TX 75235
(214) 357-9196
Engineering and computer science.

The Personnel Connection
305 One Galleria Tower
Dallas, TX 75240
(214) 922-9855
Clerical.

Roth Young Management Search Consultants
12890 Hillcrest Rd., Suite 105
Dallas, TX 75230
(214) 392-0100
Sales, marketing, manufacturing, and food.

Salesworld, Inc.
6600 LBJ Frwy., Suite 4184
Dallas, TX 75240
(214) 458-0920
Sales and marketing.

Secretaries of Dallas, Inc.
1700 Pacific Ave., Suite 1575
Dallas, TX 75201
(214) 744-4331
Administrative support, secretaries, and word processors.

Snelling & Snelling
4324 N. Belt Line Rd., Suite C102
Irving, TX 75062
(214) 258-5973
Office and clerical.

Snelling & Snelling
611 Ryan Plaza Dr., Suite 533
Arlington, TX 76011
(817) 860-3885
Office, engineering, and professional.

Wright Johnson & Johnson Personnel Consultants
400 N. Olive St., Suite 3500
Dallas, TX 75201
(214) 979-1166
Administrative support and accounting.

Executive Search Firms

An executive search firm is one that is compensated by a company to locate a person with specific qualifications that meet a precisely defined employment need. Most reputable executive search firms belong to an organization called the Association of Executive Recruiting Consultants (AERC). The association publishes a code of ethics for its membership.

A search firm never works on a contingency basis. Only employment agencies do that. The usual fee for a search assignment is 30 percent of the annual salary of the person to be hired, plus out-of-pocket expenses. These are billed on a monthly basis. During hard times, many companies forego retaining search firms because it's so expensive.

It's difficult to get an appointment to see a search specialist. Executive search consultants have only their time to sell. If a specialist spends time with you, he or she can't bill that time to a client. If you can use your personal contacts to meet a search professional, however, by all means do so. Executive specialists know the market and can be very helpful in providing advice and leads.

Search firms receive dozens of unsolicited resumes every day. They seldom acknowledge receipt and usually retain only a small portion for future search needs or business development. They really can't afford to file and store them all. Sending your resume to every search firm in the Dallas/Fort

Worth area will be useful only if one firm coincidentally has a search assignment to find someone with *exactly* your background and qualifications. It's a long shot, similar to answering blind want ads.

If you are ever contacted by an executive search firm, says A. Robert Taylor, author of *How to Select and Use an Executive Search Firm*, take the time to listen to what the consultant has to offer. Even if it isn't the job for you, establishing rapport with the consultant is important. You never know when a more appealing job might become available.

The following is a selected list of executive search firms in the Dallas/Fort Worth area.

Major Executive Search Firms

Peter W. Ambler Associates
500 W. 7th St., Suite 1210
Fort Worth, TX 76102
Metro (817) 429-6450

Boyden International
5420 LBJ Frwy., Suite 1868
Dallas, TX 75240
(214) 387-7973

Brooks, Weitzel & Associates
5757 Alpha Rd., Suite 502
Dallas, TX 75240
(214) 387-3300
Data processing.

Catterton, Inc.
580 Two Lincoln Center
5420 LBJ Frwy.
Dallas, TX 75240-6215
(214) 934-9000
Financial, accounting, and data processing.

Computer Careers, Inc.
4020 McEwen Rd., Suite 123
Dallas, TX 75244
(214) 387-4010
Accounting, banking, and engineering.

Corporate Advisors, Inc.
5420 LBJ Frwy., Suite 1100
Dallas, TX 75240
(214) 386-8642

R.J. Dishaw and Associates
5440 Harvest Hill Rd., Suite 125
Dallas, TX 75230
(214) 788-1740

Eastman & Beaudine, Inc.
1 Galleria Tower
13355 Noel Rd., Suite 1370
Dallas, TX 75240
(214) 661-5520

Ernst & Whinney/Executive Search
2001 Ross Ave., Suite 2800
Dallas, TX 75201
(214) 979-1700
Financial, insurance, and real estate.

Executive Search Personnel
5952 Royal Ln., Suite 270
Dallas, TX 75230
(214) 696-2201
Sales, marketing, and financial.

Executive Search Professionals
5952 Royal Ln.
Dallas, TX 75230
(214) 369-5161
Financial and banking.

Leon A. Farley Associates
2323 Bryan St., Suite 1730
Dallas, TX 75201
(214) 969-0370
Technology, health care, and real estate.

First Main Capital Corp.
4975 Preston Park Blvd., Suite 380
Plano, TX 75075
(214) 964-7100

Hayman & Co.
2101 Skyway Tower/Southland Center
Dallas, TX 75201
(214) 748-0944
Banking and insurance.

Henard Associates, Inc.
15301 Dallas Pkwy., Suite 1050
Dallas, TX 75248
(214) 991-7151
Food.

Ward Howell International, Inc.
1601 Elm St., Suite 900
Dallas, TX 75201
(214) 749-0099

Jack Hurst & Associates
First City Bank Center, Suite 706
Richardson, TX 75080
(214) 231-5075
High-tech, manufacturing, and banking.

Hyde, Danforth & Co.
5950 Bershire Ln., Suite 1600
Dallas, TX 75225
(214) 691-5966
Legal and financial.

Ketchum, Inc. Executive Recruiting Service
914 One Main Place
Dallas, TX 75250
(214) 741-4591
Non-profit organizations, colleges, and health care.

Korn/Ferry International
350 N. St. Paul St., Suite 1675
Dallas, TX 75201
(214) 651-1801

LMJ Company
5151 Belt Line Rd., Suite 847
Dallas, TX 75240
(214) 239-6969

Lamalie Associates
1601 Elm St., Suite 4246
Dallas, TX 75201
(214) 754-0019

LeClair Sutton Associates, Inc.
15851 Dallas Pkwy., Suite 820
Dallas, TX 75248
(214) 387-5711
Financial and compensation/benefits.

Lineback Associates
5720 LBJ Frwy., Suite 101
Dallas, TX 75240
(214) 458-8100
Banking, sales, data processing, and high-tech.

Martin, Harris & Associates
7515 Greenville Bank Tower, Suite 800
Dallas, TX 75231
(214) 691-3430
Financial, data processing, and accounting.

Meador-Wright and Associates
5520 LBJ Frwy., Suite 204
Dallas, TX 75240
(214) 788-1804

Odell & Associates
7557 Rambler Rd., Suite 720
Dallas, TX 75231
(214) 692-1221
Financial and telecommunications.

Page-Wheat Croft & Co.
1900 Pacific Ave.
Dallas, TX 75201
(214) 742-5656
Financial and management information systems.

Peat Marwick Mitchell & Co.
1601 Elm St., Suite 1400
Dallas, TX 75201
(214) 754-2000

Paul R. Ray & Co., Inc.
RepublicBank, Suite 1208
Fort Worth, TX 76116
Metro (817) 429-0127

Russell Reynolds Associates, Inc.
2001 Ross Ave., Suite 1900
Dallas, TX 75201
(214) 220-2033

Search America Personnel Consultants
12700 Hillcrest Rd., Suite 172
Dallas, TX 75230
(214) 233-3302
Telecommunications, hotels, and restaurants.

Search Systems, Inc.
14110 Dallas Pkwy., Suite 150
Dallas, TX 75240
(214) 980-0366
Administrative support.

Source Engineer
12700 Park Central Place, Suite 213
Dallas, TX 75251
(214) 239-9010
Engineering and scientific.

Source Finance
10300 N. Central Expwy., Suite 479
Dallas, TX 75231
Metro (214) 429-9772
Accounting and financial.

Spencer Stuart
1200 First City Center
Dallas, TX 75201
(214) 880-0400

Sumrall Personnel Consultants, Inc.
4020 McEwen Rd., Suite 123
Dallas, TX 75244
(214) 387-4801
Computer, accounting, banking, and manufacturing.

Western Executive Search
6816 Camp Bowie Blvd.
Fort Worth, TX 76116
Metro (817) 429-2231
Financial and accounting.

Bob White Associates
11325 Pegasus West, Suite 133
Dallas, TX 75238
(214) 343-1921
Data processing, sales, and marketing.

Youngs & Co.
12221 Merit Dr., Suite 1330
Dallas, TX 75251
(214) 458-2222

Career Consultants

If you open the employment section of the Sunday *Morning News* or the Southwest edition of *The Wall Street Journal*, you'll see several ads for career consultants. Many of the ads are directed to "executives" earning yearly salaries of $30,000 or more. Some ads suggest that the consultants have access to jobs that are not listed elsewhere. Others claim, "We do all the work." Most have branch offices throughout the country.

Career consultants vary greatly in the kind and quality of services they provide. Some may offer a single service, such as vocational testing or resume preparation. Others coach every aspect of the job search and stay with you until you accept an offer. The fees vary just as broadly and range from $100 to several thousand dollars. *You*, not your potential employer, pay the fee.

A qualified career consultant can be a real asset to your job search. But *no consultant can get you a job.* Only you can do that. You are the one who will participate in the interview, and you are the one who must convince an employer to hire you. A consultant can help you focus on an objective, develop a resume, research the job market, decide on a strategy, and train you in interviewing techniques. But you can't send a consultant to interview in your place. It just doesn't work that way.

Don't retain a career consultant if you think that the fee will buy you a job. The only reason you should consider a consultant is that you've exhausted all the other resources we've suggested here and still feel you need expert and personalized help with one or more aspects of the job search. The key to choosing a career consultant is knowing what you need and verifying that the consultant can provide it.

There are many reputable consulting firms in the Metroplex area. But as is true of employment agencies, some career consultants have been in trouble with the law. Before engaging a career consultant, check with the Better Business Bureau and other resources listed in Chapter 2. Has anyone lodged a complaint against the firm you're considering?

Check references. A reputable firm will gladly provide them. Before you sign anything, ask to meet the consultant who will actually provide the services you want. What are his or her credentials? How long has the consultant been practicing? Who are the firm's corporate clients?

Read the contract carefully before you sign it. Does the contract put the consultant's promises in writing? Has the consultant told you about providing services that are not specified in the contract? What does the firm promise? What do *you* have to promise? Are all fees and costs spelled out? What provisions are made for refunds? For how long a time can you use the firm's or the consultant's services?

Be sure to do some comparison shopping before you select a consultant. A list of Dallas/Fort Worth-area firms you might want to investigate is provided in Chapter 2.

Social Service Agencies

Unlike professional employment agencies, career consultants, and executive search firms, social service agencies are not-for-profit organizations. They offer a wide range of services—from counseling and vocational training to job placement and follow-up—and their services, in general, are free.

How do you locate these agencies? The most comprehensive guides are *First Call for Help: Directory of Community Resources in Fort Worth and Tarrant County*, published by the United Way of Metropolitan Tarrant County, and *Directory of Health, Welfare & Recreation Services*, published by the Community Council of Greater Dallas. Each directory listing includes the agency's name, address, phone number, fees (if any), and a brief description of all programs offered.

The following social service agency listings include resources for women, minorities, seniors, the disabled, and young people.

Social Service Agencies

The Bethlehem Foundation
2603-A Idaho St.
Dallas, TX 75376-0633
(214) 371-3407
Tutoring, job readiness, and some placement programs for the economically disadvantaged.

Better Influence Association
4616 E. Lancaster Ave., Suite 200
Fort Worth, TX 76103
Metro (817) 429-9462
Fees: Sliding scale
Career development and employment services for residents of the Southside, Poly, Stop Six, Eastwood, Forest Hill, and Highland Hill neighborhoods.

Citizen's Development Center
8800 Ambassador Row
Dallas, TX 75247
(214) 637-2911
Vocational evaluations, work adjustment training, job placement, and follow-up for disabled persons 16 years old and older.

Dallas Alliance of Businessmen
4501 Lemmon Ave.
Dallas, TX 75219
(214) 528-6130
Sponsors several different job programs for youths and adults. Pays 50 percent of on-the-job training expenses.

Dallas Center for Independent Living
8625 King George Dr., Suite 210
Dallas, TX 75235
(214) 631-6900
Employment assistance for physically and mentally disabled individuals.

Dallas Inter-Tribal Center
209 E. Jefferson Blvd.
Dallas, TX 75203
(214) 941-6535
Job training, counseling, and placement through job bank for American Indians and others.

Dallas Urban League
2606 Martin Luther King Blvd., Suite 215
Dallas, TX 75215
(214) 426-5486
Assists minority groups and economically disadvantaged in vocational counseling and employment. Sponsors Seniors in Community Service Employment Program for older workers.

Family Service of Tarrant County
Central Office
716 W. Magnolia Ave.
Fort Worth, TX 76104
(817) 335-2401
One of six area offices offering counseling and an employee assistance program.

Girls Club of Dallas, Inc.
5415 Maple Ave., Suite 222
Dallas, TX 75235
(214) 630-5213
Pre-employment programs and job placement for males and females from 16 to 21 years old who are from low-income families. Younger workers assisted in finding after-school work or summer employment, and in using learning center to earn GED.

Goodwill Industries of Dallas, Inc.
2800 N. Hampton Rd.
Dallas, TX 75112
(214) 638-2800
Counseling, training, and job placement for disabled adults.

Jewish Family Service
7800 Northaven Rd.
Dallas, TX 75230
(214) 696-6400
Multiple services with priority given to Jewish community and North Dallas residents. Has programs for the elderly and the emotionally, physically, or mentally handicapped. Provides vocational services for self-directed job search.

Liberation Community
3540 E. Rosedale Ave.
Fort Worth, TX 76105
(817) 534-7186
Some job-search assistance provided for Poly Technic and Stop Six area residents of Fort Worth.

Project Link/Mainstream, Inc.
2121 San Jacinto, Suite 855
Dallas, TX 75201
(214) 969-0118
Job placement services for disabled persons 16 years old and older who have a marketable job skill.

Restart, Inc.
P.O. Box 191294
Dallas, TX 75219
(214) 521-9704
Provides life-skill training programs for homeless and jobless to help them get established in productive roles.

Washington Street Presbyterian Mission
3525 State St.
Dallas, TX 75204
(214) 824-6801
Employment and job training for homeless and needy.

Woman's Center in Richardson
532 Lockwood Dr.
Richardson, TX 75080
(214) 238-9516
Variety of free programs, including Pathways to Achievement sessions on finding potential, considering lifework planning, and preparing for the job-hunt. Women-In-Transition program helps women re-enter the job market after losing spouse through death, divorce, or separation. Befrienders program offers immediate job-search assistance. Resource center and informal network helps women locate employment.

Women's Center of Tarrant County
1203 Lake St., Suite 208
Fort Worth, TX 76102
(817) 338-4456
Employment assistance through counseling, workshops on resume-writing, job-search techniques, Models and Mentors program. Several special programs, including one that assists senior citizens.

Women's Center of Dallas
3220 Lemmon Ave., Suite 210
Dallas, TX 75204
(214) 521-9606
Special employment-related programs sponsored by the center. Referrals made to other agencies.

Women's Resource Center
Young Women's Christian Association
4621 Ross Ave.
Dallas, TX 75204
(214) 827-5600
Career counseling.
Employment services available at the YWCA's headquarters at 4621 Ross Ave. and seven branches in Dallas County. Services include individual career counseling, testing, support groups, and quarterly YWCA Breakfast with networking opportunities and guest speakers. Pathways I 12-hour program prepares women for the job search. Pathways II nine-hour program helps women become even more successful once they are employed.

Government and County Agencies

Many job-seekers do not take advantage of the employment listings available through city, state, and federal government agencies because they assume most of the positions will be for lower-paying, unskilled jobs. Actually, that's not always the case. Most of these services are free, so you may as well stop by one or more of the following offices and see what is available.

American G.I. Forum, Inc.
Veterans Outreach Program
1200 W. Berry St., Suite B
Fort Worth, TX 76134
(817) 926-6873
Job placement for unemployed veterans.

City of Garland Neighborhood Service Center
701 Clark St.
Garland, TX 75040
(214) 494-7106
Employment referral and placement. GED and ESL classes.

Dallas County Community Action Committee, Inc.
2208 Main St.
Dallas, TX 75201
(214) 939-0588
Community Development Division in neighborhood centers offers information and referrals about employment.

Dallas County Department of Human Services
Employment and Training Division
4917 Harry Hines Blvd., North Building
Dallas, TX 75235
(214) 920-7843
Employment and training program for low-income Dallas County residents who live outside Dallas City limits. Programs include in-school youth employment, classroom vocational training, job placement, and on-the-job training with private sector employers. Five area offices in Garland, Grand Prairie, Irving, Lancaster, and Mesquite.

Dallas Opportunities Industrialization Center
500 S. Ervay St., Suite 110C
Dallas, TX 75201
(214) 748-6001
Job-training and placement program for economically disadvantaged.

Dallas Urban League
2606 Martin Luther King Blvd., Suite 215
Dallas, TX 75215
(214) 426-5486
Job counseling and placement for economically disadvantaged.

Deaf Action Center
3115 Crestview Dr.
Dallas, TX 75235
(214) 521-0407
Career Center with assistance in job placement for deaf and multi-disabled persons.

Department of Human Services/Employment and Training
4917 Harry Hines Blvd.
Dallas, TX 75235
(214) 920-7843
Employment and training program for low-income county residents who live outside Dallas city limits. Field offices in Garland, Grand Prairie, Irving, Lancaster, and Mesquite.

Employment and Training Programs/City of Dallas
1500 Marilla St., 6B South
Dallas, TX 75201
(214) 670-5472
Employment and training program for economically disadvantaged City of Dallas residents.

Employment and Training Programs/Fort Worth
1100 Monroe St.
Fort Worth, TX 76102
(817) 870-7555
Employment and training for economically disadvantaged Fort Worth residents.

Federal Information Center
819 Taylor St.
Fort Worth, TX 76102
(817) 334-3624
Provides referrals and information about federal services.

Martin Luther King Jr. Community Center
2922 Martin Luther King Blvd.
Dallas, TX 75215
(214) 670-8397
City of Dallas multi-purpose center that provides employment counseling and training.

Neighborhood Resources Development Program
City of Fort Worth
1000 Throckmorton St.
Fort Worth, TX 76102
(817) 870-7541
Development program for economically disadvantaged, providing job referrals at seven area offices.

North Texas Rehabilitation Service
3802 Cavalier Dr.
Garland, TX 75042
(214) 272-6531
Work adjustment training for physically and mentally disabled adults through on-the-job training, vocational evaluation, and follow-up.

Opportunities Industrialization Center, Inc.
1411 E. 18th St.
Fort Worth, TX 76102
(817) 870-8716
Training and employment program for economically disadvantaged residents.

SER Jobs for Progress, Inc.
2514 Harry Hines Blvd.
Dallas, TX 75201
(214) 871-7575
Provides training and employment for Spanish-speaking people in the Dallas/Fort Worth area.

Senior Employment Program
2727 Inwood Rd.
Dallas, TX 75235
(214) 956-8704
On-the-job training in community service or nonprofit agency leads to permanent job in the public or private sector. Promotes meaningful, part-time work for persons 55 years and older whose income doesn't exceed U.S. Department of Labor guidelines.

Tarrant County Employment and Training
100 E. Weatherford St., Suite 302
Fort Worth, TX 76196
(817) 334-1464
Provides employment and training for economically disadvantaged Tarrant County residents who live outside the Fort Worth city limits.

Texas Commission for the Blind
6301 Gaston Ave., East Tower Suite 450
Dallas, TX 75214
(214) 823-1700
Job placement services for blind/visually impaired individuals in an 11-county area.

Texas Employment Commission
Dallas District Office
8300 John Carpenter Frwy.
Dallas, TX 75247
(214) 631-6050
Provides counseling, job bank, unemployment insurance, and special assistance at nine area centers.

Texas Employment Commission
Fort Worth District Office
301 W. 13th St.
Fort Worth, TX 76102
(817) 335-5111
Same services offered at four area centers.

Texas Rehabilitation Commission
2415 W. Northwest Hwy., Suite 102
Dallas, TX 75220
(214) 387-8695
Job training and other services to help disabled individuals return to employment.

U.S. Department of Labor
Employment and Training Administration
555 Griffin Sq., Suite 502
Dallas, TX 75202
(214) 767-4993
Administers apprenticeship program.

U.S. Office of Personnel Management
Federal Job Information Center
Dallas Area Office
1100 Commerce St., Rm. 6BY
Dallas, TX 75242
(214) 767-8035
Conducts recruiting and examining for federal employment. Provides information on how to apply for federal jobs and advertises job openings in the Dallas/Fort Worth area.

Veterans Administration
1100 Commerce St., Rm. 1B29
Dallas, TX 75242
(214) 824-5440
Job assistance program to link veterans with employment and training opportunities.

Veterans Employment and Training Service
525 Griffin Sq., Suite 204
Dallas, TX 75202
(214) 767-4987
Referral and counseling program for veterans. Keeps available jobs on file.

Women's Bureau
U.S. Department of Labor
525 Griffin Sq., Suite 731
Dallas, TX 75202
(214) 767-6985
Employment referrals and other assistance.

7

How to Succeed In an Interview

If you've read straight through this book, you already know that networking (see Chapter 5) is one of the most important and useful job-hunting techniques around. Networking is nothing more or less than using personal contacts to research the job market and to generate both exploratory and formal job interviews. Networking and interviewing go hand in hand: all the contacts in the world won't do you any good if you don't handle yourself well in an interview. No two interviews are ever identical, except that you always have the same goal in mind: to convince the person to whom you're talking that he or she should help you find a job or hire you personally. An interview is also an exchange of information. But you should never treat it as you would a casual conversation, even if the "interviewer" is an old friend.

Preparing for the Interview

Whether you're talking to the housewife next door about her brother-in-law who knows someone you want to meet, or going through a final, formal interview with a multinational corporation, you are essentially making a sales presentation—in this case, selling yourself. Your goal is to convince the interviewer that you have the ability, experience, personality, maturity, and other characteristics required to do a good job, and to enlist the interviewer's help in getting you that job.

In an informal interview you'll be talking first to friends and acquaintances. Most of the people you'll be talking to will want to help you. But they need to know who you are, what you've done, what you want to do, and most important, how they can help you.

To prepare for any interview, first perfect what we like to call the five-minute resume. Start by giving a rough description, not too detailed, of what you're doing now (or did on your last job), so that when you're telling your story the listener isn't distracted by wondering how it's going to end.

Then go all the way back to the beginning—not of your career, but of your life. Talk about where you were born, where you grew up, what your folks did, whether or not they're still living, what your brothers and sisters do, and so on. Then trace your educational background briefly, and finally, outline your work history from your first job to your latest.

"What!" say many of our clients. "Drag my PARENTS into this? Talk about my crazy BROTHER and the neighborhood where we grew up?"

Yes, indeed. You want to draw the listener into your story, to make him or her interested enough in you to work for you in your search. You want the interviewer to know not only who you are and what you have achieved, but also what you are capable of. You also want to establish things you have in common with the listener. The more you have in common, the harder your listener will work for you.

Author Tom Camden, we are not ashamed to admit, is a master of the five-minute resume. Here's how he would begin a presentation to someone like the neighbor down the street:

"Would it be all right with you if I gave you a broad-brush review of my background? Let you know what I've done, what I'd like to do? That'll give us some time to talk about how I should go about this job search. Maybe I could pick your brain a little about how you can help me. OK?

"Currently, I'm president of Camden and Associates, a consulting firm specializing in corporate outplacement.

"Originally, I'm from Chicago. I'm 49 years old, married, with five kids.

"My father is a security guard at IIT Research Institute; my mother is retired. She used to work for Walgreens—made aspirins, vitamins, and pills. I'm the oldest of four children. My brother John does the traffic 'copter reports for a Chicago radio station. Another brother is a cop with the Chicago police force. My sister Connie is a consultant for an industrial relations firm.

"I went to parochial schools. When I was 14, I left home and went into a monastery. I stayed there until I was nineteen. Then I went to Loyola University, studied psychology, got my degree in '59. I was also commissioned in the infantry.

"I started my graduate work in Gestalt psychology. In 1960 Kennedy called up troops for the Berlin crisis. That included me, so I spent a year on active duty. Following that I came back and continued my graduate work in industrial relations. . . . " Tom took exactly a minute and a half to make this part of his presentation, and he's already given his neighbor several areas in which they may have something in common. He's volunteered enough information, not only to get the neighbor interested in his story, but also to let the neighbor form judgments about him.

People don't like to play God, says Tom. Yet it's a fact of life that we constantly form judgments about each other. In an interview—even an exploratory, informal one—you may as well provide enough information to be judged on who you *are*, and not on what someone has to guess about your background. What does it mean to be the oldest of four kids? What can you deduce from Tom's middle-class background?

The typical personnel professional will tell you that the number of brothers and sisters you have has nothing to do with getting a job. Technically, that's true. The law says that an employer can't ask you how old you are, your marital status, and similar questions. Yet anyone who's considering hiring you will want to know those things about you.

The typical applicant begins a presentation with something like, "I graduated from school in June, nineteen-whatever, and went to work for so-and-so." Our task in this book is to teach you how not to be typical. Our experience has convinced us that the way to get a job offer is to be *different* from the rest of the applicants. You shouldn't eliminate the first twenty years of your life when someone asks you about your background! That's the period that shaped your basic values and personality.

Neither should you spend *too* much time on your personal history. A minute or two is just about right. That gives you from three to eight minutes to narrate your work history. Most exploratory interviews, and many initial employment interviews, are limited to half an hour. If you can give an oral resume in five to ten minutes, you have roughly 20 minutes left to find out what you want to know (more on that shortly).

A word about your work history. If you've done the exercises in Chapter 2, or written your own resume, you ought to be able to rattle off every job you've had, from the first to the latest, pretty easily. In the oral resume you want especially to *emphasize your successes and accomplishments* in each job. This will take some practice. We are not accustomed to talking about ourselves positively. From childhood we're conditioned that it's not nice to brag. Well, we are here to tell you that if you *don't* do it in the interview, you *won't* get the offer.

We repeat: *the interview is a sales presentation.* It's the heart of your job search, your effort to market yourself. In an exploratory interview, the listener will be asking, "Should I help this person?" In a formal interview, the employer will be asking, "Should I hire this person?" In either case, the answer will be "yes" only if you make a successful presentation, if you convince the interviewer that you're worth the effort.

So, the first step in preparing for any interview, formal or informal, is to *practice your five-minute resume.* Go through it out loud enough times so that you're comfortable delivering it. Then work with a tape recorder and critique yourself. Try it out on a couple of friends.

When you're preparing for a formal employment interview, *do your homework on the company.* This advice is merely common sense. But it's surprising how many candidates will ask an interviewer, "What does this company do?" Don't be one of them. Before you go in for an employment interview, find out everything you can about the company—its history, organization, products and services, and growth expectations. Get hold of the company's annual report, catalogs, and brochures. Consult your networking contacts, and use the resources listed in Chapter 4.

Getting to Know You Personally

Your resume gives a prospective employer the bare-bones facts about your skills and accomplishments. But the interview, eye-to-eye with a company representative, determines whether your personal and professional assets form a nice "fit" with the company. So says the employment manager of a major telecommunications company.

"In the interview we can measure skill and capability, and we also find out about personality. Skills can be taught, but you're hard pressed to change your personality.

"We always place the most competitive person for the job,

and the ability to fit in and get along well with others is as important as knowledge of the job."

This employment manager has a few tips for making the most of your interview. "Prepare yourself psychologically for the interview," he says. "Be there on your best day, if it fits the company's schedule. It's critical to look the part, in your manner and dress. Don't hesitate to ask questions. Be persistent, and don't lie. An experienced interviewer will have you figured out in fifteen minutes."

The timing of your application can minimize your having to deal with the stress of rejection, or what the employment manager calls "job-seeking psychosis."

"Many companies hire in high numbers at certain times of the year," he says. "December is the worst month; February and March are better in our industry, then it begins to slow again in October. Find out what the hiring season is for the company you have in mind. This will increase your chances for success."■

▶ **What to wear?**

A young friend of ours who wanted to break into broadcasting finally landed her first big interview—with WFAA-TV. It was fairly easy for her to do her homework on a company of that size. Two days before the interview, it suddenly dawned on her that she had no idea how to dress. How did she solve her problem?

"It was pretty easy, actually, and fun, too," says Hillary. "All I did was go and hang around outside the office for fifteen minutes at lunchtime to see what everybody else was wearing."■

Handling the Interview

In an exploratory, or informal, interview, most of the people you'll talk with will want to help you. But they need to know how. After you've outlined your personal and work history, ask your contact how he or she thinks your experience fits into today's market. What companies should you visit? Specifically, what people should you talk with?

When someone gives you advice or a recommendation to call someone else, do it! Few things can be more irritating than to provide free counsel to someone who then ignores it. If your contact suggests that you call Jan Billingsley, call her!

In a formal employment interview, there are several typical questions you can expect to encounter, though not necessarily in this order:

Tell me about yourself. (This is your cue for the five-minute resume.)

Why do you want to change jobs?
What kind of job are you looking for now?
What are your long-range objectives?
What are your salary requirements?
When could you be available to start here?
Tell me about your present company.
What kind of manager are you?
How would you describe yourself?
What are your strengths and weaknesses?

(In the course of his career, Tom Camden has posed this question to untold numbers of applicants. "They'll list two or three strengths," he says, "and then can't wait to tell me about their weaknesses." Don't be one of those people! Accentuate the positive. Remember, this is a competitive interview.)

Describe your present boss.
To whom can I talk about your performance?
Are you open to relocation?
How long have you been looking for a new job?
Why are you interested in this company? (This is your golden opportunity to show the interviewer that you've done your homework on the company.)

Practice your answers to these questions *before* you go in for the interview. Anticipate other questions you might be asked, and develop answers for them. In general, keep your responses positive. Never volunteer a negative about yourself, another company, or a former employer. Even if you hate your present boss, describe your areas of disagreement in a calm, professional manner. You are selling *yourself*, not downgrading others. Even if you're not particularly interested in the company, always conduct the interview as if you were dead set on getting the job. The interviewer will apply your responses to the questions he or she *really* wants answered.

Does the applicant have the ability to do the job?
Can he or she manage people?
How does he or she relate to people?
What kind of person is this? A leader? A follower?
What strengths does he or she have that we need?
Why the number of job changes so far?

In what areas is he or she weak?
How did the applicant contribute to present and past companies?
What are his or her ambitions? Are they realistic?
Is he or she too soft or too tough on subordinates?
What is this person's standard of values?
Does he or she have growth potential?
Is there a health problem anywhere?
What is the nature of the "chemistry" between us?
What will the department manager think of this applicant as opposed to the others?
Should this person get an offer?

The interview should not be a one-sided affair, however. Questions that you should ask the interviewer are equally important in this exchange of information. For example, you have to know about the job, the company, and the people in your future employment situation. It's necessary to use your judgment to determine how and when to ask questions in an interview. But without the answers, it will be next to impossible for you to make a sound decision if you receive an offer. Some of the questions you want answered are:

What are the job's responsibilities?
What is the company's recent history? Its current objectives?
Its market position? Where are its plants located? What distribution systems does it use?
To whom will I report? What's his or her background?
Why is the job available?
Where does the job lead?
What about travel requirements?
Where is the job located?
Are there any housing, school, or community problems that will develop as a result of this job?
What is the salary range?
What is the detailed benefit picture?
What is the company's relocation policy?
When will an offer be made?
What references will be required?
When would I have to start?
What is the personality of the company?
Do the job and company fit my plan for what I want to do now?
What's the next step?

Psyching out the office decor

"You can tell a lot about a company by carefully scrutinizing the office environment during a job interview," says Ennis Sullivan. He made a careful study of the decor, layout, and orderliness of several offices the last time he went job-hunting.

"Each office has a distinct personality," he says. During his survey he finds that a boss's office with soft, comfortable furniture often indicates that the supervisor is easy-going—the type who doesn't mind if people linger to chat. Firmer, more utilitarian chairs could be a tip-off that the person in charge is a no-nonsense type.

Sullivan used the office decor to determine how he would handle himself in an interview. In an office lined with sports trophies, he inevitably mentioned his football experience. When he noticed during one interview that a manager had a cluttered desk and briefcase, he stressed his organizational skills.

"Use your powers of observation and gut feelings to your advantage in an interview," Sullivan says. We agree wholeheartedly.■

Following the Interview

Many job-seekers experience a kind of euphoria after a good interview. Under the impression that a job offer is imminent, a candidate may discontinue the search. This is a serious mistake. The decision may take weeks, or may not be made at all. On the average, about six weeks elapse between the time a person makes initial contact with a company and the time he or she receives a final answer. If you let up on the search, you will prolong it. Maintain a constant sense of urgency. Get on with the next interview. Your search isn't over until an offer is accepted and you actually begin the new job.

Always follow up an interview with correspondence. The purpose of the letter is to supplement the sales presentation you made. Thank the interviewer for his or her time and hospitality. Express interest in the position (ask for the order). Then mention three additional points to sell yourself further. Highlight how your specific experience or knowledge is directly applicable to the company's immediate needs. Try to establish a date by which a decision will be made.

If you think you could benefit from professional counseling in interviewing skills, consider the resources suggested in Chapters 2 and 6. You may also find it helpful to refer to some of the following books.

Allen, Jeffrey. *How to Turn an Interview Into a Job.* New York: Simon and Schuster, 1983.

Biegelein, J. I. *Make Your Job Interview a Success: A Guide for the Career-Minded Jobseeker.* New York: Arco, 1984.

Goodale, James G. *The Fine Art of Interviewing.* Englewood Cliffs, N.J.: Prentice-Hall, 1982.

Grice, Charles R. *Fifteen Tips on Handling Job Interviews.* Orange, Calif.: Career Publishers, 1981.

Krannich, Caryl R. *Interview for Success.* San Luis Obispo, Calif.: Impact, 1982.

McHugh, John J., Jr. *Interview for Jobs.* St. Paul, Minn.: EMC, 1981.

Pell, Arthur R. *How to Sell Yourself In an Interview.* New York: Monarch Press, 1982.

Price, Jonathan. *How to Find Work.* New York: New American Library, 1983.

Buttering up the boss

The general manager of a major television station tells this story about an interview that almost destroyed his career before it started:

"They took me to dinner at the Oak Room and presented me with the first lobster I had ever laid eyes on. You know how lobster comes with those little bowls of melted butter? Well, I was so nervous I thought it must be orange juice, so I picked it up and drank. After the first sip, of course, I knew I had made a mistake. But there was nothing to do but finish what I had started. . . . "■

8

What to Do If Money Gets Tight

Any job search takes time. One particularly pessimistic career counselor we know suggests you plan to spend about two weeks of search time for every thousand dollars you want to earn per year. (Pity the poor soul who wants to make $60,000!) A more optimistic estimate for a job search is around three months, provided the search is conducted full-time.

If you already have a full-time job, it will take you longer to find a new one. But at least you will be receiving a paycheck while you're looking. This chapter is intended for those who are unemployed and facing the prospect of little or no income during the search.

When the financial squeeze is on, the first thing to do is make a thorough review of your liquid assets and short-term liabilities. Ask yourself how much cash you can expect to receive during the next three months from the following sources, plus any others you might come up with:

Savings
Securities
Silver and gold
Insurance loan possibilities
Second mortgage possibilities
Unemployment compensation
Severance pay
Accrued vacation pay
Personal loan sources (relatives, friends)
Sale of personal property (car, boat, stamp collections, etc.)

Then you should consider exactly what bills absolutely *must* be paid. Don't worry about your total outstanding debt. Many creditors can be stalled or might be willing to make arrangements to forego principal as long as interest payments are made. Talk to each of your creditors to see if something can be worked out.

The final step is easy—if sometimes painful. You compare the amount of money you have on hand or expect to receive with the amount you know you'll have to spend. The difference tells you exactly what kind of financial shape you're in.

The old adage has it that it's better to be unemployed than underemployed. If you can afford it, it's wise not to take a part-time or temporary job. The more time you spend looking for a good full-time position, the sooner you're likely to succeed. But if the cupboard looks pretty bare, it may be necessary to supplement your income any way legally possible in order to eat during the search.

Try to find part-time or temporary work that leaves you as free as possible to interview during the day. For this reason, many people choose to drive a cab at night, or work in a bar or restaurant during the evenings. This kind of job gives you the advantage of flexible hours, but the pay is not always desirable. Commissioned sales positions abound in almost every industry. But if your personality isn't suited to sales work, don't pursue it. You'll find it very frustrating.

It's best if you can locate part-time work in your chosen field. The pay is usually more attractive, and you can continue to develop your network of contacts. Many professionals can freelance. An administrative assistant, for example, might be able to find part-time work at a law firm. An accountant might be able to do taxes on a part-time basis and still gain access to new referrals.

Here are some additional sources to consider when the money is really tight and you need part-time or temporary work.

Selected Sources for Part-time and Temporary Work

Accountemps
433 E. Las Colinas Blvd.
Irving, TX 75039
(214) 869-2706
Accountants, bookkeepers, and data processors.

Availability Temporary Services
211 N. Ervay St., Suite 1610
Dallas, TX 75201
(214) 748-0551
Office, light industrial, and bookkeeping.

Best Labor Service
4021 Birchman Ave.
Fort Worth, TX 76107
(817) 654-3530
General laborers, skilled carpenters, and equipment operators.

Burns International Security Services, Inc.
8150 Brookriver Dr., Suite 103A
Dallas, TX 75247
Metro (214) 638-1666
Security guard service.

CDI Temporary Services
4255 LBJ Frwy.
Dallas, TX 75244
(214) 233-0046
Data processing, word processing, and clerical.

Durham Temporaries, Inc.
4015 Main St.
Dallas, TX 75226
(214) 747-3612
Industrial, technical, and clerical.

Firstword Temporaries
14755 Preston Rd.
Dallas, TX 75240
(214) 788-4900
General office, legal secretaries, and data processors.

Fast talk nets big part-time $$$

People who need to earn money while job hunting might consider the telemarketing, or telephone sales, industry. Debra Schwartz, who has worked as a telemarketing manager, feels that the field offers a variety of challenges and rewards.

"Being a telemarketer is almost like being an actor in a radio play," says Debra. "Your success depends on how well you control your voice. You also have to be able to receive feedback from people without the benefit of eye contact or body language."

We asked Debra what telemarketing managers look for in the people they hire. "The crucial element is the person's voice. Telemarketers must speak clearly and have pleasing voices. They also must use standard English grammar. Previous sales experience is a plus, although it's not necessary. Managers also look for people who can handle rejection. A person might get rejected 25 or 30 times before making a sale."

According to Debra, most telemarketers work in four-hour shifts. "You can't work on the phone for more than four hours without becoming ineffective. Also, many firms operate only in the afternoons and evenings. But some firms do have morning hours—those involved in corporate sales, for example."

How much can a telemarketer expect to make?

"Top people can make over $10 per hour," says Debra. "The average telemarketer makes about $4–$8 per hour. The pay varies depending on whether you are working on a straight commission basis or are being paid a base hourly wage plus commissions."

Debra suggests investigating a telemarketing firm carefully before accepting a job, since there are quite a few fly-by-night operations. But she emphasizes the many benefits to working for a reputable firm: "Telemarketing is a great experience for job hunters. Many of the basic sales techniques that you learn are usable when promoting yourself to a potential employer."

Getting a part-time job in telemarketing requires persistence, since managers receive hundreds of calls and applications. "Don't give up," advises Debra. "Have your sales pitch ready when you call. Sell yourself on the phone in the same way that you would sell a product once you're hired."■

Greyhound Temporary Personnel, Inc.
101 Mallick Tower
One Summit Ave.
Fort Worth, TX 76102
(817) 335-6333
Clerical, industrial, and mechanical.

Help Unlimited, Inc.
3300 Main St.
Dallas, TX 75226
(214) 748-0561
Clerical to light industrial.

Jess Temporaries
3501 Airport Frwy.
Fort Worth, TX 76111
(817) 831-0906
General and some electrical.

Kelly Services (The "Kelly Girl" People)
2424 One Main Place
Dallas, TX 75250
(214) 742-1721
Office, light industrial, and records management.

Labor Force, Inc.
4248 Harry Hines Blvd.
Dallas, TX 75219
(214) 744-4611
General, clerical, and construction.

Manpower Temporary Services
500 N. Akard St.
Dallas, TX 75201
(214) 954-0093
Office, light industrial, sales promotion, and data processing.

Good advice from a bartender

One of our friends, a successful freelance video producer, spent several years tending bar part-time in various popular Dallas nightclubs to support his television habit.

"The best places to look for part-time work," he says, "are those where you're already known. Bar owners will rarely hire a bartender who walks in off the street, or fresh out of Famous Bartending School's two-week course. That's because it's very easy for bartenders to steal. An owner wants to know someone, to have a sense of a person's character, before he hires a bartender. So if you're looking for part-time work—and this goes for waiters and waitresses, too—spend some time in the place for a couple of weeks. Get to know the people who work there and the regular customers, and become one of the regulars yourself. Learn how the place operates. Every bar or restaurant has its own way of doing things, from handling special orders to taking care of rowdy customers. The more you know about a place, the easier it is to step in when somebody calls in sick or quits."■

Medical Temps, Inc.
13877 Brookgreen Dr.
Dallas, TX 75240
(214) 234-4575
Pharmacy, lab, and X-ray staff.

Norrell Temporary Services
2001 Bryan Tower
Dallas, TX 75201
(214) 742-8831
Clerical, light industrial, and word processing.

Olsten Temporary Services
9400 N. Central Expwy., Suite 112
Dallas, TX 75231
(214) 373-7400
Secretarial, word processing, and accounting.

Peakload Temporary Services
118 Hemphill St.
Fort Worth, TX 76104
Metro (817) 654-4409
Furniture moving, warehousing, and construction.

The Personnel Connection, Inc.
4001 Airport Frwy.
Irving, TX 75062
(817) 589-1741
Secretaries, bookkeepers, and receptionists.

Personnel Pool, Inc.
911 N. Peak St.
Dallas, TX 75204
(214) 826-6290
Industrial, technical, and clerical.

Pinkertons, Inc.
1140 Empire Central, Suite 330
Dallas, TX 75247
(214) 631-6924
Security guard service.

Pinkertons, Inc.
6421 Camp Bowie Blvd.
Fort Worth, TX 76116
(817) 737-7237
Security guard service.

Regency Temporaries, Inc.
600 Six Flags Dr., Suite 400
Arlington, TX 76011
(817) 640-6640
Temporary accounting, general office, and light industrial.

Smith Protective Services, Inc.
8918 John Carpenter Frwy.
Dallas, TX 75235
(214) 358-3333
Security guard service.

Stanley Smith Security Service, Inc.
1525 W. Mockingbird Ln., Suite 308
Dallas, TX 75235
(214) 634-9911
Security guard service.

Southwest Temporaries
2501 Parkview Dr.
Fort Worth, TX 76102
(817) 877-5757
Secretarial, legal, and data processing.

State Taxicab Co.
1231 E. Illinois Ave.
Dallas, TX 75216
(214) 823-2161
Taxicab leasing.

Temporaries' Network
1255 W. 15th St.
Plano, TX 75075
(214) 881-0373
Secretarial, clerical, and technical.

Temporary Employment Associates, Inc.
510 RepublicBank Oak Cliff
Dallas, TX 75208
(214) 941-4063
Secretarial, keypunch, and payroll.

TempsAmerica
350 N. St. Paul St., Suite 1665
Dallas, TX 75201
(214) 922-9229
Word processors, accounting clerks, and bookkeepers.

Terminal Cab
6303 Cedar Springs Rd.
Dallas, TX 75235
(214) 350-4445
Taxicab leasing.

Todays Temporary
4100 McEwen Rd.
Dallas, TX 75234
(214) 788-2833
Office, marketing, and project services.

Yellow Cab of Dallas
1610 S. Ervay St.
Dallas, TX 75215
(214) 565-9132
Taxicab leasing.

Yellow Checker Cab
1010 Stayton St.
Fort Worth, TX 76107
(817) 335-3331
Taxicab leasing.

Government and Private Assistance Programs

If you've exhausted all your resources and can't find part-time or temporary work, you might consider state, federal, or private assistance. Many people bridle at the mere mention of "charity" or "welfare." But the help you receive is needed—and temporary. It's a way of bridging the gap until you land a job. More people take advantage of these sources of assistance than you might imagine. In the case of state and federal aid, your tax dollars have helped to provide the benefits. Your taxes have also paid for the salaries of the people distributing the benefits.

Don't pass judgment on the merits of the following sources until you talk with the professionals who administer their respective programs. Pros can advise you on eligibility and benefits, and can also provide you with other ideas and resources.

City of Dallas Health and Human Services
Food Stamp Services
2922 Martin Luther King Jr. Blvd.
Dallas, TX 75215
(214) 421-7722
Food stamp assistance for Dallas residents only. Eligibility determined on the basis of income, dependents, and employment record.

Dallas County Community Action Committee, Inc.
2208 Main St.
Dallas, TX 75201
(214) 939-0588
Neighborhood centers offer limited emergency assistance, food, and clothing.

Dallas County Public Health Department
1936 Amelia Ct.
Dallas, TX 75235
(214) 920-7900
Public health services for Dallas County residents who live outside Dallas city limits.

Filing for unemployment benefits

Here are three good reasons to check with the Texas Employment Commission: There's no charge for any of the services. You'll probably find leads for better jobs than you expected. And you may qualify for one of the programs assisting special interest groups.

An average of two thousand available positions are listed in the TEC's computerized job bank. On weekdays, you can drop by any one of the 13 area offices to check on what's available. At least 50 percent are professional, clerical, and sales jobs. And a majority are permanent, full-time positions.

The government-funded public employment agency also provides free employment testing and counseling, and makes referrals to social agencies. Special assistance is provided to veterans, disabled workers, older workers, mothers with dependent children, ex-offenders, youths, minorities, and disadvantaged individuals.

A new pilot program called Job Search Seminars is offered in the downtown Fort Worth office and the Richardson-Plano office. Anyone who is receiving unemployment compensation is eligible to attend the five-day workshop. Participants prepare for the job search by watching a video job-hunting course developed by Karli and Associates. In addition, they learn to communicate more effectively with employers by having mock job interviews videotaped, so they can see where they need to improve.

The TEC also helps people find seasonal employment. Several weeks before the State Fair of Texas opens in October, a TEC booth is set up on the Dallas fairgrounds to sign up as many as one thousand people for temporary jobs. The TEC also assists storeowners in large shopping malls to find workers for the Christmas rush.

Anyone who can't find a suitable job should register at the TEC for unemployment insurance. The amount of money individuals are eligible to receive depends on their former income and reasons for being out of work.

For example, people who have been laid off because a company went out of business should find out if they are eligible for the maximum benefits. The TEC requires people to actively search for a job while they receive unemployment compensation. Checks are mailed twice a month for 26 weeks to those who qualify for the maximum benefits.

To sign up for benefits, bring your social security card and the name and mailing address of your last employer to one of the 12 offices in the Dallas/Fort Worth area. If you were employed outside of Texas during the past 24 months, you will need the names and addresses of all the companies you worked for during that time.

For more information, call the Fort Worth office at (817) 335-5111 or the Dallas office at (214) 631-6050.

Here are the phone numbers and addresses of TEC offices in the Dallas area:

Central City, 2405 Cedar Springs Rd., Suite 125, (214) 651-0550
Garland, 217 10th St., (214) 276-8361
Grand Prairie, 202 W. Hwy. 303, (214) 264-5881
Irving, 201 S. Rogers St., (214) 254-9135
Lancaster-Kiest Office, 408 Lancaster-Kiest Shopping Center, (214) 372-1471
Martin Luther King Jr. Community Center, 2922 Martin Luther King Jr. Blvd., (214) 421-2460
Northwest-Carrollton, 1718 Trinity Valley Dr., (214) 620-1351
Pleasant Grove, 313 Pleasant Grove Mall, (214) 398-0611
Richardson-Plano, 1240 E. Campbell Rd., Suite 202, (214) 234-5391
Westmoreland Heights Office, 3217 Dawes Dr., (214) 330-5183

Offices in Tarrant County include:

Arlington, 979 N. Cooper St., (817) 265-8431

Downtown Fort Worth, 301 W. 13th St., (817) 335-5111
Hurst, 1225 Precinct Line Rd., (817) 282-9845 ■

Dallas County Public Welfare
4917 Harry Hines Blvd.
Dallas, TX 75235
(214) 920-7850
Emergency assistance program providing food and rent vouchers and payment to utility companies for individuals and families who meet eligibility requirements and live in Dallas County outside the Dallas city limits.
Area offices:
Grand Prairie Unit, 1401 Densman St., (214) 262-1328
Martin Luther King Jr. Community Center, 2922 Martin Luther King Jr. Blvd., (214) 670-8367
Mesquite Unit, 207 W. Main St., (214) 288-5446

Neighborhood Resources Development Program
1000 Throckmorton St.
Fort Worth, TX 76102
(817) 870-7540
Assistance for qualified individuals in paying utility bills, dental services, distribution of surplus commodities, and referrals.
Tarrant County Centers:
Como Office, 4900 Horne St., (817) 731-0521
Eastside NRD Center, 5565 Truman Dr., (817) 457-2076
Kennedale/Mansfield NRD Center, 341 Debbie Ln., (817) 473-0253
North Tri-ethnic, 2950 Roosevelt St., (817) 625-8257
Riverside Office, 201 S. Sylvania Ave., (817) 831-0355
Sansom Park NRD Center, 5428 Cowden St., (817) 624-3139
Southside NRD Center, 959 E. Rosedale St., (817) 332-7786
Stockyards NRD Center, 2501 Houston St., (817) 625-2886
Worth Heights Office, 3551 New York Ave., (817) 921-5321

Parkland Memorial Hospital
5201 Harry Hines Blvd.
Dallas, TX 75235
(214) 637-8000
Low-cost medical services for Dallas County residents, including emergency, surgical, psychiatric, and outpatient care.

John Peter Smith Hospital
1500 S. Main St.
Fort Worth, TX 76104
(817) 921-3431
Low-cost outpatient and hospital care for Tarrant County residents.

Social Security Administration
Dallas Area Office
10910 N. Central Expwy.
Dallas, TX 75231
(214) 263-5861
Financial aid, Medicare, retirement, and disability insurance.

Social Security Administration
Fort Worth Area Office
819 Taylor St., Rm. 1A07
Fort Worth, TX 76102
(817) 263-5861
Same as Dallas office.

Tarrant County Department of Human Services
208 E. Weatherford St.
Fort Worth, TX 76102
(817) 877-2770
Financial assistance through vouchers for food, rent, and utility payments. Referrals, counseling and shelter for eligible homeless families with children.
Branch offices:
724 E. Border St., Arlington, (817) 277-8176
645 Grapevine Hwy., Suite 8, Hurst, (817) 281-5061
3212 Miller Ave., Fort Worth, (817) 531-3995

Tarrant County Welfare
3125 E. Lancaster Ave.
Fort Worth, TX 76103
(817) 531-3797
Emergency assistance program providing food and rent vouchers and payment to utility companies for individuals and families who meet eligibility requirements.

Texas Department of Health
Public Health Region 5
701 Directors Dr.
Arlington, TX 76011
Metro (817) 261-2911
Provides information and referrals to inexpensive health service programs for children under 12 years of age.

Texas Department of Human Services
Region Five
631 106th St.
Arlington, TX 76011
Metro (817) 261-3376
Food stamps, medical, and social services for adults and children who meet financial requirements.
Food Stamp program offered at the following Tarrant County sites:
308 E. 4th St., Fort Worth, (817) 335-5171
3128 S. Riverside Dr., Fort Worth, (817) 921-5511
2526 Jacksboro Hwy., Fort Worth, (817) 625-2161
203 W. Main St., Arlington, (817) 460-6491

Texas Employment Commission
Dallas District Office
8300 John Carpenter Frwy.
Dallas, TX 75247
(214) 631-6050
Provides unemployment insurance for those who are eligible and cannot find employment through the commission's job bank. Special help provided for elderly, youths, handicapped, ex-offenders, women with dependent children, and others.

Texas Employment Commission
Fort Worth District Office
310 W. 13th St.
Fort Worth, TX 76101
(817) 335-5111
Same as Dallas District Office.

Private Charitable Organizations

American Red Cross
2300 McKinney Ave.
Dallas, TX 75201
(214) 871-2175
Limited financial aid and shelter for families experiencing short-term crisis.

Arlington Charities
215 W. Main St.
Arlington, TX 76010
(817) 275-1511
Clothing and food provided on a short-term basis for Arlington residents.

Baptist Community Center
915 E. Peach St.
Fort Worth, TX 76102
(817) 336-1922
Food and clothing for people living near the center.

Baptist Family Services
4520 James Ave.
Fort Worth, TX 76115
(817) 927-1911
Food, clothing, and emergency financial assistance.

Bethlehem Foundation
2603-A Idaho St.
Dallas, TX 75376
(214) 371-3407
Food assistance, clothing, and limited funds available for housing and utilities.

Bread Basket Ministries
704 Pennsylvania Ave.
Fort Worth, TX 76104
(817) 335-7283
Financial counseling, food, rent, and utility assistance.

Broadway Baptist Church
411 May St.
Fort Worth, TX 76104
(817) 336-5761
Clothing, food vouchers, and assistance with prescription medicines.

Casa San Jose
2024 N. Houston St.
Fort Worth, TX 76106
(817) 626-3402
Hot lunches, emergency shelter, clothing, and gasoline for finding employment.

Catholic Charities
3845 Oak Lawn Ave.
Dallas, TX 75219
(214) 528-4870
Limited emergency financial aid. Emergency assistance to low-income families in East Dallas provided by component agency: Brady Social Service Center, 4009 Elm St., (214) 826-8330.

Catholic Charities
Fort Worth Office
1404 Hemphill St.
Fort Worth, TX 76104
(817) 921-5381
Food, clothing, furniture, and limited financial assistance for travelers and Tarrant County residents.
Other sites:
405 E. Pipeline Rd., Bedford, (817) 282-6646
208 W. Main St., Arlington, (817) 274-2534

Cliff Temple Baptist Church/Weekday Ministries
123 W. 10th St.
Dallas, TX 75208
(214) 942-8601
Non-perishable food, clothing, and limited financial assistance available for Oak Cliff residents only. Free lunch served at church.

Consumer Credit Counseling Service of Greater Dallas, Inc.
5415 Maple Ave., Suite 205
Dallas, TX 75235-7490
(214) 634-1560
Credit counseling for financially distressed individuals. Nominal fee charged based on family income and size.

Consumer Credit Counseling Services of Greater Fort Worth
807 Texas St., Suite 104
Fort Worth, TX 76102
(817) 334-0151
Same as Dallas office.

Consumer Credit Counseling Services of North Central Texas
Plano Office
555 Republic Dr., Suite 319
Plano, TX 75074
(214) 423-5175
Same as Dallas office.

Dallas Life Foundation
100 Cadiz St.
Dallas, TX 75221
(214) 421-1380
Provides three meals a day and a place to stay for $5 a day. Offers some counseling and assistance in finding temporary work.

East Dallas Cooperative Parish
5200 Bryan St.
Dallas, TX 75206
(214) 823-9149
Provides food twice a month and clothing once a month for East Dallas residents. Placement service with job bank available to anyone in community.

First Call For Help
Tarrant County
210 E. 9th St.
Fort Worth, TX 76102
(817) 335-3473
Refers individuals to appropriate community resource and checks to determine if problem was resolved.
Other offices:
208 W. Main St., Arlington, (817) 274-2534
405 E. Pipeline Rd., Bedford, (817) 282-6646

First Methodist Church/Epworth Hall
807 W. 5th St.
Fort Worth, TX 76102
(817) 336-8543
Provides food, clothing, and referrals.

First United Methodist Church of Lancaster
Welfare Fund
201 S. Dallas Ave.
Lancaster, TX 75146
(214) 227-1554
Contact: Margaret Robinson
Assists needy Lancaster residents.

The Food Bank of Greater Tarrant County
2101 Brennan Ave.
Fort Worth, TX 76106
(817) 625-1673
Supplemental food to chronically needy families.

Grace Union Presbytery, Good Shepherd Community Center
4931 Bernal Dr.
Dallas, TX 75212
(214) 638-1688
Emergency aid and referrals.

Grand Prairie United Charities
1415 Densman St.
Grand Prairie, TX 75051
Metro (214) 263-0010
Offers information, referrals, and limited assistance when other resources are not available.

Bill Harrod Memorial Mission
3444 Palacios St.
Dallas, TX 75212
(214) 638-2196
Supplies food and clothing on short-term basis.

Information and Referral
Community Council of Greater Dallas
2121 Main St., Suite 500
Dallas, TX 75201
(214) 747-3711
24-hour emergency referral service to health, welfare, and social service agencies.

Irving Aid, Inc.
201 E. Union Bower Rd., Suite 3
Irving, TX 75060
(214) 254-3132
Information and referral service for Irving residents only. Food and financial assistance provided on a limited basis.

Jewish Family Service
7800 Northaven Rd.
Dallas, TX 75230
(214) 696-6400
Food bank and referrals for the Jewish community and North Dallas residents.

Ladies of Charity of Dallas, Inc.
2710 Samuell Blvd.
Dallas, TX 75223
(214) 821-5775
Short-term emergency help for individuals who are waiting for assistance from established social service agencies.

Liberation Community
3110 E. Rosedale Ave.
Fort Worth, TX 76105
(817) 534-7186
Assistance in locating food, clothing, and housing.

Loaves & Fishes/The Metroplex Food Bank
1424 Hemphill St.
Fort Worth, TX 76133
(817) 924-2541
Soup kitchen open for lunch Monday through Saturday. Referrals made to other agencies.

Mesquite Social Services
207 W. Main St.
Mesquite, TX 75149
(214) 285-3000
Information and referrals about resources available to Mesquite and Balch Springs residents. Food and financial assistance available on a limited basis.

Methodism's Breadbasket
5710 E. R.L. Thornton Frwy.
Dallas, TX 75223
(214) 821-2970
Must be referred by another agency to receive food.

Metrocrest Service Center
1508 Belt Line Rd., Suite 101
Carrollton, TX 75006
(214) 446-2100
Food, clothing, and limited financial assistance provided for residents of Carrollton, Addison, Coppell, and Farmers Branch.

Mt. Olive Volunteer Effort
3100 Martin Luther King Blvd.
Dallas, TX 75215
(214) 428-2892
Food provided on short-term basis.

Network of Community Ministries
300 Bishop Ave., Suite 11N
Richardson, TX 75081
(214) 234-8880
Serves people who live in the Richardson Independent School District. Provides food, clothing, and financial assistance for rent, utilities, and prescriptions. Offers some job referrals to other agencies.

North Dallas Shared Ministries
3450 Forest Ln.
Dallas, TX 75234
(214) 353-0495
Emergency food and financial assistance for rent, utilities, and transportation provided for one-time crisis situation.

Northeast Emergency Distribution (NEED)
801-B Glenda Dr.
Bedford, TX 76022
(817) 280-0286
Twenty-six churches in Tarrant County provide food, clothing, and utility assistance.

Oak Cliff Churches for Emergency Aid
123 W. 10th St.
Dallas, TX 75208
(214) 943-7757
Emergency food and limited funds available to Oak Cliff residents.

Presbyterian Housing Coalition
2906 Swiss Ave.
Dallas, TX 75206
(214) 827-7220
Temporary housing and assistance with food, clothing, and transportation for up to 90 days for families with one member employed or employable.

Salvation Army
City Command
201 Jones St.
Fort Worth, TX 76102
(817) 332-1961
Shelter for men, women, and families. Free dinner served at 5 p.m. Referrals made to other agencies.

Salvation Army
Social Services Center
2215 N. Akard St.
Dallas, TX 75201
(214) 742-9131
Meals and temporary shelter provided for men, women, and children. Food bank available for area residents.

Salvation Army Corps of Garland
451 W. Ave. D
Garland, TX 75046
(214) 272-4531
Temporary aid for Garland-area residents and transients. Provides food and limited financial assistance for medical prescriptions, utility bills, and rent.

SEARCH (Southeast Area Churches) Association
3540 E. Rosedale Ave.
Fort Worth, TX 76105
(817) 531-2211
Clothing and emergency funds for medical, housing, and utilities for Southeast area residents.

SHARE
East Dallas Christian Church
629 N. Peak St.
Dallas, TX 75246
(214) 824-8185
Food and assistance provided from 10 a.m. to noon Monday through Friday for East Dallas residents.

Southside Area Ministries
305 W. Broadway St.
Fort Worth, TX 76104
(817) 332-3776
Food box distributed third Wednesday of each month for southside Fort Worth residents.

Stewpot
First Presbyterian Church
408 Park Ave.
Dallas, TX 75201
(214) 748-8051
Coffee and donuts served in morning and hot meal served at lunch Monday through Friday at the church. Church also sponsors a Step-Up Housing Ministry, providing temporary housing.

Union Gospel Mission
922 Park Ave.
Dallas, TX 75201
(214) 747-5606
Provides free lodging, meals, and clothing for men and women.

Union Gospel Mission and Family Center
1331 E. Lancaster Ave.
Fort Worth, TX 76102
(817) 332-3019
Temporary shelter, food, clothing, and transportation for medical assistance.

United Community Centers, Inc.
617 7th Ave.
Fort Worth, TX 76104
(817) 332-7332
Emergency food, clothing, assistance with naturalization documents and bilingual programs.
Sites:
Bethlehem Community Center, 970 E. Humbolt St., (817) 332-7911
Bethlehem Community Center Annex, 1000 New York Ave., (817) 332-8767
Englewood Community Center, 3101 Ave. J, (817) 531-2803
Maddox Community Center, 1200 Maddox St., (817) 926-5329
Southeast Center, 4716 Richardson St., (817) 534-6137
Wesley Community Center, 3600 Crump St., (817) 625-8205

Urban Ministries
1721 E. Vickery Blvd.
Fort Worth, TX 76104
(817) 332-4543
Financial assistance, food, and clothing.

Washington Street Presbyterian Mission
3525 State St.
Dallas, TX 75204
(214) 824-6801
Funds and referrals for emergency food, clothing, and legal assistance.

YWCA of Fort Worth and Tarrant County
512 W. 4th St.
Fort Worth, TX 76102
(817) 332-6191
Low-cost housing provided for women 18 years old and older. Referrals and information provided to other agencies.

Help with mounting debts

Feel overwhelmed by mounting debts? If so, contact the Consumer Credit Counseling service in your area for help in easing your temporary financial crisis.

Counselors can review your monthly living expenses and debts and suggest ways to survive financially while you're out of work. In some cases, they will contact your creditors to make arrangements for lower monthly payments.

The service assists people from all income levels who are unable to cope with their situation. "People express their frustration in very emotional terms. We tell them there is always a solution," says Pamela Gray, executive director of Consumer Credit Counseling of North Central Texas, Inc.

For some, the remedy is to discard credit cards. As a reminder, Gray's office contains large jars filled with hundreds of severed credit cards.

The best time to contact one of the area offices is when you are first unable to meet your monthly financial obligations, Gray says. Don't wait until the day someone comes out to repossess your car, she says.

Nominal fees for the nonprofit community service are based on a sliding scale and determined by a person's income and family size.

It's worth your peace of mind to get your money matters in order, Gray says, so you can concentrate on your main priority—finding a job.■

9 Where to Turn If Your Confidence Wilts

Recently a bank fired a loan officer who had worked there for more than 10 years. The employee was 58 years old, about five feet, six inches tall, weighed almost 300 pounds, and did not have a college degree. His written communication skills were negligible. His poor attitude and appearance, lack of enthusiasm, and dismal self-esteem suggested he would be unemployed a long time.

The bank decided to use Tom Camden and Associates' outplacement service to help the person get another job. "There wasn't much we could do about changing his age, education, size, or communication skills," Tom recalls. "But we certainly could—and did—work with him on improving his self-esteem and changing his attitude toward interviewing for new jobs."

After a four-month search, the loan officer succeeded in landing a position that exactly suited his needs. His new job even was located in the neighborhood where he lived. It seemed like a typical success story—until the bank informed Tom Camden about how dissatisfied that person was with the counsel he had received. The man told the bank that they would have been better off paying *him* the consulting fee instead of retaining outside help.

"He was really angry," Tom recalls. "And also full of stress, guilt, fear, anxiety, desire for vengeance, and a host of other emotions."

Such feelings, unfortunately, are not at all unusual. In fact, they're a *normal* part of any job search, particularly for those who have been laid off or fired. That's because rejection, unfortunately, is inevitable in any job search.

If you've read Chapter 5, you know that you may speak with as many as 300 people on a formal or informal basis while you're looking for suitable work—and a healthy percentage of those people will be unable or unwilling to help you. Every job-seeker must anticipate rejection—it comes with the territory. Being turned down in an interview is a painful experience, and it's normal to feel hurt. The trick is to keep those hurt and angry feelings from clouding your judgment or affecting your behavior.

If you're beginning to feel your confidence wilt, reread the tips for treating yourself well in Chapter 5. Put yourself on a regular schedule. Make sure you're eating healthy foods and getting enough rest and exercise. Don't punish yourself for being unemployed or losing a job offer.

One of the worst things that can happen in any job search is to let rejection undermine your self-confidence. Like the little boy at the door who asks, "You don't want to buy a magazine, do you?", a person who doesn't feel good about himself will not easily convince an employer that he should be hired. Each new rejection further erodes self-esteem, and the job search stalls or takes a nose dive: "Maybe I *am* a loser. Perhaps I was lucky to have my old job as long as I did. Maybe my sights are set too high. I suppose I should look for something less responsible at a lower salary."

Thoughts such as these cross most people's minds at some time or other in the job search. As we've said, it's normal to feel hurt, angry, and depressed after a series of rejections. It's important, however, to recognize these feelings and learn to work them out in some non-destructive way. It is *not* normal to let such feelings sabotage your job search. Just because you're unemployed or looking for a new job doesn't mean you're a bad or worthless person. The only

What to do if you get fired

Being fired ranks just after the death of someone you love and divorce when it comes to personal traumas. If it should happen to you, **take time to evaluate the bad news before accepting a settlement offer.** If you quickly accept what your employer has to offer, it will be much more difficult to change your situation later. Tell the boss you want some time to think about a settlement. Then go back in a day or two and negotiate.

Stay on the payroll as long as you can, even if your pride hurts. Find out if you are eligible for part-time work or consulting jobs to tide you over until you find your new job. You may be able to hang on to insurance and other benefits until you've found new employment.

Try to negotiate a generous severance payment. In the last five years, severance agreements have risen dramatically in some industries. What the company offers at first may not be the maximum. Negotiation doesn't always work, but you certainly ought to try to get the most for your years of service.

Check with your personnel office to make sure you're getting all the benefits to which you are entitled, such as vacation pay and profit sharing. Check your eligibility for unemployment compensation before you accept an offer to resign instead of being terminated.

Don't attack management during your termination interview. It may cost you good references and hurt your chances of finding a new job.■

thing "wrong" with you is that you haven't found the offer that you want.

When your confidence starts to wilt, turn to a trusted friend or relative. Talk about your feelings frankly. Get mad, or sad, or vengeful. Then get back to work on your job search. Don't let fear of rejection keep you from making that next call. It may be just the lead you're looking for.

There are no hard and fast rules on when to seek professional counseling and support, but we can offer certain guidelines. If you seriously think you need professional help, you ought to investigate two or three sources. Besides the ones we've listed below, check with your minister, priest, or rabbi. Many clerics are trained counselors, and their help is free.

If you feel you have nowhere else to turn, or if you don't want to share your feelings with anyone you know, you should consider psychiatric or psychological counseling. If you're not making calls, or not preparing for interviews, or not doing what you know you have to do to get the job you want, you could probably use some counseling. *Everybody* feels bad about being rejected. But if you allow those feelings to overwhelm you, or if they're interfering with finding a job, it's probably time to talk with a professional. Another sure sign is if you're waking up most mornings too sick or lethargic from overeating, overdrinking, or abusing some other substance to do what you have to do..

A listing in this book does not constitute an endorsement of any institution, therapist, or school of therapy. Therapy depends a great deal upon the "chemistry" between therapist and patient—something only you can evaluate. A basic rule of thumb is that if you're not comfortable with or confident in a particular therapist, it may not be wise to continue seeing him or her.

Therapy is offered by quite a variety of people, from psychiatrists and psychologists with years of post-graduate training to those with considerably lower levels of education and experience. Before engaging a therapist, check his or her credentials. Where was the therapist trained? What degrees does the therapist hold? How long has the therapist been practicing? Does he or she belong to any professional associations?

Not all therapists have to be licensed in the state of Texas. While psychologists must be licensed and social workers certified, professional counselors do not have to be licensed to practice.

Various state and local agencies can help you check up on a therapist. You can telephone state agencies to find out if a therapist has been licensed, and if so, whether any complaints have been registered.

You can call the Texas State Board of Examiners of Psychologists in Austin at (512) 835-2036 to ask about licensing and complaints. For social workers, call the Texas Department of Human Resources at (512) 450-3255.

Many professional counselors are licensed, even though it isn't mandatory. Call the Texas State Board of Examiners of Professional Counselors at (512) 458-7511. Marriage and family counselors do not have to be licensed in Texas, but many are accredited through the American Association for Marriage and Family Therapy. To find out if a therapist is a member, check the yellow pages of the phone book or call the national headquarters at (202) 429-1825, or write 1717 K St. NW, Suite 407, Washington D.C. 20006.

You can also check with the Mental Health Association of Dallas County at (214) 871-2420 or the Mental Health Association of Tarrant County at (817) 335-5405. Staff members provide information and referrals to the Mental Health and Mental Retardation Centers. Also, the association serves as a clearinghouse for information about self-help groups.

Selected Crisis Centers and Institutions

Alcoholics Anonymous
Fort Worth Central Office
316 Bailey Ave.
Fort Worth, TX 76107
(817) 332-3533
Offers referrals to numerous AA groups in Tarrant County. Free.

Alcoholics Anonymous
Metropolitan Dallas
3798 Forest Ln., Suite 9
Dallas, TX 75234
(214) 956-7333
Provides information and referrals to alcoholics and families. Offers counseling, support groups, and halfway houses. Free.

American Indian Center
818 E. Davis St.
Grand Prairie, TX 75050
(214) 262-1349
Crisis counseling for American Indians and a halfway house for alcohol rehabilitation. Free.

Baptist Marriage and Family Counseling Center
2001 W. Seminary Dr.
Fort Worth, TX 76122
(817) 926-1441
Personal and family counseling. Free.

Catholic Charities
3845 Oak Lawn Ave.
Dallas, TX 75219
(214) 528-4870
Staff members provide crisis intervention counseling and assessment for families and individuals. Free emergency help. Counseling billed on sliding scale.

Center for Creative Living
2401 Oakland Blvd., Suite 100
Fort Worth, TX 76103
Metro (817) 429-0521
Psychotherapy, vocational counseling, and crisis intervention. Sliding scale fees.

Community Psychotherapy Center, Inc.
3626 N. Hall St., Suite 600
Dallas, TX 75219
(214) 528-3722
Individual and group therapy. Psychiatric evaluations available for those in therapy. Sliding scale fees and contributions.

Community Resource Center (Gayline)
P.O. Box 190835
Dallas, TX 75219
(214) 368-6283
Volunteers provide information, referrals, and informal counseling for gay men and women from 7:30 p.m. to midnight. Accepts contributions.

Community Service Clinic, University of Texas at Arlington
211 S. Cooper St., Center B
Arlington, TX 76019
(817) 273-2165
Individual and family counseling. Sliding scale.

CONTACT—Dallas/Telephone Counseling
P.O. Box 25574
Dallas, TX 75225
(214) 233-2233
Trained volunteers provide 24-hour telephone counseling and referrals for distressed persons.

CONTACT—Tarrant County
P.O. Box 1431
Arlington, TX 76010
(817) 277-2233
Trained volunteers provide 24-hour telephone counseling and referrals for distressed individuals.

Crisis Intervention
716 W. Magnolia St.
Fort Worth, TX 76104
Hot Line: (817) 336-3355
Trained volunteers provide 24-hour telephone counseling and referrals.

Church groups offer support

Churches and synagogues have found special ways to minister to the needs of the unemployed.

In addition to providing food and clothing in emergency situations, congregations have formed support groups to help people find jobs.

Here's how the program works in one church:

Each Monday night, an average of 30 people gather at Christ United Methodist Church in Plano. One by one, they introduce themselves and state what type of job they are seeking. Some are out of work, others are thinking about making a career change, and several women are eager to re-enter the job market.

They pass along news about job openings and discuss what's happened to them. Then they spend the next hour listening to a guest speaker discuss such pertinent topics as interviewing effectively, resume writing, changing careers, networking, marketing, and the emotional aspects of losing a job.

"This group helps us realize we're not alone in this situation. It meets an acute need because some people have heard the job hunt is easy and it's not," says Carol Kepner, task force coordinator of the Job Transition Support Group.

Sessions are videotaped for those who can't attend, and copies of the tape can be checked out of the church library. Available job positions are listed on a bulletin board along with notices from people who indicate they are seeking a position. A list of resource people is available in a card file.

Church members and visitors are encouraged to drop by the meetings at 2640 Glencliff Dr. They begin with a networking session at 7 p.m. Monday followed by the program at 7:30 p.m. For more information, call the church office at (214) 596-4303.■

Dallas Alcoholic Center, Inc.
614 S. Harwood St.
Dallas, TX 75201
(214) 742-0872
Shelter, food, clothing, and job referrals for rehabilitation of male alcoholics.

Dallas Council on Alcoholism and Drug Abuse
5415 Maple Ave., Suite 316
Dallas, TX 75235
(214) 638-7090
Provides public education, information and referrals, employee assistance program. Sliding scale fees.

Dallas Vet Center (Vietnam Veterans Outreach Center)
5415 Maple Ave., Suite 114
Dallas, TX 75235
(214) 634-7024
Counseling, referrals, and psychotherapy provided for veterans and their families. Free.

Drug & Family Counseling Center of Arlington
812 W. Division St.
Arlington, TX 76012
(817) 459-5940
Counseling provided for Arlington residents. Free to residents.

Family Guidance Center
2200 Main St.
Dallas, TX 75201
(214) 747-8331
Crisis intervention and general counseling for individuals, couples, and families. Sliding scale fees.

Family Outreach Program
6434 Maple Ave.
Dallas, TX 75235
(214) 350-9711
Information, referrals, and counseling provided for parents experiencing family stress. Accepts contributions.

The Family Resource, Inc.
4901 W. Lovers Ln.
Dallas, TX 75209
(214) 350-6621
Individual, family, couples, and group counseling. Sliding scale fees.

Family Service
716 W. Magnolia Ave.
Fort Worth, TX 76104
(817) 335-2401
Several centers provide counseling for individuals and families. The crisis intervention hotline number is (817) 336-3355. Sliding scale fees.
Other sites:
3212 W. Park Row Ave., Suite E, Arlington, (817) 277-1337
530 Bedford Rd., Bedford, (817) 283-6686
2315 N. Main St., Suite 304, Fort Worth, (817) 625-6321

First United Methodist Church Counseling Service
800 W. Fifth St.
Fort Worth, TX 76102
(817) 924-8521
Counseling for couples, individuals, and groups. Fees vary from $40 for individual counseling to sliding scale.

First United Methodist Church of Arlington Counseling Service
313 N. Center St.
Arlington, TX 76011
(817) 274-2571
Counseling programs for individuals, couples, and families. Ongoing support groups. Fees vary from $35 per individual session to $10 for group sessions. Adjustments made for income.

Galaxy Center
451 W. Ave. D
Garland, TX 75040
(214) 272-4429
Group, individual, and family counseling for Garland residents. Sliding scale fees.

Jewish Family Service
7800 Northaven Rd., Suite B
Dallas, TX 75230
(214) 696-6400
Individual, vocational, and family counseling. Sliding scale fees.

Jewish Social Service Agency
6801 Dan Danciger Rd.
Fort Worth, TX 76133
(817) 294-2660
Individual and family counseling. Sliding scale fees.

Mental Health Association of Dallas County
2500 Maple Ave.
Dallas, TX 75201
(214) 748-7825
Referrals and information for counseling and self-help groups that deal with a variety of mutual concerns.

Metroplex Psychotherapy Services, Inc.
12606 N. Greenville Ave., Suite 244
Dallas, TX 75243
(214) 238-1267
Counseling, treatment, crisis intervention, and psychiatric consultation for individuals, couples, and families. Offers group psychotherapy. Sliding scale fees.

Nexus, Inc.
3116 Fairmount St.
Dallas, TX 75201
(214) 871-2467
Alcohol, drug, and employment counseling for women 18 to 65 years old. Sliding scale fees.

Pastoral Care and Training Center of Texas Christian University
2828 W. Lowden St.
Fort Worth, TX 76129
(817) 921-7573
Counseling services. Sliding scale fees.

Pastoral Counseling and Education
2727 Oak Lawn Ave., Suite 101
Dallas, TX 75219
(214) 871-1069
Counselors with theological, psychotherapy, and social work training provide range of counseling services. Sliding scale fees.

Richardson Crisis Center
(214) 783-0008
(Telephone inquiries only.)
Telephone counseling service for help in stressful situations.

Richland Hills Church of Christ Counseling Center
6720 NE Loop 820
Richland Hills, TX 76180
Metro (817) 498-6970
Various counseling programs. Fees vary.

▶ Tips for out-of-work executives

The higher you climb the corporate ladder, the harder you may fall if you get laid off or fired.

Out-of-work executives can profit from the advice of Bob Inman, who's worked with hundreds of managers as an outplacement specialist and senior partner of Inman, McLean and Gaddy in Dallas.

Here are three ways Inman says you can be more successful in your job hunt:

1. Find a position that fits you rather than trying to conform to the position: You should identify your skills and interests and find a job that is a good match. The higher up you go, the more important this is. Too often people limit themselves by looking for work in a familiar field. For example, people who lose jobs in real estate may look for work only in that industry. Then when there is an opening, they will turn themselves inside-out trying to fit it. This process leads to job dissatisfaction.

2. Look for ways to expand your opportunities by finding ways to transfer your skills and talents: Employers may try to typecast you, so it's good to think of ways you can apply your talents to other fields. Someone with a petroleum engineering managerial background, for instance, might be well suited for a petroleum and minerals lending section of a large bank or for an oil and gas or engineering consulting company.

3. Relax and program yourself to succeed: We encourage clients to turn negative thoughts into positive ones. Rather than lingering over thoughts of being middle-aged and out of work, tell yourself that you're a valuable person with lots of experience who happens to be unemployed. Reaffirm the things that are good about you rather than dwelling on what's going wrong.■

The Salvation Army Social Services Center
2215 N. Akard St.
Dallas, TX 75201
(214) 742-9131
Rehabilitation through counseling and work therapy. Free.

The Salvation Army of Tarrant County
2901 NE 28th St.
Fort Worth, TX 76111
(817) 834-6271
Work programs and counseling for socially handicapped and substance abusers. Free.

Soul's Harbor Rehabilitation Center
13134 Nile Dr.
Dallas, TX 75253
(214) 286-1940
Counseling and work therapy for homeless men who are alcoholics.

Southwest Family Institute, Inc.
12532 Nuestra Dr.
Dallas, TX 75230
(214) 960-0050
Counseling for individuals, couples, and families. Sliding scale fees.

The Suicide and Crisis Center
2910 Swiss Ave.
Dallas, TX 75204
(214) 828-1000
24-hour telephone crisis counseling for suicidal individuals or someone facing a crisis. Community education and preventive services are offered. Accepts contributions.

Swiss Avenue Counseling Center
3611 Swiss Ave.
Dallas, TX 75204
(214) 821-3680
Provides counseling for individuals and groups, including help for substance abuse. Sliding scale fees and contributions.

Turtle Creek Manor, Inc.
2707 Routh St.
Dallas, TX 75201
(214) 871-2454
Vocational and group counseling for people with mental/emotional problems and/or chemical dependency.

Urban Ministries
1721 E. Vickery Blvd.
Fort Worth, TX 76104
(817) 332-4543
Provides crisis counseling for individuals and families. Accepts donations of money or clothing.

Vietnam Veterans' Center
Seminary South Building
Suite B-10
Fort Worth, TX 76115
(817) 821-3733
Psychological counseling and referrals. Free.

Welcome House, Inc.
1111 S. Haskell Ave.
Dallas, TX 75223
(214) 823-7522
Counseling, employment assistance, and residential service for male alcoholics. Fees vary.

Welcome House II
3024 Park Row Ave.
Dallas, TX 75215
(214) 421-3948
Counseling, employment assistance, and residential service for men and women who have alcohol or drug problems. Fees vary.

10

Selecting the Right Job For You

Welcome to the most pleasant chapter of this book—and the one that's the most fun. You've figured out what you want to do, developed an acceptable resume, and used your network of contacts and other resources to research the job market and generate all sorts of interviews. At this point in the process you've probably received or are pretty close to landing at least a couple of offers that come fairly close to your objective.

You have a problem if one of your possibilities becomes a firm offer that demands an immediate response while you're still investigating other promising leads. The employer making this offer is essentially telling you, "We think you have everything we're looking for, and we want you to start as soon as possible."

It is difficult to stall or delay your acceptance just because other promising leads still haven't yielded firm offers. You have to use your best judgment in such a case, but try to delay a final decision until all likely offers are in. Unless you're absolutely desperate, there's no reason to jump at the first offer you receive.

A job involves much more than a title and base salary. For any firm offer, be sure you understand what your responsibilities will be, what benefits you'll receive besides salary (insurance, vacation, profit sharing, training, tuition reimbursement, and the like), how much overtime is required (and whether you'll be paid for it), how much travel is involved in the job, who your superior will be, how many people you'll be supervising, and where the position might lead. (Is it a dead-end job, or are people in this slot often promoted?) In short, find out anything and everything you need to know to evaluate the offer.

For many positions, especially those requiring several years' experience, it's appropriate to ask for an offer in writing. Such a document would specify the position's title, responsibilities, reporting relationship and compensation, and include a statement of company benefits.

At the very least, before you make a firm decision, be sure to obtain a copy of the company's personnel policy. It will fill you in on such details as the number of paid sick days, overtime and vacation policy, insurance benefits, profit sharing, and the like. These so-called fringe benefits can really add up. It's not a bad idea to try to assign a dollar value to them to help you evaluate the financial pros and cons of each offer.

Compare the Offers on Paper

You've talked with each employer and taken notes about the responsibilities and compensation being offered. Where possible, you've obtained a job offer in writing. You have also read through the company's personnel policy. Make yourself a checklist for comparing the relative merits of each offer. We've provided a sample here, but if another format suits your purposes better, use it. The idea is to list the factors that you consider important in any job, and then assign a rating for how well each offer fills the bill in each particular area.

We've listed some of the factors that we think ought to be considered before you accept any offer. Some may not be relevant to your situation. Others that we've left out may be of great importance to you. So feel free to make any additions, deletions, or changes you want.

Once you've listed your factors, make a column for each job offer you're considering. Assign a rating (say, 1 to 5, with

1 the lowest and 5 the highest) for each factor and each offer. Then, total the scores for each offer.

The offer with the most points is not necessarily the one to accept. The chart doesn't take into account the fact that "responsibilities" may be more important to you than "career path," or that you promised yourself you'd never punch a time clock again. Nevertheless, looking at the pros and cons of each offer in black and white should help you make a much more methodical and logical decision.

Factor	**Offer A**	**Offer B**	**Offer C**
Responsibilities	______	______	______
Salary	______	______	______
Insurance	______	______	______
Paid vacation	______	______	______
Pension	______	______	______
Profit sharing	______	______	______
Tuition reimbursement	______	______	______
On-the-job training	______	______	______
Career path (where can you	______	______	______
go from this job?)	______	______	______
Company future	______	______	______
Quality of product or service	______	______	______
Location (housing market,	______	______	______
schools, transportation)	______	______	______
Boss(es)	______	______	______
Other workers	______	______	______
Travel	______	______	______
Overtime	______	______	______
Other	______	______	______
____________	______	______	______
____________	______	______	______
TOTAL POINTS	______	______	______

For advice on how to get the salary you want, we recommend two books:

Cohen, Herb. *You Can Negotiate Anything.* New York: Bantam Publishing Co., 1982.

Kennedy, Marilyn Moats. *Salary Strategies: Everything You Need to Know to Get the Salary You Want.* New York: Rawson Wade, 1982.

A Final Word

Once you have accepted a job, it's important that you notify each of the people in your log of your new position, company, address, and phone number. Be sure to thank these people; let them know you appreciated their assistance.

After all, you never know when you may need to ask them to help you again.

On each anniversary date of your new job, take the time to run through the self-appraisal process to evaluate your situation and the progress you are making (as measured by increased responsibilities and abilities). Consider how they compare with the objectives you set at the start of your search. Although you may be completely satisfied in your new assignment, remember that circumstances can change overnight, and you must always be prepared for the unexpected. So make an employment "New Year's resolution" to weigh every aspect of your job annually and compare the result with what you want and expect from your life's work.

We hope that you have made good use of the job search techniques outlined in this book. Indeed, we hope that the resulting experiences not only have won you the job you want but—equally important—also have made you a better person. Perhaps the next time you talk to an unemployed person or someone who is employed but seeking a new job, you will look at that person with a new insight gained from your own search experiences. We hope you'll gladly share what you've learned about how to get a job in Dallas/Fort Worth.

Special perks and benefits: Dallas/Fort Worth's Big Ten

We were curious about the "extras" provided by Dallas/Fort Worth businesses. So we asked career counselors, academicians, management consultants, and headhunters to select 10 places that offered the best working conditions for employees. They based their choices on companies that engender a team spirit, offer competitive salaries and benefits, have low turnover, promote people from within the ranks, and provide such special services as physical fitness centers or Employee Assistance Programs.

Here are the employers that were mentioned most often as being good places to work:

- All Saints Episcopal Hospital, which has the largest employer-run child care facility in Texas. They sponsor physical fitness programs, and schedule regular employee meetings with the administrators.
- Trammell Crow Company, which

offers employees a profit-sharing trust. Five percent of the work staff have become millionaires through sales commissions and ownership of properties. And they serve employees free hot lunches!

- Delta Air Lines, where if you're hired, you're practically guaranteed a lifetime job. There's free health care for employees and their families, and layoffs are avoided during slack times.
- Diamond Shamrock, which encourages personnel to reach their potential through goal-setting and regular evaluations. Personal counseling is available to staff members and their families.
- Home Interiors and Gifts, which has a generous profit-sharing plan, and rewards employees with a one-hour holiday grocery "shopping spree." Employees celebrate five-year anniversaries with the company by taking a free trip to Disney World.
- Lomas & Nettleton, which encourages employee input in problem-solving through quality-circles called Employee Participation Ideas Councils. Employees enjoy subsidized lunches in a center overlooking pond and golf course. Even retirees are given a cost-of-living increase.
- Miller Business Systems, where new employees receive a "success kit" on the day they arrive and are later invited to a "Meet the Prez" lunch with company president Jim Miller. Employees are encouraged to make suggestions for improvements.
- Recognition Equipment, where outstanding staff members are recognized during quarterly Friday afternoon "beer busts." The company encourages fitness by providing a company gym and organizing team sports. Hosts company picnics and welcoming

parties for new "team members" and their families.

■ The Southland Corporation, where the best employee ideas are rewarded with cash prizes and trips. The Employee Assistance Program helps individuals with personal problems. Southland sponsors lunch and after-work seminars to stimulate personal and professional growth.

■ Vick's Restaurants & Catering, where there's relatively low turnover in this high-turnover business. Monetary rewards given regularly to the friendliest employee and those who go above and beyond.■

Where Dallas/ Fort Worth Works

This chapter contains the names, addresses, and phone numbers of the area's top 1,300 employers. The companies are arranged in categories according to the major products and services they manufacture or provide. Where appropriate, entries contain a brief description of the company's business and the name of the personnel director or other contact.

This listing is intended to help you survey the major potential employers in fields that interest you. It is *selective*, not exhaustive. We have not, for example, listed *all* the advertising agencies in the area, as you can find that information in the *Yellow Pages*. We have simply listed the top 25 or so, that is, the ones with the most jobs.

The purpose of this chapter is to get you started, both looking and thinking. This is the kickoff, not the final buzzer.

Browse through the whole chapter, and take some time to check out areas that are unfamiliar to you. Many white-collar skills are transferable. People with marketing, management, data processing, accounting, administrative, secretarial, and other talents are needed in a huge variety of businesses.

Ask yourself in what areas your skills could be marketed. Use your imagination, especially if you're in a so-called specialized field. A dietician, for instance, might look first under Health Care, or maybe Hotels. But what about insurance companies, museums, banks, or the scores of other places that run their own dining rooms for employees or the public? What about food and consumer magazines? Who makes up all those recipes and tests those products?

The hints and insider interviews that are scattered throughout this chapter are designed to nudge your creativity and suggest additional ideas for your job search. Much more detailed information on the area's top employers and other, smaller companies can be found in the directories and other resources suggested in Chapter 4. We can't stress strongly enough that *you have to do your homework when you're looking for a job,* both to unearth places that might need a person with your particular talents, and to succeed in the interview once you've lined up a meeting with the hiring authority.

A word about hiring authorities: if you've read Chapter 5, you know that the name of the game is to meet the person with the power to hire you, or get as close to that person as you can. You don't want to go to the chairman or the personnel director if the person who actually makes the decision is the marketing manager or customer service director. Obviously, we can't list every possible hiring authority in the area's "Top 1,300." If we tried, you'd need a wagon to haul this book around. Besides, printed directories go out of date—even those that are regularly and conscientiously revised. So always double-check a contact whose name you get from a book or magazine, including this one. If necessary, call the company's switchboard to confirm who heads a particular department or division.

Here, then, are Dallas/Fort Worth's greatest opportunities. Happy hunting!

The Dallas/Fort Worth area's top 1,300 employers are arranged in the following categories:

Accounting/auditing firms and services
Advertising/public relations agencies
Aerospace manufacturers, services, and sales

Apparel and textile manufacturers
Architectural firms
Automobile, truck, and transportation equipment manufacturers
Banks: commercial and savings
Book publishers
Broadcasting
Chemicals
Computers: data processing services
Computers: equipment manufacturers
Contractors and construction companies
Drugs and pharmaceuticals manufacturers and wholesalers
Educational institutions
Electronic, telecommunications, and office automation systems
Engineering firms and services
Entertainment
Film, videotape, recording, and talent services
Food and beverage producers and distributors
Furniture and fixtures manufacturers
Government
Health care
Hotels
Human services
Insurance underwriters and brokers
Investment bankers and brokers
Law firms
Management consultants
Manufacturers, general
Media: newspapers and magazines
Metal products manufacturers
Museums and art galleries
Oil and gas companies
Paper and allied products
Printers
Real estate: development, brokerage, and finance
Restaurants
Retailers and other merchandisers
Sports, recreation, and fitness
Travel and shipping
Utilities

▶Accounting/auditing firms and services

To learn more about **accounting** and related fields, check out these professional organizations listed in Chapter 5:

American Society of Women Accountants
Certified Public Accountants
Council of Petroleum Accountants Societies

Dallas Society of Accounting Librarians
National Association of Accountants

For additional information, you can write to:

American Institute of CPAs
666 5th Ave.
New York, NY 10019

National Association of Accountants
919 3rd Ave.
New York, NY 10022

National Association of Minority CPAs
1625 I St., NW
Washington, DC 20006

National Society of Public Accountants
1717 Pennsylvania Ave., NW
Washington, DC 20006

Professional Publications:
Accounting & Business Research
The Accounting Review
Cash Flow
The CPA Journal
D & B Reports
Dun's Business Month
Journal of Accountancy
Journal of Accounting, Auditing & Finance
Management Accounting
The Practical Accountant

Directories:
Accounting Firms and Practitioners (American Institute of Certified Public Accountants, New York, NY)
National Directory of Certified Public Accountants (Peter Norback Publishing Co., Princeton, NJ)
Who Audits America (Data Financial Press, Menlo Park, CA)

Arthur Andersen & Co.
Dallas Office
5600 InterFirst Plaza
Dallas, TX 75265
(214) 741-8300
Partner: Ron Ebest

Arthur Andersen & Co.
Fort Worth Office
801 Cherry St., Suite 1200
Fort Worth, TX 76102
(817) 870-3000
Contact: Kathy Sullivan

Coopers & Lybrand
Dallas Office
1999 Bryan St., Suite 3000
Dallas, TX 75201
(214) 754-5000
Personnel Director: Ron Castleman

Coopers & Lybrand
Fort Worth Office
1800 Texas American Bank Bldg.
Fort Worth, TX 76102
Metro (817) 429-2410
Personnel Director: Carolyn Drews

Deloitte, Haskins & Sells
500 N. Akard St., Suite 1400
Dallas, TX 75201
(214) 954-4500
Recruiting Manager: David Sparks

Dohm & Wolff
2121 San Jacinto St., Suite 1850
Dallas, TX 75201
(214) 922-0088
Partner: Joe Dolm, Jr.

Ernst & Whinney
Dallas Office
2001 Ross Ave., Suite 2800
Dallas, TX 75201
(214) 979-1700
Southwest Regional Manager: Bill Fleming

Ernst & Whinney
Fort Worth Office
2700 Texas American Bank Bldg.
Fort Worth, TX 76102
Metro (817) 429-1410
Partner: Dave Keller

Lane, Gorman Trubitt & Co.
2301 N. Akard St., Suite 200
Dallas, TX 75201
(214) 871-7500
Partner: Jerry Lane

Laventhol & Horwath
2121 San Jacinto St., Suite 1700
Dallas, TX 75201
(214) 754-7100
Recruiting Director: Ed Swalm

Kenneth Leventhal & Co.
2001 Ross Ave., Suite 1600
Dallas, TX 75201
(214) 969-0900
Partner: David Steinfield

James B. Lewis
1515 8th Ave.
Fort Worth, TX 76104
(817) 926-8066
President: James B. Lewis

Oppenheim, Appel, Dixon & Co.
700 N. Pearl St., Suite 400
Dallas, TX 75201
(214) 969-5333
Office Manager: Janet Sheehan

Pannell, Kerr, Forster
6500 Greenville Ave., Suite 200
Dallas, TX 75206
(214) 369-1551
Office Manager: Virginia Matthews

Peat, Marwick, Mitchell & Co.
Dallas Office
1601 Elm St., Suite 1400
Dallas, TX 75201
(214) 754-2000
Personnel Director: Lisa Rabenaldt

Peat, Marwick, Mitchell & Co.
Fort Worth Office
2300 First City Bank Tower
Fort Worth, TX 76102
(817) 335-2655
Partner: Clyde Womack

Pittman O'Daniel & Co.
1000 S. Main St., Suite 200
Grapevine, TX 76051
(817) 481-7505
Partner: Jerry Pittman

Price Waterhouse
Dallas Office
1400 First City Center
Dallas, TX 75201-4698
(214) 922-8040
Human Resources Director: Kevin O'Neil

Price Waterhouse
Fort Worth Office
1600 Two Tandy Center
Fort Worth, TX 76102
(817) 335-6271
Partner: Bob Mann

Seidman & Seidman
4200 Renaissance Tower
Dallas, TX 75270
(214) 741-4200
Partner: Robert Watts

Snow Tomerlin & Garrett
4200 S. Hulen St., Suite 435
Fort Worth, TX 76109
(817) 738-3202
Partner: Wayne Burchfield

Tabor & Hankins
3801 Hulen St., Suite 100
Fort Worth, TX 76107
(817) 731-7000
Partner: Paul Tabor

Grant Thorton
1800 One Dallas Centre
Dallas, TX 75201
(214) 922-9010
Office Manager: Betty Jones

Touche Ross & Co.
2001 Bryan Tower, Suite 2400
Dallas, TX 75201
(214) 741-3553
Recruiter: Lindsey Green

Accounting firms big and small

Donald Menton has been with a Dallas data processing financial services firm for 13 years. He is currently Senior Vice President of Finance. Menton began his career in public accounting at Touche Ross, one of the country's Big Eight accounting firms. We talked with him about how large and small accounting firms differ.

"Usually, working for a larger firm means learning a specific task," says Menton. "Staffs are larger, so each job is more specialized. You don't usually handle as many components of a job as you would in a smaller firm. You sometimes have more opportunity for hands-on experience in a smaller firm and gain more general management experience.

"Whether you work for a large firm or a small one is really a matter of personal preference and what career path you wish to embark on. I started out with a large public accounting firm for the experience and the opportunity to become certified as a public accountant.

"But regardless of the size of the firm where you begin your career, you should remain flexible during your first five years if you wish to advance. If your job is not what you expected, be willing to make a change.

"Also, if you want a manager's position, you may have to move around to gain general managerial experience. Sometimes that will mean a transfer to a department that would not necessarily be your first choice. But if the position rounds out your background, it is usually worth at least a temporary stay."■

Philip Vogel & Co.
12221 Merit Dr., Suite 1200
Dallas, TX 75251-2212
(214) 386-4200
Comptroller: Shirley Johnson

Weaver & Tidwell
105 W. 5th St., Suite 1500
Fort Worth, TX 76102
(817) 332-7905
Partner: Ronnie Coulson

Arthur Young Co.
Dallas Office
2121 San Jacinto St., Suite 700
Dallas, TX 75201
(214) 969-8000
Personnel Director: Sally Neal

Arthur Young Co.
Fort Worth Office
500 Throckmorton St., Suite 2200
Fort Worth, TX 76102
Metro (817) 429-7780
Partner: Turner Almond

▶Advertising/public relations agencies

To learn more about **advertising and public relations,** check out the following professional organizations listed in Chapter 5:

Advertising Club of Fort Worth
Dallas Advertising League
Dallas Professional Photographers Association
Dallas Society of Illustrators
Dallas Society of Visual Communication
International Association of Business Communicators
Press Club of Dallas
Public Relations Society of America
Southwestern Association of Advertising Agencies
Texas Association of Film & Tape Professionals
Women in Communication, Inc.

For additional information, you can write to:

The Advertising Council, Inc.
1200 18th St., NW
Washington, DC 20036

American Association of Advertising Agencies
200 Park Ave.
New York, NY 10017

Direct Mail Marketing Association
230 Park Ave.
New York, NY 10017

International Public Relations Association
United States Section
P.O. Box 1001
Little Rock, AK 72203

Public Relations Exchange
425 Lumber Exchange Bldg.
Minneapolis, MN 55402

Professional Publications:
Ad Forum
Advertising Age
Advertising World
Adweek
Direct Marketing Magazine
Journal of Advertising
Journal of Advertising Research
Journal of Business Communication
Potentials in Marketing
PR Reporter
Public Relations Journal
Public Relations Quarterly
Public Relations Review
O'Dwyer's Newsletter

Directories:
Advertising Research Foundation Yearbook (Advertising Research Foundation, New York, NY)
Bacon's Publicity Checker (Bacon's Publishing Company, Chicago, IL)
Graphics Pages (Graphics Publishers, Inc., Dallas, TX)
O'Dwyer's Directory of Corporate Communications and O'Dwyer's Directory of Public Relations Firms (J. R. O'Dwyer Co., New York, NY)
Standard Directory of Advertising Agencies (National Register Publishing Co., Skokie, IL)

Ackerman & McQueen, Inc.
12790 Merit Dr., Suite 616
Dallas, TX 75251
(214) 458-0376
Senior Vice President: Patti Weinbrenner

Advertising, Graphics & Marketing
Electric Service Bldg., Suite 1215
Fort Worth, TX 76102
Metro (817) 429-0348
Vice President: Larry Hutchins

Anderson Fischel Advertising Agency
5151 Belt Line Rd., Suite 700
Dallas, TX 75240
(214) 233-8461
Vice President: Steve Braasch

Arnold/Foster/Sherrill/Carrithers, Inc.
4131 N. Central Expwy., Suite 510
Dallas, TX 75204
(214) 521-6400
Personnel: Sue Spence

Berry-Brown Advertising
2602 McKinney Ave., Suite 300
Dallas, TX 75204
(214) 871-1001
President: Robert Brown

The Bloom Co., Inc.
7701 Stemmons Frwy.
Dallas, TX 75247
(214) 638-8100
Personnel Director: Paula Simmons

Bozell, Jacobs, Kenyon & Eckhardt
201 E. Carpenter Frwy.
Irving, TX 75038
(214) 556-1100
Personnel Director: Linda Jeffers

Cox-Pippin Communications
7007 Twin Hills Ave.
Dallas, TX 75231-5118
(214) 691-4888
Office Manager: Sunny Brewer

Crume
1303 Walnut Hill Ln., Suite 300
Irving, TX 75038
(214) 580-1520
Office Manager: Debbie Shaw

DBG&H Unlimited
3131 McKinney Ave., Suite 100
Dallas, TX 75228
(214) 871-2151
Human Resources Director: Carrie Bradley

Dally Advertising, Inc.
1320 S. University Dr., Suite 501
Fort Worth, TX 76107
(817) 332-5299
Vice President: Charles Jeffreys

Sissy Day & Associates
1701 N. Market St., Suite 204
Dallas, TX 75202
(214) 742-2717
President: Sissy Day

Direct Response Group, Inc.
8701 Carpenter Frwy., Suite 150
Dallas, TX 75247
(214) 631-5111
President: James E. Dunne III

Emerson/Nichols/Bailey
4425 W. Airport Frwy., Suite 500
Irving, TX 75062
(214) 257-0123
President: Stan Emerson

GSD&M–Dallas, Inc.
750 N. St. Paul St.
Dallas, TX 75201
(214) 969-7373
Office Manager: Mary Graves

Goodman & Associates, Inc.
601 Penn St.
Fort Worth, TX 76102
(817) 332-2261
President: Gerry Goodman

Graphics 2
701 Pennsylvania Ave.
Fort Worth, TX 76104
(817) 731-9941
President: Ben Herman

Graphics Concepts Group
2630 West Frwy., Suite 205
Fort Worth, TX 76102
(817) 332-4546
President: Scott Turner

Hill & Knowlton, Inc.
One Dallas Centre, Suite 1500
Dallas, TX 75201
(214) 979-0090
Administrative Assistant: Hazel Jones

Howe Associates
2019 N. Lamar St., Suite 220
Dallas, TX 75202
(214) 954-0847
President: Janet Howe

Keller-Crescent/SW
102 Decker Ct., Suite 100
Irving, TX 75062
(214) 659-9220
Personnel Director: Onie Webb

Levenson, Levenson & Hill, Inc.
5215 N. O'Connor Blvd.
Irving, TX 75039
(214) 556-0944
Personnel Director: Candace Ramsey

Magnussen Advertising Agency
906 Mallick Tower
Fort Worth, TX 76102
(817) 332-1145
President: Neil Ross

May Advertising Corp.
400 W. Vickery Blvd.
Fort Worth, TX 76104
(817) 336-5671
Contact: Personnel

McKone & Co.
1900 Westridge Dr.
Irving, TX 75038
(817) 550-7433
Office Manager: Nancy Harper

McStay-Regian Associates, Inc.
219 S. Main St.
Fort Worth, TX 76104
(817) 870-1128
President: Paula McStay

Moroch & Associates, Inc.
2727 Cedar Springs Rd.
Dallas, TX 75201
Metro (214) 263-8801
Office Manager: Debbie Wells

The Oakley Co., Inc.
3625 N. Hall St., Suite 500
Dallas, TX 75219
(214) 742-5511
Office Manager: Kathy Difiore

Ogilvy & Mather
5430 LBJ Frwy., Suite 900
Dallas, TX 75240
(214) 770-2727
Administrative Assistant: Jody Daniel

Ottmann Advertising Agency, Inc.
1020 Summit Ave.
Fort Worth, TX 76102
(817) 335-4473
President: Harry Ottmann

Pavlik & Associates
100 E. 15th St., Suite 320
Fort Worth, TX 76102
(817) 429-0062
President: Linda Pavlik

C. Pharr & Co., Inc.
12700 Hillcrest Rd., Suite 208
Dallas, TX 75230
(214) 661-2490
President: Cynthia Pharr

Point Communications, Inc.
4050 Alpha Rd., Suite 1300
Dallas, TX 75244
(214) 851-1100
Executive Vice President: Willard Moon

Read-Poland Associates
411 Adolphus Tower
Dallas, TX 75202
(214) 742-9238
Contact: Austin office

The Richards Group, Inc.
10000 N. Central Expwy., Suite 1200
Dallas, TX 75231
(214) 987-2700
Creative Director: Gary Gibson

Rominger Advertising Agency
3600 Commerce St., Suite A
Dallas, TX 75226
(214) 826-9141
President: David Dunnigan

Rosenberg & Co.
4225 Office Pkwy.
Dallas, TX 75204
(214) 821-8312
Senior Vice President: Carol Smith

Saunders, Lubinski & White, Inc.
7610 Stemmons Frwy., Suite 100
Dallas, TX 75247
(214) 630-6160
President's Assistant: Pat Stevenson

Jane Schlansker & Co.
610 Grove St.
Fort Worth, TX 76102
Metro (817) 429-4682
Administrative Assistant: Jan Green

Stern/Monroe Advertising, Inc.
2905 Maple Ave.
Dallas, TX 75201
(214) 871-7171
Personnel: Mary O'Brian

Tracy-Locke, Inc.
600 N. Pearl St.
Dallas, TX 75201
(214) 969-9000
Personnel Manager: Lee Schwartz

The West Agency, Ltd.
13601 Preston Rd., Suite 400W
Dallas, TX 75240
(214) 991-3501
President: Gus Gregory

Witherspoon Advertising
1000 W. Weatherford St.
Fort Worth, TX 76102
(817) 335-1373
Office Manager: Mackey Beard

Breaking into advertising production

Tracey Barnett was working in public relations when she decided to break into advertising film production. Although she didn't know anyone in the industry when she began, today she is a successful freelance production manager. We asked her how she did it.

"Most important was that I had the desire to do it," says Tracey, "and I didn't get discouraged. I began by making a few contacts in the industry through people I knew in related fields. Then I set up interviews with these contacts. At the end of each interview, I asked for the names of three to five other contacts in the industry. This strategy opened a lot of doors for me. I followed up each interview with a phone call. I also kept in touch with my contacts on a monthly basis."

We asked Tracey what jobs are available for beginners in the film business and what qualifications are needed for these jobs.

"Entry-level positions include production assistant, assistant prop manager, assistant stylist, assistant wardrobe manager, and grip," says Tracey. "There are no special requirements for these jobs. You don't need a degree in film to work in the business. In fact, people with film degrees begin at the same level as everybody else. What does count is intelligence and the ability to get things done quickly and efficiently. You need to think on your feet and be able to anticipate what needs to be done."

According to Tracey, free-lance production assistants begin at about $75-$100 per day. More experienced production assistants can make as much as $175 per day. "But keep in mind that as a freelancer, you don't have the security of a regular paycheck," says Tracey. "You may not work every day." She advises those who need a more reliable income to look for a staff position in the industry.

Tracey advises those who want to break into the film business to keep at it: "Don't count your inexperience as a negative. Tenacity and enthusiasm will get you the first job. Approach your contacts and keep approaching them—over and over and over again."■

▶Aerospace manufacturers, services, and sales

To learn more about **aerospace** and related fields, you might want to contact the **American Institute of Aeronautics and Astronautics.**

For additional information, you can write to:

Aerospace Education Foundation
1750 Pennsylvania Ave., NW
Washington, DC 20006

Aerospace Electrical Society
Box 24BB3 Village Station
Los Angeles, CA 90024

American Institute of Aeronautics and Astronautics
9841 Airport Blvd.
Los Angeles, CA 90045

Int'l. Association of Machinists & Aerospace Workers
8411 S. Pioneer
Whittier, CA 90601

National Space Institute
600 Maryland Ave., SW
Washington, DC 20034

Professional Publications:
Air Cargo Magazine
Airfair Interline Magazine
Aviation Week and Space Technology
Business and Commercial Aviation
Frequent Flyer

Directories:
Aviation Week & Space Technology, Marketing Directory issue (McGraw-Hill Publishing Co., New York, NY)

Aero Components Company
419 W. Fork Dr.
Arlington, TX 76012
(817) 265-3007
Contact: Becky Kate
Government contractor that manufactures small aircraft components.

Aerospace Optics, Inc.
3201 Sandy Ln.
Fort Worth, TX 76112
(817) 451-1141
Contact: Personnel
Manufactures panels and switches for aircraft.

Aerospace Technology
7445 E. Lancaster Ave.
Fort Worth, TX 76112
(817) 451-0620
Personnel Manager: Dan Perkins
Manufactures aircraft components.

Aerospatiale Helicopter Corp.
2701 Forum Dr.
Grand Prairie, TX 75053-4005
(214) 641-0000
Personnel Director: Don Black
Reassembles and modifies helicopters for commercial and government use.

Anadite/Anacast Division
701 W. Mansfield Hwy.
Kennedale, TX 76060
(817) 478-9231
Contact: Personnel
Manufactures metal castings.

Associated Air Center
8321 Lemmon Ave.
Dallas, TX 75209
(214) 350-4111
Contact: Carolyn Dalton
Customizes aircraft.

Aviall
7555 Lemmon Ave.
Dallas, TX 75209
(214) 357-1811
Contact: Human Resources Department
Services and repairs turbine engines, installs avionic systems, refurbishes general aviation airframes, and operates terminal hangar and refueling complex at Dallas Love Field. Also distributes engine and aircraft-related parts and supplies.

Bell Helicopter/Textron, Inc.
600 E. Hurst Blvd.
Hurst, TX 76053
(817) 280-2011
Personnel: D. L. Stockton
Large government contractor involved in research and manufacturing of helicopters.

Bidco Products, Inc.
206 N. Sentry Dr.
Mansfield, TX 76063
(817) 477-3145
Personnel: Jud Mitchell
Manufactures fiberglass aircraft parts.

Chaparral Aviation, Inc.
4451 Glenn Curtis Dr.
Dallas, TX 75248
(214) 931-8400
General Manager: John Thomason
Sales and service of Beechcraft airplanes.

Clark-Aiken Co. of Texas
941 Ave. G East
Arlington, TX 76011
(817) 640-1806
President: Paul Hart
Machine shop for aircraft parts.

Dynalectron Corp.
6801 Calmont Ave.
Fort Worth, TX 76116
(817) 732-4481
Personnel Administrator: Daphne Eley
Government service contractor for aircraft maintenance and modification.

EDM of Texas
14042 Distribution Way
Dallas, TX 75234
(214) 241-2501
Personnel Director: Tom Glidewell
Repairs aircraft parts.

Euless Aero Components, Inc.
1100 S. Pipeline Rd.
Euless, TX 76039
(817) 267-1371
President: Tony Shelton
Manufactures aircraft machine parts.

GEC Avionics, Inc.
6410 Southwest Blvd.
Fort Worth, TX 76109
(817) 763-0281
Contact: Atlanta, GA office
Develops and produces electronic devices used in aircraft.

General Aviation Industries, Inc.
7150 Midway Rd.
Fort Worth, TX 76118
(817) 284-4848
Personnel Director: Bonnie Nix
Government defense contractor for airplane parts.

General Dynamics Corp.
Grants Ln.
Fort Worth, TX 76106
(817) 777-2000
Employment Manager: Jerre Yoder
Major employer and government contractor that manufactures aircraft, radar systems, and related equipment in the Fort Worth division.

Glover Machine Co.
210 S. Morocco St.
Dallas, TX 75211
(214) 331-8373
Personnel Manager: Ygnacio Lopez
Manufactures aircraft parts.

HAC Corp.
537 Camden Dr.
Grand Prairie, TX 75051
(214) 263-4387
Plant Manager: Phillip Hoffman
Manufactures aircraft parts and does composite bondings.

K–C Aviation, Inc.
7350 Cedar Springs Rd.
Dallas, TX 75235
(214) 350-4177
Personnel Director: Mrs. Floy Green
Aircraft maintenance and modification.

LTV Corp.
9314 W. Jefferson St.
Dallas, TX 75211
(214) 266-2011
Contact: J. V. Johnson, Jr. at (214) 266-4600 for engineering division and Ken Slawson at (214) 266-7281 for missiles division
Government contractor producing aircraft, missiles, launch vehicles, and space vehicle components.

Menasco Aerosystems Division
Hwy. 157 and Pipeline Rd.
Euless, TX 76039
(817) 283-4471
Personnel Director: Ed Bianchi
Multi-industry firm producing marine weapons, handling systems, aircraft landing gear, helicopter rotor assemblies, and heat-treated metals.

Murdock Engineering Co. of Texas
5100 W. Airport Frwy.
Irving, TX 75061
(214) 790-1122
Personnel Administration Manager: Julius Farris
Manufactures aircraft parts and equipment, flexible pipe fittings for marine and oil industries, and bonded metal parts.

Perkins Plastics, Inc.
3724 N. Commerce St.
Fort Worth, TX 76106
(817) 625-4106
Personnel: Frank Gordoa
Builds replacement parts for helicopters.

Progressive, Inc.
1030 N. Commercial Blvd.
Arlington, TX 76017
(817) 467-0031
Owner: Gwen Crousen
Aircraft machine shop.

Putoma Corp.
5101 E. California Pkwy.
Fort Worth, TX 76119
(817) 536-1271
Personnel Director: Leslie Ratliff
Manufactures aircraft parts.

Skyline Industries, Inc.
4909 Northeast Pkwy.
Fort Worth, TX 76106
(817) 624-4991
Vice President: Jack Roach
Government contractor with machine shop for small aircraft parts. Also manufactures fishing rods.

Stratoflex, Inc.
220 Roberts Cutoff Rd.
Fort Worth, TX 76114
(817) 738-6543
Personnel Director: Janice Looper
Manufactures hose fittings for aircraft and automobiles.

Apparel and textile manufacturers

To learn more about the **apparel and textile industries** and related fields, check out the following professional organizations listed in Chapter 5:

American Fashion Association
American Society of Interior Designers

For additional information, you can write to:

Educational Foundation for the Fashion Industries
227 W. 27th St.
New York, NY 10001

Federation of Apparel Manufacturers
450 7th Ave.
New York, NY 10001

National Association of Textilo and Apparel Distributors
401 7th Ave.
New York, NY 10001

Textile Research Institute
Box 625
Princeton, NJ 08540

Professional Publications:
American Fabrics and Fashions
Apparel World
Fabricnews
Fashion Newsletter
Home Fashions Textiles
Homesewing Trade News
Impressions
New York Apparel World
Textile Products
Textile Research Journal
Textile World
Women's Wear Daily

Directories:
Apparel Industry Sourcebook (Denyse & Co., Inc., North Hollywood, CA)
Apparel Trades Book (Dun & Bradstreet, Inc., New York, NY)
Models Mart Directory (Peter Glenn Publications, New York, NY)
Textile Blue Book (Davison Publishing Co., Glen Rock, NJ)

Byn-Mar
2920 Anode Ln.
Dallas, TX 75220
(214) 350-7011
Personnel: Kathy O'Donnell
Manufactures women's clothing.

Victor Costa, Inc.
3000 Irving Blvd.
Dallas, TX 75247
(214) 634-1133
Contact: Roland Micrahi
Manufactures women's clothing.

Designers Collection, Inc.
1207 Round Table Dr.
Dallas, TX 75247
(214) 634-8040
Contact: Personnel
Manufactures table linens.

Dickson-Jenkins Manufacturing Co.
202 St. Louis Ave.
Fort Worth, TX 76101
(817) 335-4489
Personnel Manager: Tom Barnett
Manufactures Western wear.

H.B. Manufacturing
2527 W. Dickson St.
Fort Worth, TX 76109
(817) 926-5244
Contact: Personnel
Manufactures ladies' sportswear.

The Haggar Co.
6113 Lemmon Ave.
Dallas, TX 75209
(214) 352-8481
Contact: George Greer
Manufactures sportswear.

Jerell, Inc.
1365 Regal Row
Dallas, TX 75247
(214) 637-5300
Personnel Manager: Bill Summers
Manufactures women's and juniors' clothing.

Jones of Dallas Manufacturing
8505 Chancellor Row
Dallas, TX 75247
(214) 638-0321
Contact: Personnel
Manufactures women's clothing.

The Lorch Co.
4949 Beeman Ave.
Dallas, TX 75223
(214) 826-7500
Contact: Department Head
Manufactures misses' and juniors' dresses and sportswear.

Malouf Co., Inc.
944 S. Lamar St.
Dallas, TX 75202
(214) 565-0126
Contact: Department Head
Manufactures women's and juniors' clothing.

Miller Bros. Industries, Inc.
2300 Stemmons Frwy.
Dallas, TX 75207
(214) 631-0566
Personnel Manager: Charles Wood
Manufactures men's hats.

Niver Western Wear, Inc.
1221 Hemphill St.
Fort Worth, TX 76104
(817) 336-2389
Contact: Personnel
Manufactures Western clothing.

Prophecy Corp.
1302 Champion Circle
Carrollton, TX 75006
(214) 247-1900
Personnel Manager: Diana Walker
Manufactures women's sportswear.

RLM Fashion Industries, Inc.
2220 Canton St.
Dallas, TX 75201
(214) 747-4812
Contact: Personnel
Manufactures women's apparel.

Resistol Hats
601 Marion Dr.
Garland, TX 75040
(214) 494-0511
Personnel Manager: Juanita Kimbrell
Manufactures cowboy hats and other headwear.

Salty's Cap & Apparel, Inc.
3209 Stuart Dr.
Fort Worth, TX 76110
(817) 927-8408
Contact: Personnel
Manufactures misses' and juniors' clothing.

Sidran Sportswear, Inc.
2875 Merrell Rd.
Dallas, TX 75229
(214) 352-7979
Personnel Manager: Sandra Phillips
Manufactures Western clothing.

Sunny Isle, Inc.
9106 Chancellor Row
Dallas, TX 75247
(214) 631-2910
Personnel Director: Dorothy Phillips
Manufactures juniors' and misses' dresses and sportswear.

Sunny South Fashions, Inc.
7777 Hines Place
Dallas, TX 75235
(214) 637-4333
Personnel Manager: Paula Hultsman
Manufactures women's blouses.

Williamson-Dickie Manufacturing Co.
509 W. Vickery Blvd.
Fort Worth, TX 76104
(817) 336-7201
Personnel Manager: Jack Marr
Manufactures women's and men's clothing.

Howard B. Wolf
3809 Parry Ave.
Dallas, TX 75226
(214) 823-9941
Contact: Personnel
Manufactures women's clothing.

▶Architecture firms

To learn more about **architecture** and related fields, check out the following professional organizations listed in Chapter 5:

American Institute of Architects
American Society of Landscape Architects
Institute of Business Designers

For additional information, you can write to:

American Institute of Architects
1735 New York Ave., NW
Washington, DC 20006

American Institute of Building Design
1412 19th St.
Sacramento, CA 95814

Association of Women in Architecture
7440 University Dr.
St. Louis, MO 63130

National Organization of Minority Architects
c/o Marshall E. Purnell
1215 Connecticut Ave., NW
Washington, DC 20036

Society of American Registered Architects
600 S. Michigan Ave.
Chicago, IL 60601

Professional Publications:
AIA Journal
Architectural Forum
Architectural Record
Building Design & Construction
Progressive Architecture

Directories:
AIA Membership Directory (American Institute of Architects, New York, NY)
Profile: Professional File Architectural Firms (American Institute of Architects, Philadelphia, PA)

Beran & Shelmire
1800 Mercantile Commerce Bldg.
Dallas, TX 75201
(214) 748-5779
Managing Partner: Overton Shelmire

CRS Sirrine, Inc.
414 W. 5th St.
Fort Worth, TX 76102
(817) 429-7262
Managing Partner: Bob Kumlin

Corgan Associates Architects
501 Elm St., Suite 500
Dallas, TX 75202
(214) 748-2000
Managing Partner: Jack Corgan

EDI Architects, Inc.
8440 Walnut Hill Ln., Suite 100
Dallas, TX 75231
(214) 750-1945
Managing Partner: Val Hawes

F&S Partners, Inc.
3535 Travis St., Suite 201
Dallas, TX 75201
(214) 559-4851
Managing Partner: Ronald Shaw

Good Haas & Fulton Architects
2001 Ross Ave., Suite 300
Dallas, TX 75201
(214) 979-0028
Managing Partner: R. Lawrence Good

HMBH Architects
15303 Dallas Pkwy., Suite 300
Dallas, TX 75248
(214) 701-9000
Managing Partner: Edward B. Haldeman, Jr.

Hellmuth/Obata & Kassabaum
2501 Cedar Springs Rd., Suite 700
Dallas, TX 75201
(214) 742-7000
Managing Partner: Larry Self

Henningson, Durham & Richardson, Inc.
12700 Hillcrest Rd., Suite 125
Dallas, TX 75230
(214) 980-0001
Managing Partner: Dan Jeakins

JPJ Architects, Inc.
900 Jackson St., Suite 700
Dallas, TX 75202
(214) 749-0904
Managing Partner: Bill D. Smith

Albert S. Komatsu & Associates, Inc.
1300 S. University Dr., Suite 200
Fort Worth, TX 76107
(817) 332-1914
Managing Partner: Albert Komatsu

Frank Meier Architects International
3400 Carlisle St., Suite 300
Dallas, TX 75204
(214) 871-0020
Managing Partner: Frank L. Meier

O'Brien O'Brien Callaway
3131 McKinney Ave., Suite 850-LD113
Dallas, TX 75204
(214) 871-9100
Managing Partner: Jack O'Brien

The Office of Pierce Goodwin Alexander
2121 San Jacinto St., Suite 1900
Dallas, TX 75201
(214) 969-6888
Managing Partner: J. Allen Pierce

OmniPlan Architects
400 S. Record St.
Dallas, TX 75202
(214) 742-1261
Managing Partner: E. G. Hamilton

Parker/Croston Partnership, Inc.
3111 Hamilton Ave.
Fort Worth, TX 76107
(817) 332-8464
Managing Partner: Merwyn Croston

RTKL Associates, Inc.
8330 Meadow Rd., Suite 100
Dallas, TX 75231
(214) 373-6900
Managing Partner: Joseph Scalabrin

SHWC, Inc.
5601 MacArthur Blvd.
Irving, TX 75062
(214) 550-0700
Managing Partner: J. W. Hiester

SNTW, Inc.
8235 Douglas Ave., Suite 900
Dallas, TX 75225
(214) 691-2900
Managing Partner: Phillip W. Shepherd

Harwood K. Smith & Partners, Inc.
1111 Plaza of the Americas, Suite 307
Dallas, TX 75201
(214) 969-5599
Managing Partner: Ronald M. Brame

Taylor-Hewlett, Inc.
14951 Dallas Pkwy., Suite 200
Dallas, TX 75240
(214) 960-1136
Managing Partner: Dallas J. Taylor

WZMH Group, Inc.
1600 Southland Center, North Tower
Dallas, TX 75201
(214) 747-3445
Managing Partner: Bernard P. Himel

Womack-Humphreys Architects
5430 LBJ Frwy., Suite 3100
Dallas, TX 75240
(214) 770-2300
Managing Partners: Charles R. Womack and Mark Humphreys

Woo James Harwick Peck Architects/Planners, Inc.
7557 Rambler Rd., Suite 300
Dallas, TX 75231
(214) 363-5687
Managing Partner: George C. T. Woo

▶Automobile, truck, and transportation equipment manufacturers

Some of the major trade publications covering the **auto industry** are:

Automotive Industries
Automotive News
Motor
Motor Age

Directories:
ASIA Membership Directory (Automotive Service Industries Association, Chicago, IL)
Automotive Age, Buyers Guide Issue (Freed-Crown Publishing Co., Van Nuys, CA)
Automotive News, Market Data Book issue (Crain Automotive Group, Detroit, MI)
Jobber Topics, Annual Marketing Directory Issue (Irving-Cloud Publishing Co., Chicago, IL)

ARA Manufacturing Co.
606 Fountain Pkwy.
Grand Prairie, TX 75050
Metro (817) 647-4111
Personnel Director: Robert Barkholtz
Manufactures automobile air conditioners.

Big 4 Automotive, Inc.
512 S. Jennings Ave.
Fort Worth, TX 76104
(817) 332-3171
General Manager: Marty Buckles
Warehouse distributor for automotive parts.

Champion Parts Rebuilders, Inc.
200 W. Vickery Blvd.
Fort Worth, TX 76104
(817) 336-9741
Personnel Manager: A. C. Hamann
Major remanufacturer and marketer of functional automotive, truck, and tractor parts.

Cummins Sales & Service, Inc.
600 N. Watson Rd.
Arlington, TX 76010
Metro (817) 640-6801
Personnel Director: Don Watson
Distributes and services diesel engines.

Darr Equipment Co.
2000 E. Airport Frwy.
Irving, TX 75062
(214) 721-2000
Personnel Director: Michael Shropshire
Caterpillar dealership and parts distributor.

ESI Industries
6440 N. Central Expwy., Suite 200
Dallas, TX 75206
(214) 361-6663
Vice President & Treasurer: Kenneth Uselton
Truck body manufacturer.

Four Seasons Division
500 Industrial Park Dr.
Grapevine, TX 76051
Metro (817) 481-7881
Personnel Director: Shirley DeCoopman
Remanufactures and distributes automotive parts.

Freight Master
8600 Will Rogers Blvd.
Fort Worth, TX 76140
(817) 293-4220
Personnel Manager: Jack Adams
Manufactures hydraulic cushioning devices for railroad freight cars.

Frigette Corp.
800 W. Risinger Rd.
Fort Worth, TX 76140
(817) 293-5313
Personnel Director: Nita Pound
Manufactures automotive air conditioners and parts.

General Automotive Parts Corp.
2221 W. Mockingbird Ln.
Dallas, TX 75235
(214) 357-3900
Personnel Director: Suzanne Moore
Wholesaler and retailer of automotive parts.

General Motors Corp.
2525 E. Abram St.
Arlington, TX 76010
(817) 649-6211
Personnel Director: R. E. Lee
Major international automobile manufacturer. Oldsmobiles and Chevrolets built in Arlington plant.

Hobbs Trailers
4800 Blue Mound Rd.
Fort Worth, TX 76106
(817) 625-2181
Contact: Dick Haub
Manufactures semi-trailers.

International Harvester Co.
1850 N. Greenville Ave., Suite 150
Richardson, TX 75081
(214) 238-3500
Administration Manager: R. O. Harris
Manufactures and sells heavy machinery.

Interstate Battery System of America, Inc.
9304 Forest Ln., Suite 200
Dallas, TX 75243
(214) 340-0432
Personnel Director: Violet Lewis
Battery distributor.

Lone Star Manufacturing & Affiliates
1900 SE Loop 820
Fort Worth, TX 76140
(817) 293-6303
Personnel Director: Sonia Tschaekofske
Manufactures automotive air conditioners.

Long Mile Rubber Co.
5550 LBJ Frwy., Suite 200
Dallas, TX 75240
(214) 788-0731
Personnel Director: Carolyn Ghoston
Manufactures tire retreads.

Mass Merchandisers, Inc.
4221 Shilling Way
Dallas, TX 75137
(214) 263-7069
Division Manager: Bob Dehart
Wholesaler of automotive supplies, housewares, and other non-food items.

Micro Products, Inc.
210 E. Buckingham Rd.
Garland, TX 75040
(214) 276-0577
Personnel Director: George Turek
Rebuilds and distributes auto parts.

Rhino Products, Inc.
1000 Singleton Blvd.
Dallas, TX 75212
(214) 651-0733
Personnel Director: Robert Ford
Manufactures farm and industrial equipment.

Scotti Muffler Centers, Inc.
5959 E. Rosedale St.
Fort Worth, TX 76112
(817) 451-0753
Marketing Vice President: Cecil Reaves
Manufactures and distributes benders and lifts for muffler installation.

TIC United Corp.
4645 N. Central Expwy.
Dallas, TX 75205
(214) 559-0580
Personnel Director: Harold Hatley
Manufactures farm machinery.

Texas Kenworth Co.
4040 Irving Blvd.
Dallas, TX 75247
(214) 920-7300
Employment Director: Ron Fulmer
Heavy-duty truck sales and service.

Volkswagen of America, Inc.
4401 Blue Mound Rd.
Fort Worth, TX 76106
(817) 624-4941
Personnel Director: J. P. Derderian
Manufactures Volkswagen air conditioners and heaters.

▶Banks: commercial and savings

To learn more about the **banking industry** and related fields, check out the following professional organizations listed in Chapter 5:

Dallas American Institute of Banking
Dallas Business League
Fort Worth Security Dealers Association
National Association of Bank Women

For additional information, you can write to:

American Bankers Association
1120 Connecticut Ave., NW
Washington, DC 20036

Bank Marketing Association
309 W. Washington Blvd.
Chicago, IL 60606

Mortgage Bankers Association of America
1125 15th St., NW
Washington, DC 20005

National Bankers Association
490 l'Enfant Plaza East, Suite 320
Washington, DC 20024

National Savings & Loan League
1101 15th St., NW
Washington, DC 20005

Professional Publications:
ABA Banking Journal
American Banker
American Business
Bank Marketing Magazine
The Banker
Bankers Digest
Bankers Monthly
Banking Law Journal
Banking Magazine
Barron's National Business and Financial Weekly
Boardroom Reports
Business and Society Review
D & B Reports
Federal Home Loan Bank Board Journal
Journal of Bank Research
Journal of Banking & Finance
The Journal of Commercial Bank Lending
Journal of Money, Credit and Banking
Mortgage Banking
Savings Bank Journal
Savings & Loan News

Directories:
American Bank Directory (McFadden Business Publications, Norcross, GA)
American Banker's Guide to the First 5,000 U.S. Banks (American Banker, New York, NY)
Money Market Directory (Money Market Directories, Charlottesville, VA)
Moody's Bank and Finance Manual (Moody's Investors Service, New York, NY)
Texas Banking Red Book (Bankers Digest, Inc., Dallas, TX)
Western Bank Directory (Western Banker Publications, Inc., San Francisco, CA)

Allied Lakewood Bank
6301 Gaston Ave.
Dallas, TX 75214
(214) 823-9924
Personnel Director: Lucy Finger

Bank of Dallas
3333 Lee Pkwy.
Dallas, TX 75219
(214) 521-4171
Personnel Manager: Terry Hollingshead

Bright Banc
Corporate Office
2355 Stemmons Frwy.
Dallas, TX 75207
(214) 638-9784
Vice President: Elaine Gress

Cullen/Frost Bank of Dallas
2001 Bryan St.
Dallas, TX 75221
(214) 979-2000
Vice President of Personnel: Carolyn Nance

Dallas Federal Savings & Loan Association
Corporate Headquarters
8333 Douglas Ave.
Dallas, TX 75225
(214) 750-5000
Vice President: Elaine Gress

Empire of America FSA
1600 W. 7th St.
Fort Worth, TX 76102
(817) 336-8161
Personnel Manager: Susan Simons

Farm & Home Savings Association
5644 LBJ Frwy.
Dallas, TX 75240
(214) 661-3043
Personnel Manager: David Cason

First City Bank/Dallas
1700 Pacific Ave.
Dallas, TX 75201
(214) 939-8000
Personnel Director: Lourdes Cordero

First City National Bank/Arlington
201 E. Abram St.
Arlington, TX 76010
(817) 588-0100
Personnel Director: Ester Thomason

First Texas Savings
300 W. 7th St.
Fort Worth, TX 76102
(817) 336-9766
Contact: Branch manager at each office

Grand Bank/R. L. Thornton
5201 R. L. Thornton Frwy.
Dallas, TX 75223
(214) 823-4191
Personnel Director: Nikki Dancer

InterFirst Bank/Dallas
1401 Elm St.
Dallas, TX 75202
(214) 977-2610
Personnel: Pearl Smith for clerical and Lucy Neary for professional

InterFirst Bank/Fort Worth
One Burnett Plaza
Fort Worth, TX 76197
(817) 390-6161
Human Resources Director: Dick Andrews

InterFirst Bank/DFW
8445 Freeport Pkwy.
Irving, TX 75063
(214) 929-8100
Personnel: Cynthia Sindric Smith

InterFirst Bank/Park Cities
5315 Preston Rd.
Dallas, TX 75205
(214) 526-8100
Personnel Manager: Debbie Wren

Lomas & Nettleton Financial Corp.
2001 Bryan Tower
Dallas, TX 75201
(214) 746-7111
Vice President of Human Resources: Charles Werner

MBank/Dallas
1704 Main St.
Dallas, TX 75201
(214) 698-6000
Personnel Director: Ann Rhodes

MBank/Preston
8111 Preston Rd.
Dallas, TX 75225
(817) 363-1511
Personnel Director: Hoyt Neal

MCorp
1807 Commerce St.
Dallas, TX 75201
(214) 698-5000
Personnel Director: Leslie Lieberman

Metropolitan Financial Savings & Loan Association
Corporate Office
5944 Luther Ln.
Dallas, TX 75225
(214) 369-2700
Personnel Manager: Scott Campbell

NorthPark National Bank
1300 NorthPark Center
Dallas, TX 75225
(214) 890-5100
Personnel Director: Culver Wilson

RepublicBank/Dallas
Pacific & Ervay
Dallas, TX 75201
(214) 922-5000
Personnel Manager: Roger Dunn

RepublicBank/Greenville Ave.
7515 Greenville Ave.
Dallas, TX 75231
(214) 369-8400
Personnel Director: Ed Whitmore

RepublicBank/Oak Cliff
400 S. Zang Blvd.
Dallas, TX 75208
(214) 942-2161
Personnel Director: Linda Wood

RepublicBank/Ridglea
6300 Ridglea Place
Fort Worth, TX 76116
(817) 737-3111
Personnel Manager: Brenda Clark

Texas American Bank/Dallas
100 Exchange Park North
Dallas, TX 75235
(214) 353-8100
Personnel Manager: Shane Winkles

Texas American Bank/Fort Worth
500 Throckmorton St.
Fort Worth, TX 76113
(817) 338-8011
Personnel Director: Robert Herchert

Texas Commerce Bank/Arlington
500 E. Border St.
Arlington, TX 76010
Metro (817) 469-3100
Personnel Manager: Sarah Francis

Texas Commerce Bank/Dallas
600 Pearl St.
Dallas, TX 75201
(214) 922-2300
Human Resources Representative: Barbara Wagley

Texas Independent Bank
5205 N. O'Connor Blvd., Suite 1200
Irving, TX 75039
(214) 869-4600
Personnel Manager: Connie Rickard

▶Book and directory publishers

To learn more about **book publishing** and related fields, check out the following professional organizations listed in Chapter 5:

Southwestern Booksellers Association
Women in Communications, Inc.

For additional information, you can write to:

American Booksellers Association
122 E. 42nd St.
New York, NY 10017

Association of American Publishers
One Park Ave.
New York, NY 10016

Trade Publications:
American Bookseller
Coda: Poets and Writers Newsletter
Editor and Publisher
Library Journal
Publishers Weekly
Small Press

Directories:
American Book Trade Directory (R. R. Bowker, New York, NY)
Literary Market Place (R. R. Bowker, New York, NY)

Business Publications, Inc.
1700 Alma Rd., Suite 390
Plano, TX 75075
(214) 422-4389
Personnel: Susie Hegg
Publishes college textbooks.

Harcourt Brace Jovanovich, Inc.
1875 Monetary Ln.
Carrollton, TX 75006
(214) 245-1118
Contact: M. G. Halsey
Regional sales office of educational publishing company.

Houghton Mifflin Co.
13400 Midway Rd.
Dallas, TX 75244-5165
(214) 980-1100
Contact: Personnel
Regional sales division of educational publishing company.

MAPSCO, Inc.
5308 Maple Ave.
Dallas, TX 75235
(214) 521-2131
Personnel: Ryan McClin
Publishes street maps and reference guides.

McGraw Hill Book Co.
8301 Ambassador Row
Dallas, TX 75247
(214) 631-0096
District Manager: Tim O'Leary
Sales office for textbook publishing company.

Pressworks Publishing, Inc.
2800 Routh St., Suite 249
Dallas, TX 75201
(214) 369-3113
Contact: Personnel
Book publishing company.

Southwest Offset, Inc.
1809 S. Lamar St.
Dallas, TX 75215
(214) 421-5900
Personnel Director: Sygale Lamas
Publication firm.

Sweet Publishing
3934 Sandshell Dr.
Fort Worth, TX 76137
(817) 232-5661
President: Byron Williamson
Publishes Christian books.

Taylor Publishing Co., Inc.
1550 W. Mockingbird Ln.
Dallas, TX 75235
(214) 637-2800
Personnel Director: Scott Latham
Publishes yearbooks and general interest books.

The Underground Shopper
Route 4, Box 176 H
Roanoke, TX 76266
(817) 430-0101
President: Sue Goldstein
Publishes bargain shopping guides and fitness books.

▶Broadcasting

To learn more about **radio, television, cable,** and related fields, check out the following professional organizations listed in Chapter 5:

Dallas Cable Club
Dallas Communications Council
Dallas/Fort Worth Association of Black Communicators
Network of Hispanic Communicators
Press Club of Dallas
Society of Professional Journalists, Sigma Delta Chi
Texas Association of Film and Tape Professionals
Women in Communications, Inc.

For additional information, you can write to:

Broadcasters Promotion Association
Box 5102
Lancaster, PA 17601

National Association of Broadcasters
1771 N St., NW
Washington, DC 20036

National Association of Television Program Executives
Box 5272
Lancaster, PA 17601

Radio-Television News Directors Association
1735 DeSales St., NW
Washington, DC 20036

Television Information Office
745 5th Ave.
New York, NY 10022

Professional Publications:
Billboard
Broadcast Communications
Broadcasting Magazine
Communications News
Television/Radio Age

Directories:
Broadcasting Cable Source Book (Broadcasting Publishing Co., Washington, DC)
Broadcasting Yearbook (Broadcasting Publishing Co., Washington, DC)
Creative Directory of the Sun Belt (Ampersand, Inc., Houston, TX)
Metroplex Mediaguide (Bob Lawler Public Relations, Dallas, TX)
Television Fact Book (Television Digest, Washington, DC)

Heritage Cablevision
6464 Jim Miller Rd.
Dallas, TX 75228
(214) 328-2882
General Manager: Joe King
Cable company with franchise to serve Dallas, Farmers Branch, and Mesquite.

KAAM–AM
15851 Dallas Pkwy., Suite 1200
Dallas, TX 75248
(214) 770-7777
General Manager: William Steding
24-hour Big Band Music.

KCBI–FM
1600 Patterson St.
Dallas, TX 75201
(214) 954-4444
Station Manager: Carl Singer
24-hour religious radio music.

KDAF–TV
8001 Carpenter Frwy.
Dallas, TX 75247
(214) 634-8833
General Manager: Raymond Schonbak
Channel 33 independent TV station.

KDFI–TV
433 Regal Row
Dallas, TX 75247
(214) 637-2727
General Manager: John McKay
Channel 27 independent TV station.

KDFW–TV
400 N. Griffin St.
Dallas, TX 75202
(214) 744-4000
General Manager: Bill Baker
Channel 4 CBS–TV affiliate.

KDLZ–FM
3601 Kimbro Rd.
Fort Worth, TX 76111
(817) 630-3488
General Manager: Gary Lewis
Urban contemporary radio music.

KEGL–FM
222 Las Colinas Blvd., Suite 1400
Irving, TX 75039
(214) 869-9700
General Manager: Norman Rau
Contemporary hit radio music.

KERA–FM
3000 Harry Hines Blvd.
Dallas, TX 75201
Metro (214) 263-3151
General Manager: Richard Meyer
NPR news, jazz and classical radio music.

KERA–TV
3000 Harry Hines Blvd.
Dallas, TX 75201
Metro (214) 263-3151
General Manager: Richard Meyer
Channel 13 PBS–TV station.

KESS–FM
2601 Scott Ave., Suite 218
Fort Worth, TX 76103
(817) 535-1519
General Manager: Marcos Rodriguez
24-hour Spanish radio music.

KFJZ–AM
2214 E. 4th St.
Fort Worth, TX 76111
(817) 336-7175
General Manager: David Button
Daytime "music of your life" radio programming.

KHYI–FM
2216 S. Cooper St.
Arlington, TX 76013
Metro (817) 265-3101
General Manager: Paul Jacobs
24-hour contemporary radio programming.

KKDA–AM
621 N. W. 6th St.
Grand Prairie, TX 75050
Metro (817) 263-9911
General Manager: Hymen Childs
Daytime contemporary music.

KKDA–FM
621 N. W. 6th St.
Grand Prairie, TX 75050
Metro (817) 263-9911
Station Manager: Hymen Childs
24-hour urban contemporary radio music.

KLIF–AM
411 Ryan Plaza Dr.
Arlington, TX 76011
Metro (817) 461-0995
Station Manager: Dan Halyburton
24-hour all talk.

Breaking into broadcasting

If you're fresh out of school and want to break into the Dallas/Fort Worth broadcast market, KRLD radio personality Alex Burton has one word of advice: Wait.

"There's no reason any broadcaster in this market should accept someone without experience. Those with degrees should go to a smaller market, so they can unlearn everything they learned in school," Burton says.

While working in smaller towns, get a broad-based education on what makes a radio station run. Volunteer to do EVERYTHING, Burton recommends. That means sales, sports, news, copywriting, deejaying, and even engineering. "Engineering experience helps you know what is possible, that you're not at the mercy of an engineer, and what to do in case your equipment breaks down," he says.

When you have at least six months of experience, begin building your tape of your best pieces and critique them as if they're by someone else. Then you can take your best work to apply in D/FW's tough broadcast market, which is the ninth largest in the nation.

After working at 17 stations during his 33-year career, Burton says, "I would never suggest that anyone go into the broadcasting business. It's such a tenuous life. So few people have contracts. You work long hours, strange hours. It's hard on the wives and kids."

The image of the hard-living, hard-drinking broadcaster is deceptive, Burton adds. "The only people who stay in the business are the ones who do their work straight—all the time," he says.■

KLTJ–TV
1957 E. Irving Blvd.
Irving, TX 75060
(214) 721-0104
Station Manager: Eldred Thomas
Channel 49 Christian independent TV station.

KLUV-FM
5217 Ross Ave.
Dallas, TX 75205
Metro (214) 263-3187
General Manager: Steven Dienetz
24-hour solid gold oldies radio music.

KMEZ AM-FM
9900 McCree Rd.
Dallas, TX 75247
Metro (214) 348-3800
Vice President/General Manager: Chester Maxwell
Easy listening radio music.

KMGC-FM
1353 Regal Row
Dallas, TX 75247
Metro (214) 688-0641
General Manager: Ross Reagan
Adult contemporary radio music.

KMIA-AM
616 One Tandy Center
Fort Worth, TX 76102
(817) 336-1540
General Manager: Alberto Soto
6 a.m. to midnight. Religious radio music.

KPBC-AM
3201 Royalty Row
Irving, TX 75062
Metro (214) 445-1700
Station Manager: Bill MacCormick
Sunrise to sunset adult Christian contemporary radio music.

KPLX-FM
411 Ryan Plaza Dr.
Arlington, TX 76011
Metro (817) 461-0995
Station Manager: Dan Halyburton
Contemporary country radio music.

KQZY-FM
400 S. Houston St., Suite 105
Dallas, TX 75202
Metro (214) 263-0875
General Manager: Ted Jordan
Adult contemporary music.

KRLD–AM
1080 Metromedia Place
Dallas, TX 75247
Metro (214) 634-1080
General Manager: Ed Wodka
24-hour radio news and sports.

KRQX–AM
Communications Center
Dallas, TX 75202
(214) 748-9631
General Manager: Gene Boivin
Good-time rock 'n' roll radio music.

KSCS–FM
One Broadcast Hill
Fort Worth, TX 76103
Metro (817) 429-2330
General Manager: Warren Potash
Contemporary country radio music.

KSKY–AM
2727 Inwood Rd.
Dallas, TX 75235
(214) 352-3975
General Manager: Andy Bell
Sunrise to sunset religious radio music.

KSSA–AM
7700 Carpenter Frwy.
Dallas, TX 75247
Metro (214) 263-6577
General Manager: Chuck Gratner
Spanish language station.

KTKS–FM
8235 Douglas Ave., Suite 300
Dallas, TX 75225
(214) 891-3400
General Manager: John Hare
Contemporary hit radio.

KTVT–TV
4801 West Frwy.
Fort Worth, TX 76107
Metro (817) 654-1100
Vice President/General Manager: Charles Edwards
Channel 11 independent TV station.

KTXQ–FM
4131 N. Central Expwy., Suite 700
Dallas, TX 75204
Metro (214) 263-0804
General Manager: Clint Culp
Album rock radio music.

KVIL–FM
5307 Mockingbird Ln., Suite 500
Dallas, TX 75206
Metro (214) 263-7045
General Manager: Dave Spence
Adult contemporary radio music.

KVTT–FM
2618 Electronics Ln.
Dallas, TX 75220
Metro (214) 263-8713
General Manager: Rayne Nell Thomas
Religious non-commercial radio music.

KWJS–AM
3001 W. 5th St.
Fort Worth, TX 76107
(817) 335-2400
General Manager: Jack Rabito
24-hour religious radio music.

KXAS–TV
3900 Barnett St.
Fort Worth, TX 76103
Metro (817) 429-1550
General Manager: Frank O'Neil
Channel 5 NBC–TV affiliate.

KXTA–TV
1712 E. Randol Mill Rd.
Arlington, TX 76011
Metro (817) 265-2100
President/General Manager: William Castleman
Channel 21 independent TV station.

KXTX–TV
3900 Harry Hines Blvd.
Dallas, TX 75219
(214) 521-3900
General Manager: Dick Bove
Channel 39 independent TV station.

KZEW–FM
Communications Center
Dallas, TX 75202
(214) 748-9898
General Manager: Gene Bolvin
Album rock radio music.

KZPS–FM
15851 Dallas Pkwy., Suite 1200
Dallas, TX 75248
(214) 770-7777
General Manager: William Steding
Contemporary-hit radio music.

Sammons Communications
4528 W. Vickery Blvd.
Fort Worth, TX 76104
(817) 737-4731
Marketing Manager: Karen Cantrell
Cable system serving Fort Worth.

Scott Cable Communications, Inc.
700 W. Airport Frwy.
Irving, TX 75062
(214) 438-9450
Personnel: Lyn Masterman
Corporate headquarters for cable television systems.

Southern Baptist Radio-Television Commission
6350 West Frwy.
Fort Worth, TX 76150
(817) 737-4011
Vice President for Production Services: Bob Taylor
Baptist broadcast network producing radio and TV shows.

Texas State Network
7901 Carpenter Frwy.
Dallas, TX 75247
(214) 688-1133
General Manager: Gene Ashcraft
Statewide radio news network.

WBAP–AM
One Broadcast Hill
Fort Worth, TX 76103
Metro (817) 429-2330
General Manager: Warren Potash
Country radio music.

WFAA–TV
Communications Center
Dallas, TX 75202
(214) 748-9631
General Manager: Dave Lane
Channel 8 ABC–TV affiliate.

WRR–FM
Fair Park
Dallas, TX 75226
(214) 670-8888
General Manager: Maurice Lowenthal
24-hour classical radio music.

Chemicals

To learn more about the **chemical** industry and related fields, you may want to check out the **American Institute of Chemical Engineers,** listed in Chapter 5.

For additional information, you can write to:

American Chemical Society
1155 16th St., NW
Washington, DC 20036

Professional Publications:
Chemical and Engineering News
Chemical Marketing Reporter
Chemical Week

Directories:
Chemical and Engineering News, Career Opportunities issue (American Chemical Society, Washington, DC)
Chemical Week: Buyer's Guide issue (McGraw Hill, New York, NY)

American Cyanamid Co.
7611 John Carpenter Frwy.
Dallas, TX 75247
(214) 631-2130
Contact: Becky Rollheiser for sales positions or Edna Oden for clerical and office positions
A diversified corporation with several area divisions: Agriculture Division, Formica Corp., Household Products Division, Lederle Laboratories, and Cyro Acrylics.

Ashland Chemical Co.
3101 Wood Dr.
Garland, TX 75041
(214) 840-0206
Contact: Main office in Columbus, Ohio (614) 889-3333
Supplies solvents and chemicals and handles hazardous waste disposal. Three other Dallas locations.

Buckley Oil & Chemical Co., Inc.
1809 Rock Island St.
Dallas, TX 75207
(214) 421-4147
Personnel: Bess Buckley
Buys and sells alcohol, ketones, hexane, lacquer, enamel, motor oil, paint stripper, and screen cleaners.

Delta Distributors
11344 Plano Rd.
Dallas, TX 75243
(214) 341-0510
Vice President: Art Adams
Distributes acetates, acids, ethers, ektones, and pine oil.

DeSoto, Inc.
701 Shiloh Rd.
Garland, TX 75042
(214) 276-5181
Personnel Director: Bob Highland
Manufactures paints and resins.

Dow Chemical USA
One Galleria Tower
13355 Noel Rd., Suite 1025
Dallas, TX 75240
(214) 387-2211
Contact: Linda Neal for clerical positions; company headquarters in Midland, Mich. (517) 636-1000 for sales and lab work positions
Produces agricultural and industrial chemicals, including herbicides, insecticides, plastics, and latex.

DuBois Chemicals Division
8770 S. Central Expwy.
Dallas, TX 75239
(214) 376-6491
Contact: Department heads
Produces industrial and institutional cleaning products.

Hancock Industries, Inc.
7101 Burns St.
Richland Hills, TX 76118
(214) 589-2410
President: Dean Hancock
Distributes more than 750 varieties of chemicals to 47 companies.

Jett Research Center, Inc.
Hwy. 1187
Mansfield, TX 76063
(817) 483-0933
Personnel: Phil Hester
Produces explosive devices, including shaped charges and pyrotechnic devices.

Jones-Blair Co.
2728 Empire Central Dr.
Dallas, TX 75235
(214) 353-1600
Personnel Manager: C. E. Isom
Produces and distributes paints.

NCH Corporation
2727 Chemsearch Blvd.
Irving, TX 75062
(214) 438-0211
Contact: Personnel
Maintenance of industrial and chemical products.

Petrochemical/Desoto, Inc.
2001 N. Grove St.
Fort Worth, TX 76106
(817) 625-2111
Personnel Manager: Mark Renfro
Manufactures specialty chemicals, stearates, and detergents.

Plastics Manufacturing Co.
2700 S. Westmoreland Rd.
Dallas, TX 75233
(214) 330-8671
Contact: Billy Crow for office work and C. R. Whited for plant jobs
Produces resin adhesives and plastic dinnerware.

Poly-America
2000 W. Marshall Dr.
Grand Prairie, TX 75051
(214) 647-2950
Personnel: Myrtle Walker
Manufactures polyethylene film for agriculture and commercial uses.

Roach Paint Co., Inc.
2121 French Settlement Rd.
Dallas, TX 75212
(214) 630-5511
Contact: Department Head
Manufactures paints and drywall supplies.

Southwestern Petroleum Corp.
534 N. Main St.
Fort Worth, TX 76106
(817) 332-2336
Personnel Director: Rachel Newman
Manufactures protective coatings and specialty lubricants.

Texas Refinery Corp.
840 N. Main St.
Fort Worth, TX 76106
(817) 332-1161
Personnel Director: R. O. Phillips
Produces industrial coatings, lubricants, and industrial cleaners.

Texstyrene Plastics, Inc.
3607 N. Sylvania Ave.
Fort Worth, TX 76111
(817) 831-3541
Personnel Director: Chuck Sparkman
Manufactures polystyrene resin.

Thompson-Hayward Chemicals
2627 Weir St.
Dallas, TX 75212
(214) 638-8034
Operations Manager: Barbara Rudiger
Distributes industrial and oil field chemicals, laundry and dry cleaning supplies, and pest control chemicals.

Valley Solvents
2573 NE 33rd St.
Fort Worth, TX 76111
(817) 831-0001
Branch Manager: Robert Rumford
Distributes industrial solvents and chemicals.

Virginia KMP Corp.
4100 Platinum Way
Dallas, TX 75237
(214) 330-7731
Contact: Department Heads
Produces water-treating chemicals and manufactures air-conditioning and refrigeration components.

Zoecon Industries
12005 Ford Rd., Suite 800
Dallas, TX 75234
(214) 243-2321
Human Resources Manager: Andrew Arrington
Two area locations produce a variety of insecticide products, including baited traps and dog and cat flea collars.

▶Computers: Data Processing

To learn more about **data processing** and related fields, check out the following professional organizations listed in Chapter 5:

Association for Systems Management
Association of Information Systems Professionals
Women in Computing

Directories:
IWP Word Processing Directory (International Word Processing Association, Willow Grove, PA)

Automatic Data Processing, Inc.
2735 Stemmons Frwy.
Dallas, TX 75207
(214) 630-9311
Personnel: Virginia Vanscoy
A computing services company with several divisions.

AIC Analysts Corporation
9901 E. Valley Ranch Pkwy., L. B. 27
Irving, TX 75063
(214) 869-1881
Corporate Recruiter: Kay Dorr
Consulting firm for systems analysts.

Business Computer Systems Corp.
13600 LBJ Frwy., Suite 1640
Garland, TX 75041
(214) 681-1331
Administrative Assistant: Monica Hamilton
Data processing services company that works primarily with property and casualty insurance companies.

Commercial Computer Service, Inc.
309 W. 7th St.
Fort Worth, TX 76102
Metro (817) 589-0333
Data Control: Bill Campbell
Provides packaged programs, systems programming, and data preparation.

CompuServe, Inc.
717 N. Harwood St., Suite 520, LB6
Dallas, TX 75201
(214) 742-2888
Branch Manager: Tom Fry
Nationwide computer time-sharing service.

Computer Assistance, Inc.
11498 Luna Rd., Suite 108
Dallas, TX 75234
(214) 869-1161
Contact: Kae Bailey
Provides consulting, designing, and programming services for every industry.

Computer Data Processing, Inc.
2307 Oak Ln., Suite 100
Grand Prairie, TX 75051
(214) 263-4761
Owner: Murray Procell
Data processing service bureau.

Computer Language Research, Inc.
2395 Midway Rd.
Carrollton, TX 75006
(214) 250-7000
Contact: David Swanson
Provides computing services for tax processing.

CompuTrac, Inc.
222 Municipal Dr.
Richardson, TX 75080
(214) 234-4241
Business Manager: Linda Phillips
Computerized law firm management systems.

Control Data Business Centers
14801 Quorum Dr., Suite 200
Addison, TX 75240
(214) 385-5750
Data Processing Manager: Anthony N. Mitcham
Service bureau company that provides batch services for payroll and other financial needs.

Cutler/Williams Information Management Services
2655 Villa Creek Dr., Suite 205
Dallas, TX 75234
(214) 243-3421
Recruiting Manager: Cal Henline
Information management services company.

DataLogic
1800 N. Glenville Dr., Suite 136
Richardson, TX 75081
(214) 644-6373
Personnel: Jackie Clark
Data entry service bureau.

Electronic Data Systems Corporation
7171 Forest Ln.
Dallas, TX 75230
(214) 661-6000
Corporate Recruiting: Jay Salem
Designs, programs, consults, and operates computer services for major commercial and governmental customers worldwide.

Ericsson Information Systems
715 N. Glenville Dr., Suite 401
Richardson, TX 75081
(214) 669-9900
Contact: Personnel
Develops and maintains software products in the microprocessor and PC areas.

Leardata Info-Services
900 Texas Commerce Bank Tower
600 N. Pearl St.
Dallas, TX 75201
(214) 969-7300
Vice President of Personnel: Barbara Martin
Provides contract data processing.

Byte into data processing management

Jerry Dalton, director of computer services for a suburban school district, works with students and professionals alike. He tracks movement in the field and says, "For a recent graduate to get a first job as a computer center manager would take luck. It has been done, but it's unusual. A manager needs not only technical expertise, but competence with budgetary matters and with the handling of money for the installation—in other words, some accounting is extremely beneficial. A manager is also responsible for personnel and needs those skills.

"To get a foot in the door generally means starting out as a programmer or operator, moving into systems analysis and then manager. And this would likely be in a small- to medium-size installation," Jerry continues.

"Turnover is high in data processing and more often than not, a person is expected to step in and take over. There's not much on-the-job training. I advise young people to have a good, strong resume and to take sample programs they've written to the interview.

"Of industries using computer specialists, banking and hospitals seem to be unique situations with unique clientele," Jerry adds. "I tend to put those in a different category from manufacturing and education. Applications for the latter differ but the theory is the same: in warehouses you track inventory and in schools you track student absenteeism, etc."■

Lomas & Nettleton Information Systems, Inc.
1750 Viceroy Dr.
Dallas, TX 75235
(214) 879-1600
Human Resources: Joan McEachen
Provides data processing for Lomas & Nettleton and contract services for mortgage and savings and loan companies.

Merit Computer Systems, Inc.
12201 Merit Dr., Suite 690
Dallas, TX 75251
(214) 788-4100
Corporate Recruiting: Mary Beth Shaffer
Data processing consulting company.

MTech
1712 Commerce St.
Dallas, TX 75222
(214) 742-7100
Contact: Human Resources Department
Corporate office for one of the nation's leading bank data processors and developers of MPACT automated teller machines.

STSC
14901 Quorum Dr., Suite 485
Dallas, TX 75240
(214) 239-3723
Branch Manager: Judy Feld
Provides remote access computer timesharing and consulting.

StaffWare Consulting
5220 Spring Valley Rd., Suite 625
Dallas, TX 75240
(214) 991-9752
Technical Recruiter: Robert Waring
Data processing consulting firm.

▶Computers: equipment manufacturers and services

To learn more about the **computer industry,** check out the following professional organizations listed in Chapter 5:

Association for Systems Management
Association of Information Systems Professionals
Women in Computing

Professional Publications:
Byte
Design News
Electronic Products
Electronics Distributor
Electronics News
Semiconductors International

Directories:
Data Sources: Hardware-Data Communications Directory (Ziff-Davis, New York, NY)

Directory of Computer Facilities in the Southwest (Texas A&M University, College Station, TX)
Directory of Electrical Wholesale Distributors (McGraw-Hill, New York, NY)
Directory of High-Technology Firms (Dallas Chamber of Commerce, Dallas, TX)
Directory of Member Firms (Electronics Association of California, Sunnyvale, CA)
EIA Trade Directory (Electronic Industries Association, Washington, DC)
SIA Yearbook (Semiconductor Industry Association, Cupertino, CA)
Who's Who in Electronics (Harris Publishing Co., Twinsburg, OH)

Amdahl Corp.
9441 LBJ Frwy., Suite 208
Dallas, TX 75243
(214) 234-8553
Contact: Personnel
Manufactures computers.

Apple Computer, Inc.
12770 Merit Dr., Suite 1000
Dallas, TX 75251
(214) 770-5800
Contact: Human Resources Department
Sales office for Apple personal computers.

Applied Data Research, Inc.
9101 LBJ Frwy.
Dallas, TX 75243
(214) 680-8200
Personnel Manager: Peggy Taylor
Develops and supports computer software.

Banc Tec, Inc.
4435 Spring Valley Rd.
Dallas, TX 75244
(214) 450-7700
Human Resources Director: Jim Wimberley
Manufactures check processing equipment.

Business Computer Systems Corp.
13600 LBJ Frwy., Suite 1640
Garland, TX 75041
(214) 681-1331
Administrative Assistant: Monica Hamilton
Data processing servicing company working with property and casualty insurance companies.

Business Records Corp.
7505 Carpenter Frwy.
Dallas, TX 75247
(214) 688-1800
Manager: John Harvell or William Gerwick
Record-keeping company with 11 divisions that provides services for county governments and other agencies.

CE Services
2509 Dalworth St.
Grand Prairie, TX 75050
(214) 647-2255
Contact: Department Head
Computer service company.

CompuServe, Inc.
717 N. Harwood St., Suite 520 LB6
Dallas, TX 75201
(214) 742-2888
Branch Manager: C. Michael White, Jr.
Nationwide computer time-sharing, data communications, network sales, and financial information services.

Computer Assistance, Inc.
11498 Luna Rd.
Dallas, TX 75234
(214) 869-1161
Personnel Manager: Kaye Bailey
Computer consulting firm involved in project engineering, equipment purchase, and software programs.

Computer Language Research & Fast-Tax
2395 Midway Rd.
Carrollton, TX 75006
(214) 250-7000
Employment Recruiter: Mark Whitehead
Provides time-sharing services for tax applications.

CompuTrac, Inc.
222 Municipal Dr.
Richardson, TX 75080
(214) 234-4241
Business Manager: Linda Phillips
Sells computer systems for legal profession.

Cutler Williams, Inc.
2655 Villa Creek Dr., Suite 205
Dallas, TX 75234
(214) 243-3421
Recruiting Manager: Cal Henline
Provides contract programming services.

Electronic Data Systems Corp.
7171 Forest Ln.
Dallas, TX 75230
(214) 661-6000
Corporate Recruiting: Jay Salem
Designs, programs, consults, and operates computer services for major commercial and government customers.

Final Test
10858 Harry Hines Blvd.
Dallas, TX 75220
(214) 352-4500
Personnel Director: Wilma Hughes
Assembles, tests, and repairs computer boards.

Flexible Computer Corp.
1801 Royal Ln.
Dallas, TX 75229
(214) 869-1234
Personnel Manager: Rick Jangemi
Multi-computer hardware and software.

Fox Computers
150 Bank St.
Southlake, TX 76092
(817) 488-2000
Personnel Manager: Suzie Collier
Manufactures, programs, and services computer systems for pharmacies.

General Railway Signal
4747 Irving Blvd., Suite 230
Dallas, TX 75247
(214) 630-7566
Personnel Manager: Ginger Lane
Provides software for mass transit and railway yards.

GenRad, Inc.
1601 N. Collins Blvd.
Richardson, TX 75080
(214) 234-3357
Sales Manager: Gary Russell
Designs and manufactures computer-controlled test, measurement, and development systems in three high-technology markets.

Closing the deal on computer sales

Jerry Packer put in a long and successful stint as a salesman for Xerox, then got an MBA and went to work as district manager for Paradyne Corp., a comparatively risky, aggressive new computer company. We asked him about the differences between selling for a giant and taking a risk with a relatively unknown firm.

"Xerox is probably fairly typical of any large corporation," says Jerry, "in that they are very structured. It was a good place to work, but it didn't provide much opportunity for individual decision making. A company like Paradyne offers a fantastic chance to exercise some entrepreneurial skills. The corporation sets general goals, but it's up to me how I meet them. I can try out different marketing techniques, divide up the territory in new ways, create teams, whatever. It's neat to be able to exercise that kind of flexibility."

We asked Jerry what it takes to be a good salesperson.

"A lot of people think that salesmen are forever buying people lunches and playing golf," says Jerry. "But in order to be really successful, you have to work hard. I don't necessarily mean 80 hours a week. But you need to put in sufficient time to do the things that are necessary. A second important requirement is an absolutely thorough understanding of the products you're selling. Not only your own products, but also your competitors'.

"In high-level selling, sales people have to be especially sharp in terms of interpersonal skills. There's an old saying, and it's true: people don't buy from companies, they buy from people. When you're selling systems that range upwards of $5 million, you're also selling yourself. It's important that your clients feel you'll be around even after the sale to handle any problems that might come up. To establish that kind of rapport, you have to look presentable and be very articulate. It also helps if you have good written communication skills."■

Harris Corporation
16001 Dallas Pkwy.
Dallas, TX 75380-9022
(214) 386-2000
Professional Recruiter: Judy Estabrook
Manufactures, designs, sells, and services high-technology communications and information processing equipment, including computer terminals, line printers, card punchers, and readers.

Harris-Lanier Business Products, Inc.
2777 Stemmons Frwy., Suite 1022
Dallas, TX 75207
(214) 630-0692
District Sales Manager: Pat Brown
Regional sales office for word processing and data processing equipment.

Hogan Systems, Inc.
5080 Spectrum Dr.
Dallas, TX 75248
(214) 386-0020
Facilities Administrator: Shirley Wilkerson
Develops, markets, maintains, and supports integrated line of standard banking applications software packages.

IBM Corp.
2727 LBJ Frwy.
Dallas, TX 75381
(214) 620-6683
Contact: Central Employment Office
Manufactures, sells, and services computers and office equipment.

Logic, Inc.
9330 LBJ Frwy., Suite 600
Dallas, TX 75243
(214) 238-1898
Personnel Manager: Winston Kimzey
Provides software for insurance firms.

Micronyx, Inc.
1901 N. Central Expwy., Suite 400
Richardson, TX 75080
(214) 690-0595
Vice President of Administration: Gladys Denton
Computer hardware and software design.

MTech
1712 Commerce St.
Dallas, TX 75222
(214) 742-7100
Contact: Human Resources Department
Corporate office for one of the nation's leading bank data processors and developers of MPACT automated tellers.

NCR Corp.
6777 Oakbrook Blvd.
Dallas, TX 75235
(214) 638-5130
Regional Personnel Manager: M. O. DePalma
Sells and services computer systems and financial and retail terminals.

National Data Corporation
12000 Ford Rd.
Dallas, TX 75234
(214) 620-1851
Contact: Home office in Atlanta, GA (404) 982-8372
Sells computer systems and software to pharmacies and health care organizations.

Olivetti USA
5615 Highpoint Dr.
Irving, TX 75038
(214) 550-5400
Personnel Director: Tim Jehli
Manufactures, sells, and maintains automated financial transaction systems, including computers, automated bank teller machines, and office machines.

Pinetree Computer Systems
8600 Freeport Pkwy., Suite 2000
Dallas, TX 75063
(214) 929-8080
Vice President of Finance: Bill Frazier
Manufactures hand-held computers.

Reynolds & Reynolds Co.
1010 Ave. J. East
Grand Prairie, TX 75050
(214) 647-1722
Contact: Personnel
Sells and services computers.

Rubicon Corporation
1200 E. Campbell Rd.
Richardson, TX 75081
(214) 231-6591
Personnel Manager: Andrea Marshall
Provides computer software for the medical industry.

S.W.P. Microcomputer Products
1000 W. Fuller Ave.
Fort Worth, TX 76115
(817) 924-7759
President: John McFarlen
Manufactures computer products.

Sterling Software, Inc.
8080 N. Central Expwy., Suite 1140
Dallas, TX 75206
(214) 891-8600
Administrative Assistant: Karen McFarlin
Acquires, develops, markets, and supports a broad range of computer software products and services through Informatics and other wholly owned subsidiaries.

Tandem Computers
4001 McEwen Rd., Suite 321
Dallas, TX 75244
(214) 980-0311
Personnel Manager: Allison Felsted
Manufactures, sells and services computers.

Tandy Corp.
500 One Tandy Center
Fort Worth, TX 76102
(817) 390-3700
Vice President & Personnel Director: George Berger
Manufactures and sells microcomputers.

UCCEL Corp.
6303 Forest Park Rd.
Dallas, TX 75235
(214) 353-7100
Employee Relations Director: Lon Davis
Manufactures turnkey systems, software, and timeshare computer services.

VMX, Inc.
One Synergy Park
17217 Waterview Pkwy.
Dallas, TX 75252
(214) 907-3000
Human Resources: C. L. Carter, Jr.
Designs, assembles, markets, and services patented microprocessor-based software-driven computer systems called Voice Message Exchange systems.

Xerox Corp.
222 W. Las Colinas Blvd.
Irving, TX 75039
(214) 830-4616
Contact: Employment Office
One of the world's largest manufacturers of computer systems, copy machines, and other office products.

▶Contractors and construction companies

To learn more about the **construction** industry and related fields, check out the following professional organizations listed in Chapter 5:

American Subcontractors Association
Builders Association of Fort Worth/Tarrant County
Home & Apartment Builders Association of Metropolitan Dallas
Mechanical Contractors Association of Dallas
National Association of Women in Construction
National Electrical Contractors Association

For additional information, you can write to:

National Asphalt Pavement Association
6811 Kenilworth Ave.
Riverdale, MD 20840

National Association of Home Builders
15th & M Streets, NW
Washington, DC 20005

National Construction Industry Council
2000 L St., NW, Suite 612
Washington, DC 20036

Professional Publications:
Building Design & Construction
Construction Review
Engineering News-Record
Glass Industry
Pit and Quarry
Texas Contractor

Directories:
Blue Book of Major Homebuilders (CMR Associates, Inc., Crofton, MD)
Directory of Construction Associations (Metadata, Inc., New York, NY)
Guide to Information Sources in the Construction Industry (Construction Products Manufacturers Council, Arlington, VA)
Texas Contractor, Buyers Guide and Directory issue (P.O. Box 28351, Dallas, TX)

APAC–Texas, Inc.
505 NW 5th St.
Fort Worth, TX 76101
(817) 336-0521
Personnel Director: Edwin Slimp
Contractor for highway, street, and parking facilities.

Austin Industries, Inc.
2949 Stemmons Frwy.
Dallas, TX 75247
(214) 630-5100
Personnel Director: Evelyn Hulhouser
Commercial construction.

Brown & Blakney, Inc.
3700 Reagan Dr.
Fort Worth, TX 76116
(817) 244-6024
Secretary-Treasurer: Bill Evans
Highway and heavy construction.

Thomas S. Byrne, Inc.
464 Bailey Ave.
Fort Worth, TX 76107
(817) 335-3394
Contact: Department Head
General contractor.

Centex Corp.
3333 Lee Pkwy.
Dallas, TX 75219
(214) 748-7901
Director of Corporate Communication: Sheila Gallagher
Residential and commercial construction.

Dallas Construction Co., Inc.
5518 Dyer St., Suite 11
Dallas, TX 75206
(214) 691-9271
President: Tom Martin
Commercial and industrial construction.

Fox & Jacobs, Inc.
2800 Surveyor Blvd.
Carrollton, TX 75011-0934
(214) 245-8511
Personnel Director: Jean Parnell
Home builder.

GMD Engineered Systems, Inc.
305 W. Arlington Ave.
Fort Worth, TX 76110
(817) 926-9294
Contact: Carol Webb
Industrial construction.

HCB Contractors
4600 InterFirst One
Dallas, TX 75202
(214) 747-8541
Director of Human Resources: Jerry Cooper
Commercial construction.

Haws & Tingle General Contractors, Inc.
909 W. Magnolia Ave.
Fort Worth, TX 76104
Metro (817) 429-8310
President: Paul R. Tingle
General contracting.

Huber, Hunt & Nichols
2040 Empire Central Dr.
Dallas, TX 75235
(214) 350-7991
Vice President: Larry Duggan
Commercial construction.

J.A. Jones Construction Co.
14875 Landmark Blvd., Suite 110
Dallas, TX 75240
(214) 233-3095
Vice President: William G. Tucker
Commercial and industrial construction.

SRO Asphalt, Inc.
1007 Harrison Ave.
Arlington, TX 76010
(817) 261-2991
Secretary-Treasurer: Kathy Morrison
Road and street construction.

Speed Fab-Crete Corp.
1150 E. Mansfield Hwy.
Kennedale, TX 76060
(817) 478-1137
Personnel Director: David Bloxom, Jr.
General contractor and precast concrete manufacturer.

Walker Construction Co.
4028 Daily Dr.
Fort Worth, TX 76118
(817) 284-9208
Controller: Glenn Jones
Commercial building construction.

▶Drugs and pharmaceuticals manufacturers and wholesalers

To learn more about the **drug industry** and related fields, you can write to:

American Pharmaceutical Association
2215 Constitution Ave., NW
Washington, DC 20037

Drug Wholesalers Association
1101 Connecticut Ave., NW
Washington, DC 20036

National Association of Chain Drugstores
1911 Jefferson Davis Hwy.
Arlington, VA 22209

National Association of Retail Druggists
1750 K St., NW
Washington, DC 20006

Pharmaceutical Manufacturers Association
1155 15th St., NW
Washington, DC 20005

Professional Publications:
American Druggist
Cosmetic Technology
Drug & Cosmetic Industry
Drug Store News
Drug Topics
Soap/Cosmetics/Chemical Specialties

Directories:
Drug Topics Red Book (Litton Publications, Oradell, NJ)
Health Care Directory (Litton Publications, Oradell, NJ)
NACDS Membership Directory (National Association of Chain Drugstores, Arlington, VA)
NWDA Membership Directory (National Wholesale Druggists Association, Scarsdale, NY)
Pharmaceutical Manufacturers of the U.S. (Noyes Data Corp., Park Ridge, NJ)

AKM Distributing
10790 N. Stemmons Frwy.
Dallas, TX 75220
(214) 350-7814
Vice President: Carolyn McLellan
Manufactures vitamins, health, and beauty aids.

Abbott Laboratories
1921 Hurd Dr.
Irving, TX 75038
(214) 257-6008
Personnel Administrator: Martin Potisek
Designs, develops, and manufactures automated diagnostic instruments.

Alcon Laboratories, Inc.
6201 South Frwy.
Fort Worth, TX 76134
(817) 293-0450
Contact: Placement and Development
Produces ophthalmic products, including contact lens solutions and eye care products.

Carrington Lab
9200 John W. Carpenter Frwy.
Dallas, TX 75247
(214) 638-7686
Contact: Personnel
Produces skin and health care products.

Dexide, Inc.
7509 Flagstone Dr.
Fort Worth, TX 76118
(817) 589-1454
Contact: Texas Employment Commission to take aptitude test
Manufactures surgical scrub devices.

Hoffmann LaRoche, Inc.
5101 Rondo Dr.
Fort Worth, TX 76106
(817) 626-8278
Contact: Main office for application and instructions for applying at New Jersey headquarters
Manufactures vitamin premixes for animal food.

Nortex Drug Distributors, Inc.
1201 N. Central Expwy.
Plano, TX 75075
(214) 424-2127
Contact: Individual store managers
Parent company for Drug Emporium chain.

Quest Medical, Inc.
4103 Billy Mitchell St.
Addison, TX 75244
(214) 387-2740
Human Resources Manager: Corinne Olszowka
Assembles medical and surgical products.

Scherer Laboratories, Inc.
14335 Gillis Rd.
Dallas, TX 75244
(214) 233-2800
Personnel: Nancy Wendeboren
Manufactures vitamins and dental products.

Surgikos, Inc.
2500 Arbrook Blvd.
Arlington, TX 76014
(817) 465-3141
Contact: Personnel
Produces disposable packs, gowns, and specialty surgical products. Johnson & Johnson subsidiary.

TPC Products, Inc.
2021 N. Grove St.
Fort Worth, TX 76106
(817) 626-5408
Executive Vice President: Don Luttrell
Manufactures veterinary drugs for cattle, horses, sheep, and goats.

Tecnol, Inc.
7450 Whitehall St.
Fort Worth, TX 76118
(817) 284-2206
Contact: Vickie Carter
Manufactures health care products.

Traders Oil Mill
3501 S. Jennings Ave.
Fort Worth, TX 76110
(817) 923-4641
Contact: Personnel
Processor of cottonseeds for vegetable oil, cattle feeds, and high-protein nutrients for the pharmaceutical industry.

Travenol Laboratories, Inc.
2501 N. Great Southwest Pkwy.
Grand Prairie, TX 75050
(214) 647-1633
Personnel: Jan Waneck
Distributes medical products.

▶Educational institutions

To learn more about **education** and related fields, check out the following professional organizations listed in Chapter 5:

Administrative Women in Education
American Association of University Women
Classroom Teachers of Dallas
Dallas Association for Childhood Education
Dallas Association of Counselors
Dallas Association of Texas Professional Educators
Dallas County Federation of Teachers
Dallas Educational Secretaries Association
Dallas Music Teachers Association
Dallas School Administrators Association
Educational Secretaries Association of Grand Prairie
Fort Worth Art Education Association
Fort Worth Association for the Education of Young Children
Fort Worth Classroom Teachers Association
Fort Worth Federation of Teachers
Irving Association of Educational Office Personnel
Irving Music Teachers Association
Mesquite Area Music Teachers Association
Mesquite Education Association
Richardson Music Teachers Association
Texas Federation of Teachers
United Teachers of Dallas

For additional information, you can write to:

American Association of School Administrators
1801 N. Moore St.
Arlington, VA 22209

American Federation of Teachers
11 DuPont Circle, NW
Washington, DC 20036

Association of Independent Colleges and Universities
P.O. Box 10186
Lansing, MI 48901

Council for Educational Development and Research
1518 K St., NW
Washington, DC 20005

National Association of College and University Business Officials
One DuPont Circle, Suite 510
Washington, DC 20036

National Association of College Stores
528 E. Lorain St.
Oberlin, OH 44074

National Education Association
1201 16th St., NW
Washington, DC 20036

Professional Publications:
Chronicle of Higher Education
Instructor
Learning
School Administrator

Directories:
College Placement Annual (College Placement Annual, Bethlehem, PA)
Directory of Education Associations (Marquis Publishing Co., Chicago, IL)
Yearbook of Higher Education (Marquis Publishing Co., Chicago, IL)

PUBLIC SCHOOL DISTRICTS

Arlington Independent School District
1203 W. Pioneer Pkwy.
Arlington, TX 76013
(817) 460-4611
Personnel Administrative Assistant: Mary Moore
Enrollment: 39,000

Birdville Independent School District
6125 E. Belknap St.
Haltom City, TX 76117
(817) 831-0951
Personnel: Robert L. Cox
Enrollment: 16,100

Carrollton-Farmers Branch Independent School District
1445 N. Perry Rd.
Carrollton, TX 75006
(214) 323-5700
Personnel: Dr. Betty Jo Monk
Enrollment: 15,100

Castleberry Independent School District
315 Churchill Rd.
Fort Worth, TX 76114
(817) 737-7235
Personnel: Dr. Clarence L. Winn
Enrollment: 2,650

Cedar Hill Independent School District
333 S. Hwy. 67
Cedar Hill, TX 75104
(214) 291-1581
Personnel: Carmyn Douglas
Enrollment: 2,600

Dallas Independent School District
3700 Ross Ave.
Dallas, TX 75204
(214) 824-1620
Personnel: Debra Gomez
Enrollment: 130,000

DeSoto Independent School District
200 E. Belt Line Rd.
DeSoto, TX 75115
(214) 223-6666
Personnel: James Daniels
Enrollment: 5,000

Duncanville Independent School District
802 Main St.
Duncanville, TX 75137
(214) 296-4761
Personnel: Carl Smith
Enrollment: 9,000

Eagle Mountain-Saginaw Independent School District
1200 Old Decatur Rd.
Saginaw, TX 76179
(817) 232-0880
Personnel: Truett Absner
Enrollment: 4,200

Everman Independent School District
608 Townley Dr.
Everman, TX 76140
(817) 293-0631
Personnel: Nelda Winnett
Enrollment: 3,000

Fort Worth Independent School District
3210 W. Lancaster Ave.
Fort Worth, TX 76107
(817) 336-8311
Personnel: Joe Ross
Enrollment: 65,500

Garland Independent School District
720 Stadium Dr.
Garland, TX 75040
(214) 494-8201
Personnel: Gary Reeves
Enrollment: 33,500

Grand Prairie Independent School District
202 W. College St.
Grand Prairie, TX 75050
(214) 264-6141
Personnel: Don Pennock
Enrollment: 15,100

Grapevine-Colleyville Independent School District
3051 W. Hwy. 26
Grapevine, TX 76051
(817) 488-9588
Personnel: JoAnn Houston
Enrollment: 5,600

Highland Park Independent School District
7015 Westchester Dr.
Dallas, TX 75205
(214) 521-4103
Personnel: Dr. Tom Parker
Enrollment: 4,000

Hurst-Euless-Bedford Independent School District
1849 Central Dr.
Bedford, TX 76022
(817) 283-4461
Personnel: Sammie Wester
Enrollment: 17,200

Irving Independent School District
901 N. O'Connor Rd.
Irving, TX 75061
(214) 259-4575
Personnel: Dr. Barry Tacker
Enrollment: 20,200

Kennedale Independent School District
120 W. Mansfield Hwy.
Kennedale, TX 76060
(817) 478-1166
Superintendent: Jay W. Teague
Enrollment: 1,300

Lake Worth Independent School District
6800 Telephone Rd.
Lake Worth, TX 76135
(817) 237-1491
Superintendent: Arthur Gregory
Enrollment: 1,450

Lancaster Independent School District
1105 Westridge Ave.
Lancaster, TX 75146
(214) 227-2747
Personnel: Dr. Don Sykes
Enrollment: 3,750

Mansfield Independent School District
609 E. Broad St.
Mansfield, TX 76063
(817) 473-1178
Personnel: Glenn Harmon
Enrollment: 5,500

Mesquite Independent School District
405 E. Davis St.
Mesquite, TX 75149
(214) 288-6411
Personnel: Dr. Don Woolley
Enrollment: 22,000

Plano Independent School District
1517 Ave. H
Plano, TX 75074
(214) 881-8100
Personnel: Keith Sockwell
Enrollment: 27,500

Richardson Independent School District
400 S. Greenville Ave.
Richardson, TX 75081
(214) 238-8111
Personnel: Dr. Dan Lair
Enrollment: 33,000

White Settlement Independent School District
431 S. Cherry Ln.
White Settlement, TX 76108
(817) 246-6271
Superintendent: Clabe Welch
Enrollment: 3,400

Wilmer-Hutchins Independent School District
3820 E. Illinois Ave.
Dallas, TX 75216
(214) 376-7311
Personnel: Wade O. Cummins
Enrollment: 1,500

UNIVERSITIES AND COLLEGES

Amber University
1700 Eastgate Dr.
Garland, TX 75041
(214) 279-6511
Personnel: Melinda Reagan
Business and technology undergraduate and graduate courses.
Enrollment: 900

Arlington Baptist College
3001 W. Division St.
Arlington, TX 76012
(817) 461-8741
Personnel: David Clogston
Bible studies, education, and music education programs.
Enrollment: 190

The Art and Fashion Institute of Dallas
2829 W. Northwest Hwy.
Dallas, TX 75220
(214) 350-8874
Personnel: Dr. Jackie Brewster
Private institution offering associate degrees in applied arts with majors in fashion merchandising, interior design, and commercial arts.
Approximate enrollment: 325

Baylor College of Dentistry
3302 Gaston Ave.
Dallas, TX 75246
(214) 828-8100
Personnel: John Gilbert
Private college for dentists, dental hygienists, and graduate students.
Enrollment: 450

Baylor University School of Nursing
3700 Worth St.
Dallas, TX 75246
(214) 820-3700
Personnel: Dr. Lorraine Gentner
Four-year R.N. program.
Enrollment: 150

Bishop College
3837 Simpson-Stuart Rd.
Dallas, TX 75241-9899
(214) 372-8000
Contact: President's Office
Private college offering liberal arts and education degrees.
Supported by the United Negro College Fund.
Enrollment: 1,000

Criswell Center for Biblical Studies
525 N. Ervay St.
Dallas, TX 75201
(214) 954-0012
Personnel: Dr. Richard Land
Graduate and undergraduate Bible studies program.
Enrollment: 370

Dallas Baptist University
7777 W. Kiest Blvd.
Dallas, TX 75211-9800
(214) 263-7595
Personnel: Norma McDow
Private liberal arts school offering undergraduate and graduate programs.
Enrollment: 1,500

There *is* life after English 101

Our friend Jane Curtis was an English major in college. Today, she is Assistant Dean of the College of Engineering at a major Dallas university. We asked her how a liberal arts major can become an administrator in a technical field like engineering.

"I never intended to get into academic administration," says Jane. "But I did want to work at the university, which was located near my home. I was exploring job possibilities when I finally attracted the attention of a personnel manager at the university. She felt that I had an interesting background and a good education, and that I would be good in a junior-level administrative position. Eventually I was hired as assistant to a department chairman in the Health Sciences Center. A year later, I moved to a newly created position in the Center, Assistant to the Dean for Student Affairs. During my years with the Center I became a real expert in health sciences education, even though I didn't have any background in the field.

"As I gained experience as an administrator, I also worked at expanding and nurturing my contacts within the university. When higher-level jobs became available, I began applying for them. I was nominated and recommended for the position of Assistant Dean of the College of Engineering. In my current position, I'm transferring my knowledge of student affairs in the Health Sciences Center to the College of Engineering."

We asked Jane if it's unusual to become an administrator in a field in which one has no academic training. "It depends on the university. At older, more tradition-bound schools, it would be more difficult to do what I did. But in a fairly young, evolving university, things are more open. I'm certainly not unique in the system; there are other administrators who do not have academic training in their particular fields. In fact, in some of the professional schools here, people see a need for someone on the senior administrative staff to be from outside the field. Such a person can bring a perspective that is not quite so narrow. Also, as an English major, I have writing, editing, and public speaking skills that those with a more technical background may lack. These skills are very helpful to an administrator."

Jane points out that you don't necessarily need a master's degree or a Ph.D. to become a college administrator. "I'm sure that in some schools you need an advanced degree, but in our university you don't," says Jane. "I did eventually get a master's degree because I felt that I would need it to advance at the university. But keep in mind that there's an awful lot of administrative work to be done that does not require specialized education at an advanced level."

We asked Jane what it takes to become a good academic administrator. "You have to be methodical and good at handling details. You cannot gloss over things. It's important to be able to operate within the university's rules, regulations, and bylaws. You also have to care about the job. Academic administration is not really a 9-to-5 job. You must be willing to work nights and weekends at certain times of the year."

What advice would Jane give to people interested in the field? "Get the attention of someone who has the power to get you in the door. That's the hardest part. It took me a long time to get the attention of the personnel manager who helped me get my first administrative job. So be incredibly persistent, as I was. Don't give up."■

Dallas Christian College
2700 Christian Pkwy.
Dallas, TX 75234
(214) 241-3371
Academic Dean: John C. Ketchen
Four-year private college for ministerial students.
Enrollment: 120

Dallas County Community College District
701 Elm St.
Dallas, TX 75202
(214) 746-2149
Personnel: Barbara Corvey
Offers associate degrees at seven campuses, including Brookhaven Community College, Cedar Valley Community College, Eastfield Community College, El Centro Community College, Mountain View Community College, North Lake Community College, and Richland Community College.
Approximate enrollment: 49,500

Dallas Theological Seminary
3909 Swiss Ave.
Dallas, TX 75204
(214) 824-3094
Personnel: Chet Toole
Nondenominational graduate seminary.
Enrollment: 1,500

Devry Institute of Technology
4250 N. Belt Line Rd.
Irving, TX 75038
(214) 258-6330
Human Resources Director: Glyn Williams
Private institution offering training and placement in electronics, technology, and computer science with associate and bachelor's degrees.
Approximate enrollment: 2,500

Harris College of Nursing
2800 S. University Dr.
Fort Worth, TX 76129
(817) 921-7652
Personnel: Patricia Scearse
Four-year undergraduate nursing program associated with Texas Christian University.
Enrollment: 280

Independent Baptist College
3940 Blue Ridge Blvd.
Dallas, TX 75233
(214) 337-3144
Personnel: Wendell McHargue
Associate and undergraduate programs in church-related work.
Enrollment: 70

Northwood Institute of Texas
FM Rd. 1382
Cedar Hill, TX 75104
(214) 291-1541
Personnel: John Castle
Accredited private business management college with two-year associate degrees in accounting, automotive, computer science, fashion, hotel/restaurant, and marketing.
Enrollment: 200

Southern Methodist University
Hillcrest and University
Dallas, TX 75275
(214) 692-2000
Personnel: Bill Detwiler
Private Methodist university offering undergraduate and graduate programs.
Enrollment: 9,150

Southern Bible Institute
830 S. Buckner Blvd.
Dallas, TX 75217
(214) 398-1454
President: Gordon Mumford
Bible studies program.
Enrollment: 450

Southwestern Baptist Theological Seminary
2001 W. Seminary Dr.
Fort Worth, TX 76115
(817) 923-1921
Personnel: Mina Bickerstaff
World's largest Baptist graduate theological seminary.
Approximate enrollment: 5,000

Tarrant County Junior College District
1500 Houston St.
Fort Worth, TX 76102
(817) 336-7851
Personnel: Erma Johnson
Community college offering associate degrees at TCJC Northeast Campus, TCJC Northwest Campus, TCJC South Campus, and Community Campus in downtown Fort Worth.
Approximate enrollment: 25,000

Texas A&M University, Research and Extension Center at Dallas
17360 Coit Rd.
Dallas, TX 75252
(214) 231-5362
Contact: Texas A&M University in College Station (409) 845-2423
Agriculture and urban studies research. (No courses are offered.)

Texas Christian University
2800 S. University Dr.
Fort Worth, TX 76129
(817) 921-7000
Personnel: Raul Armendariz
Private university affiliated with the Christian Church, offering undergraduate and graduate programs.
Enrollment: 7,000

Texas College of Osteopathic Medicine
Camp Bowie at Montgomery
Fort Worth, TX 76107
(817) 870-5320
President: Dr. David Richards
State medical school for osteopathic doctors.
Enrollment: 450

Texas Wesleyan College
1201 Wesleyan St.
Fort Worth, TX 76105
(817) 531-4403
Personnel: Ann Borriceno
Private Methodist college offering undergraduate and graduate programs.
Enrollment: 1,350

Texas Woman's University, Institute of Health Sciences
1810 Inwood Rd.
Dallas, TX 75235
(817) 898-3555
Personnel: Jeff Ferguson
Offers degrees in health-related fields.
Enrollment: 3,000

University of Dallas
1845 E. Northgate Dr.
Irving, TX 75062-4799
(214) 445-0110
Personnel: Shane Wilbanks
Private Catholic university offering undergraduate and graduate programs.
Enrollment: 2,600

The University of Texas at Arlington
800 S. Cooper St.
Arlington, TX 76019
(817) 273-2011
Personnel: Jim Wise
Largest area state university offering undergraduate and graduate programs.
Enrollment: 21,000

University of Texas at Dallas
2601 Floyd Rd.
Richardson, TX 75080
(214) 690-2111
Personnel: Jerry Robinson
State university offering undergraduate and graduate programs.
Enrollment: 7,300

The University of Texas Health Science Center at Dallas
5323 Harry Hines Blvd.
Dallas, TX 75235
(214) 688-3111
Personnel: Johnnie R. Reynolds
State health science center, which includes the Southwestern Medical School, Southwestern Graduate School of Biomedical Sciences, and the School of Allied Health Sciences.
Enrollment: 2,150

▶Electronic and telecommunications, and office automation systems

To learn more about **electronics** and related fields, check out the following professional organizations listed in Chapter 5:

Data Processing Managers Association
Texas Electronics Association

For additional information, you can write:

Information Management and Processing Association
P.O. Box 16267
Lansing, MI 48901

Institute of Electrical and Electronics Engineers
345 E. 47th St.
New York, NY 10017

Urban and Regional Information Systems Association
1340 Old Chain Bridge Rd.
McLean, VA 22101

Women in Data Processing
P.O. Box 22818
San Diego, CA 92122

Women in Information Processing
P.O. Box 39173
Washington, DC 20016

Professional Publications:
Electronic Business
Electronic News
Electronics
Information and Records Management
Information and Word Processing Report
Technology News of America
Telecommunications
Telecommunications Retailer

Directories:
IWP Word Processing Directory (International Word Processing Association, Willow Grove, PA)
NOMDA Who's Who (National Office Machine Dealers Association, Elk Grove Village, IL)
NOPA Directory (National Office Products Association, Alexandria, VA)

AT&T Information Systems
2777 Stemmons Frwy., Suite 1425
Dallas, TX 75207
(214) 879-1800
Contact: Employment Office
Sales, service, and maintenance for AT&T products.

Airborn, Inc.
4321 Airborn Dr.
Addison, TX 75001
(214) 931-3200
Contact: Personnel
Manufactures electronic connectors.

American Medical Electronics
4125 Keller Springs Rd., Suite 144
Dallas, TX 75244
(214) 248-6000
Personnel Manager: Wesley Johnson
Manufactures proprietary medical equipment.

Armiger Company
2525 Ridgmar Blvd.
Fort Worth, TX 76116
(817) 737-2900
Personnel Director: Jan McKinley
Manufactures telecommunications apparatus.

Centel Business Systems
2350 Valley View Ln., Suite 200
Dallas, TX 75234
(214) 620-8300
Office Manager: Helen Cobb
Sells and services phone systems.

Communications Corporation of America
8585 N. Stemmons Frwy., Suite 500
Dallas, TX 75247
(214) 638-7650
Administrative Assistant: Sheri Grubbs
Sells, installs, and services telephone systems.

Contel Executone Systems, Inc.
4445 Sigma Rd.
Dallas, TX 75244
(214) 661-5646
Contact: Gail Wayrynen
Manufactures and sells telecommunications systems.

Continental Electronics
4212 S. Buckner Blvd.
Dallas, TX 75227
(214) 381-7161
Senior Vice President: Pat Hopper
Manufactures high-power radio transmitters for radio stations.

Cronus Industries, Inc.
12700 Park Central Dr., Suite 300
Dallas, TX 75251
(214) 386-2900
Assistant Corporate Secretary: Pat Dugan
Multi-industry corporation that includes Business Records Corporation, which micrographically records and electronically indexes special records.

DSC Communications Corp.
1000 Coit Rd.
Plano, TX 75075
(214) 519-3000
Contact: Personnel
Designs, develops, manufactures, and markets digital telecommunications switching and transmission systems.

Electronic Modular Systems, Limited
4546 Beltway Dr.
Dallas, TX 75244
(214) 991-9585
Executive Vice President: Jess Turner
Sales of VME and CPU products for industrial uses.

Electrospace Systems, Inc.
1301 E. Collins Blvd.
Richardson, TX 75081
(214) 470-2000
Contact: Personnel
Designs, manufactures, installs, and repairs telecommunications and switching systems.

Elfab Corp.
10907 Yeats St.
Lewisville, TX 75067
(214) 221-8776
Personnel Vice President: Linda Sanders
Manufactures printed circuit boards and assemblies for computer and electronics industries.

Environmental Processing
1321 Plano Rd.
Richardson, TX 75081
(214) 669-0830
Personnel Director: Mrs. Bobby Pribble
Semi-conductor testing.

E–Systems, Inc.
6250 LBJ Frwy.
Dallas, TX 75240
(214) 661-1000
Human Resources Director: Tom Clark
Corporate headquarters for major worldwide developer and producer of high-technology electronic systems and products for government uses.

GNB, Inc.
1880 Valley View Ln.
Farmers Branch, TX 75234
(214) 243-1011
Contact: Personnel
Manufactures automotive and boat batteries.

GTE/Business Phone Systems
290 E. Carpenter Frwy.
Irving, TX 75062
Metro (214) 659-7700
Personnel Manager: Mildred Hooper
Sells, installs, and maintains business communications systems.

Booting up big $$$ in computer sales

Phyllis Daniels competes in the fast lane of a man's world, as a computer sales engineer. Her clients are Fortune 500 companies and her products are communications boards, controllers, and disk and tape subsystems manufactured by a relatively new specialty company.

"It's an emotionally and physically stressful environment where I constantly have to prove myself," says Phyllis, one of seven women in a sales force of 60. We asked how she got there, and what keeps her successful.

"I use every skill and experience I've ever had," said the former teacher and editorial assistant for a steel company's community relations department. "When I decided to go back to school for an associate degree in computers, I needed a job as well. So I sold cars, and that provided invaluable marketing and people experience, plus communications skills that are absolutely essential in my present business.

"Once I got into computer courses, I realized I couldn't settle for a $20,000 programming job, and began laying more plans. And incidentally, you must prepare yourself for the entry position in this field. My first job—strictly commission—was with a small systems house, and within a year I was director of marketing with a sales staff of six. I got a total overview of the business so that I could talk from that perspective on my next round of interviews.

"I used an agent who specializes in computer sales to get this position and was very specific with him about my requirements."

Asked to explain her current success, Phyllis responds: "I'd have to say the number one factor is technical expertise—with sales ability second. I read, listen and pick brains to stay on top of the product and a changing market place, so that my company has provided a service to the client by sending me. By the way, with little more education than a $20,000 programmer, I'll make at least twice that this year. And the perks are great, too."■

Hall-Mark Electronics Corp.
11333 Pagemill Dr.
Dallas, TX 75243
(214) 343-5000
Personnel Supervisor: Vi New
Distributes electronic components.

Honeywell, Inc.
1111 W. Mockingbird Ln.
Dallas, TX 75247
(214) 688-7600
Field Relations Manager: Cynthia Allison
Researches, develops, manufactures, and sells advanced technology products for information processing, electronics, automation, and controls industries.

Howell Instruments, Inc.
3479 W. Vickery Blvd.
Fort Worth, TX 76107
(817) 336-7411
Personnel Manager: Corene Cloud
Manufactures ground test equipment for jet engines.

International Power Machine Corp.
3328 Executive Blvd.
Mesquite, TX 75149
(214) 288-7501
Personnel Manager: Monica Robinson
Manufactures UPS systems.

Lorain Products
722 N. Great Southwest Pkwy.
Arlington, TX 76011
(214) 640-1134
Contact: Dennis Bennett
Manufactures telephone power equipment.

Motorola, Inc.
5555 N. Beach St.
Fort Worth, TX 76113
(817) 232-6000
Contact: Employment Manager
Electronic equipment and components manufacturer, including two-way communications equipment.

Northern Telecom, Inc.
2100 Lakeside Blvd., Greenway Bldg.
Richardson, TX 75081
(214) 437-8000
Human Resources: Mary Saathoff
Sales office for telecommunications company that offers a complete line of digital switching and transmissions systems.

Pac Tel Gencom
12221 Merit Dr.
Dallas, TX 75251
(214) 960-1977
Human Resources: Jack Wiggins
Sells and services telecommunications systems.

Pacific Telesis Communications Industries
3811 Turtle Creek Blvd., Suite 610
Dallas, TX 75219-4419
(214) 651-4250
Benefits Administrator: Jodi Boyer
Corporate office for mobile communications company.

Panduit Corp.
3321 Towerwood Dr., Suite 113
Farmers Branch, TX 75234
District Manager: Gary Weaver
(214) 620-7717
Manufactures mass-terminated connectors, plastic wiring devices, and terminals.

Recognition Equipment, Inc.
2701 E. Grauwyler Rd.
Irving, TX 75061
(214) 579-6000
Staffing Administration Supervisor: Barbara Resnick
Manufactures and distributes optical character recognition equipment.

Rockwell International Corp.
1200 N. Alma Rd.
Richardson, TX 75081
(214) 996-5000
Staffing Representative: C. V. Shepard
Manufactures electronics and communications systems for commercial and defense applications.

Rolm Corporation
15303 Dallas Pkwy.
Dallas, TX 75248
(214) 980-0098
Contact: Personnel
Telecommunications sales and service.

Scientific Communications, Inc.
2908 National Dr.
Garland, TX 75041
(214) 840-4900
Personnel Manager: Beverly Killgo
Manufactures complete line of surveillance systems.

Siecor Corp.
Hwy. 377
Keller, TX 75248
(817) 431-1521
Personnel Manager: Bill McVay
Manufactures telephone apparatus and electronic components.

Spectradyne, Inc.
1501 N. Plano Rd.
Richardson, TX 75081
(214) 234-2721
Personnel Director: Bob Carr
Manufactures, sells, and services television entertainment systems.

Tandy Corp.
500 One Tandy Center
Fort Worth, TX 76102
(817) 390-3700
Vice President and Personnel Director: George Berger
Manufactures and sells consumer electronic parts and equipment, including microcomputers, cellular mobile telephones, and satellite dishes.

Teccor Electronics, Inc.
1801 Hurd Dr.
Irving, TX 75038
(214) 252-7651
Personnel Director: Myran Dill
Manufactures electronic power controls, semiconductor power devices, solid state relays, silicon chips, and rectifiers.

Teleci, Inc.
1915 West Ridge Dr.
Irving, TX 75038
(214) 550-0066
Personnel Director: Billie Miller
Sells and services business telephone systems.

Texas Instruments, Inc.
13500 N. Central Expwy.
Dallas, TX 75265
(214) 995-5201
Corporate Staffing Manager: George Berryman
Largest Texas-based high-tech firm. Designs, develops, and manufactures semiconductor memories, microprocessors, large-scale integrated circuits, electronic calculators, home and professional computers, electronic data terminals, and electro-optics equipment.

Thermalloy, Inc.
2021 W. Valley View Ln.
Farmers Branch, TX 75234
(214) 243-4321
Executive Vice President/Personnel: Larry Craddock
Manufactures electronic components and systems, including semiconductor equipment and semiconductor insulating covers.

Thomson Components-Mostek
1310 Electronic Dr.
Carrollton, TX 75006
(214) 466-6509
Employment Manager: Richard Holtry
Designs, manufactures, and sells large-scale integrated circuits.

UTL Corp.
1508 W. Mockingbird Ln.
Dallas, TX 75235
(214) 350-7601
Personnel: Tim O'Brien
Manufactures electronic warfare systems.

Varo, Inc.
2800 W. Kingsley Rd.
Garland, TX 75046
(214) 271-8511
Corporate Staffing Manager: Jim Guy
Manufactures defense systems.

Westronics, Inc.
2441 Northeast Pkwy.
Fort Worth, TX 76161
(817) 625-2311
Personnel Administrator: Carol Sullivan
A division of Tracor, Inc. that manufactures potentiometric indicators and recorder and digital data systems.

▶Engineering firms and services

To learn more about **engineering** and related fields, check out the following professional organizations listed in Chapter 5:

American Institute of Chemical Engineers
American Institute of Industrial Engineers
American Society of Civil Engineers
American Society of Heating, Refrigeration and Air-Conditioning Engineers
The American Society of Mechanical Engineers
American Society of Safety Engineers
Illuminating Engineering Society
Society of Hispanic Professional Engineers
Society of Women Engineers
Texas Environmental Health Association
Texas Society of Professional Engineers

For additional information, you can write:

American Institute of Plant Engineers
3975 Erie Ave.
Cincinnati, OH 45208

American Society of Civil Engineers
345 E. 47th St.
New York, NY 10017

Institute of Industrial Engineers
25 Technology Park
Atlanta, GA 30092

National Society of Professional Engineers
2924 Stuart Dr.
Falls Church, VA 22042

Trade Publications:
Building Design and Construction
Chemical & Engineering News
Chemical Engineering Progress
Civil Engineering
Engineering News-Record
Journal of Petroleum Technology

Directories:
Directory of Contract Service Firms (C. E. Publications, Kenmore, WA)
Electronic News and Financial Factbook and Directory (Fairchild Publications, New York, NY)
Peterson's Guide to Careers (Peterson's Guides, Princeton, NJ)
Who's Who in Engineering (Engineers Joint Council, New York, NY)
Who's Who in Technology Today (Technology Recognition Corp., Pittsburgh, PA)

ATEC Associates, Inc.
11310 Newkirk St.
Dallas, TX 75229
(214) 243-8931
Vice President: Mark Kawalek

Biar & Frost, Inc.
12720 Hillcrest Ave., Suite 1080
Dallas, TX 75230
(214) 661-2726
Owner: Richard T. Biar

Black & Veatch Engineering and Architects
5728 LBJ Frwy., Suite 300
Dallas, TX 75380
(214) 770-1500
Recruitment Director: Bill Davis

B. R. Blackmarr & Associates
1 Turtle Creek Village, Suite 606
Dallas, TX 75219
(214) 522-5580
Office Manager: Leslie Chapman

Blum Consulting Engineering, Inc.
4144 N. Central Expwy., Suite 400
Dallas, TX 75204
(214) 821-8010
Executive Administrative Assistant: Barbara Rutherford

Camp Dresser & McKee, Inc.
8800 N. Central Expwy., Suite 400
Dallas, TX 75231
(214) 987-1900
Vice President: Ashok Varma

Carter & Burgess, Inc.
1100 Macon St.
Fort Worth, TX 76113
(817) 335-2611
Personnel Supervisor: Mary Conn

Ellisor & Tanner, Inc.
12750 Merit Dr., Suite 602
Dallas, TX 75251
(214) 387-8393
Vice President: Dr. Leo Galletta

Freese and Nichols, Inc.
811 Lamar St.
Fort Worth, TX 76102
(817) 336-7161
Office Manager: John Kendro

Raymond Goodson, Jr., Inc.
10300 N. Central Expwy., Bldg. 1, Suite 200
Dallas, TX 75231
(214) 739-8100
Executive Vice President: Robert Wood

Greiner Engineering Sciences, Inc.
8585 Stemmons Frwy., M24
Dallas, TX 75247
(214) 638-2249
Vice President of DFW Operations: Donald Henderson

Gunnin-Campbell Consulting Engineers
4514 Cole Ave., Suite 1000
Dallas, TX 75205
(214) 559-2600
President: Stephen J. Campbell

Hunter Associates
8350 N. Central Expwy., M2100
Dallas, TX 75206
(214) 369-9171
Supervisor: Erene Jacobsen

Lockwood Andrews & Newnam, Inc.
2710 N. Stemmons Frwy., Suite 1200
Dallas, TX 75207
(214) 630-1414
Vice President: Mike Wilson

Lockwood Green Engineers
2665 Villa Creek Dr.
Dallas, TX 75234
(214) 243-6303
Personnel Director: Judy Schosield

Mason-Johnston Associates, Inc.
235 Morgan Ave.
Dallas, TX 75203
(214) 941-3808
President: Pete Henley

Powell & Powell Engineers
3988 N. Central Expwy., Suite 1130
Dallas, TX 75204
(214) 522-4660
Partner: Mike McKenzie

Purdy-McGuire, Inc.
14901 Quorum Dr., Suite 900
Dallas, TX 75240
(214) 239-5357
Executive Vice President: Diane Fletcher

Romine, Romine & Burgess, Inc.
300 Greenleaf St.
Fort Worth, TX 76107
(817) 336-4633
Vice President: Jack Burgess

Teague, Nall & Perkins, Inc.
915 Florence St.
Fort Worth, TX 76102
(817) 336-5773
Partner: John Nall

Entertainment

To learn more about the **entertainment** industry, check out the following professional organizations listed in Chapter 5:

American Guild of Organists
Dallas Communications Council
Pro-Musica
Texas Music Association

For more information, you can write to:

Academy of Motion Pictures Arts & Sciences
8949 Wilshire Blvd., Suite 800
Beverly Hills, CA 90211

American Film Institute
Kennedy Center for the Performing Arts
Washington, DC 20566

American Theater Association
101 Wisconsin Ave., NW
Washington, DC 20005

Amusements & Music Operators Association
2000 Spring Rd.
Oak Brook, IL 60521

International Theatrical Agencies Association
P.O. Box 99004
Louisville, KY 40299

National Academy of Recording Arts and Sciences
4444 Riverside Dr.
Burbank, CA 91505

World Leisure and Recreation Association
345 E. 46th St.
New York, NY 10017

Trade Publications:
American Film
Back Stage
Billboard
Cashbox
Film Comment
Music Journal
Performance
Show Business
Theater Times
Variety
Video Business

Directories:
Back Stage Film/Tape/Syndication Directory (Back Stage Publications, New York, NY)
Blue Book (Hollywood Reporter, Hollywood, CA)
Music Business Handbook & Career Guide (Sherwood Co., Los Angeles, CA)

Acapulco Bar
5111 Greenville Ave.
Dallas, TX 75231
(214) 692-9856
Contact: Bruce Davis
Recorded music nightclub for over-21 crowd.

Belle Starr
7724 N. Central Expwy.
Dallas, TX 75106
(214) 750-4787
Owner: Jim Leske
Country music nightclub.

Billy Bob's Texas
2520 N. Commerce St.
Fort Worth, TX 76106
Metro (817) 429-5979
Personnel Manager: Patsy Andrews
World's largest honky-tonk with indoor bull-riding arena, concerts by national entertainers, gift shops, and restaurants.

Caravan of Dreams
312 Houston St.
Fort Worth, TX 76102
(817) 877-3000
Manager: Greg Dugan
Jazz/blues nightclub featuring local and national entertainers, theater, and restaurant.

Casa Manana Musicals, Inc.
3101 W. Lancaster Ave.
Fort Worth, TX 76107
(817) 332-6221
Contact: Marion Searcy
Theater with summer musicals, children's plays, and theatrical productions.

Club Clearview
2625 Elm St.
Dallas, TX 75226
(214) 939-0006
Contact: Jeff Swaney
Avant-garde nightclub with music, art, video, and fashion displays.

Comedy Corner
8202 Park Ln.
Dallas, TX 75231
(214) 361-7461
Contact: Kevin Talbot
Comedy nightclub with national and local entertainers.

Confetti
5201 Matilda St.
Dallas, TX 75231
(214) 369-6977
General Manager: Mark Vasu
Recorded music nightclub with video screens.

Crystal Chandelier
I-35 at Bear Creek Rd.
Lancaster, TX 75146
(214) 223-5898
Manager: Doug Horn
Country music nightclub.

Dallas Ballet Association, Inc.
1925 Elm St., Suite 300
Dallas, TX 75201
(214) 744-4396
Contact: Personnel

The Dallas Opera
1925 Elm St., Suite 400
Dallas, TX 75201
(214) 747-8600
Comptroller: John Sleeper
Opera association.

Dallas Repertory Theatre
1030 NorthPark Center
Dallas, TX 75225
(214) 369-8966
Managing Director: Edmond DeLatte
Legitimate theater.

Dallas Symphony Orchestra
Fair Park
P.O. Box 26207
Dallas, TX 75226
(214) 565-9100
Executive Director: Leonard Stone

Dallas Theater Center
3636 Turtle Creek Blvd.
Dallas, TX 75219
(214) 526-8857
Executive Director: Peter Donnelly
Legitimate theater.

Dallas Zoo
621 E. Clarendon Dr.
Dallas, TX 75203
(214) 946-5155
Personnel: Steve Renda

Fast & Cool Club
3606 Greenville Ave.
Dallas, TX 75206
(214) 827-5544
Co-owner: John Kenyon
Dance club with recorded and live music.

Fort Worth Ballet
6841 B. Green Oaks Rd.
Fort Worth, TX 76116
(817) 763-0207
Executive Director: Jane E. Brown
Ballet company.

Fort Worth Opera Association
3505 W. Lancaster Ave.
Fort Worth, TX 76107
(817) 731-0833
Business Manager: Beth Evans
Opera company.

Fort Worth Symphony Orchestra
4401 Trail Lake Dr.
Fort Worth, TX 76109
(817) 921-2676
Personnel Manager: Don Thomas

Fort Worth Zoological Park
2727 Zoological Park Dr.
Fort Worth, TX 76109
(817) 870-7050
Contact: Personnel
More than 4,000 animals, amusement rides, and exhibits.

Funny Bone
12101 Greenville Ave.
Dallas, TX 75243
(214) 437-2000
Manager: Dan Fleshman
Comedy club with local and national entertainers.

That's entertainment

Theater Three director Jac Alder appreciates the struggle involved when people pursue a career in the theater. He was an architect for seven years before his avocation became his vocation.

"In a true sense, when I chose my wife (Norma Young), I chose the theater; because she was the founder of this institution (Theater Three)," Alder says. "She was not only the love of my life but my teacher."

His interests motivated him to get more involved in the theater, although he says, "I haven't given up architecture. In the service of the theater, I design sets. I use every bit of training I got as an architect on virtually a daily basis. Right now I'm standing over a computer doing a spread sheet on construction costs."

Alder describes how terrified parents have approached him and said, "My God, my son or daughter is in theater. What's going to happen?"

"They can't see it as a paying profession and they are right," he says.

He tells parents that the theater teaches young people to work in a team situation, meet deadlines, and deal with great ideas of the Western world.

"My feeling is that any task can be followed with a sense of ethics and a sense of industry," Alder says. "If any job offers you an opportunity to do that, you've got a wonderful life; because that implies creativity, responsibility, and all the things that we think are important."■

Hip Pocket Theatre
1620 Las Vegas Trail North
Fort Worth, TX 76108
(817) 927-2833
Director: Johnny Simons
Outdoor theater.

International Wildlife Park
601 Wildlife Pkwy.
Grand Prairie, TX 75050
(214) 263-2203
Office Manager: Mickey Hunt
Drive-through animal park.

Longhorn Ballroom
216 Corinth St.
Dallas, TX 75207
(214) 428-3128
Manager: Brandy Pence
Concert facility for national shows and private events.

Monopoly's Park Place
6532 E. Northwest Hwy.
Dallas, TX 75231
(214) 696-3720
Contact: Manager
Nightclub with recorded music and bands.

New Arts Theatre
702 Ross Ave.
Dallas, TX 75202
(214) 761-9064
Managing Director: Barry Steinman
Legitimate theater.

Shakespeare Festival of Dallas
5609 Yale Blvd.
Dallas, TX 75206
(214) 987-1993
Managing Director: Jeff West
Annual outdoor Fair Park production.

Showco, Inc.
9011 Governors Row
Dallas, TX 75247
(214) 630-1188
Personnel Director: Sandy Murrell
Sound and lighting company.

Six Flags Over Texas
2201 Road To Six Flags
Arlington, TX 76010
Metro (817) 640-8900
Personnel: Larry Cox
Family theme park and Texas' No. 1 tourist attraction.

Stage West
821 W. Vickery St.
Fort Worth, TX 76104
(817) 332-6238
Manager: Jerry Russell
Legitimate theater.

Starck Club
703 McKinney Ave.
Dallas, TX 75265
(214) 720-0130
Manager: Greg McCone
Recorded music nightclub with concerts, fashion shows, and video presentations.

State Fair of Texas
P.O. Box 26010
Dallas, TX 75226
(214) 565-9931
Contact: Personnel for staff positions and Texas Employment Commission for seasonal jobs during annual October fair.

Texas Stadium
2401 E. Airport Frwy.
Irving, TX 75062
(214) 438-7676
Contact: Department Head
Major stadium for Dallas Cowboys football games and other events.

Theatre Three
2800 Routh St.
Dallas, TX 75201
(214) 871-3300
Director: Jac Alder
Legitimate theater.

▶Film, videotape, recording, and talent

To learn more about the **film, videotape, and recording** fields, check out the following professional organizations listed in Chapter 5:

Dallas Communications Council
Dallas Producers Association
Texas Association of Film & Tape Professionals
Texas Music Association
Third Coast Screenwriters Forum
Women of the Motion Picture Industry

For additional information, you can write:

American Film Institute
Kennedy Center for the Performing Arts
Washington, DC 20566

Professional Motion Picture Equipment Association
10000 Riverside Dr., Suite 6
Toluca Lake, CA 91602

Academy of Recording Arts and Sciences
4444 Riverside Dr.
Burbank, CA 91505

National Academy of Television Arts and Sciences
110 W. 57th St.
New York, NY 10019

Directories:
Audio-Visual Communications . . . Who's Who (United Business Publications, New York, NY)
Back Stage Film/Tape/Syndication Directory (Back Stage Publications, New York, NY)
Creative Directory of the South (Ampersand, Inc., Houston, TX)
NAVA Membership Directory (National Audio-Visual Association, Inc., Fairfax, VA)

Tanya Blair Agency, Inc.
4131 N. Central Expwy., Suite 810
Dallas, TX 75204
(214) 559-2990
Contact: Harold Bach
Full-service agency; casting and auditioning facilities for commercial film, industrial, theatrical, and voice talent for all media, with a complete children's division.

Creative Communications Group
2015 McKenzie Dr.
Carrollton, TX 75006
(214) 243-2100
President: Pam Rost
Full-service production company that specializes in meetings, conventions, training programs, live business theater, and industrial films.

Dallas Sound Lab
Four Dallas Communications Complex, Suite 119
6305 N. O'Connor Rd.
Irving, TX 75039
(214) 869-1122
Accepts resumes by mail only.
Contact: Bec Moore
Specializes in post-production audio services for film and video, including film/video interlock and scoring; mixing, demos, and albums.

Kim Dawson Agency, Inc.
1643 Apparel Mart
P.O. Box 585060
Dallas, TX 75258
(214) 638-2414
Attention: Sue Gallo
Talent and modeling agency for film, television, radio, theater, and fashion promotions.

Victor Duncan, Inc.
Four Dallas Communications Complex, Suite 100
6305 N. O'Connor Rd.
Irving, TX 75039
(214) 869-0200
Personnel: Carol Chamberlain
Rental, sales, and service company specializing in film and video production equipment and accessories.

FPS, Inc.
11250 Pagemill Rd.
Dallas, TX 75243
(214) 340-8545
Accepts resumes by mail only.
Personnel: Ben Hogan
Equipment rental, sound stage rental, pre-production, and production service.

Fort Worth Productions, Inc.
1423 W. Terrell Ave.
Fort Worth, TX 76104
(817) 336-0777
Accepts resumes by mail only.
Contact: Lyn Downing
Independent television production company providing programming for network syndicators, public broadcasting, and cable.

Goodnight Audio
11260 Goodnight Ln.
Dallas, TX 75229
(214) 241-5182
Studio Manager: Don Cei
Complete 24-track recording studio.

Industry Dallas
4319 Oak Lawn Ave.
Dallas, TX 75204
(214) 520-1135
Contact: Mike Beaty
Talent agency for TV, radio, film, print, and conventions.

Move over, Brooke Shields

On an average day, 30 phone calls and even more letters are directed to George Dawson, new talent coordinator for the Kim Dawson Agency, Inc. Here's what he tells eager applicants who want to break into the area's growing fashion, film, and talent industries:

Send several color photographs along with your measurements, height, phone number, and address where you can be reached. "Most people think you have to pay for expensive portfolio photographs, and that's not the case," Dawson says.

Out of 50 or 60 inquiries, he may find one person who has the potential to make it in the highly competitive Dallas market. Many people don't meet one necessary requirement—height. A woman must be 5 feet 7½ inches to 5 feet 10 inches and a man should be between 5 feet 11 inches to 6 feet 1 inch.

Dawson interviews promising candidates. If he thinks they have potential, he advises them to get a series of quality pictures taken. If those turn out well, the person is signed with the agency and they are assisted in putting together a "head sheet" and portfolio.

The first year can be rough financially for new models, Dawson says. They should be prepared to moonlight during the first six months to a year because few novices make a livable income.

People who sign with the agency can take modeling and grooming classes, but it's not a requirement. "We never tell a person she will be a model after taking a certain number of courses," he says. "Models are usually born, not made."■

January Sound Studios, Inc.
3341 Towerwood Dr., Suite 205
Dallas, TX 75234
(214) 243-3735
Studio Manager: Les Studdard
Sound studio featuring two full-service 24-track studios.

K&H Productions
3601 Oak Grove Ave.
Dallas, TX 75204
(214) 526-5268
Contact: Personnel
Produces graphic animation, film/tape TV commercials, A/V presentations, and corporate films.

Richard Kidd Productions, Inc.
5610 Maple Ave.
Dallas, TX 75235
(214) 638-5433
Contact: Barbara Ratliff
Full-service production company for film, video, and A/V presentations.

The Norton Agency
3900 Lemmon Ave.
Dallas, TX 75219
(214) 528-9960
Contact: Personnel
Represents models, talent, and celebrities for film and commercial industry.

Omega Audio & Productions, Inc.
8036 Aviation Place, Box 71
Dallas, TX 75235
(214) 350-9066
Contact: Donna Christensen
Complete remote audio multi-track recording service for records, film, and video.

Southwest Teleproductions, Inc.
2649 Tarna Dr.
Dallas, TX 75229
(214) 243-5719
Contact: Susan Bilbrey
Production and post-production services for 35mm and 16mm film, as well as ¾-inch, 1-inch and 2-inch videotape.

Spindletop Productions, Inc.
1328 Inwood Rd.
Dallas, TX 75247
(214) 634-7206
President: Jim Row
Full-service film and tape production.

Bill Stokes Associates
5642 Dyer St.
Dallas, TX 75206
(214) 363-0161
President: Bill Stokes
Full production facility for 35mm and 16mm commercials, industrials, and feature films.

Sumet-Bernet Sound Studios, Inc.
7027 Twin Hills Ave.
Dallas, TX 75231
(214) 691-0001
President: Ed Bernet
Complete recording services for record, jingle, film producers, and ad agencies.

Sundance Productions
7141 Envoy Ct.
Dallas, TX 75247
(214) 688-0081
Contact: Doyle Williams
Produces industrial and commercial films.

TM Productions
1349 Regal Row
Dallas, TX 75247
(214) 634-8511
Contact: Omey King
Sound studio specializing in the production of custom music, including film scoring, theme music, A/V, commercials, radio, and TV imagery.

Peggy Taylor Talent, Inc.
2309 Springlake Rd., Suite 600
Farmers Branch, TX 75234
(214) 241-1800
Contact: Personnel
Talent agency for film and television.

Tele-Image, Inc.
6305 N. O'Connor Rd.
Irving, TX 75039
(214) 869-0060
Operations Manager: Sunny McDonnieal
Video production facility for ¾-inch and 1-inch formats. Specializes in conventions, seminars, teleconferencing, cable programming, concerts, and industrials.

Video Post and Transfer, Inc.
Love Field Terminal
8036 Aviation Place
Dallas, TX 75235
(214) 350-2676
Send resumes by mail only.
Complete video post-production services, including film-to-tape transfer, graphics, animation, and special effects.

Zimmersmith/Radio Ranch, Inc.
6311 N. O'Connor Rd., Suite 113
Dallas Communications Complex, Bldg. #3
Irving, TX 75039
(214) 869-4611
Contact: Paula Rogers
Full-service radio creative production company.

▶Food and beverage producers and distributors

To learn more about the **food industry** and related fields, check out the following professional organizations listed in Chapter 5:

Metroplex Retail Bakers Association
Southwestern Meat Packers Association
Women's Association of Allied Beverage Industries

For more information, you can write to:

Food Marketing Institute
1750 K St., NW
Washington, DC 20006

National Association of Alcoholic Beverage Importers
1025 Vermont Ave.
Washington, DC 20005

National Food Distributors Association
111 E. Wacker Dr.
Chicago, IL 60601

United States Brewers Association
P.O. Box 1435
Topeka, KS 66601

Wine & Spirits Wholesalers of America
2033 M St., NW
Washington, DC 20036

Trade Publications:
Beverage World
Food and Beverage Marketing
Food and Wine
Food Industry Newsletter
Food Management
Foodservice Product News
Forecast for Home Economics
Institutional Distribution
Progressive Grocer
Quick Frozen Foods

Directories:
Foodservice/West—Manufacturers, Brands & Sources (Harlequin Publications, Palos Verdes, CA)
Frozen Food Fact Book (National Frozen Food Association, Hershey, PA)
Grocers/West—Manufacturers, Brands & Sources (Harlequin Publications, Palos Verdes, CA)
National Beverage Marketing Directory (Beverage Marketing Corp., New York, NY)
NFBA Directory (National Food Brokers Association, Washington, DC)

Affiliated Food Stores, Inc.
100 Nat Gibbs Dr.
Keller, TX 76248
(817) 498-4042
Personnel Manager: Jerry Blakeney
Food store chain.

American Bakeries Co.
411 S. Ballinger St.
Fort Worth, TX 76104
(817) 336-9444
Personnel Director: Angelita Parsons
Wholesale bakery.

American Produce & Vegetable Co.
4721 Simonton Rd.
Farmers Branch, TX 75234
(214) 233-5750
Contact: Personnel Department
Distributes canned and fresh food to hotels, caterers, restaurants, and airlines.

Arrow Industries, Inc.
2625 Belt Line Rd.
Carrollton, TX 75006
(214) 242-0525
Personnel Director: David Swanson
Packages dry food products.

Mrs. Baird's Bakeries
Dallas Office
5230 E. Mockingbird Ln.
Dallas, TX 75205
(214) 526-7201
Personnel Director: Lila Farmer
Produces bread and baked goods.

Mrs. Baird's Bakeries
Fort Worth Office
7301 South Frwy.
Fort Worth, TX 76134
(817) 293-6230
Personnel Director: Bob Jenkins
Same as Dallas.

Big Value Super Markets, Inc.
2012 N. Riverside Dr.
Fort Worth, TX 76111
(817) 834-7173
General Manager: H. E. Howard
Retail grocery chain.

Borden, Inc.
5327 S. Lamar St.
Dallas, TX 75215
(214) 565-0332
Personnel Manager: Lou Ray
Produces milk, ice cream, and dairy products.

Martin Brower Corp.
721 Parkway Dr.
Grand Prairie, TX 75051
(214) 647-1918
Contact: Personnel
Distribution center for McDonald's restaurants.

Cabell's Dairy
4017 Commerce St.
Dallas, TX 75226
(214) 821-9164
Personnel Manager: Diane Lewis
Produces and distributes dairy products.

Campbell Taggert
6211 Lemmon Ave.
Dallas, TX 75209
(214) 358-9211
Vice President of Personnel: R. C. Clark
Produces white breads, earth grains, and sweet goods.

Cargill Inc.-Burrus Milling Dept.
401 E. Industrial Blvd.
Saginaw, TX 76179
(817) 232-1160
Contact: Tom Wright
Produces flour, cornmeal, cereal, and wafers.

Coca-Cola Bottling of North Texas
3400 Fossil Creek Blvd.
Fort Worth, TX 76137
(817) 232-8600
Personnel Manager: Tina Perrin
Bottlers of soft drink beverage.

Continental Grain Co.
2301 Terminal Rd.
Fort Worth, TX 76106
(817) 624-4171
Operations Manager: Bill Naughton
Buys and sells grains, mills flour and feed, and processes oil.

Coors Distributing Co.
2550 Gemini Pkwy. S.
Fort Worth, TX 76111
(817) 831-4211
Contact: Personnel
Beer distributor.

Cullum Companies, Inc.
14303 Inwood Rd.
Dallas, TX 75234
(214) 661-9700
Personnel Director: Mike Kissner
Operates chain of supermarkets, drug stores, wholesale grocery distribution, and meat packing, including Tom Thumb Page Food & Drug Centers.

Dallas Cash and Carry
1135 S. Lamar St.
Dallas, TX 75215
(214) 565-1311
Personnel Manager: Wayne Kizer
Wholesale grocer.

The Jimmy Dean Meat Co., Inc.
1341 W. Mockingbird Ln., Suite 1100 E
Dallas, TX 75247
(214) 638-1190
Personnel Assistant: Janet Kelley
Produces sausage and prepared meats.

Jacob E. Decker & Sons
3200 W. Kingsley Rd.
Garland, TX 75041
(214) 278-6192
Personnel Manager: Michael Hake
Processes bacon, sausage, boiled ham, and smoked and cured pork.

Dr Pepper
5523 E. Mockingbird Ln.
Dallas, TX 75206
(214) 824-0331
Personnel Manager: Scott Brown
Soft drink beverage bottlers.

Foremost Foods Co.
8033 Ambassador Row
Dallas, TX 75246
(214) 631-2330
Contact: Personnel
Produces milk, ice cream, and other dairy products.

Frito-Lay, Inc.
National Headquarters
7701 Carpenter Rd.
Plano, TX 75024
(214) 624-7000
Personnel Director: Fred Ley
Produces and markets snack products.

Glazer's Wholesale Drug Co., Inc.
508 Park Ave.
Dallas, TX 75201
(214) 748-9301
Contact: Department Head
Wholesale wine and liquor distributor.

Herby's Foods, Inc.
901 Santerre Dr.
Grand Prairie, TX 75050
(214) 647-0371
Personnel Manager: Alicia Allen
Produces and distributes wholesale sandwiches, snacks, and Mexican food.

George A. Hormel & Co.
4114 Mint Way
Dallas, TX 75224
(214) 333-3251
Personnel Manager: Brian Zastoopil
Processes and distributes fresh and canned meat products, frozen and prepared foods, and institutional food.

ITT Continental Baking Co.
9000 Denton Dr.
Dallas, TX 75235
(214) 358-0232
Personnel Director: Stan Whitesel
Produces and distributes bread and bakery items.

Keebler Co.
4300 Diplomacy Rd.
Fort Worth, TX 76155
(214) 267-2445
Contact: Personnel
Distributes cookie, cracker, and snack products.

Ben E. Keith Co., Inc.
8220 Forney Rd.
Dallas, TX 75227
(214) 388-5411
Contact: Personnel
Beer distributor and wholesaler of frozen foods and produce.

Kreck Foods
4115 S. Lamar St.
Dallas, TX 75215
(214) 428-3551
Personnel Manager: Beverly Allen
Produces processed meats and meat products.

Kroger Food Co.
1901 Gateway Dr.
Irving, TX 75038
(214) 580-3000
Personnel Manager: Jim Sneyd
Major food retailer and operator of food processing, dairies, bakeries, and egg-producing facilities.

Lone Star Co.
4000 Spring Valley Rd.
Dallas, TX 75244
(214) 243-1009
Contact: Personnel
Wholesale wine and liquor distributor.

Manor Baking Co.
3500 Manor Way
Dallas, TX 75235
(214) 357-1754
Personnel Director: Harless Rattan
Produces bread and bakery products.

Miller Brewing Co.
7001 South Frwy.
Fort Worth, TX 76134
(817) 551-3300
Personnel Manager: Dominic Feragotti
Produces, bottles, and distributes beer and malt beverages.

Miller Distributing of Dallas
2730 Irving Blvd.
Dallas, TX 75207
(214) 689-4101
Personnel Director: Kristi Jenkins
Miller Beer distributor.

Minyard Food Stores, Inc.
777 Freeport Pkwy.
Coppell, TX 75019
Metro (817) 462-8700
Contact: Mary Benson
Retail grocery chain with 52 stores in Dallas and Tarrant counties.

Morton Foods, Inc.
6333 Denton Dr.
Dallas, TX 75235
(214) 350-9971
Personnel Director: Billie Eddy
Produces snack foods, tea, spices, and syrup.

Owens Country Sausage, Inc.
1403 Lookout Dr.
Richardson, TX 75080
(214) 235-7181
Personnel Manager: Gerald Kelly
Produces sausage and pork products.

Pepsi Cola Bottling Group
4532 Hwy. 67
Mesquite, TX 75150
(214) 324-8500
Personnel Manager: Ron Parker
Bottles soft drink beverages.

Pilgrim Pride Foods
2411 Ferris St.
Dallas, TX 75226
(214) 421-7611
Personnel Director: Dr. Art Wolf
Poultry wholesaler.

▶ Mouth-watering opportunities in food service management

Kate Williams, manager of the dietary department of a suburban hospital, sees the food service industry as a growing field with tremendous potential. The many hospitals in the Dallas/Fort Worth area offer varied opportunities in food services, according to Kate. Some of the jobs, such as clinical or administrative dietitian, require a college degree in nutrition. But many do not.

"Some employees have experience working at a fast-food restaurant," says Kate. "Others just learn on the job. Still others have completed one- or two-year programs in food service offered by various colleges." Besides registered dietitians, Kate's staff includes food service supervisors, who manage the personnel who prepare food; diet technicians, who prepare and implement menus based on information about the patient; diet aides, who perform such tasks as delivering meals to patients; a chef and a cooking staff; and a food purchasing agent.

Kate is optimistic about employment prospects in the food service industry as a whole. "There are tremendous opportunities for those with culinary arts skills, as well as for hotel or restaurant food service managers. Opportunities exist in food equipment companies, public and private schools, contract food companies, and food service consulting firms. Right now the possibilities in food marketing are phenomenal.

"The nutritional needs of the growing elderly population," Kate adds, "will also create many new jobs in the food service business as hospitals and other organizations become involved in the field of long-term care."■

Purity Cheese Co.
7839 Churchill Way
Dallas, TX 75251
(214) 247-2377
Contact: Employment Office
Diversified food products manufacturer of several brands of cheese, soy bean oil, and salad dressing mixes.

Quaker Oats Co.
13745 Jupiter Rd.
Dallas, TX 75238
(214) 340-0370
Personnel Manager: Lindy Vernon
Distributor for foods, pet foods, and specialty chemicals.

Ralston Purina Co.
1501 E. 4th St.
Fort Worth, TX 76101
(817) 336-4041
Personnel Director: Steve Jones
Produces commercial livestock and poultry feed.

Rodriguez Festive Foods
913 N. Houston St.
Fort Worth, TX 76106
(817) 624-2123
Personnel Manager: Leslie Stubbs
Produces Mexican food products.

Safeway Stores, Inc.
2325 Lakeland Dr.
Dallas, TX 75228
(214) 324-9600
Personnel Manager: Pat Robins
Retail grocery chain and warehouse.

Seven-Up Bottling Co.
2817 Braswell Dr.
Fort Worth, TX 76111
(817) 625-1553
Office Manager: Mary Mead
Bottler and distributor of soft drinks.

Shaklee Corp.
1900 SE Loop 820
Fort Worth, TX 76140-1095
(817) 478-0885
Contact: Personnel
Regional field service center and manufacturer of energy bars and fruit bars.

Skaggs Alpha Beta
1100 Executive Dr., Suite 100
Richardson, TX 75081
(214) 238-7231
Contact: Store Manager
Grocery and drug store chain.

Southland Corp.
2828 N. Haskell Ave.
Dallas, TX 75204
(214) 828-7011
Personnel Manager: Wanda Williams
Corporate headquarters for 7-Eleven convenience stores and dairy products producer.

Standard Meat Co.
3709 E. First St.
Fort Worth, TX 76111
(817) 831-0981
Personnel Manager: Mark Nerio
Produces meats for institutional and commercial customers.

Supreme Beef Co.
5219 2nd Ave.
Dallas, TX 75210
(214) 428-1761
Personnel Manager: Ron Tracey
Beef processing plant.

Sysco Food Systems, Inc.
14330 Gillis Rd.
Farmers Branch, TX 75244
(214) 233-9700
Personnel Manager: Kyle Killingsworth
Institutional food distributor.

Vandervoort Dairy Foods
900 S. Main St.
Fort Worth, TX 76104
(817) 332-7551
Personnel Manager: Louis Herrera
Dairy foods processor.

White Swan, Inc.
1515 Big Town Blvd.
Mesquite, TX 75149
(214) 388-7700
Personnel Manager: Bobbie Jackson
Institutional food distributor.

Willow Distribution
2601 Cockrell Ave.
Dallas, TX 75215
(214) 426-5636
Personnel Manager: Larry Hachtel
Beer distributor.

Winn-Dixie Texas, Inc.
5500 S. Frwy.
Fort Worth, TX 76115
(817) 921-1100
Personnel Director: Oscar McCullough
Grocery store chain and dairy products producer.

▶Furniture and fixtures manufacturers

To help you learn more about the **furniture** industry, you can write:

International Home Furnishings Representatives Association
518 Davis St.
Evanston, IL 60201

National Home Furnishings Association
405 Merchandise Mart Plaza
Chicago, IL 60654

Trade Publications:
Home Furnishings Daily
Textile Products
Textile World

Directories:
Professional Furniture Merchant Resource Directory (Gralla Publications, New York, NY)
Who's Who in the Furniture Industry (Southern Furniture Manufacturers Association, High Point, NC)

A. Brandt Co., Inc.
1300 E. Berry St.
Fort Worth, TX 76119
(817) 926-5141
Vice President of Human Resources: Dale Ulbrich
Manufactures furniture for homes and hotels in the United States and abroad.

Duro Metal Manufacturing Co.
440 Hilburn St.
Dallas, TX 75217
(214) 391-3181
Executive Vice President: Chuck Siegel
Manufactures bed frames, mirror supports, bed rails, and trundle beds.

Inca Metal Products Corp.
One Inca Place
501 E. Purnell St.
Lewisville, TX 75067
(214) 436-5581
Contact: Department Heads
Manufactures workbenches, shop desks, and industrial shelving.

Levolor Lorentzen, Inc.
14310 Gillis Rd.
Dallas, TX 75244
(214) 387-9095
Personnel Director: Edna Gallington
Manufactures venetian blinds.

Massould Furniture Manufacturer
8208 Moberly Ln.
Dallas, TX 75227
(214) 388-8655
Personnel Director: Mary Goad
Manufactures household furniture.

Pillowtex Corp.
4111 Mint Way
Dallas, TX 75237
(214) 333-3225
Personnel Manager: Mary Urbas
Manufactures bedding, pillows, mattress pads, and comforters.

Simmons Co.
8600 Harry Hines Blvd.
Dallas, TX 75235
(214) 637-0460
Contact: John Cannon or Nina Torres
Manufactures mattresses and box springs.

Smith System Manufacturing Co.
1714 E. 14th St.
Plano, TX 75074
(214) 424-6591
Marketing Director: Herbert H. Taylor
Manufactures plastic furniture for schools and offices.

Southland Bedding Co.
1207 W. Crosby Rd.
Carrollton, TX 75006
(214) 242-7666
General Manager: Grady McAlum
Manufactures mattresses.

From housework to spousework

Ruth Glover is well acquainted with the need for "transplacement"—assisting individuals who have moved to a new city because their spouse has been transferred. With the rise in the number of dual-career couples, many of these people need help in finding another job. As a result, Glover made spouse re-employment one of the specialties of her Career Consultations company.

She's often asked, "What do you say during job interviews about your spouse's transfer? What if they want to know how long you plan to live in the area?"

Glover urges people to be honest. "If you know you are going to be here for a specific length of time, say so. Depending on the position, the company may be investing a lot of training dollars.

"You want to emphasize that you are a hard worker and that the company will get its money's worth. Don't dwell on your relocation—downplay it, and tell them what you can contribute," she says.

The employer's reaction to this situation may depend on the company's philosophy. Firms such as IBM expect people to remain for many years. Other businesses that have higher turnover may not be as concerned about hiring someone who might have to move again.

Spouses who anticipate being uprooted on a regular basis may want to consider "suitcase" careers, Glover suggests. These are jobs in high-demand fields, such as health care or sales, which are easy to find in almost any city.

When employees are asked to transfer, she encourages them to ask the company for assistance in helping their spouses find work. Part of the relocation expenses provided by companies could include career counseling and job placement for their marriage partner.

After all, more couples now depend on two incomes. So the success of the transfer can depend on how quickly the trailing spouse finds a satisfying job.■

Stamco-Stationers Manufacturing Co.
420 S. Ballinger Rd.
Fort Worth, TX 76104
(817) 332-8311
Personnel Director: Jim Pipes
Manufactures tables, office chairs, and sofas.

Universal Carrier Co.
613 Easy St.
Garland, TX 75042
(214) 276-8335
Personnel Manager: Marsha Flenner
Manufactures wire and tubular display racks.

Vecta Contract, Inc.
1800 S. Great Southwest Pkwy.
Grand Prairie, TX 75051
(214) 641-2860
Personnel Director: Betty Miller
Manufactures contemporary office furniture.

▶Government

To learn more about **government** and related fields, check out the following professional organizations listed in Chapter 5:

Dallas County Library Association
Dallas County Sheriffs Association
Dallas Fire Fighters Association
Dallas Planning Association
Dallas Police Association
Fort Worth Librarians Association
League of Women Voters
Mesquite Fire Fighters Association
National Organization for Women
North Texas State Juvenile Officers Association
Texas Recreation & Park Society
Urban Management Assistants of North Texas

You can also contact:

Council of State Governments
P.O. Box 11910
Iron Works Pike
Lexington, KY 40578

Federal Bar Association
1815 H St., NW
Washington, DC 20006

Government Finance Officers Association of U.S. and Canada
180 N. Michigan Ave.
Chicago, IL 60601

National Council of County Association Executives
440 First St., NW
Washington, DC 20001

Professional Publications:
The Chief
Government Executive
Public Works Magazine

Directories:
Directory of Texas City Officials (Texas Municipal League, Austin, TX)
Legislative Directory (North Central Texas Council of Government, Arlington, TX)
Texas Legislative Handbook (Legislative Associates, Dallas, TX)

CITY

Town of Addison
5300 Belt Line Rd.
Addison, TX 75001
(214) 450-7000
Personnel Director: Betty Salem

City of Arlington
101 W. Abram St.
Arlington, TX 76010
Metro (817) 265-3311
Personnel Director: Norman Clark

City of Balch Springs
3117 Hickory Tree Rd.
Balch Springs, TX 75180
(214) 286-4444
City Manager: Mozelle Strain

City of Bedford
2000 Forest Ridge Dr.
Bedford, TX 76021
Metro (817) 267-1396
Personnel Director: Doug Rivers

City of Burleson
141 W. Renfro St.
Burleson, TX 76028
(817) 295-1113
Personnel Director: Jean Beckwith

City of Cedar Hill
502 Cedar St.
Cedar Hill, TX 75104
(214) 291-4211
City Manager: Greg Vick

City of Cockrell Hill
4125 W. Clarendon Dr.
Cockrell Hill, TX 75211
(214) 330-6333
City Secretary: Jackie Smith

City of Colleyville
5400 Bransford Rd.
Colleyville, TX 76034
(817) 281-4044
City Secretary: LaVada Johnson

City of The Colony
5576 N. Colony Blvd.
The Colony, TX 75056
(214) 248-4341
Administration Secretary: Sharon Sebera

City of Dallas
1500 Marilla St.
Dallas, TX 75201
(214) 670-3011
Personnel Director: Troy Coleman

City of DeSoto
119 S. Hampton Rd.
DeSoto, TX 75115
(214) 223-6316
Personnel: Gary Whittle

City of Duncanville
100 E. Center St.
Duncanville, TX 75116
(214) 780-5000
Personnel Director: Greg Weaver

City of Euless
201 N. Ector Dr.
Euless, TX 76039
(817) 283-5381
Personnel Director: K. B. Fuller

City of Everman
212 N. Race St.
Everman, TX 76140
(817) 293-0525
Personnel Director: Jerry Schlangenstein

City of Farmers Branch
13000 William Dodson Pkwy.
Farmers Branch, TX 75234
(214) 247-3131
Personnel Director: Norman Reynolds

City of Forest Hill
6800 Forest Hill Dr.
Forest Hill, TX 76140
(817) 293-3695
Personnel Director: Cheryl Thompson

City of Fort Worth
1000 Throckmorton St.
Fort Worth, TX 76102
(817) 870-7750
Personnel Director: Charlie Shapard

City of Garland
200 N. Fifth St.
Garland, TX 75040
(214) 494-7100
Personnel Director: Nancy Carney

City of Grand Prairie
317 College St.
Grand Prairie, TX 75050
Metro (214) 263-5221
Acting Personnel Director: Gay McCollough

City of Grapevine
413 Main St.
Grapevine, TX 76051
Metro (817) 481-2546
Personnel Director: Kelvin Knauf

City of Haltom City
5024 Broadway Ave.
Haltom City, TX 76117
(817) 834-7341
Personnel Director: Ruby Leath

Town of Highland Park
4700 Drexel Dr.
Dallas, TX 75205
(214) 521-4161
Personnel Director: Margie Shelton

City of Hurst
1505 Precinct Line Rd.
Hurst, TX 76054
(817) 281-6160
Personnel Director: Dale Schultz

City of Irving
825 W. Irving Blvd.
Irving, TX 75060
(214) 721-2532
Personnel Director: Howard Day

City of Lake Worth
6720 Telephone Rd.
Lake Worth, TX 76135
(817) 237-1211
City Manager: Robert Turner

City of Lancaster
211 N. Henry St.
Lancaster, TX 75146
(214) 227-2111
Personnel Director: Steve Harris

City of Mansfield
1305 E. Broad St.
Mansfield, TX 76063
(817) 473-9371
Personnel Officer: Barbara Parker

City of Mesquite
711 N. Galloway Ave.
Mesquite, TX 75149
(214) 288-7711
Personnel Director: Ben Franklin

City of North Richland Hills
7301 NE Loop 820
North Richland Hills, TX 76180
(817) 281-0041
Personnel Director: Ron McKinney

City of Plano
1520 Ave. K
Plano, TX 75074
(214) 424-6531
Personnel Director: Martha Royal

City of Richardson
411 Arapaho Rd.
Richardson, TX 75050
(214) 235-8331
Personnel Director: Howard Weaver

City of Richland Hills
3200 Diana Dr.
Richland Hills, TX 76118
(817) 284-4901
Personnel Director: Dennis Woodard

City of Saginaw
333 W. McLeroy Blvd.
Saginaw, TX 76179
(214) 577-0333
Personnel Director: Nan Stanford

City of Seagoville
702 N. Hwy 175
Seagoville, TX 75159
(214) 287-2050
Personnel Director: Debbie Littlejohn

City of University Park
3800 University Blvd.
Dallas, TX 75205
(214) 363-1644
Personnel Director: Mary Boehning

City of Watauga
7101 Whitley Rd.
Watauga, TX 76148
(817) 281-8047
City Secretary: Nancy Meadows

COUNTY

Dallas County
600 Commerce St.
Dallas, TX 75202
(214) 749-8637
Personnel Director: Sylvia Reaves

How a police chief decided on his career

Dallas Police Chief Billy Prince says it was pure fate that led him to his job, but he's never regretted what happened.

"In our high school, we didn't have career planning or anything to help you systematically go through a thought process of determining what you wanted to do with your life," he says.

Prince had just completed his Army reserve training at Fort Bliss in El Paso and was on his way home to Antlers, Oklahoma. Along the way, he stopped to visit his aunt and uncle in Dallas and happened to glance at the want ads. He saw an opening for a Dallas policeman that paid $370 a month.

The job and money looked appealing, so he applied the next day. At the time, Prince recalls, "I had very little idea of what police work in a big city would be like after growing up in a small town where there was only one sheriff in the county."

He liked the work and was encouraged by others to move up through the ranks. "Each time you reach a new step, you think about the next one," Prince says.

He advises other people to take a close look at the jobs they are considering and find something that is interesting and rewarding.

"In police work, you get a lot of self-satisfaction if you like to help people," he says. "Obviously, the pay isn't that good, but there are other rewards. When you cut through everything in life, they are much more important than the monetary part. If people get into something that they enjoy and get a good feeling from, they are going to do well in other aspects, too. The money and promotions will come."■

Tarrant County
100 E. Weatherford St.
Fort Worth, TX 76196-0105
(817) 334-1188
Personnel Director: Gerald Wright

Fort Worth State School
5000 Campus Dr.
Fort Worth, TX 76119
(817) 534-4831
Personnel Director: Fred Miler

Highways and Public Transportation
Dallas District Office
9700 E. R. L. Thornton Frwy.
Dallas, TX 75228
(214) 320-6100
Personnel Director: Fred White

Highways and Public Transportation
Fort Worth District Office
2501 SW Loop 820
Fort Worth, TX 76115
(817) 292-6510
Personnel Director: Frank Durda

Human Services
Regional Office
631 106th St.
Arlington, TX 76005-5128
Metro (817) 640-5090
Personnel Director: Claudia McDowell

Parks & Wildlife
Fort Worth Office
5200-A Airport Frwy.
Fort Worth, TX 76117
(817) 831-3128
Office Manager: Joann King

Public Health
Region 5 Office
2561 Matlock Rd.
Arlington, TX 76015
Metro (817) 261-2911
Personnel Assistant: Sandy Evarts

Public Safety
Region 1
350 W. Interstate 30
Garland, TX 75043
(214) 226-7611
Personnel Director: Bill Dawson

Public Safety
Fort Worth District Office
624 NE Loop 820
Hurst, TX 76053
(817) 284-1490
Contact: Glenda Evans

Rehabilitation Commission
Regional Office
3005 Alta Mere Dr.
Fort Worth, TX 76116
(817) 731-7343
Personnel Director: Robert Garner

Texas Employment Commission
Administrative Office
8300 John W. Carpenter Frwy.
Irving, TX 75247
(214) 631-6050
Personnel Director: Bill Allmon

UNITED STATES GOVERNMENT

Agriculture Department
Food & Nutrition Division
1100 Commerce St., Rm. 5C30
Dallas, TX 75242
(214) 767-0224
Administration Director: Sally Vela

Agriculture Department
Fruit and Vegetable Division
819 Taylor St., Rm. 9C03
Fort Worth, TX 76102
(817) 334-2624
Director: Bryon White

Army Corps of Engineers
Dallas Personnel Office
1114 Commerce St., Rm. 403
Dallas, TX 75242
(214) 767-2480
Personnel Officer: Parker Greenwell

Army Corps of Engineers
Fort Worth District Office
819 Taylor St., Rm. 4A18
Fort Worth, TX 76102-0300
(817) 334-2208
Personnel Director: Gerald Slusher

Carswell Air Force Base
Hwy. 183 and White Settlement Rd.
Carswell Air Force Base, TX 76127
(817) 735-5000
Chief of Civilian Personnel: Lynn James

Commerce, Department of
International Trade Office
1100 Commerce St., Rm. 7A5
Dallas, TX 75242
(214) 767-0544
Contact: Office of Personnel Management

Dallas Naval Air Station
3100 W. Jefferson Blvd.
Dallas, TX 75211
(214) 266-6129
Civilian Personnel Director: Hollis Shultz

Defense, Department of
Dallas Office
1100 Commerce St., Rm. 3B17
Dallas, TX 75242
(214) 767-0458
Branch Manager: W. J. Froning

Defense Contract Administration, Department of
Fort Worth Office
819 Taylor St.
Fort Worth, TX 76102
(817) 334-3307
Contact: Civilian Personnel Director at 1200 Main St., Dallas, TX 75202, (214) 670-9222

Education, Department of
Regional Office
1200 Main Tower Bldg., Rm. 2125
Dallas, TX 75202
(214) 767-3626
Personnel Director: Pauline Torres

Environmental Protection Agency
Regional Office
1201 Elm St., Rm. 2772A
Dallas, TX 75270
(214) 767-2600
Personnel Director: Evelyn Daniels

Federal Bureau of Investigation
Dallas Office
1801 N. Lamar St.
Dallas, TX 75202
(214) 720-2200
Special Agent: Tom Cotton

General Services Administration
Personnel Division
819 Taylor St., Rm. 9A00
Fort Worth, TX 76102
(817) 334-2361
Personnel Director: Larry Hathaway

Health and Human Services, Department of
Dallas Office
1900 Pacific Ave.
Dallas, TX 75201
(214) 767-3126
Regional Personnel Officer: Frank Fajardo

Housing & Urban Development, Department of
Fort Worth Office
221 W. Lancaster Ave.
Fort Worth, TX 76102
(817) 885-5541
Personnel Director: James Farrington

Interior, Department of
Fish and Wildlife Ecological Services
819 Taylor St., Rm. 9A33
Fort Worth, TX 76102
(817) 334-2961
Contact: Regional Headquarters, P.O. Box 1306, Albuquerque, NM 87103, (505) 766-2033

Interior, Department of
Geological Survey
1100 Commerce St., Rm. 1C45
Dallas, TX 75242
(214) 767-0198
Contact: Regional Headquarters, P.O. Box 1306, Albuquerque, NM 87103, (505) 766-2033

Internal Revenue Service
Dallas Office
1100 Commerce St., Rm. 11A20
Dallas, TX 75242
(214) 767-1441
Recruitment Coordinator: Evelyn Butler

Internal Revenue Service
Fort Worth Office
819 Taylor St., Rm. 11A01
Fort Worth, TX 76102
(817) 334-3477
Contact: Dallas IRS Office

Interstate Commerce Commission
Fort Worth Office
411 W. 7th St., Suite 500
Fort Worth, TX 76102
(817) 334-3101
Regional Compliance Officer: Haldon West

Justice, Department of
Dallas Office, Anti-trust Division
1100 Commerce St., Rm. 8C6
Dallas, TX 75242
(214) 767-8051
Personnel: James Backstrom

Justice, Department of
Fort Worth Office
10th St. and Lamar St., Rm. 310
Fort Worth, TX 76102
(817) 334-3291
Personnel Director: Don Leaf

Labor, Department of
Office of Information
525 Griffin St.
Dallas, TX 75202
(214) 767-4776
Personnel Director: Gayla Coleman

Labor, Department of
Fort Worth Office
819 Taylor St., Rm. 7A08
Fort Worth, TX 76102
(817) 334-3341
Contact: Dallas Labor Department Office

Office of Personnel Management
1100 Commerce St., Rm. 6B4
Dallas, TX 75242
(214) 767-8235
Staffing Specialist: Carol Green

Postal Service
Main Post Office-Dallas
401 Interstate 30
Dallas, TX 75260
(214) 741-5508
Personnel Director: Jimmy Lamb

Postal Service
Main Post Office-Fort Worth
4600 Mark IV Pkwy.
Fort Worth, TX 76161
(817) 885-1564
Personnel Director: Joe Bob Clendenin

Small Business Administration
Regional Office
8625 King George Dr.
Dallas, TX 75235
(214) 767-7643
Chief of Personnel: Ruby Rachal

Transportation, Department of
Southwest Regional Office
4400 Blue Mound Rd.
Fort Worth, TX 76106
(817) 877-2000
Human Resources Management Division: Melvin N. Asher

Treasury, Department of
Dallas Office
1114 Commerce St.
Dallas, TX 75242
(214) 767-2250
Administrative Assistant: Sharon Rhine

Veterans Administration
Dallas Office
1100 Commerce St., Rm. 1B29
Dallas, TX 75242
(214) 824-5440
Contact: Office of Personnel Management

Health care

To learn more about the **health care** industry, check out the following professional organizations listed in Chapter 5:

American Association for Respiratory Therapy
American Association of Medical Transcription
American Orthodontics Society

Analytical Psychology Association of Dallas
Association of American Dentists
Christian Medical Society
Dallas Association of Speech Pathologists & Audiologists
Dallas County Chiropractic Society
Dallas County Dental Society
Dallas County Medical Society
Dallas County Podiatric Medical Society
Dallas Dental Hygienists Society
Dallas Dietetic Association
Dallas Group Psychotherapy Society, Inc.
Dallas Metropolitan Black Nurses Association
Dallas Psychological Association
Dallas Southwest Osteopathic Physicians, Inc.
Fort Worth Area Medical Records Association
Fort Worth Area Medical Staff Services Association
Fort Worth District Dental Society
Greater Fort Worth Dental Hygienists Society
Licensed Vocational Nurses Association
National League for Nursing
North Central Texas Registry of Interpreters for the Deaf
North Texas Optometric Society
Nurses Association
Official Professional Nursing Bureau, Inc.
Registered Nurses of Arlington
Society of Diagnostic Medical Sonographers
Southwest Council of Optometry
Texas Association of Nurse Anesthetists
Texas Nurses Association
Texas Society of Medical Assistants

For additional information, you can write to:

American Health Care Association
1200 15th St., NW
Washington, DC 20005

American Hospital Association
840 N. Lake Shore Dr.
Chicago, IL 60611

American Public Health Association
1015 18th St., NW
Washington, DC 20036

American Society for Hospital Personnel Administrators
American Hospital Association
840 N. Lake Shore Dr.
Chicago, IL 60611

National Association of Social Workers
59 E. Main St.
Washington, DC 20005

National Council of Community Mental Health
2233 Wisconsin Ave., NW
Washington, DC 20007

Professional Publications:
American Journal of Nursing
Contemporary Administration
Health Care Management Review
Health Care Product News
Healthcare Financial Management
Hospital Physician
Hospital Practice
Hospital Purchasing News
Hospitals
Journal of the American Medical Association
Modern Healthcare
Nursing Outlook
Physician Assistant and Health Practitioner

All Saints Episcopal Hospital
1400 8th Ave.
Fort Worth, TX 76104
(817) 926-2544
Personnel Director: Kathy Maxwell

American Healthcare Management, Inc.
14160 Dallas Pkwy., Suite 900
Dallas, TX 75240
(214) 385-7000
Human Resources Specialist: Julie Johnson

Arlington Community Hospital
3301 Matlock Rd.
Arlington, TX 76015
Metro (817) 467-7486
Personnel Director: Sandra Van Dyke

Arlington Memorial Hospital
800 W. Randol Mill Rd.
Arlington, TX 76012
(817) 274-5581
Personnel Director: Aleyne Brochet

Baylor Medical Center
3500 Gaston Ave.
Dallas, TX 75246
(214) 820-1111
Personnel Director: Elvis Bates

Cook Children's Medical Center
1212 W. Lancaster St.
Fort Worth, TX 76102
(817) 336-5521
Personnel Director: David Blackwell

Dallas/Fort Worth Medical Center
2709 Hospital Blvd.
Grand Prairie, TX 75051
Metro (214) 647-1141
Personnel Director: Hazel Hensley

Dallas Memorial Hospital
5003 Ross Ave.
Dallas, TX 75206
(214) 824-3071
Personnel Director: Rick Thomssen

Doctors Hospital
9440 Poppy Dr.
Dallas, TX 75218
(214) 324-6100
Contact: Personnel

Fort Worth Children's Hospital
1400 Cooper St.
Fort Worth, TX 76104
(817) 336-9861
Personnel Director: David Blackwell

Fort Worth Osteopathic Hospital
1000 Montgomery St.
Fort Worth, TX 76107
(817) 731-4311
Personnel Director: Sue Spalding

Garland Community Hospital
122 S. International Rd.
Garland, TX 75042
(214) 276-7116
Personnel Director: Inga Kirby

Grapevine Medical Center
1650 W. College St.
Grapevine, TX 76051
Metro (817) 481-1588
Personnel Director: Cynthia Johnson

Harris Hospital – H.E.B.
1600 Hospital Pkwy.
Bedford, TX 76022
Metro (817) 267-3956
Contact: Personnel

Harris Hospital-Methodist
1300 W. Cannon Ave.
Fort Worth, TX 76104
(817) 334-6308
Personnel Manager: Peter Kleven

Horizon Recovery Center
2345 Reagan St.
Dallas, TX 75219
Metro (214) 263-8838
Program Director: Myra Byanka

Irving Community Hospital
1901 N. MacArthur Blvd.
Irving, TX 75061
(214) 579-8180
Human Resources Director: Christopher Spanos

Mansfield Community Hospital
1802 Hwy. 157 North
Mansfield, TX 76063
(817) 473-6101
Personnel Coordinator: Carol Sprinkle

Medical Care International, Inc.
15110 Dallas Pkwy., Suite 600
Dallas, TX 75248
(214) 490-3190
Administrative Assistant: Cyrene Dacanti

Medical City-Dallas
7777 Forest Ln.
Dallas, TX 75230
(214) 661-7000
Personnel Director: Steve Melton

Medical Plaza Hospital
1612 W. Humbolt St.
Fort Worth, TX 76104
(817) 336-2100
Personnel Director: Richard Ward

Memorial Hospital of Garland
2300 Marie Curie Dr.
Garland, TX 75042
(214) 276-9511
Personnel Director: Larry Hughes

Mesquite Community Hospital
3500 Hwy. 67 East
Mesquite, TX 75150
(214) 270-3300
Personnel Director: Cindy Bennett

Methodist Medical Center
301 W. Colorado Blvd.
Dallas, TX 75208
(214) 944-8181
Personnel Director: Roger Fay

North Hill Medical Center
4401 Booth Calloway Rd.
North Richland Hills, TX 76180
(817) 284-1431
Personnel Director: Martin Ethridge

Northeast Community Hospital
1301 Airport Frwy.
Bedford, TX 76021
(817) 282-9211
Personnel Director: Paul Winton

Parkland Memorial Hospital
5201 Harry Hines Blvd.
Dallas, TX 75235
(214) 637-8000
Personnel Director: Melinda Stevens

Plano General Hospital
3901 W. 15th St.
Plano, TX 75075
(214) 596-6800
Personnel: Ted Smith

Presbyterian Hospital of Dallas
8200 Walnut Hill Ln.
Dallas, TX 75231
(214) 369-4111
Personnel Director: Ken Alexander

R.H.D. Memorial Medical Center
7 Medical Pkwy.
Farmers Branch, TX 75381-9094
(214) 247-1000
Personnel Director: Norma Resneder

Republic Health Corp.
14951 Dallas Pkwy., Suite 1100
Dallas, TX 75240
(214) 851-3100
Recruitment Manager: Herb Cox

Richardson Medical Center
401 W. Campbell Rd.
Richardson, TX 75080
Metro (214) 231-1441
Personnel Director: Terri Williams

St. Joseph Hospital
1401 S. Main St.
Fort Worth, TX 76104
(817) 336-9371
Personnel Director: Kerry Little

St. Paul Medical Center
5909 Harry Hines Blvd.
Dallas, TX 75235
(214) 879-1000
Personnel Director: Steve Franks

Schick Shadel Hospital of DFW
4101 Frawley Dr.
North Richland Hills, TX 76118
Metro (817) 589-0444
Personnel Director: Pat Brooks

John Peter Smith Hospital
1500 S. Main St.
Fort Worth, TX 76104
(817) 921-3431
Personnel Director: Susan Willis

Southeastern Methodist Hospital
9202 Elam Rd.
Dallas, TX 75217
(214) 372-7600
Personnel Manager: Jim Clark

Texas Scottish Rite Hospital
2222 Welborn St.
Dallas, TX 75219
(214) 521-3168
Personnel Director: Carrie Fish

Timberlawn Psychiatric Hospital
4600 Samuell Blvd.
Dallas, TX 75228
(214) 381-7181
Personnel Director: Judy Redd

Twin Oaks Medical Center
2919 Markum Dr.
Haltom City, TX 76117
(817) 831-0311
Personnel Director: Leah Trim

▶Hotels

To learn more about the **hospitality** industry and related fields, check out the following professional organizations listed in Chapter 5:

Dallas Restaurant Association
Hotel and Motel Association of Greater Dallas

For more information you can write to:

American Hotel and Motel Association
888 7th Ave.
New York, NY 10019

Hospitality Lodging & Travel Research Foundation
888 7th Ave.
New York, NY 10019

Hotel Sales Management Association
1235 Jefferson Davis Hwy., Suite 610
Arlington, VA 22202

Trade Publications:
Club Management
The Cornell Hotel and Restaurant Administration Quarterly
Hotel and Motel Management
Hotel and Resort Industry
Meetings and Conventions

Directories:
Directory of Hotel and Motel Systems (American Hotel Association Directory Corp., New York, NY)

Hotel and Motel Redbook (American Hotel Association Directory Corp., New York, NY)
Meetings and Conventions Magazine, Directory issue (Ziff Davis Publishing Co., New York, NY)

AMFAC Hotel and Resort
P.O. Box 619025
Dallas/Fort Worth Airport, TX 75261
Metro (817) 453-8400
Employment Manager: Olivia Mongaras

Adolphus Hotel
1321 Commerce St.
Dallas, TX 75202
(214) 742-8200
Contact: Karen Ranker

Arlington Rodeway Inn
833 N. Watson Rd.
Arlington, TX 76011
Metro (817) 265-8241
Personnel Director: Patty Shipley

Crescent Court Hotel
400 Crescent Court
Dallas, TX 75201
(214) 871-0303
Personnel Director: Becky Murdock

Dallas/Fort Worth Marriott
8440 Freeport Pkwy.
Irving, TX 75063
(214) 258-4800
Personnel Director: Bob Cropp

Dallas Hilton Inn
5600 N. Central Expwy.
Dallas, TX 75206
(214) 827-4100
Personnel Director: Janet Fein

DoubleTree Inn
8250 N. Central Expwy.
Dallas, TX 75206
(214) 691-8700
Personnel: Daisy Jimenez

Downtown Dallas Hilton Hotel
1914 Commerce St.
Dallas, TX 75201
(214) 747-7000
Personnel Director: Rene Hartman

Fairmont Hotel at the Arts District
1717 N. Akard St.
Dallas, TX 75201
(214) 720-2020
Personnel Director: Bob Minier

Fort Worth Hilton Hotel
1701 Commerce St.
Fort Worth, TX 76102
(817) 335-7000
Personnel Director: Rick Salinas

Green Oaks Inn/Conference Center
6901 West Frwy.
Fort Worth, TX 76116
(817) 738-7311
Personnel Director: Karin Naron

Holiday Inn-Brook Hollow
7050 Stemmons Frwy.
Dallas, TX 75247
(214) 630-8500
Contact: Heidi Plagge

Holiday Inn-D/FW Airport South
4440 W. Airport Frwy.
Irving, TX 75061
(214) 399-1010
Personnel Director: Edie Short

Holiday Inn-Midtown
1401 S. University Dr.
Fort Worth, TX 76107
(817) 336-9311
Personnel Director: Annette Jenkins

Hyatt Regency Dallas
300 Reunion Blvd.
Dallas, TX 75207
(214) 651-1234
Personnel Director: Barbara Hoover

Hyatt Regency Fort Worth
815 Main St.
Fort Worth, TX 76102
(817) 870-1234
Personnel Director: Humberto Peraza

Hotel business: more than puttin' on the Ritz

The hotel business offers people unparalleled opportunities, says Randy Gantenbein, general manager of the Loews Anatole Hotel. Often, executives work their way up from the bottom as he did.

While still in high school, Gantenbein began busing tables and working as a waiter and bartender. He didn't intend to stay in the business after college graduation, until he realized that he could get a job at a higher management level at a hotel than if he transferred into another field.

He moved swiftly through the ranks from catering director to food and beverage manager and finally to general manager of the 1,620-room Loews Anatole, the largest hotel in the Southwest and the 19th largest in the world.

Gantenbein advises aspiring hotel managers to get a degree in business and be willing to start in a less glamorous position to establish a solid understanding of the operation.

"The hotel business is more of a lifestyle than a career because of its odd hours, such as working on holidays and weekends," he says. But, adds Gantenbein, the rewards are great for people who prove their abilities.■

The Lincoln Hotel
5410 LBJ Frwy.
Dallas, TX 75240
(214) 934-8400
Personnel Director: Carol Taylor

Loews Anatole Hotel
2201 N. Stemmons Frwy.
Dallas, TX 75207
(214) 748-1200
Personnel Director: Jody Larkin

Mandalay Four Seasons Hotel
221 E. Las Colinas Blvd.
Irving, TX 75039
(214) 556-0800
Personnel Director: Don Griffin

The Mansion on Turtle Creek Hotel
2821 Turtle Creek Blvd.
Dallas, TX 75219
(214) 559-2100
Personnel Director: Carolyn Mann

Marriott Hotel/Market Center
2101 N. Stemmons Frwy.
Dallas, TX 75207
(214) 748-8551
Personnel Director: Bob Fitzwater

Marriott Hotel/Quorum
14901 Dallas Pkwy.
Dallas, TX 75240
(214) 661-2800
Personnel Director: Bob O'Brien

Marriott Park Central Hotel
7750 LBJ Frwy.
Dallas, TX 75251
(817) 233-4421
Personnel Director: Ken Brown

Plaza of the Americas Hotel
650 N. Pearl St.
Dallas, TX 75201
(214) 747-7222
Assistant Personnel Director: Andrea Aviar

Pratt Hotel Corp.
4099 McEwen St.
Dallas, TX 75244
(214) 386-9777
Personnel Director: Gini Shippole

Ramada Hotel/Dallas
1055 Regal Row
Dallas, TX 75247
(214) 634-8550
Personnel Director: Carl Heimann

The Regent Hotel
1241 W. Mockingbird Ln.
Dallas, TX 75247
(214) 630-7000
Personnel Director: Julie Friedman

Registry Hotel/Dallas
15201 Dallas Pkwy.
Dallas, TX 75248
(214) 386-6000
Personnel Director: Susan Hershman

The Rosewood Corporation
1601 Elm St.
Dallas, TX 75201
(214) 880-7000
Personnel Director: Mike Graham

Sheraton Dallas Hotel & Tower
400 N. Olive St.
Dallas, TX 75201
(214) 922-8000
Personnel Director: Jan Butler

Sheraton Inn Mockingbird West
1893 W. Mockingbird Ln.
Dallas, TX 75235
(214) 634-8850
Personnel Director: Paul Allen

Sheraton Park Central Hotel
12720 Merit Dr.
Dallas, TX 75251
(214) 385-3000
Personnel Director: Bob O'Neil

The Summit Hotel
2645 LBJ Frwy.
Dallas, TX 75234
(214) 243-3363
Personnel Director: Anne Pomerantz

The Westin Hotel Galleria
13340 Dallas Pkwy.
Dallas, TX 75240
(214) 934-9494
Personnel Director: Nancy Lebrecht

Worthington Hotel
200 Main St.
Fort Worth, TX 76102
(817) 870-1000
Personnel Director: Leonard Bade

Wyndham Hotel at Market Center
2222 Stemmons Frwy.
Dallas, TX 75207
(214) 631-2222
Personnel Director: Betty Corner

Human services

To learn more about **human services** and related fields, check out the following professional organizations listed in Chapter 5:

National Society of Fund Raising Executives
Salesmanship Club of Dallas

For more information, you can write to:

Center for Human Services
5530 Wisconsin Ave.
Chevy Chase, MD 20815

National Federation of Societies for Clinical Social Work
c/o Sidney H. Grossberg, Ph.D.
25835 Southfield Rd., Suite 101
Southfield, MI 48075

Volunteers of America
3813 N. Causeway Blvd.
Metairie, LA 70002

Trade Publications:
Children and Youth Services Review
Modern Times
Society

Directories
Consumer Assistance Directory (Federal Executive Board, Dallas, TX)
Directory of Agencies (National Association of Social Workers, Washington, DC)
Directory of Community Resources for Fort Worth and Tarrant County (United Way, Fort Worth, TX)
Directory of Human Resources in Health, Physical Education and Recreation (ERIC Clearing House on Teacher Education, Washington, DC)
Directory of Human Services & Resources for the North Texas Area (Junior League of Wichita Falls, Wichita Falls, TX)
National Directory of Children and Youth Services (CPR Directory Services Co., Washington, DC)
National Directory of Private Social Agencies (Croner Publications, Queens Village, NY)

Open Dallas: A Guide to Services and Special Resources (Dallas Public Library, Dallas, TX)

American Cancer Society
Area V Office
8900 Carpenter Frwy.
Dallas, TX 75247
(214) 631-3850
Executive Director: Chris Torti
Charitable organization that provides counseling, cancer screening, public and professional education, and conducts research.

American Cancer Society
Texas Division
2222 Montgomery St.
Fort Worth, TX 76107
(817) 737-3185
Office Manager: Debra Elias
Same as Dallas Office.

American Heart Association
National Center Office
7320 Greenville Ave.
Dallas, TX 75231
(214) 750-5300
Personnel Representative: Sally Stalnaker
National headquarters for association that provides education, research, CPR instruction, and blood pressure screenings.

American Red Cross
Dallas County Chapter
2300 McKinney Ave.
Dallas, TX 75201
(214) 871-2175
Executive Director: Michael F. Giard
Services provided for military families, 24-hour disaster assistance, and community volunteer programs.

American Red Cross
Tarrant County Chapter
6640 Camp Bowie Blvd.
Fort Worth, TX 76116
(817) 732-4491
Executive Director: Eddy Herrera
Provides first-aid classes, disaster training programs, community volunteer service, military family assistance, and transportation for the elderly.

Arthritis Foundation, Northwest Texas Chapter
3145 McCart Ave.
Fort Worth, TX 76110
(817) 926-7733
Executive Director: Marty Cook
Public education and special help for arthritis victims.

Association for Retarded Citizens
National Headquarters
2501 Ave. J
Arlington, TX 76006
(817) 640-0204
Executive Director: Alan Abeson
Information and referral services for mentally retarded and their families. Also includes respite care, citizen advocacy, and continuing education for mentally retarded adults.

Boy Scouts of America
National Office
1325 Walnut Hill Ln.
Irving, TX 75038-3096
(214) 580-2122
Employment Director: Richard Christian
Headquarters for national organization that sponsors education and character-building programs for boys 7 years old through high school.

Boys' Clubs of Dallas, Inc.
4804 Worth St.
Dallas, TX 75246
(214) 821-2950
Executive Director: Ralph Pahel
Physical, educational, and vocational guidance program for boys between the ages of 6 and 18.

Buckner Baptist Benevolences
5200 S. Buckner Blvd.
Dallas, TX 75227
(214) 328-3141
Contact: Department Head
Baptist General Convention of Texas supports adoption services, Buckner's Children's Home, Ryburn Home for Aging, and Mary E. Trew Home for Aging.

Catholic Charities Diocese of Dallas
3845 Oak Lawn Ave.
Dallas, TX 75219
(214) 528-4870
Director: Father Killian Broderick
Manages the Catholic Counseling Service, Marillac Social Center, St. Joseph Youth Center, St. Joseph Residence, and migration and refugee services.

Tips for senior citizens

Job-hunting techniques that work for younger people aren't always as effective for individuals over the age of 55, says Dorothy McLaughlin, project director of the **Dallas Senior Community Service Employment Program.**

The good-ol'-boy network begins breaking down for senior citizens as their friends retire, she says.

"It's especially hard for people who didn't plan on working past a certain age and thought they could live off savings, Social Security benefits, or pensions," she says. "Everyone thinks, 'This won't happen to me,' but inflation and health costs can wipe out savings."

As a result, older workers need special help, and Ms. McLaughlin's agency is one that can provide it. Applicants must take a free physical and meet U.S. Department of Labor income guidelines for the economically disadvantaged.

They receive training and counseling to prepare for a part-time job and are placed in non-profit agencies. After working there for six months to a year, workers are encouraged to find work in the public or private sector.

Call (214) 956-8704 for information about the program, which is funded by the U.S. Department of Labor and sponsored by the American Association of Retired Persons and the National Retired Teachers Association. The agency's address is 2727 Inwood Rd., Dallas, TX 75235.

Other senior employment programs include:

Experience Unlimited
911 State St.
Garland, TX 75040
(214) 494-7271
City of Garland Office on Aging sponsors program for Garland, Rowlett, and Sachse residents who are at least 55 years old. Referral service for part-time, full-

time, and temporary positions in all fields.

Senior Community Service Project
1100 Monroe St.
Fort Worth, TX 76102
(817) 870-8797
Part-time work for people who are at least 55 years old. On-the-job training in community service or non-profit organizations. Assists in job search. Must meet low-income guidelines and pass medical examination.

Senior Workers Program
2208 Main St.
Dallas, TX 75201
(214) 939-0588 ext. 138
Dallas County Community Action Committee sponsors program for people who are 55 years old or older and meet the U.S. Department of Labor low-income wage guidelines. Individuals undergo assessment of skills and two-week job-hunting training course. Assists in finding full-time and part-time jobs in private companies with benefits.

Seniors in Community Service
2606 Martin Luther King Blvd.
Dallas, TX 75215
(214) 421-0233
Workers who are at least 55 years old and meet low-income qualification are eligible for program that assesses needs and abilities and prepares person for work in a non-profit agency. Once individuals learn new job skills, they find work in the private sector.

Women's Center of Tarrant County, Inc.
1203 Lake St., Suite 208
Fort Worth, TX 76102
(817) 338-4456
Employment program for men and women who are 60 years old and older.■

Catholic Charities Diocese of Fort Worth
1300 S. Lake St.
Fort Worth, TX 76104
(817) 921-5381
Director: Karen Spicer
Programs for underprivileged families, counseling, foster care, and adoption service. Also manages St. Theresa's Home.

Community Council of Greater Dallas
2121 Main St., Suite 500
Dallas, TX 75201-4321
(214) 741-5851
Executive Director: Rus Delator
Organization for public and nonprofit voluntary service agencies. Council provides information and referral to social services, publishes a directory, conducts surveys, and provides management assistance and planning.

Dallas County Mental Health and Mental Retardation Services
1353 W. Westmoreland Rd.
Dallas, TX 75207
(214) 330-7726
Personnel Director: Phyllis Allen
Comprehensive community mental health and mental retardation program with hospital, day treatment, and outpatient services. Also drug treatment clinic, Mental Diagnostic Center, and Mexican-American Family Center.

Fort Worth State School
5000 Campus Dr.
Fort Worth, TX 76119
Metro (817) 429-0810
Contact: Personnel
Residential campus and non-residential programs for mentally retarded.

Girl Scout Council
4411 Skillman Ave.
Dallas, TX 75206
(214) 823-1342
Executive Director: Judy Nash
Worldwide organization for girls between the ages of 5 and 17.

Edna Gladney Center
2300 Hemphill St.
Fort Worth, TX 76110
(817) 926-3304
Executive Director: Eleanor Tuck
Services for unwed mothers and adoption agency.

Goodwill Industries of Dallas, Inc.
2800 N. Hampton Rd.
Dallas, TX 75212
(214) 638-2800
Personnel Director: Joy Jones
Rehabilitation services for handicapped adults. Operates stores with donated and repaired merchandise.

Goodwill Industries of Fort Worth
1701 E. Lancaster Ave.
Fort Worth, TX 76102
(817) 332-7866
Executive Director: Sam Rea
Same as Dallas Center.

Jewish Federation of Fort Worth and Tarrant County
6801 Dan Danciger Rd.
Fort Worth, TX 76133
(817) 292-3081
Executive Director: Harvey Freiman
Plans and coordinates health, recreation, and social services for the Tarrant County Jewish community, including the Dan Danciger Jewish Community Center and Jewish Social Agency.

Jewish Federation of Greater Dallas
7800 Northaven Rd., Suite A
Dallas, TX 75230
(214) 369-3313
Executive Director: Morris Stein
Plans and coordinates health, recreation, and social services for the Dallas Jewish community, including the Dallas Home for Jewish Aged, Jewish Community Center of Dallas, and Jewish Family Services.

March of Dimes, Birth Defects Foundation
North Central Texas Chapter
1801 Royal Ln., Suite 500
Dallas, TX 75229
(214) 263-1045
Executive Director: Kathy Bowser
Provides public health education, conducts fund-raising campaigns, and provides services for polio patients.

Multiple Sclerosis Association, Inc.
Tarrant County
617 7th Ave.
Fort Worth, TX 76104-2776
(817) 877-1222
Executive Director: Nancy Walters
Counseling, support groups, physical therapy, and education.

National Kidney Foundation of Texas
13500 Midway Rd., Suite 213
Dallas, TX 75234
(214) 934-8057
Executive Director: Charles Chadwick
Provides education about kidney disease, supports research, and sponsors organ donor program.

National Multiple Sclerosis Society
North Texas Chapter
4406 Beltway Dr.
Dallas, TX 75244
(214) 490-3222
Executive Director: Carolyn Rice
Sponsors education programs, supports research, and provides patient services and counseling.

Salvation Army
Social Services Headquarters
2215 N. Akard St.
Dallas, TX 75201
(214) 742-9131
Division Commander: Lt. Col. John Mikles
Provides meals, lodging, and casework services for transient men, women, and families.

Salvation Army
Tarrant County City Command
201 Jones St.
Fort Worth, TX 76102
(817) 332-1961
City Commander: Major Neal Keeton
Same services as Dallas Divisional Headquarters.

Sickle Cell Anemia Association of Texas
617 7th Ave., Suite 402
Fort Worth, TX 76104
(817) 332-5300
Executive Director: Fontainette White
Screening, counseling, and educational programs.

Tarrant County Mental Health & Mental Retardation Services
1319 Summit Ave.
Fort Worth, TX 76112
(817) 335-5371
Assistant Director of Personnel: Margaret Bonner
Provides treatment, training, and social services for mental health patients in Tarrant County, including programs for the elderly, alcohol center, family services, diagnosis service, sheltered workshops, and industrial training for the retarded.

United Way of Metropolitan Dallas, Inc.
901 Ross Ave.
Dallas, TX 75202
(214) 720-1801
President: J. J. Guise, Jr.
Voluntary nonprofit organization providing support to local, state, and national health agencies and character-building organizations. Conducts annual fund-raising campaign.

United Way of Metropolitan Tarrant County
210 E. 9th St.
Fort Worth, TX 76102
(817) 335-3473
Contact: Department Head
Same as Dallas Division.

YMCA–Dallas Metropolitan Offices
601 N. Akard St.
Dallas, TX 75201
(214) 954-0550
President: John W. Davis
Recreational and social activities for all ages and sexes at 17 area branches.

YMCA–Tarrant County Offices
540 Lamar St.
Fort Worth, TX 76102
(817) 335-6147
President: Art Thompson
Offers similar programs as Dallas YMCA at 10 Tarrant County centers.

YWCA–Metropolitan Dallas
4621 Ross Ave.
Dallas, TX 75204
(214) 827-5600
Executive Director: Mary Fife
Provides social and recreational activities, licensed day care, and year-round special programs at seven branches.

YWCA–Tarrant County
512 W. 4th St.
Fort Worth, TX 76102
(817) 332-6191
Executive Director: Nancy Marchant
Provides residential and support services for women, child care, Y–Teens, and handicapped programs.

▶Insurance underwriters and brokers

To learn more about **insurance** and related fields, check out the following professional organizations listed in Chapter 5:

Dallas Association of Life Underwriters
Independent Insurance Agents of Dallas
Insurance Women

For more information, you can write to:

National Association of Independent Insurers
2600 River Rd.
Des Plaines, IL 60018

National Association of Life Underwriters
1922 F St., NW
Washington, DC 20006

Professional Publications:
Business Insurance
Independent Agent
Insurance Advocate
The Insurance Record
The Journal of Risk and Insurance
National Underwriter

Directories:
Best's Directory of Recommended Insurance Adjusters (A. M. Best Co., Oldwick, NJ)
Insurance Almanac (Underwriter Publishing Co., Englewood, NJ)
Kirschner's Insurance Directory (Kirschner's Publishing Co., Santa Cruz, CA)
New York Insurance Brokers Directory (American Underwriter, Media, PA)

Aetna Life & Casualty
611 Plaza Dr., Suite 300
Arlington, TX 76011
(817) 273-5500
Personnel Director: Angie Aguero

Alexander & Alexander of Texas, Inc.
Dallas Office
717 N. Harwood St., 19th Fl.
Dallas, TX 75201
(214) 880-0321
Personnel Manager: Dorothy King

Alexander & Alexander of Texas, Inc.
Fort Worth Office
6100 Western Place, Suite 100
Fort Worth, TX 76113
Metro (817) 429-3653
Personnel Director: Tamia Smith

Allstate Insurance Co.
200 W. Hwy. 114
Irving, TX 75038
Metro (214) 256-4570
Personnel Director: Debra Bell

American International Co.
2001 Bryan Tower
Dallas, TX 75201
(214) 658-6000
Human Resources Manager: Jackie Quigley

Associates Insurance Group
250 E. John Carpenter Frwy.
Irving, TX 75062
(214) 659-4000
Personnel Director: Bill Mathers

Auto Club Insurance Agency
4425 N. Central Expwy.
Dallas, TX 75205
(214) 526-7911
Personnel Director: Jolynn Senkel

Bayly Martin & Fay Insurance Agency, Inc.
5310 Harvest Hill Rd., Suite 160
Dallas, TX 75230
(214) 233-6841
Personnel Director: Millie Stovall

Blue Cross-Blue Shield of Texas
901 S. Central Expwy.
Richardson, TX 75080
Metro (214) 669-6900
Employment Director: Ed Toogood

Bright Insurance Services, Inc.
2355 Stemmons Frwy., Suite 901
Dallas, TX 75207
(214) 637-6320
Operations Manager: J. Carlton Sims

Chubb Group of Insurance Companies
717 N. Harwood St., Suite 300
Dallas, TX 75201
(214) 744-0331
Personnel Manager: Janice Wilsford

Combined Insurance Co. of America
3141 Hood St.
Dallas, TX 75219
(214) 521-2174
Divisional Administrator: Lou White

Commercial Union Insurance Co.
9330 Amberton Pkwy.
Dallas, TX 75243
(214) 783-6100
Personnel Manager: Rich Tremblay

Corrigan Jordan Insurance Agency
700 N. Pearl St., Suite 840
Dallas, TX 75201
(214) 754-0022
Office Manager: Terry Cook

Crump Insurance Services
12720 Hillcrest Rd., Suite 802
Dallas, TX 75230-2010
(214) 661-5050
Personnel Manager: Diane Combs

Employers Insurance of Texas
1301 Young St.
Dallas, TX 75202
(214) 760-6100
Personnel Director: Louis Rosen

Fidelity Union Life Insurance Co.
2323 Bryan St., 8th Fl.
Dallas, TX 75201
(214) 978-7000
Attention: Recruiting

Fireman's Fund Insurance Co.
1999 Bryan St., 9th Fl.
Dallas, TX 75201
(214) 220-4000
Regional Director: Dan McColl

Globe Life & Accident Insurance Co.
2909 N. Buckner Blvd.
Dallas, TX 75228
(214) 324-1202
Personnel: Chris Gaddis

Gulf Insurance Group
4600 Fuller Dr.
Irving, TX 75038
(214) 257-2800
Personnel Manager: John McRae

Hartford Insurance Group
5001 LBJ Frwy.
Dallas, TX 75234
(214) 980-1900
Personnel Manager: Carol Neff

Fred S. James & Co. of Texas, Inc.
3811 Turtle Creek Blvd.
Lock Box 1
Dallas, TX 75219-4419
(214) 651-4000
Personnel: Ruth Goodenough

Johnson & Higgens of Texas, Inc.
One Dallas Centre, Suite 2300
Dallas, TX 75201
(214) 655-3200
Personnel: Doris Kinsey

Kemper Group
1800 Eastgate Dr.
Garland, TX 75041
(214) 270-6601
Personnel Director: Tina Ashley

Kirby Head-Teas Insurance
777 N. Rosedale Dr., Suite 260
Fort Worth, TX 76104
(817) 332-1278
President: Arthur B. Kirby, Jr.

Life Insurance Co. of the Southwest
1300 W. Mockingbird Ln.
Dallas, TX 75247
(214) 638-7100
Personnel Director: Glo Calhoun

Lone Star Life Insurance Co.
4050 Alpha Rd.
Farmers Branch, TX 75244
(214) 233-2510
Personnel Director: Michael Brown

Marsh & McLennan Cos., Inc.
2121 San Jacinto St., Suite 1300
Dallas, TX 75201
(214) 979-9900
Personnel Director: Ellie Pamplin

Members Insurance Group
4455 LBJ Frwy., Suite 917
Dallas, TX 75244
(214) 980-5441
Personnel Director: Diane Stevenson

Millers Insurance Group
300 Burnett St.
Fort Worth, TX 76102
(817) 332-7761
Personnel Manager: Elaine Hargett

The Mills Co.
3434 Fairmount Dr.
Dallas, TX 75219
(214) 528-2580
President's Assistant: Mona Robertson

Kenneth Murchison & Co.
4104 McEwen Rd., Suite 800
Dallas, TX 75244
(214) 458-0080
Agency Manager: Colin Williams

Mutual of Omaha Insurance Co.
6263 Harry Hines Blvd.
Dallas, TX 75235
(214) 630-4100
Personnel Director: Laverne Bechtol

Noel, Greaves & Strother, Inc.
4211 Cedar Springs Rd., Suite 200
Dallas, TX 75219
(214) 526-4700
Contact: Personnel

Arthur Owen Co., Inc.
714 Jackson St., Suite 1000
Dallas, TX 75202
(214) 747-6500
Personnel: Pam Sublett

J.C. Penney Life Insurance Co.
2700 W. Plano Pkwy.
Plano, TX 75074
(214) 881-8400
Personnel Director: Connie Amesquita

Reserve Life Insurance Co.
403 S. Akard St.
Dallas, TX 75202
(214) 670-9700
Personnel Director: Bill Boykin

William Rigg Co.
410 W. 7th St., Suite 1800
Fort Worth, TX 76102
Metro (817) 429-0040
Executive Vice President: Bill Meadows

Roach, Howard, Smith & Hunter
1661 Northwest Hwy.
Garland, TX 75041
(214) 840-1300
Contact: Personnel

Royal Insurance
3725 Blackburn St.
Dallas, TX 75219
(214) 522-1600
Personnel Director: Gail Stafford

SCOR Reinsurance Co.
222 W. Las Colinas Blvd., Suite 1900
Irving, TX 75039
(214) 869-6300
Personnel Director: Betty Ivy

Shelton & Bowles, Inc.
7007 Twin Hills Ave., Suite 300
Dallas, TX 75231
(214) 363-1600
Operations Supervisor: Marsha Lavenant

Southland Life Insurance Co.
400 N. Olive St., Suite 1220
Dallas, TX 75201
(214) 922-1200
Personnel Director: Kim Ragsdale

Southwestern Life Insurance Co.
500 N. Akard St., 6th Fl.
Dallas, TX 75221
Metro (214) 954-7407
Personnel Vice President: Jerolyn Jones

State Farm Insurance Companies
17301 Preston Rd.
Dallas, TX 75252
(214) 248-4000
Personnel Director: Ed Hudson

Transport Insurance Co.
4100 Harry Hines Blvd.
Dallas, TX 75219
(214) 526-3876
Personnel Director: Jenna Mattix

Transport Life Insurance Co.
714 Main St., 20th Fl.
Fort Worth, TX 76102
Metro (817) 429-1620
Personnel Director: Amy Kruckemeyer

Travelers Insurance Co.
1137 S. Jupiter Rd.
Garland, TX 75042
(214) 272-6560
Personnel Manager: Shirley Mathis

Trinity Universal Insurance Co.
2000 Ross Ave.
Dallas, TX 75201
(214) 979-2400
Personnel: Judith Fagen

Underwriters Adjusting Co.
600 N. Pearl St.
Plaza of the Americas South Tower
Dallas, TX 75201
(214) 760-1100
Personnel Director: Al Roberts

Union Bankers Insurance Co.
2551 Elm St.
Dallas, TX 75226
(214) 939-0821
Personnel Manager: Fred Dean

United American Insurance
2909 N. Buckner Blvd.
Dallas, TX 75228
(214) 328-2841
Personnel: Christine Gaddis

Wausau Insurance Co.
1333 Corporate Dr., Suite 300
Irving, TX 75015
Metro (214) 550-1615
Personnel Director: Ken Haynes

World Service Life Insurance Co.
2300 Continental Plaza
Fort Worth, TX 76101
(817) 390-1011
Personnel Vice President: Maryann Goss

▶Investment bankers and brokers

To learn more about **finance** and related fields, check out the following professional organizations listed in Chapter 5:

Dallas Association of Investment Analysts
Dallas Security Dealers Association
Dallas Society of the Institute of Certified Financial Planners

For more information, you can write to:

The Financial Analysts Federation
219 E. 42nd St.
New York, NY 10017

National Association of Securities Dealers
1735 K St., NW
Washington, DC 20007

Trade Publications:
Commodity Journal
Corporate Financing Week
Credit and Financial Management
D & B Reports
Dun's Business Month
Finance & Development
Finance, the Magazine of Money and Business
Financial Analysts Journal
Financial Executive
Financial Management
Financial World
Financier
Institutional Investor
Investment Dealer's Digest
Securities Week
Security Industry and Product News
Security Letter
Stock Market Magazine
Wall Street Transcript

Directories:
CUSIP Master Directory (Standard & Poors, New York, NY)
Money Market Directory (Money Market Directories, Inc., Charlottesville, VA)
Security Dealers of North America (Standard and Poor's, New York, NY)
Who's Who in the Securities Industry (Economist Publishing Co., New York, NY)

Associates Corp. of North America
250 E. John Carpenter Frwy.
Irving, TX 75062
(214) 659-4000
Personnel Director: Bill Mathers

Bear, Stearns & Co.
1601 Elm St., 40th Fl.
Dallas, TX 75201
(214) 741-8100
Administrative Manager: Paula Castonguay

Cullum & Sandow
2001 Bryan Tower
Dallas, TX 75201
(214) 754-0111
Contact: Tim Cullum

Dallas Securities Investment Corp.
8585 Stemmons Frwy., Suite 1106
Dallas, TX 75247
(214) 638-7044
Contact: Chuck Marretsky

Dean Witter Reynolds, Inc.
2300 Lincoln Plaza
Dallas, TX 75201
(214) 740-2000
Branch Manager: Allen Schroder

Donaldson, Lufkin & Jenrette Securities Corp.
717 N. Harwood St., Suite 400
Dallas, TX 75201
(214) 979-4000
Contact: William Barker

Drexel Burnham Lambert, Inc.
350 N. St. Paul St., Suite 1900
Dallas, TX 75201
(214) 979-0193
Manager: Chuck Best

A.G. Edwards & Sons, Inc.
411 N. Akard St., Suite 100
Dallas, TX 75201
(214) 954-4466
Assistant Branch Manager: J. T. Allen

Eppler, Guerin & Turner, Inc.
2001 Bryan Tower
Dallas, TX 75201
(214) 880-9000
Senior Vice President: Ellen Gray

First Southwest Co.
800 Mercantile Dallas Bldg.
Dallas, TX 75201
(214) 742-6461
Executive Vice President: W. Stewart Storie

E.F. Hutton Co., Inc.
2001 Bryan Tower, Suite 3308
Dallas, TX 75201
(214) 744-2511
Personnel and Operations Manager: Al Hines

Kidder, Peabody & Co., Inc.
1201 Elm St., Suite 3939
Dallas, TX 75270
(214) 761-7000
Branch Manager: Patrick McLochlin

MSecurities Corp.
1802 Main St.
Dallas, TX 75201
(214) 698-6877
Office Manager: Norma Galbraith

Merrill Lynch, Pierce, Fenner & Smith, Inc.
8350 N. Central Expwy., Suite 688
Dallas, TX 75206
(214) 750-2111
Contact: Personnel

Minton Schmid Landers Vinton Reuther & Smith, Inc.
916 One Tandy Center
Fort Worth, TX 76102
Metro (817) 429-6282
Office Manager: Ed Ford

Paine Webber, Inc.
1601 Elm St., Suite 2000
Dallas, TX 75201
(214) 978-6000
Office Manager: Elaine Look

Prudential Bache Securities, Inc.
3 NorthPark East, Suite 100
Dallas, TX 75231
(214) 373-2700
Branch Manager: Charles Grose

Rauscher Pierce Refsnes, Inc.
Plaza of the Americas, Suite 2500 North Tower
Dallas, TX 75201
(214) 978-0111
Personnel Director: Kay Greenhaw

Rotan Mosle, Inc.
InterFirst Two, Suite 2600
Dallas, TX 75270
(214) 651-6000
Office Manager: Louis Riggsby

Schneider, Bernet & Hickman, Inc.
2400 Renaissance Tower
Dallas, TX 75270
(214) 761-5100
Contact: Eva Janousck

Shearson Lehman Brothers, Inc.
1999 Bryan St., Suite 2600
Dallas, TX 75201
(214) 979-7000
Administrative Assistant: Ms. Bobbi Walker

Smith Barney Co., Inc.
5300 InterFirst Two Bldg.
Dallas, TX 75270
(214) 744-5300
Branch Manager: George Longino

Southwest Securities, Inc.
1704 Main St., Suite 711
Dallas, TX 75201
(214) 651-1800
Personnel Manager: Ivy Lindloff

Weber, Hall, Sale & Associates, Inc.
1525 Elm St., Suite 1800
Dallas, TX 75201
(214) 954-9472
Contact: Rick Hall

▶Law firms

To learn more about the **law** and related fields, check out the following professional organizations listed in Chapter 5:

Dallas Association of Black Women Attorneys
Dallas Association of Law Librarians
Dallas Association of Legal Assistants
Dallas Association of Young Lawyers
Dallas Bar Association
Dallas Business League
Dallas Women Lawyers Association
Fort Worth/Tarrant County Young Lawyers Association
Irving Bar Association
Mesquite Bar Association
Richardson Bar Association
Tarrant County Bar Association
Tarrant County Women's Bar Association

For more information, you can write to:

American Bar Association
750 N. Lake Shore Dr.
Chicago, IL 60611

American Bar Association Foundation
750 N. Lake Shore Dr.
Chicago, IL 60611

National Association of Bar Executives
425 Lumber Exchange Bldg.
Minneapolis, MN 55402

Professional Publications:
ABA Journal
American Business Law Journal
American Lawyer
Banking Law Journal
Criminal Law Bulletin
For the Defense
Labor Law Journal
Law Enforcement Communications
Trial

Directories:
ABA Directory (American Bar Association, Chicago, IL)

Akin, Gump, Strauss, Hauer & Feld
4100 First City Center
1700 Pacific Ave.
Dallas, TX 75201-4618
(214) 969-2800
Managing Partner: Edward Copley

Baker, Smith & Mills
2001 Ross Ave.
600 LTV Center
Dallas, TX 75201
(214) 220-8200
Managing Partner: Robert Baker

Barlow & Garsek
3815 Lisbon St.
Fort Worth, TX 76107
(817) 731-4500
Office Manager: Elizabeth Bush

Bishop, Payne, Lamsens & Brown
1800 InterFirst Bank Bldg.
Fort Worth, TX 76102
(817) 335-4911
Office Manager: Carl Albert

Brice & Mankoff
300 Crescent Court, Suite 700
Dallas, TX 75201
(214) 855-3700
Contact: Kim DiLallo

Brown, Herman, Scott, Dean & Miles
306 W. 7th St., Suite 203
Fort Worth, TX 76102
(817) 332-1391
Partner: Richard Wiseman

Camp, Jones, O'Neill, Hall & Bates
2400 City Center
301 Commerce St.
Fort Worth, TX 76102
(817) 336-2400
Managing Partner: Kenneth Jones

Cantey, Hanger, Gooch, Munn & Collins
2100 InterFirst Tower
801 Cherry St.
Fort Worth, TX 76102
Metro (817) 877-2800
Managing Partner: John Johndroe III

Carrington, Coleman, Sloman & Blumenthal
200 Crescent Court, Suite 1500
Dallas, TX 75201
(214) 855-3000
Recruitment Coordinator: Pam Mueller

Clark, West, Keller, Butler & Ellis
1201 Elm St., Suite 4949
Dallas, TX 75270
(214) 741-1001
Managing Partner: Mike Tabor

Cowles & Thompson
4000 InterFirst Plaza
901 Main St.
Dallas, TX 75202
(214) 670-1100
Recruiting Coordinator: Brent Cooper

Dushman, Friedman & Gray
2620 Airport Frwy.
Fort Worth, TX 76111
(817) 834-8851
Managing Partner: Lowell Dushman

Freytag, Perry, LaForce, Rubinstein, Stutzman & Teofan
500 N. Akard St.
2000 Lincoln Plaza
Dallas, TX 75201
(214) 740-3000
Recruitment Administrator: Margret O'Connell

Gandy, Michener, Swindle, Whitaker & Pratt
2501 Parkview Dr., Suite 600
Fort Worth, TX 76102
(817) 335-4417
Managing Partner: Charles Lundelius

Gardere & Wynne
1500 Diamond Shamrock Tower
Dallas, TX 75201
(214) 748-7211
Recruitment Coordinator: Ramona Jones

Geary, Stahl & Spencer
2800 One Main Place
Dallas, TX 75250
(214) 748-9901
Recruitment Coordinator: Marge Penson

Godfrey & Decker
3200 Continental Plaza
Fort Worth, TX 76102
(817) 336-0361
Contact: Richard Bourland

Harris, Finley, Creel & Bogle
3100 Continental Plaza
Fort Worth, TX 76102
(817) 335-5050
Managing Partner: Dee Finley

Haynes & Boone
901 Main St., Suite 3100
Dallas, TX 75202
(214) 670-0550
Recruitment Coordinator: Beth Zilch

Hudson, Keltner, Smith, Brants & Sparks
2300 Texas American Bank Bldg.
Fort Worth, TX 76102
(817) 336-2300
Managing Partner: Harry Brants

Hughes & Luce
1000 Dallas Building
Dallas, TX 75201
(214) 760-5500
Personnel Supervisor: Denni Comer

Jackson, Walker, Winstead, Cantwell & Miller
901 Main St.
6000 InterFirst Plaza
Dallas, TX 75202
(214) 953-6000
Personnel Coordinator: Gail Tahn

Jenkins, Hutchison & Gilchrist
3200 Allied Bank Tower
Dallas, TX 75202-2711
(214) 855-4500
Managing Partner: Christie Flanagan

Johnson, Bromberg & Leeds
500 Lincoln Plaza, Suite 2600
Dallas, TX 75201
Metro (214) 740-2600
Contact: Al Badger

Johnson & Swanson
900 Jackson St., Suite 100
Dallas, TX 75202
(214) 977-9000
Recruiting Administrator: Kay Scoggin

Jones, Day, Reavis & Pogue
2001 Ross Ave., Suite 2300
Dallas, TX 75201
(214) 220-3939
Recruiting Coordinator: Jerrie Hawley

Kelly, Appleman, Hart & Hallman
201 Main St., Suite 2500
Fort Worth, TX 76102
(817) 332-2500
Personnel Director: Debra Cholak

Law, Snakard, Brown & Gambill
3200 Texas American Bank Bldg.
Fort Worth, TX 76102
(817) 335-7373
Personnel Director: Sharon Mullarkey

Locke, Purnell, Boren, Laney & Neely
3600 RepublicBank Tower
Dallas, TX 75201
(214) 754-7400
Contact: Mary Calhoun

McDonald Law Firm
777 Main St., Suite 1300
Fort Worth, TX 76102
(817) 336-8651
Contact: Rick Soreson

McLean, Sanders, Price, Head & Ellis
1700 Two Tandy Center
100 Main St.
Fort Worth, TX 76102
Metro (817) 429-9181
Personnel Administrator: Ann Dunkin

Moore & Peterson
2800 First City Center
Dallas, TX 75201
(214) 754-4800
Managing Partner: Mike Wylie

Murphey, Shrull, Moore & Bell
1300 S. University Dr., Suite 520
Fort Worth, TX 76107
(817) 336-4456
Managing Partner: Roswald Shrull

Rain, Harrell, Emery, Young & Doke
4200 RepublicBank Tower
Dallas, TX 75201
(214) 754-9400
Partner: Steve Gagnon

Ross, Arnn, Hartley, Irion & Wilkes
500 E. Border St., Suite 517
Arlington, TX 76010
Metro (817) 261-7711
Contact: Linda Douglas

Shank, Irwin & Conant
2200 Lincoln Plaza
Dallas, TX 75201-4713
(214) 720-9600
Recruiting Coordinator: Cynthia Scott

Shannon, Gracey, Ratliff & Miller
2200 First City Bank Tower
201 Main St.
Fort Worth, TX 76102
(817) 336-9333
Contact: Charles Curry

Simon, Anisman, Doby, Wilson & Skillern
303 W. 10th St., Suite 400
Fort Worth, TX 76071
Metro (817) 429-3245
Office Manager: Clayton McGilveray

Strasburger & Price
901 Main St.
4300 InterFirst Plaza
Dallas, TX 75202
(214) 651-4300
Managing Partner: William Rippey

Thompson & Knight
1700 Pacific Ave.
3300 First City Center
Dallas, TX 75201
(214) 969-1700
Partner: M. L. Hicks, Jr.

Touchstone, Bernays, Johnston, Bell & Smith
1201 Elm St.
4700 Renaissance Tower
Dallas, TX 75270
(214) 741-1166
Office Manager: Wade C. Smith

Vial, Icmilton, Koch & Knox
325 N. St. Paul St.
1500 RepublicBank Tower
Dallas, TX 75201
(214) 922-9393
Contact: Recruiting Committee

Winstead, McGuire, Sechrest & Minick
1807 Commerce St.
1700 Dallas Bldg.
Dallas, TX 75201
(214) 742-1700
Contact: Dominique Howard

Worsham, Forsythe, Samples & Wooldridge
2001 Bryan Tower, Suite 3200
Dallas, TX 75201
(214) 748-9365
Recruitment Coordinator: Kay Brandon

Wynn, Brown, Mack, Renfro & Thompson
201 Main St.
1800 First City Bank Tower
Fort Worth, TX 76102
(817) 335-6261
Managing Partner: Harold Brown

▶Management consultants

To learn more about **management consulting** and related fields, check out the following professional organizations listed in Chapter 5:

American Management Association
Dallas/Fort Worth Organizational Psychologists

For more information, you can write to:

Association of Management Consultants
331 Madison Ave.
New York, NY 10017

Association of Management Consulting Firms
230 Park Ave.
New York, NY 10169

National Management Association
2210 Arbor Blvd.
Dayton, OH 45439

Society of Professional Management Consultants
163 Engle St.
Englewood, NJ 07631

Professional Publications:
Academy of Management Journal
Academy of Management Review
Administrative Management
Advanced Management Journal
Business Quarterly
Executive
Harvard Business Review
Journal of Management
Management Accounting
Management Review
Management Today

Directories:

AMC Directory (Association of Management Consultants, New York, NY)
Consultants and Consulting Organizations Directory (Gale Research Co., Detroit, MI)
Directory of Management Consultants (Kennedy & Kennedy, Fitzwilliam, NH)
Directory of Management Consultants and Industrial Services (Los Angeles Chamber of Commerce, Los Angeles, CA)
IMC Directory (Institute of Management Consultants, New York, NY)

Booz, Allen & Hamilton, Inc.
2121 San Jacinto St., Suite 3100
Dallas, TX 75201
(214) 922-0454
Office Manager: Donna Hastings

Challenger, Gray & Christmas, Inc.
5501 LBJ Frwy., Suite 500
Dallas, TX 75240
(214) 788-1816
Vice President: John Challenger
Specialty: Outplacement and transplacement for helping spouses of transferred employees.

Club Corporation of America
2711 LBJ Frwy.
Dallas, TX 75243
(214) 243-6191
Corporate Recruiter: Norm Werbach
Specialty: Country clubs and private clubs.

Harris Group Management Consultants
One Turtle Creek Village
Dallas, TX 75219
(214) 522-5580
President: Lane Harris
Specialty: Financial institutions.

Holloway Associates
8210 Walnut Hill Ln., Suite 619
Dallas, TX 75231
(214) 750-6031
President: Dr. Diane Holloway
Specialty: Evaluations for prospective employees and promotions. Supervisory training.

Inman Maclean & Gaddy
4307 Newton Ct.
Dallas, TX 75219
(214) 522-2106
Senior Partner: Bob Inman
Specialty: outplacement, employee assistance programs, and organizational development.

LWFW Group, Inc.
12700 Park Central Place, Suite 1805
Dallas, TX 75251
(214) 233-5561
Contact: Personnel

M/A/R/C, Inc.
7850 N. Belt Line Rd.
Irving, TX 75063
(214) 506-3400
Personnel Director: Sharon Olson
Specialty: Custom marketing and counseling for larger consumer product and service companies.

Manersa Management Consultants, Inc.
6300 Ridglea Place, Suite 610
Fort Worth, TX 76116
(817) 738-6311
Owner: E. R. Manersa

Mok-Bledsoe International
14455 Webb Chapel Rd., Suite 102
Dallas, TX 75234
(214) 484-4444
President: Larry Bledsoe

RCM Corp.
1201 Fort Worth Club Tower
Fort Worth, TX 76102
(817) 335-9951
Owner: John W. Ratliff
Specialty: Mergers and acquisitions.

Survey Systems, Inc.
Campbell Centre, Suite 344
Dallas, TX 75206
(214) 692-5511
Contact: Personnel
Specialty: Surveys.

Taylor Management Systems, Inc.
9242 Markville Dr.
Dallas, TX 75243
(214) 690-4333
Contact: Personnel

The Wyatt Co.
RepublicBank Tower, Suite 1900
Dallas, TX 75201
(214) 979-3800
Personnel Assistant: Ray Wagner

▶Manufacturers, General

To learn more about **manufacturers** in Dallas, you may want to consult these directories:

Dallas/Fort Worth Metropolitan Area Manufacturers (Dallas Chamber of Commerce, Dallas, TX)
Directory of Texas Manufacturers (Bureau of Business Research, Austin, TX)

Acro Welch, Inc.
6200 Denton Dr.
Dallas, TX 75235
(214) 358-4631
Personnel Director: Marilyn Chase
Security locks and hardware items.

American Permanent Ware Co.
729 3rd Ave.
Dallas, TX 75226
(214) 421-7366
Personnel Director: Joyce Smith
Restaurant equipment.

Ametek Heat Transfer
2300 W. Marshall Dr.
Grand Prairie, TX 75051
(214) 647-2626
Contact: Personnel
Heat exchangers.

Anacast Division of Anadite, Inc.
701 W. Mansfield Hwy.
Kennedale, TX 76060
(817) 478-9231
Personnel Director: Ray De Los Santos
Sand castings.

Anchor Brush Co.
5012 Rondo Dr.
Fort Worth, TX 76106
(817) 625-5923
Personnel Director: Joann Henrikson
Cosmetic brushes and plastic bottles for the medical industry.

Atlas Match Corp.
1801 S. Airport Circle
Euless, TX 76039
(817) 267-1500
Contact: Sandy Stillner
Advertising matchbooks.

Bates Container, Inc.
6433 Davis Blvd.
Fort Worth, TX 76180
(817) 498-3200
Personnel Manager: Sally Hackfeld
Corrugated containers.

Beckett Corp.
2521 Willowbrook Rd.
Dallas, TX 75220
(214) 357-6421
Contact: Personnel
Float valves, drinking fountains, and submergible water pumps.

Brinkman Corp.
4215 McEwen Rd.
Dallas, TX 75244
(214) 387-4939
Personnel Director: Kathy Guttilla
Metal detectors, meat smokers, spotlights, and radar detectors.

Container Corporation of America
6701 South Frwy.
Fort Worth, TX 76134
(817) 293-4111
Personnel Director: Joe Williamson
Corrugated shipping containers.

Cook Machinery Co.
4301 S. Fitzhugh Ave.
Dallas, TX 75226
(214) 421-2135
Comptroller: Jim Corder
Commercial laundry equipment.

Susan Crane, Inc.
8107 Chancellor Row
Dallas, TX 75247
(214) 631-6490
Vice President: Mark Britain
Display materials, artificial flowers, and gift wrappings.

Dahlgren Manufacturing Co.
3305 Manor Way
Dallas, TX 75235
(214) 357-4621
Personnel Director: Tom McMillen
Dampening systems and printing press equipment.

Dallas Corporation
6750 LBJ Frwy., Suite 1200
Dallas, TX 75240
(214) 233-6611
Office Manager: Renna Carrico
Garage and truck doors.

Dallas Woodcraft/Division of Bomar Manufacturing
2829 Sea Harbour Rd.
Dallas, TX 75212
(214) 631-2782
Personnel Director: Helen Ruggles
Picture frames.

Darr Equipment Co.
549 Jim Wright Frwy.
Fort Worth, TX 76108
(817) 246-6651
Contact: Department Heads
Construction and mining equipment.

Esco Elevators, Inc.
4720 Esco Dr.
Fort Worth, TX 76140
Metro (817) 572-2384
Personnel Director: Jordan Jones
Hydraulic passenger and freight elevators.

Forney Engineering Co.
3405 Wiley Post Rd.
Carrollton, TX 75006
(214) 233-1871
Personnel Director: Edward C. Quinn
Industrial boiler burners and process control systems.

Gifford-Hill American
1003 Meyers Rd.
Grand Prairie, TX 75050
(214) 262-1571
Personnel Manager: Royce Adams
Concrete pressure pipe and pipe fittings.

Harris Corp., Commercial Press Division
501 S. Dick Price Rd.
Kennedale, TX 76060
Metro (817) 572-2311
Personnel Manager: Jim Penny
Printing presses.

Hobart Corporation
4407 Alpha Rd.
Dallas, TX 75244
(214) 233-7781
Branch Manager: Darrel Pocock
Food equipment.

Ben Hogan Co.
2912 W. Pafford St.
Fort Worth, TX 76110
(817) 921-2661
Personnel Director: Don Holland
Golf clubs, golf balls, and golf apparel.

Johnson Controls
1111 Shiloh Rd.
Garland, TX 75042
(214) 494-2461
Contact: Personnel
Auto, marine, and commercial storage batteries.

Justin Industries
2821 W. 7th St.
Fort Worth, TX 76107
(817) 336-5125
Personnel Manager: Bobby Moon
Diversified products, including Acme brick, Justin and Nocona boots, ceramic cooling towers, and concrete products.

Keystone Consolidated Industries, Inc.
4835 LBJ Frwy., Suite 345
Dallas, TX 75244
(214) 458-0028
Personnel Administration: Dottie Olsen
Steel and wire products, including nails, fences, and fasteners.

LTV Energy Products, Oil States Industries Division
7701 S. Cooper St.
Arlington, TX 76017
(817) 468-1400
Personnel Manager: Keith Steinhoss
Rubber molded products and drilling equipment.

Lennox Industries
Airport Frwy. and Maxine St.
Fort Worth, TX 76117
(817) 831-0931
Personnel Manager: Ed Mabe
Air-conditioning equipment, systems, and furnaces.

Lighthouse for The Blind, Inc.
4245 Office Pkwy.
Dallas, TX 75204
(214) 821-2375
Personnel Director: John Taylor
Household items, including brooms and mops.

MCC Powers
1311 Regal Row
Dallas, TX 75247
(214) 631-5280
Contact: Personnel
Automatic temperature controls.

MPI, Inc.
1301 Cold Springs Rd.
Fort Worth, TX 76113
(817) 335-7676
Controller: Sandy McGowan
Carpet underlay.

Martin Sprocket & Gear, Inc.
3106 Sprocket Dr.
Arlington, TX 76015
(817) 465-6377
Personnel Manager: H. L. Pettis
Mechanical power transmission equipment and bulk materials handling equipment.

National Gypsum Co.
4500 Lincoln Plaza
Dallas, TX 75201
(214) 740-4500
Vice President of Human Resources: David Byrne
Building materials.

Otis Engineering Corp.
2601 Belt Line Rd.
Carrollton, TX 75006
(214) 323-3000
Personnel Manager: Kay McInnish
Valves and controls used in oil and gas, marine, and other major industries.

PVI Industries, Inc.
3209 Galvez St.
Fort Worth, TX 76111
Metro (817) 429-1313
Personnel Director: Sue Spradling
Commercial, institutional, and industrial water heaters and heat exchangers.

Pilot Audio
1411 Greenway Dr.
Irving, TX 75038
(214) 550-8050
Personnel Director: Nancy Knoble
Stereo systems.

Publishers Equipment Corp.
3230 Commander Dr.
Carrollton, TX 75006
(214) 931-2312
Marketing Vice President: George Derby
Newspaper printing presses.

Redman Industries
2550 Walnut Hill Ln., Suite 200
Dallas, TX 75229
(214) 353-3600
Personnel Manager: Fred Slarik
Mobile homes.

Reed Mining Tools
1600 S. Great Southwest Pkwy.
Grand Prairie, TX 75051
(214) 988-3322
Personnel Director: Pat Morris
Rock drilling bits.

Republic Gypsum
3625 Miller Park Dr.
Garland, TX 75042
(214) 272-0441
Personnel Director: Jack Weis
Gypsum wallboard and paperboard.

Rochester Gauges, Inc. of Texas
11616 Harry Hines Blvd.
Dallas, TX 75229
(214) 241-2161
Personnel Director: Sam Sims
Industrial gauges.

Samsill Corporation
4301 Mansfield Hwy.
Fort Worth, TX 76119
(817) 536-1906
Personnel Director: Bill Longley
Vinyl office products.

Sargent-Sowell, Inc.
1185 108th St.
Grand Prairie, TX 75050
(214) 647-1525
Personnel Director: C. M. Wrotenbery
Street signs.

Shoreline Products, Inc.
921 W. Mayfield Rd.
Arlington, TX 76015
(817) 465-1351
Contact: Gwen Wright
Boat trailers and other pleasure trailers.

Snapper Power Equipment
5000 South Frwy.
Fort Worth, TX 76115
(817) 921-3611
Personnel: Sherrye Owen
Garden and lawn equipment.

Snow Corp.
3817 Rutledge St.
Fort Worth, TX 76107
(817) 732-5554
Personnel Director: Mae Belle Patterson
Plastic process machinery and molded plastic products.

Snyder General Corp.
2001 Ross Ave., Suite 3620
Dallas, TX 75201
(214) 979-3100
Personnel Department: Judy Wiegand
Heating and air-conditioning equipment.

Southwestern Petroleum Corp.
534 N. Main St.
Fort Worth, TX 76101
(817) 332-2336
Personnel Director: Margaret Castillo
Building products, roofing materials, and motor oils.

T.I.C. United Corp.
4645 N. Central Expwy.
Dallas, TX 75205
(214) 559-0580
Personnel Director: Harold Hatley
Farm machinery and equipment.

Telsco Industries
3301 W. Kingsley Rd.
Garland, TX 75041
(214) 278-6131
Contact: Department Head
Lawn sprinklers.

Temtex Industries, Inc.
1601 LBJ Frwy., Suite 605
Dallas, TX 75234
(214) 484-1845
Contact: Personnel
Fireplaces.

Texas Industries
715 Ave. H East
Arlington, TX 76010
(817) 640-1701
Personnel Director: Tom Bryan
Cement, concrete products, and related materials.

Texstar Plastics
802 Ave. J East
Grand Prairie, TX 75050
(214) 647-1366
Personnel Administrator: Debbie Vickers
Plastic molders and fabricators.

Trane Co.
2331 W. Northwest Hwy.
Dallas, TX 75220
(214) 358-4301
Accounting Manager: Jim Hartgraves
Air-conditioning equipment for buildings, buses, trucks, and mass transit vehicles.

Triangle Pacific Corp.
16803 Dallas Pkwy.
Dallas, TX 75248
(214) 931-3000
Personnel Director: Sue Kearins
Cabinet and hardwood floors.

Tyler Corp.
3200 San Jacinto Tower
Dallas, TX 75201
(214) 754-7800
Personnel Director: Eddie Holmes
Pipe fittings and explosives.

Universal Manufacturing Co.
900 S. Cedar Ridge Rd.
Duncanville, TX 75137
(214) 298-0531
Office Manager: Donna Smith
Steel enclosures for electrical wiring.

Weben Jarco
4007 Platinum Way
Dallas, TX 75237
(214) 637-0530
Personnel Manager: Susan Privitt
Commercial water heaters, water conditioners, car wash equipment, conveyor systems, and steel tanks.

York Air Conditioning, Inc.
13592 Stemmons Frwy.
Dallas, TX 75234
(214) 241-3694
Branch Manager: Marshall Harris
Air conditioners, refrigeration, and gas compression systems.

▶Media: newspapers and magazines

To help you learn more about the **newspaper and magazine** publishing business, check out the following professional organizations listed in Chapter 5:

American Society of Magazine Photographers
Dallas/Fort Worth Association of Black Communicators
Dallas Professional Photographers Association
Network of Hispanic Communicators
Newspaper Advertising Sales Association
Press Club of Dallas
Society of Professional Journalists, Sigma Delta Chi
Women in Communications

For additional information, you can write:

American Newspaper Publishers Association
11600 Sunrise Valley Dr.
Reston, VA 22091

Audit Bureau of Circulations
900 Meacham Rd.
Schaumburg, IL 60195

Magazine Publishers Association
575 Lexington Ave.
New York, NY 10022

Trade Publications:
Editor and Publisher
Folio
Writer's Digest
The Columbia Journalism Review

Directories:
Editor and Publisher International Yearbook (Editor and Publisher, New York, NY)
Finderbinder Media Directory (Liz Oliphant & Associates, Dallas)
Magazine Industry Market Place (R. R. Bowker, Inc., New York, NY)
Metroplex Mediaguide (Bob Lawler Public Relations, Dallas)

Adweek-Southwest
2909 Cole Ave., Suite 115
Dallas, TX 75204
(214) 871-9550
Editor: Barbara Johnson
Weekly trade publication for the advertising and marketing industry.

Arlington Citizen-Journal
1111 W. Abram St.
Arlington, TX 76010
Metro (817) 261-1191
Editor: Sharon Cox
Community newspaper published twice weekly.

Associated Press
Southland Center, Suite 2100
Dallas, TX 75201
(214) 220-2022
Assistant Chief of Bureau: Kristin Gazlay
Wire service.

Baptist Standard
2343 Lone Star Dr.
Dallas, TX 75212
(214) 630-4571
Business Manager: John Welch
Weekly religious publication.

Buddy Magazine
P.O. Box 8366
Dallas, TX 75205
(214) 826-8742
Publisher: Stoney Burns
Monthly music magazine.

Carrollton Chronicle
1712 Belt Line Rd.
Carrollton, TX 75006
(214) 446-0303
Editor: Kevin Murphy
Newspaper published three times a week.

The Colony Courier
5201 S. Colony Blvd., Suite 695
The Colony, TX 75056
(214) 370-1529
Publisher: Jack Blalock
Weekly newspaper.

D Magazine
3988 N. Central Expwy., Suite 1200
Dallas, TX 75204
(214) 827-5000
Editor: Ruth Miller Fitzgibbons
Monthly general interest magazine.

D/FW People-Airport Newspaper
201-A Martha St.
Euless, TX 76040
Metro (817) 540-4666
Editor: Darrell Day

Dallas Cowboys Weekly
6116 N. Central Expwy.
Dallas, TX 75206
(214) 369-8000
Publisher: Russ Russell
Dallas Cowboys sports publication.

Dallas Downtown News
3600 Commerce St., Suite B
Dallas, TX 75226
(214) 826-7661
Publisher: Bronson Havard
Weekly newspaper for the central business district and surrounding area.

Dallas-Fort Worth Business Journal
12200 Park Central Dr., Suite 470
Dallas, TX 75251
Metro (214) 263-0449
Editor: Darrell Mack
Weekly business newspaper.

Dallas-Fort Worth Home & Garden
2930 Turtle Creek Plaza, Suite 114
Dallas, TX 75219
(214) 522-1320
Editor: Karen Muncy
Monthly magazine that features area homes, gardens, food, and entertaining.

Dallas/Fort Worth Living
5757 Alpha Rd., Suite 400
Dallas, TX 75240
(214) 239-2399
Editor: Karen Colbert
Bimonthly publication with articles about real estate and entertainment.

Dallas/Fort Worth Suburban Newspapers
1000 Ave. H East
Arlington, TX 76001
Metro (817) 640-0146
Contact: General manager of individual newspapers.
Chain of community newspapers owned by the Belo Corporation that publishes Arlington Daily News, Garland Daily News, Grand Prairie Daily News, Irving Daily News, Mesquite Daily News, Mid-Cities Daily News, and Richardson Daily News.

Dallas Magazine
Dallas Chamber of Commerce
1507 Pacific Ave.
Dallas, TX 75201
(214) 954-1390
Managing Editor: Jeff Hampton
The Dallas Chamber of Commerce's monthly magazine.

The Dallas Morning News
Communications Center
Dallas, TX 75265
(214) 745-8222
Personnel Manager: Mel Kinch
Major daily newspaper with a morning edition.

Dallas Observer
4216 Herschel Ave.
Dallas, TX 75219
(214) 521-9450
Publisher: Ken Kirk
Weekly entertainment and features publication.

Dallas Times Herald
1101 Pacific Ave.
Dallas, TX 75202
(214) 744-6111
Human Resources Director: John Thomas
Major daily newspaper with morning and afternoon editions.

Dallas Weekly
3101 Martin Luther King Jr. Blvd.
Dallas, TX 75215
(214) 428-8958
General Managing Editor: Charles Jackson

El Sol De Texas
4255 LBJ Frwy., Suite 105
Dallas, TX 75234
Metro (214) 263-3645
Personnel Manager: Emmy Silva
Weekly Spanish-language newspaper with news about Dallas, Fort Worth, and Latin countries.

Farmers Branch Times
1712 Belt Line Rd.
Carrollton, TX 75006
(214) 446-0303
Executive Editor: Roger Cramer
Newspaper published three times a week.

Fort Worth Magazine
Fort Worth Chamber of Commerce
700 Throckmorton St.
Fort Worth, TX 76102
(817) 336-2491
Executive Editor: Barbara Winkle
The Fort Worth Chamber of Commerce's monthly magazine.

Fort Worth News-Tribune
212 S. Main St.
Fort Worth, TX 76104
(817) 338-1055
Editor: Linda Pavlik
Weekly Fort Worth business and government publication.

Fort Worth Star-Telegram
400 W. 7th St.
Fort Worth, TX 76102
Metro (817) 429-2655
Personnel Manager: Jim Mason
Fort Worth's major daily newspaper.

Grapevine Sun
322 S. Main St.
Grapevine, TX 76051
(817) 488-8561
Managing Editor: Les Cockrell
Newspaper published twice weekly.

Lancaster News
Towne Square
Lancaster, TX 75146
(214) 277-6033
Editor: Jamie Graham
Weekly newspaper.

Las Colinas Now
5215 N. O'Connor Blvd.
Las Colinas Urban Center
Irving, TX 75261
(214) 556-3750
Editor and Publisher: Roger Pendleton
Monthly business and lifestyle magazine about Las Colinas.

Lewisville Daily Leader
591 W. Main St.
Lewisville, TX 75067
(214) 436-3566
Editor: Wayne Epperson
Newspaper published five times a week.

Lewisville News
131 W. Main St.
Lewisville, TX 75067
(214) 436-5551
Editor: Charley Wilson
Newspaper published three times a week.

Metrocrest News
1430 Valwood Pkwy., Suite 125
Carrollton, TX 75006
(214) 243-0194
Editor: Sue Forney
Weekly newspaper.

Oak Cliff Advertiser
126 W. West Cliff Mall
Dallas, TX 75224
(214) 339-3111
Editor: Don Gililland
Weekly newspaper for Oak Cliff and surrounding areas.

Oak Lawn Today
2429 Reagan St., Suite 201
Dallas, TX 75219
(214) 528-4954
Publisher: Ed Frick
Weekly newspaper.

Oil & Gas Journal
4849 Greenville Ave., Suite 318
Dallas, TX 75206
(214) 739-3338
Managing Editor: Gene Kinney
Monthly magazine for the petroleum industry.

Park Cities News
6060 N. Central Expwy., Suite 134
Dallas, TX 75206
(214) 369-7570
Publisher: Marjorie Waters
Weekly newspaper.

Park Cities People
230 Expressway Tower
Dallas, TX 75206
(214) 739-2244
Publisher: Reid Slaughter
Weekly newspaper.

Performance
1020 Currie St.
Fort Worth, TX 76107
(817) 338-9444
Editor: Louis Marroquin
Weekly international touring talent magazine.

Plano Daily Star Courier
1301 19th St.
Plano, TX 75074
(214) 424-6565
Editor: Louis Moore
Newspaper published six days a week.

Texas Business
5757 Alpha Rd., Suite 400
Dallas, TX 75240
(214) 239-4481
Personnel Manager: Doug Yoder
Monthly business magazine.

Texas Catholic
3915 Lemmon Ave.
Dallas, TX 75219
(214) 528-8792
Editor: Debbie Landregan
Weekly religious publication.

Texas Homes
3988 N. Central Expwy., Suite 1200
Dallas, TX 75204
(214) 827-5000
Managing Editor: Chris Caperton
Monthly magazine featuring homes, entertaining, wine, food, and collectibles.

Texas Jewish Post
11333 N. Central Expwy., Suite 213
Dallas, TX 75243
(214) 692-7283
Contact: Jimmy Wisch
Weekly religious publication.

Texas Woman's News
15790 Dooley Rd., Suite 101
Dallas, TX 75244
(214) 960-NEWS
Executive Editor: Lorraine Bruck
Monthly publication with news and features about women.

Travelhost Magazine
6116 N. Central Expwy., Suite 1020
Dallas, TX 75206
(214) 691-1163
Personnel: Frank Black
Weekly travel magazine.

United Press International
13900 Midway Rd.
Dallas, TX 75244
(214) 980-8300
Bureau Chief: Phil Magers
Wire service.

The Wall Street Journal
1233 Regal Row
Dallas, TX 75247
(214) 631-7250
Personnel Manager: Betty Pate
Publishing office for the Southwest edition of financial newspaper published Monday through Friday.

The White Rocker News
1350 N. Buckner Blvd.
Dallas, TX 75218
(214) 327-9335
Managing Editor: Retta Hanie
Weekly newspaper.

▶Metal products manufacturers

Major trade publications read by metal products manufacturers include:

Assembly Engineering
Design News
Iron Age
Iron Age Metals
Metal Working Digest

Directories:
Dallas Area Manufacturers Directory (Dallas Chamber of Commerce Business Development Group, Dallas, TX)

A.S.C. Pacific
404 E. Dallas Rd.
Grapevine, TX 76051
(817) 481-3521
Personnel Manager: Bill Sawyer
Sheet metal work for metal buildings.

American Can Co.
2803 E. Abram St.
Arlington, TX 76010
(214) 351-3781
Acting Office Manager: Jim Dowlan
Packaging company that manufactures cans, tubes, bottles, and packaging material.

Anchor Crane & Hoist Service Co.
2020 E. Grauwyler Rd.
Irving, TX 75061
(214) 438-5100
Vice President: Marsha Sheridan
Manufactures overhead cranes and hoists.

Anchor Metals, Inc.
605 W. Hurst Blvd.
Hurst, TX 76053
(817) 268-1311
Personnel Manager: Jackie Wright
Manufactures steel towers and transmission poles.

Austin Steel Co., Inc.
1815 Coombs St.
Dallas, TX 75215
(214) 421-2141
Contact: Personnel
Steel fabricators.

Barker & Bratton Steel, Inc.
10733 Newkirk St.
Dallas, TX 75220
(214) 556-1951
Vice President of Finance: Marvin Davies
Steel fabricators.

Carnation Co. Can Division
1500 E. Broad St.
Mansfield, TX 76063
(817) 473-6123
Plant Manager: A. J. Stubenrauch
Manufactures metal containers.

Commercial Metals Co.
7800 Stemmons Frwy.
Dallas, TX 75247
(214) 631-4120
Corporate Personnel Director: Jesse Barnes
Secondary metals processing, steel manufacturing, and trading.

Cronus Industries
12700 Park Central Dr., Suite 300
Dallas, TX 75251
(214) 386-2900
Personnel Director: Wanda Wilkerson
Manufactures heat transfer equipment.

General Aluminum Corp.
1001 Crosby Rd.
Carrollton, TX 75006
(214) 242-5271
Personnel Manager: Yvonne Warren
Manufactures aluminum windows and sliding glass doors.

Glitsch, Inc.
4900 Singleton Blvd.
Dallas, TX 75212
(214) 631-3841
Vice President of Employee Relations: Ed McGee
Heavy metal fabricator that manufactures metal plates, petroleum refinery processing equipment, and pollution control devices.

G. H. Hensley Industries, Inc.
2108 Joe Field Rd.
Dallas, TX 75229
(214) 241-2321
Assistant to President: Alex Rivera
Steel foundry producing steel castings and construction equipment parts.

J&L Tank, Inc.
500 Randall St.
Rhome, TX 76078
(817) 430-1472
Personnel Director: Carl Lange
Manufactures transport tanks.

Keystone Consolidated Industries
4835 LBJ Frwy.
Dallas, TX 75234
(214) 458-0028
Personnel Director: Dorothy Olson
Manufactures wire products and locks.

Lone Star Technology
2200 W. Mockingbird Ln.
Dallas, TX 75235
(214) 352-3981
Personnel: Nancy Scott
Manufactures casing and tubing for oil and automobile industries.

M&M Manufacturing Co.
200 Adolph St.
Fort Worth, TX 76107
(817) 336-2311
Personnel Director: Fati Jones
Manufactures air-conditioning ducts and pipes and sheet metal products.

Martin Sprocket & Gear & Fairmount Tools
3600 McCart St.
Fort Worth, TX 76110
(817) 924-4255
Personnel Manager: Guy Young
Manufactures mechanical power transmission and bulk materials handling equipment.

Mesco Metal Buildings Corp.
Hwy. 114 and N. Kimball Rd.
Southlake, TX 76051
(817) 481-2501
Contact: Department Heads
Manufactures metal building systems.

Mosher Steel Co.
5101 Maple Ave.
Dallas, TX 75235
(214) 631-3311
Personnel Director: Debra Miller
Produces fabricated structural steel and steel platework.

Nasco Steel
1909 Northpark Dr.
Fort Worth, TX 76102
(817) 332-7063
President: Val Martin
Steel fabrication company.

North Texas Steel Co.
412 W. Bolt St.
Fort Worth, TX 76110
(817) 927-5333
Secretary/Treasurer: Don Wilson
Fabricated structural steel.

Prior Industries, Inc.
8330 Lovett Ave.
Dallas, TX 75227
(214) 388-2151
Personnel Director: Jewel Duckett
Manufactures axles for trailers and farm equipment.

RSR Corp.
1111 W. Mockingbird Ln.
Dallas, TX 75247
(214) 631-6070
Contact: Industrial Relations Department
Secondary lead smelter.

Skotty Aluminum Products Co.
2101 N. Union Bower Rd.
Irving, TX 75060
(214) 438-4787
Personnel Director: Georgia De La Torre
Manufactures aluminum windows.

Telsco Industries
3301 Kingsley Rd.
Garland, TX 75041
(214) 278-6131
Contact: Department Heads
Manufactures commercial and residential underground sprinkler systems.

Temtex Industries, Inc.
1601 LBJ Frwy., Suite 605
Dallas, TX 75234
(214) 484-1845
Contact: Gay Sherbert
Manufactures fabricated metal and structural clay products.

Texas Steel Co.
3901 Hemphill St.
Fort Worth, TX 76110
(817) 923-4611
Personnel Director: W. O. Pender
Manufactures steel castings for machinery parts.

Thornton Industries, Inc.
2700 W. Pafford St.
Fort Worth, TX 76109
(817) 926-3321
Contact: Personnel
Structural steel fabricators.

Trinity Industries, Inc.
2548 N. E. 28th St.
Fort Worth, TX 76111
(817) 625-4161
Personnel Director: Dewey Nance
Manufactures rail cars and structural steel products.

Trinity Industries, Inc.
3001 W. Pafford St.
Fort Worth, TX 76110
(817) 927-8421
Personnel Manager: Helga Sedler
Steel fabricators.

Trinity Valley Iron & Steel Co.
3400 Bryce Ave.
Fort Worth, TX 76107
(817) 738-1925
Personnel Director: Anna Johnson
Manufactures cast iron fittings.

Verson Allsteel Press Co.
8300 S. Central Expwy.
Dallas, TX 75215
(214) 371-1301
Personnel Director: Bill Shiplett
Manufactures metal-forming presses.

Museums and art galleries

To learn more about running **museums and art galleries** you can write to:

American Association of Museums
1055 Thomas Jefferson St., NW
Washington, DC 20007

American Federation of Arts
41 E. 65th St.
New York, NY 10021

Arts and Business Council
130 E. 40th St.
New York, NY 10016

National Assembly of Local Arts Agencies
1625 I St., NW, Suite 725 A
Washington, DC 20006

Professional Publications:
Art Direction
Art Forum
Art Material Trade News
Art World
Curator
Museum Magazine
Southwest Art

Directories:
Artsource Texas (Dallas Public Library)
Guide to Humanities Source in the Southwest (Neal-Schuman Publishers, New York, NY)
Texas Museum Directory (Texas Historical Commission, Austin, TX)

Biblical Arts Center
7500 Park Ln.
Dallas, TX 75225
(214) 691-4661
Director: Tom Gleason
Religious-theme exhibits, including Miracle at Pentacost.

Amon Carter Museum
3501 Camp Bowie Blvd.
Fort Worth, TX 76107
(817) 738-1933
Assistant to Business Manager: Kathy Goodale
Western art collection with special exhibits.

Dallas Aquarium
Fair Park
Dallas, TX 75226
(214) 670-8441
Contact: Personnel
Country's largest inland aquarium.

Dallas Fire Fighters Museum
3801 Parry Ave.
Dallas, TX 75226
(214) 821-1500
Contact: James Clay
Display of antique fire trucks and firefighting equipment in historic setting.

Dallas Museum of Art
1717 N. Harwood St.
Dallas, TX 75202
(214) 922-0220
Administration Director: Tom Libsay
Dallas' largest fine arts museum with Old Masters, modern, pre-Columbian, and American art.

Dallas Museum of Natural History
Fair Park
Dallas, TX 75226
(214) 670-8457
Contact: Personnel
Fossil, animal, and plant life of Texas.

Fort Worth Art Museum
1309 Montgomery St.
Fort Worth, TX 76107
(817) 738-9215
Director: E. A. Carmean, Jr.
Contemporary art museum with special exhibits.

Fort Worth Museum of Science & History
1501 Montgomery St.
Fort Worth, TX 76107
Metro (817) 654-1356
Executive Secretary: Jeanne Boyd
Hall of Texas history exhibit, planetarium, and Omni Theater.

Hall of State
Fair Park
Dallas, TX 75226
(214) 421-5136
Contact: Personnel
Permanent exhibit traces 400 years of Texas history.

Kimball Art Museum
3333 Camp Bowie Blvd.
Fort Worth, TX 76107
(817) 332-8451
Assistant to Director: Barbara White
Fort Worth's largest fine arts museum with extensive permanent collection and special exhibits.

Meadows Museum
Owen Fine Arts Center
SMU Campus
Dallas, TX 75275
(214) 692-2516
Director: Donald E. Knaub
Spanish drawings and prints.

Old City Park
1717 Gano St.
Dallas, TX 75215
(214) 421-5141
Dallas County Heritage Society Director: Dr. Tom Smith
Historical buildings, exhibits, and restaurant located in park near downtown Dallas.

Sid Richardson Collection of Western Art
309 Main St.
Fort Worth, TX 76102
(817) 332-6554
Director: Jan Brenneman
Western art and special exhibits.

Science Place
Fair Park
Dallas, TX 75226
(214) 428-8351
Business Officer: Marilyn Waters
Museum with permanent and special science and energy exhibits and planetarium shows.

Wax Museum of the Southwest
601 E. Safari Pkwy.
Grand Prairie, TX 75050
(214) 263-2391
Personnel Director: Bill Phillips
Some 200 life-size wax figures of famous Southwest people.

▶Oil and gas companies

To learn more about the **petroleum** industry and its related fields, check out the following professional organizations listed in Chapter 5:

American Association of Petroleum Landmen
American Petroleum Institute
Dallas Geographical Society
Desk & Derrick Club
Fort Worth Association of Petroleum Landmen
Society of Petroleum Engineers

For more information, you can write to:

American Gas Association
P.O. Box 1426
Vienna, VA 22180

Trade Publications:
Drilling-The Wellsite Publication
Energy Journal
Modern Plastics
National Petroleum News
Oil and Gas Digest
Oil and Gas Journal
Petroleum Engineer International
Petroleum Marketer
Pipeline & Gas Journal

Directories:
Directory of Producers and Drilling Contractors (Midwest Oil Register, Tulsa, OK)
Energy Job Finder (Mainstream Access, New York, NY)
Geophysical Directory (Geophysical Directory, Inc., Houston, TX)
Gulf Coast Oil Directory (Spearhead Publications, Houston, TX)

Mid-South Oil & Gas Directory (Mid-South Publishing Co., Shreveport, LA)
Modern Plastics encyclopedia issue (McGraw-Hill, New York, NY)
Oil and Gas Directory (Geophysical Directory, Inc., Houston, TX)
Oil Directory of Texas (R. W. Byram Co., Austin, TX)

American International Manufacturing Corp.
3300 N. Sylvania Ave.
Fort Worth, TX 76111
Metro (817) 429-6715
Personnel Director: Jack Kennedy
Manufactures oil field equipment.

American Quasar Petroleum Co.
500 Throckmorton St.
Fort Worth, TX 76102
(817) 335-4701
Personnel Administrator: Marsha Davee
Oil and gas exploration and production.

Arch Petroleum Co., Inc.
777 Taylor St., Suite 2A
Fort Worth, TX 76102
Metro (817) 429-0691
Contact: Department Head
Oil and gas exploration and production.

Atlantic Richfield Co.
1601 Bryan St.
Dallas, TX 75201
(214) 880-2500
Contact: Personnel
Oil and gas exploration and production.

Aztec Manufacturing Co.
400 N. Tarrant St.
Crowley, TX 76036
(817) 297-4361
Contact: Dana Perry
Manufactures oil tubing and processing drilling pipe.

Baruch-Foster Corp.
4925 Greenville Ave., Suite 1160
Dallas, TX 75206
(214) 368-5886
Office Manager: Becky Osborne
Oil and gas exploration and production.

Buffton Corporation
1415 InterFirst Tower, 801 Cherry St.
Fort Worth, TX 76102
(817) 332-4761
President: Robert McLean
Exploration and development of oil and gas. Manufactures plastic products and electrical harness and cables.

Caltex Petroleum Corp.
125 E. John W. Carpenter Frwy.
Irving, TX 75062
(214) 830-1000
Personnel: Helen Foy
Oil refining.

Cenergy Corp.
10210 N. Central Expwy., Suite 500
Dallas, TX 75231
(214) 692-3800
Personnel Administrator: Martha Huttash
Oil and gas exploration.

Champlin Petroleum Co.
801 Cherry St.
Fort Worth, TX 76102
(817) 877-6000
Personnel Director: Tom Buie
Diversified oil company.

Cimarron Corporation
2550 Lincoln Plaza
500 N. Akard St.
Dallas, TX 75201
(214) 740-2800
Contact: Pam Ridgell
Oil and gas exploration and production.

Claiborne Gasoline
InterFirst One, Suite 4500
1401 Elm St.
Dallas, TX 75202
(214) 741-4128
Controller: Larry Wallace
Refinery.

Dallas Oil & Mineral
1701 River Run, Suite 409
Fort Worth, TX 76107
(817) 870-2601
Contact: Personnel
Oil and gas exploration and production.

Diamond Shamrock Corp.
717 N. Harwood St.
Dallas, TX 75201
(214) 922-2000
Contact: Human Resources Department
Headquarters for diversified international energy corporation with five plants located in Texas.

Dresser Industries, Inc.
1600 Pacific Ave.
Dallas, TX 75201
(214) 740-6000
Personnel Manager: Marcy Schutt
Supplies technology, products, and services used by energy-related industries in the development of petroleum, natural gas, and coal.

ESI Industries, Inc.
6440 N. Central Expwy., Suite 200
Dallas, TX 75206
(214) 361-6663
Office Manager: Priss Boozer
Diversified holding company. ESI and Tidelands Geophysical Company conduct land-based geophysical surveys for the oil and gas industry.

Endevco, Inc.
8080 N. Central Expwy., Suite 1200
Dallas, TX 75206
(214) 691-5536
Personnel Manager: Carol Gardner
Energy development company.

Energy Resources Corp.
4849 Greenville Ave., Suite 1550
Dallas, TX 75206
(214) 987-2800
Contact: Personnel
Explores, develops, and produces oil and gas.

ENSERCH Corp.
300 S. St. Paul St.
Dallas, TX 75201
(214) 651-8700
Personnel Recruiters: Jim Beard, Pam Hixson
Petroleum exploration and production; natural gas transmission and distribution; engineering and construction, and oil field services.

Fina Oil & Chemical Co.
8350 N. Central Expwy., Suite 1660
Dallas, TX 75206
(214) 750-2930
Employment Manager: Paula Green
Oil and gas company.

GNC Energy Corporation
Plaza of the Americas, 2320 South Tower
Dallas, TX 75201
Office Manager: Clarice Taylor
Exploration surveys and geophysical services.

Gearhart Industries, Inc.
1100 Everman
Fort Worth, TX 76140
(817) 293-1300
Personnel Director: Ben Byrd
Manufactures oil field service equipment.

Halliburton Co.
3600 Lincoln Plaza
Dallas, TX 75201
(214) 978-2600
Director of Employee Benefits: Hayden Hankins
Headquarters for one of the world's largest and most diversified oil field services, and engineering and construction organizations. Also has casualty and life insurance companies.

Harbison-Fischer Manufacturing Co.
901 N. Crowley Rd.
Fort Worth, TX 76036
(817) 297-2211
Personnel Director: Leon Gregory
Manufactures oil field equipment, subsurface oil well pumps, and pumping equipment.

Henry Energy
1170 W. Corporate Dr., Suite 108
Arlington, TX 76006
(817) 640-8441
Administrative Assistant: Theresa Tucker
Oil and gas exploration.

Holly Corporation
2600 Diamond Shamrock Bldg.
717 N. Harwood St.
Dallas, TX 75201
(214) 979-0210
Contact: Andrea Raines
Refining and marketing of petroleum products.

Hunt Energy Corp.
1601 Elm St.
Dallas, TX 75201-4781
(214) 880-8400
Personnel Director: Bill Heidelberg
Oil and gas production.

Hunt Oil Co.
2900 InterFirst Bank Building
Dallas, TX 75202
(214) 744-7020
Personnel Director: Mike Watts
Oil and gas production, real estate, and agribusiness.

ICO, Inc.
6000 Western Place, Suite 120
Fort Worth, TX 76107
Metro (817) 429-9005
Vice President: Steve Houk
Services oil field equipment.

Intramerican Oil & Minerals
12221 Merit Dr., Suite 960
Dallas, TX 75251
(214) 934-0147
Treasurer: David Speer
Oil and gas production.

Jefferson Williams Energy Corp.
4001 Airport Frwy., Suite 580
Bedford, TX 76021
(214) 233-2792
President: Bob Jefferson
Oil and gas production.

Kendavis Industries International, Inc.
106 W. 6th St.
Fort Worth, TX 76102
(817) 335-6748
Personnel Assistant: Martha Richards
Provides support services to oil companies.

Knox Oil of Texas
4835 LBJ Frwy., Suite 800
Dallas, TX 75244
(214) 960-9663
Controller: Keith Hurd
Wholesale and retail petroleum production.

Lear Petroleum Corp.
One Energy Square, Suite 950
Dallas, TX 75206
(214) 363-6085
Human Resources Director: Michael Stewart
Oil and gas transmission.

May Petroleum Co.
5400 LBJ Frwy., Suite 800
Dallas, TX 75240
(214) 934-9600
Administrative Assistant: Barbara Cook
Exploration, production, and contract drilling.

Maynard Oil Co.
8080 N. Central Expwy., Suite 660
Dallas, TX 75206
(214) 891-8880
Vice President of Administration: Stephen Hoffner
Exploration, development, and production of oil and natural gas.

Meridian Oil Co.
801 Cherry St.
Fort Worth, TX 76102
(817) 390-9200
Placement Coordinator: Linda Harris
Oil and gas exploration and production.

Mobil Oil Corp.
1201 Main St.
Dallas, TX 75250
(214) 658-2933
Employee Relations Manager: Ed Griggs
Petroleum refining and distribution.

Moncrief Oil Co.
Ninth at Commerce
Fort Worth, TX 76102
(817) 336-7232
Contact: Department Head
Oil and gas production.

OKC Limited Partnership
4835 LBJ Frwy.
Dallas, TX 75244
(214) 233-7100
Contact: Charles Redwine
Oil and gas production.

Peerless Manufacturing Co.
2819 Walnut Hill Ln.
Dallas, TX 75229
(214) 357-6181
Personnel Director: Jennifer Wisdom
Manufactures products for oil and gas industry.

Pengo Industries
1400 Everman Rd.
Fort Worth, TX 76140
Metro (817) 572-3389
Personnel: James E. Robertson
Oil well servicing.

Penrod Drilling Co.
2200 Thanksgiving Tower
Dallas, TX 75201
(214) 880-1700
Human Resources Director: Louis Mullenix
Oil and gas driller.

Sabine Corp.
LTV Center, Suite 1000
2001 Ross Ave.
Dallas, TX 75201
(214) 979-6900
Personnel Director: Cindy Grimshaw
Exploration, development, production, and acquisition of crude oil, natural gas, and other natural resources.

Saxon Oil Co.
717 N. Harwood St.
Dallas, TX 75201
(214) 745-1300
Personnel Director: Dave Jackson
Oil and gas exploration and development.

SEDCO Forex, Inc.
1601 Munger St.
Dallas, TX 75202
(214) 720-8700
Accepts mail inquiries only.
Personnel Director: L. J. Altobell
Offshore oil drilling company.

Shanley Oil Co.
2305 Cedar Springs Rd.
Dallas, TX 75201
(214) 871-2207
Contact: Department Head
Oil and gas exploration, development, and production.

Snyder Oil Co.
2500 InterFirst Tower
Fort Worth, TX 76102
(817) 338-4043
Office Manager: Bonnie Serben
Oil and gas exploration and production.

Southern Union Co.
1201 Elm St.
Dallas, TX 75270
(214) 748-8511
Contact: Paul Zeis
Headquarters for diversified energy company that through its subsidiaries distributes and sells natural gas in Texas, New Mexico, Oklahoma, and Arizona.

Statex Petroleum, Inc.
300 E. Carpenter Frwy., Suite 1100
Irving, TX 75062
(214) 257-1771
Office Manager: Tom Covalt
Oil and gas exploration and production.

Summit Energy, Inc.
1925 Mercantile Dallas Bldg.
Dallas, TX 75201
(214) 748-0221
Office Manager: Bevely Ford
Oil and gas exploration and production.

Sunbelt Exploration
601 Fort Worth Club Bldg.
Fort Worth, TX 76102
(817) 335-3163
Contact: Margie Cullum
Oil and gas exploration and production.

Sunshine Mining Co.
500 Plaza of the Americas South Tower
600 Pearl St.
Dallas, TX 75201
(214) 979-0405
Assistant Secretary: Mary Belmeyer
Silver mining and exploration of oil and gas.

Searching for your first job out of college

Landing that first job out of school is a frightening prospect for many. But there are ways to prepare for the entry into the work world.

We asked directors of college and university career centers what's the best advice they would give someone who is starting to look for their first job after graduation. Here are their replies:

Dr. B. B. Robinson, Bishop College Dean of Student Services: "Be sure to make a good assessment of yourself and your abilities. Be prepared to present yourself in a positive manner during job interviews and indicate your willingness to be flexible and expand your horizons. That's important in today's changing job market."

Suzanne M. Fields, TCJC Northeast's Director of Counseling and Testing Services: "Try to get work experience while you're in college. If you wait until you get out, you're already behind. Don't worry about low pay because the experience will more than make up for the difference. Later on you will get back what you didn't receive in pay in terms of the extra boost to your career. Work experience also helps you know if you want to enter a field before you waste time. Also be sure to get as much experience in writing and English as you can. I have applications from Ph.D.'s who can't write or communicate effectively."

Dr. Don Hankins, TCJC South Campus Director of Counseling and Testing: "One of the most important things is to work on communications skills. People who present themselves well do better in getting a job, and once they get out, they get ahead faster than others."

Dr. Warren Robb, UTA Director of Counseling, Testing, and Career Placement Office, offers one word of advice—"Research."

Dr. Diana Ilami, University of Texas at Dallas Coordinator of Career Service: "Many people approach the job hunt backwards. How can you market yourself and write a resume when you aren't sure about what you really want to do? It's important to go through an evaluation and then begin early in the job search. Undergraduates should start at the beginning of their senior year. Then persevere because it's a tough job market now."

Jackie Tulloch, Brookhaven Director of Counseling: "A lot of people will change jobs many times over a lifetime. It's important for people to learn the process of self-examination, the process of being successful in job interviews, and how to get information about a company, so that in the future, job-hunters can call up these skills when they need them."

Judy Brewster, Eastfield Community College Coordinator of Career Placement: "To be prepared, learn how to get a job. Many people don't know about resume-writing and interviewing techniques. They are unaware of how college centers can help them get free help."

Ron Randall, TCU Director of Career Planning and Placement: "Self-assessment is important to determine your likes, dislikes, and skills. Determine what you want as opposed to what you think others might want for you. Additionally, it's important to explore the marketplace with persistance and realistic goal-setting."

Terry Kepler, Director of SMU's Career Center: "I remember what an alumnus once said: The key to getting a good job involves the 3 P's—preparation, professional stance, and persistance. Many graduates and alumni start too late. Allow two months or more for the search."■

Teledyne Geotech
3401 Shiloh Rd.
Garland, TX 75041
(214) 271-2561
Industrial Relations Manager: Ernest Stephens
Manufactures scientific equipment for oil and gas, seismology, and meteorology industries.

Teledyne Merla
300 Kirby St.
Garland, TX 75042
(214) 276-8561
Personnel Manager: Bill Stockl
Designs, manufactures, and services oil and gas production equipment for the petroleum industry.

Texas Oil & Gas Corp.
1700 Pacific Ave.
Dallas, TX 75201
(214) 954-2000
Personnel: Andy Garza
Headquarters for drilling company that produces and sells crude oil and natural gas from properties.

Triton Energy Corporation
1400 One Energy Square
Dallas, TX 75206
(214) 691-5200
Human Resources Director: Linda Smith
Oil, gas, and coal exploration and production.

United LP Gas Co.
2435 N. Central Expwy., Suite 950
Dallas, TX 75080
(214) 783-6550
Contact: Doris Wilson
Liquid and petroleum product marketing.

Universal Resources Corp.
5400 Valley View Trail
Dallas, TX 75380
(214) 661-3876
Contact: Department Head
Oil and gas exploration and production company.

Varel Manufacturing Co.
9230 Denton Dr.
Dallas, TX 75235
(214) 351-6487
Personnel Director: Donna Trotman
Manufactures mining and oil well drilling bits and equipment and tungsten carbide products.

Western Co. of North America
6000 Western Place
Fort Worth, TX 76107
(817) 731-5100
Personnel: Vince Whelan
Provides technical services for discovery and production of oil and gas, including off-shore drilling.

Whitehall Corp.
2659 Nova Dr.
Dallas, TX 75229
(214) 247-8747
Personnel: Wayne Fisher
Oil and gas exploration and production.

Woodbine Petroleum, Inc.
2130 Lincoln Plaza
Dallas, TX 75201
(214) 954-3080
Office Manager: Cricket Livengood
Oil and gas exploration and production.

▶Paper and allied products

For more information about the **paper industry,** you can write to:

American Paper Institute
260 Madison Ave.
New York, NY 10016

Paper Industry Management Association
2400 E. Oakton St.
Arlington Hts., IL 60005

Technical Association of the Pulp and Paper Industry
Technology Park, Box 105113
Atlanta, GA 30348

Trade Publications:
Fibre Market News
Paper Age
Paper Sales
Paper Trade Journal
Pima Magazine
Publications
Pulp and Paper

Directories:
Lockwood's Directory of the Paper and Allied Trades (Vance Publishing Co., New York, NY)
Paper Yearbook (Harcourt Brace Jovanovich, New York, NY)

American Excelsior Co.
900 Ave. H East
Arlington, TX 76011
(817) 640-2161
Branch Manager: John Tengvall
Manufactures protective shipping pads, fabricated polyurethane foam, and related products.

Arrow Industries
2625 Belt Line Rd.
Carrollton, TX 75006
(214) 242-0525
Personnel Director: David Swanson
Manufactures paper plates and packaged dry food products.

Bags, Inc.
3312 Garden Brook Dr.
Dallas, TX 75234
(214) 247-2914
Personnel Director: Vivian LaFayette
Manufactures roll stock, bags, tubing, military and export packaging.

Bates Container, Inc.
6433 Davis Blvd.
Fort Worth, TX 76180
(817) 498-3200
Personnel: Sally Hackfeld
Manufactures corrugated board.

Clampitt Paper Co.
2101 Franklin Dr.
Fort Worth, TX 76106
(817) 625-1695
Personnel Director: Eddie Crippin
Paper distribution company.

Contact Products, Inc.
9244 Markville Dr.
Dallas, TX 75243
(214) 231-6367
Employee Relations Manager: Jean McAllister
Manufactures pressure-sensitive labels.

Container Corp. of America
925 Ave. H East
Arlington, TX 76011
(817) 649-3341
Plant Manager: Bill Gensler
World's largest producer of paperboard packaging, including folding cartons, sanitary food containers, and sales promotional products. Fort Worth branch also.

Dairy Pak Division
1901 Windsor Place
Fort Worth, TX 76110
(817) 926-6661
Personnel Manager: Joanne Coffman
Manufactures milk cartons.

Dixico, Inc.
1415 S. Vernon Ave.
Dallas, TX 75224
(214) 943-7521
Personnel Director: Christine Hunt
Manufactures snack food packaging.

Herlitz, Inc.
3000 W. Kingsley Rd.
Garland, TX 75041
(214) 840-3594
Personnel Manager: Anita Wilkerson
A division of Herlitz AG West Germany that manufactures stationery, art paper, index cards, envelopes, and specialty items.

Kimberly-Clark Corporation
545 E. John W. Carpenter Frwy.
Irving, TX 75062
(214) 830-1483
Vice President of Human Resources: Wayne Sanders
World headquarters for producers of household, personal care, business, and health care paper products.

Olmsted-Kirk Paper Co., Inc.
2420 Butler St.
Dallas, TX 75235
(214) 637-2220
Personnel Director: Tom Harmon
Wholesale paper distributor for specialty products and industrial papers. Operates graphic art and retail centers. Branch office in Fort Worth.

Packaging Corp. of America
1001 113th St.
Arlington, TX 76011
Metro (817) 640-1888
Contact: Chris Thomas
Manufactures corrugated containers.

Princeton Packaging, Inc.
1010 Alma St.
Dallas, TX 75215
(214) 421-4161
Personnel Manager: John Bell
Manufactures food packaging products.

Rock-Tenn Co., Inc.
1100 E. Clarendon Dr.
Dallas, TX 75203
(214) 941-3400
Personnel Manager: Kent Sutherland
Manufactures paperboard and paperboard packing products.

Stone Container Corp.
2302 W. Marshall Dr.
Grand Prairie, TX 75051
(214) 647-1333
General Manager: Don Bogdanovich
Manufactures corrugated boxes.

Sweetheart Products Group
4444 W. Ledbetter Dr.
Dallas, TX 75236
(214) 339-3131
Personnel Director: Tom Pinto
National manufacturer and distributor of paper cups, plastic lids, and drinking straws.

Westvaco Corp.
10700 Harry Hines Blvd.
Dallas, TX 75220
(214) 352-9791
Contact: Personnel
Manufactures envelopes.

Willamette Industries, Inc.
1200 N. Carrier Pkwy.
Grand Prairie, TX 75050
(214) 647-1616
Office Manager: Tom Milton
Manufactures corrugated boxes.

▶Printers

To learn more about **printing** and related fields, check out the following professional organizations listed in Chapter 5:

Direct Marketing Association of North Texas
Printing Industries Association of Texas

For more information, you can write to:

National Association of Printers and Lithographers
780 Palisade Ave.
Teaneck, NJ 07666

Technical Association of the Graphic Arts
Box 3064
Federal Station
Rochester, NY 14614

Professional Publications:
American Printer
Graphic Arts Monthly
Printing News

Directories:
Directory of Typographic Services (National Composition Association, Arlington, VA)
Graphic Arts Green Book (A. F. Lewis & Co., Hinsdale, IL)
Printing Trades Blue Book (A. F. Lewis & Co., Hinsdale, IL)

Allied Printing Co.
501 N. Good-Latimer Expwy.
Dallas, TX 75204
(214) 827-5151
Owner: Roy Stein
Printing and publishing company.

American Standard Graphics
6320 Denton Dr.
Dallas, TX 75235
(214) 358-1371
Personnel Manager: Glenda Scully
Prints periodicals.

Anchor Press
820 N. Main St.
Fort Worth, TX 76106
(817) 335-4861
Personnel Manager: Richard Monzingo
Commercial printing.

Branch-Smith, Inc.
120 St. Louis Ave.
Fort Worth, TX 76104
(817) 332-6306
Personnel Manager: Charlie Hettinger
Advertising, printing, and publishing of trade magazines.

Buchanan Printing Co.
2330 Jett St.
Dallas, TX 75234
(214) 241-3311
Personnel Manager: Lynn Johnson
Commercial printing.

Deluxe Check Printers
9125 Viscount Row
Dallas, TX 75247
(214) 631-7780
Personnel Manager: Lisa Shinn
Check printing company.

Evans Press
5133 Northeast Pkwy.
Fort Worth, TX 76106
(817) 626-1901
Personnel Manager: Ronda Fuler
Prints catalogs.

Lehigh Press-Dallas
1515 Round Table Dr.
Dallas, TX 75247
(214) 631-3130
Personnel Coordinator: Judy Griffin
Prints catalogs.

Pandick Press Dallas
333 N. Stemmons Frwy.
Dallas, TX 75207
(214) 698-9777
Personnel Manager: Betty Guinn
Legal and financial printing.

Printing Center of Texas, Inc.
701 E. 5th St.
Fort Worth, TX 76102
(817) 429-2320
Personnel Manager: John Daniels
Newspapers, circulars, and books.

Riverside Press, Inc.
4901 Woodall St.
Dallas, TX 75247
(214) 631-1150
Personnel Department: Marie Burris
Commercial printing.

Texas Color, Inc.
4800 Spring Valley Rd.
Dallas, TX 75244
(214) 233-3400
Personnel Manager: David Hoogesteger
Offset printing.

VIP
2124 W. Marshall Dr.
Grand Prairie, TX 75051
(214) 647-8888
Personnel Manager: Sara Baxter
Commercial printing.

Williamson Printing Corp.
6700 Denton Dr.
Dallas, TX 75235
(214) 352-1122
Personnel Manager: Tony Lalumia
Commercial printing.

▶Real estate: development, brokerage, and finance

To learn more about **real estate** and related fields, check out the following professional organizations listed in Chapter 5:

Garland Board of Realtors
Grand Prairie Board of Realtors
Greater Dallas Board of Realtors
National Society of Real Estate Appraisers
Society of Industrial and Office Realtors
Women's Council of Realtors

For more information, you can write to:

National Association of Realtors
430 N. Michigan Ave.
Chicago, IL 60611

Trade Publications:
Journal of the American Real Estate & Urban Economics Association
The Real Estate Appraiser and Analyst
Real Estate Insider Newsletter
Real Estate News
Real Estate Review
Realty and Building
Southwest Real Estate News

Directories:
American Society of Real Estate Counselors Directory (ASREC, Chicago, IL)
Directory of Certified Residential Brokers (Retail National Marketing Institute, Chicago, IL)
Texas Association of Realtors Membership (Texas Association of Realtors, Austin, TX)

Who's Who in Creative Real Estate (Who's Who in Creative Real Estate, Inc., Glendale, CA)

Blackland Properties, Inc.
703 McKinney Ave.
Dallas, TX 75202
(214) 954-0099
Contact: Personnel

Bramalea Texas, Inc.
InterFirst Plaza, Suite 5000
Dallas, TX 75202
(214) 760-7070
Office Manager: Nancy Shelton

Cadillac-Fairview Urban Development Corp.
1901 Pacific Ave., Suite 400
Dallas, TX 75201
(214) 754-8700
Contact: Personnel

Centennial Homes, Inc.
5720 LBJ Frwy., Suite 610
Dallas, TX 75240
(214) 458-9909
Contact: Personnel

Centre Development Co., Inc.
4000 N. McEwen Rd.
Farmers Branch, TX 75234
(214) 980-8060
Personnel Director: Sandy Branick

Century 21 Real Estate of Northern Texas, Inc.
4500 Fuller Dr., Suite 401
Irving, TX 75062
(214) 258-0221
Administrative Manager: Billy Stimmel

Cityplace Development Corp.
4106 Office Pkwy.
Dallas, TX 75204
(214) 747-2489
Contact: Doug Thompson

Coldwell Banker
5400 LBJ Frwy., Suite 1100
Dallas, TX 75240
(214) 458-4800
Contact: Personnel

Criswell Development Co.
5080 Spectrum Dr., Suite 1200
Dallas, TX 75248
(214) 855-7000
Personnel Manager: Gilda Smith

Trammell Crow Co.
2001 Ross Ave., Suite 3200
Dallas, TX 75201
(214) 969-5100
Contact: Personnel

Cushman & Wakefield of Texas, Inc.
1201 Elm St., Suite 3711
Dallas, TX 75270
(214) 744-5007
Personnel: Nidia Zaitoon

Dal-Mac Development Corp.
111 W. Spring Valley Rd.
Richardson, TX 75081
(214) 238-0401
Personnel Manager: Angela Gideo

Hank Dickerson & Co.
16475 Dallas Pkwy., Suite 700
Dallas, TX 75248
(214) 931-0000
Secretary-Treasurer: Bill Roberts

ERA Real Estate, Inc.
Southwest Regional Headquarters
225 E. John W. Carpenter Frwy., Suite 535
Irving, TX 75062
(214) 556-0362
Contact: Office Managers of individual companies

Folsom Investments, Inc.
16475 Dallas Pkwy., Suite 800
Dallas, TX 75248
(214) 931-7400
Personnel: Marie Garrison

Fox & Jacobs, Inc.
2800 Surveyor Blvd.
Carrollton, TX 75006
(214) 245-8511
Contact: Personnel

▶ Location, location, location . . .

Bob Barrett is a partner in a Dallas firm that leases office space throughout the area. We talked with him recently about getting started in commercial real estate.

"Leasing commercial real estate in Dallas is a very tough business," says Barrett. "You don't make any money during your first year or two in the business. There's a very high attrition rate. But if you stick with it, you can make more money than your peers in other fields ever dreamed of. Six-figure incomes are not uncommon among people who have been in the business only five years.

"At our firm, we don't hire people right out of school; we look for people with some experience in the business world and in real estate. But many of the larger firms will hire recent grads and train them. In fact, some large firms have formal training programs. If you're a young person just starting out, I'd suggest getting a job with a bigger firm. Then be like a blotter—soak up everything they can teach you. After a few years, reevaluate your position with the company. The problem with the bigger firms is that they sometimes tend to ignore you once they've trained you. In a smaller firm, the senior people see more of a relationship between your success and the overall success of the company. Also, there's a lot of competition within a large firm. It's easy to get lost in the shuffle."

We asked Barrett what qualifications are needed to succeed in commercial real estate. "You have to be tough, because you'll face a certain amount of rejection. You have to be hungry, because this is an extremely competitive business. A college degree is helpful, but it isn't required. This business is basically sales—getting out and seeing people, convincing them that your skills and knowledge are up to snuff. When you're just starting out, it's also very important to have a mentor in the company—someone to help you and look out for you."■

GSC Development Corp.
520 Ave. H
Arlington, TX 76011
(817) 640-1660
Vice President: Gordan Rainey

Hall Real Estate Tree Line
10300 N. Central Expwy.
Dallas, TX 75231
(214) 363-1629
Contact: Personnel

Ebby Halliday Realtors
4455 Sigma Rd.
Dallas, TX 75234
(214) 980-6600
Personnel Director: Florence Willess

Hurd Development Co.
14881 Quorum Dr., Suite 500
Dallas, TX 75240
(214) 239-8196
Contact: Personnel

Kerr Development Co.
4514 Cole Ave., Suite 600
Dallas, TX 75205
(214) 969-0908
Contact: Personnel

Lehndorff Management USA Ltd., Inc.
2121 N. Akard St.
Dallas, TX 75201
(214) 658-0800
Personnel Manager: Linda Kamphaus

Lincoln Property Co.
3300 Lincoln Plaza
500 N. Akard St.
Dallas, TX 75201
(214) 740-3300
Personnel Manager: David McCoy

MBank Facilities, Inc.
1810 Commerce St., Suite 1100
Dallas, TX 75201
(214) 760-5229
President: John Cook

Merrill Lynch-Paula Stringer, Inc.
6730 LBJ Frwy., Suite 2240
Dallas, TX 75240
(214) 385-3600
Personnel Director: Jane Durbin

Henry S. Miller Real Estate Co.
2001 Bryan Tower, Suite 3000
Dallas, TX 75201
(214) 748-9171
Personnel Director: Linda Wissen

Murray Properties Co.
5520 LBJ Frwy.
Dallas, TX 75240
(214) 851-6600
Personnel Director: Martha Hartness

Raymond D. Nasher Co.
8950 N. Central Expwy., Suite 400
Dallas, TX 75231
(214) 369-1234
Personnel Director: Mary Mrozinski

Paragon Group
7557 Rambler Rd.
Dallas, TX 75231
(214) 696-8000
Contact: Personnel

Prism Development Corp.
3811 Turtle Creek Blvd., Suite 1950
Dallas, TX 75219-4419
(214) 760-6800
President: Bob Kaminski

Red Carpet Corp. of America
North Texas Service Center
2995 LBJ Frwy., Suite 101
Dallas, TX 75234
(214) 243-5151
Administrator/Trainer: Judy Drewry

Southern Union Co.
1201 Elm St., Suite 1800
Dallas, TX 75270
(214) 748-8511
Contact: Personnel

Southland Financial Corp.
4950 N. O'Connor Rd.
Irving, TX 75062
(214) 258-6166
Contact: Personnel

Southmark Corp.
1601 LBJ Frwy., Suite 800
Dallas, TX 75234
(214) 241-8787
Contact: Janice Townsend

Southwest Realty, Ltd.
7424 Greenville Ave.
Dallas, TX 75231
(214) 369-1995
Contact: Personnel

Sullivan Development Co., Inc.
8340 Meadow Rd., Suite 248
Dallas, TX 75231
(214) 987-3223
Contact: Mark Sullivan

The Thomes Corp.
4001 Airport Frwy., Suite 550
Bedford, TX 76021
(817) 540-1091
Contact: Personnel

Triland International
5400 LBJ Frwy.
Dallas, TX 75240
(214) 934-1234
Contact: Personnel

The Vantage Co.
2525 N. Stemmons Frwy., Suite 525
Dallas, TX 75207
(214) 631-0600
Personnel Director: Joe McFadden

Woodbine Development Corp.
3200 InterFirst One
Dallas, TX 75202
(214) 744-6000
Vice President of Finance: Don McDaniel

▶Restaurants

To learn more about the **restaurant industry** and related fields, check out the **Dallas Restaurant Association** listed in Chapter 5:

For more information you can write to:

Council on Hotel, Restaurant, and Institutional Education
Human Development Bldg.
University Park, PA 96802

National Restaurant Association
311 First St., NW
Washington, DC 20001

Trade Publications:
Beverage Media
Fast Service/Family Restaurant
Food and Beverage Marketing
Food and Wine
Food Industry Newsletter
Food Management
Foodservice Product News
Nation's Restaurant News
Restaurant Business
Signature Magazine

Directories:
Directory of Hotel and Restaurant Management Programs (Holiday Inn University, Olive Branch, MS)
Restaurant Hospitality—Hospitality 500 Issue (Penton/IPC, Inc., Cleveland, OH)
Restaurant and Institution—Annual 400 Issue (Cahners Publishing Co., Chicago, IL)

Bennigan's Tavern
6606 LBJ Frwy.
Dallas, TX 75240
(214) 960-5000
Personnel Director: Rob Harig

Bonanza International, Inc.
National Headquarters
8080 N. Central Expwy., 5th Fl.
Dallas, TX 75206-1666
(214) 891-8400
Personnel Director: Susan Schimek

Burger King Corp.
400 Chisolm Place, Suite 400
Plano, TX 75075
(214) 578-9575
Personnel Director: Phil Paustian

Casa Bonita
6250 LBJ Frwy.
Dallas, TX 75240
(214) 385-3300
Human Resource Director: Mike Porter

Chili's, Inc.
6820 LBJ Frwy., Suite 200
Dallas, TX 75240
(214) 980-9917
Human Resources Director: Janet Coen

Denny's Restaurant
Regional Office
850 Greenview Dr.
Grand Prairie, TX 75050
Metro (214) 988-1428
Personnel Director: Ken Agorichas

Domino's Pizza, Inc.
Regional Office
1 Galleria Tower
13355 Noel Rd., Suite 455
Dallas, TX 75240
(214) 392-4271
Personnel Coordinator: Debra Beard

El Chico Corp.
12200 Stemmons Frwy., Suite 100
Dallas, TX 75234
(214) 241-5500
Contact: Personnel

El Fenix
11075 Harry Hines Blvd.
Dallas, TX 75229
(214) 241-2171
Personnel Director: Tina Martinez

Grandy's
Corporate Office
997 Grandy's Ln.
Lewisville, TX 75229
(214) 221-3780
Personnel Director: Thomas Coch

International House of Pancakes
Southwest Regional Office
2540 Walnut Hill Ln., Suite 208
Dallas, TX 75229
(214) 956-7971
Regional Director: Lyman Bowe

Tips for younger workers

Younger workers who are looking for summer or after-school work face a common dilemma: How do you get a job when you haven't had much work experience?

Special employment programs assist youths in overcoming this problem. (See the list below.) In addition, college placement services are also good sources for job leads.

You'll often have better luck if you check with employers in the restaurant, hotel, recreation, and entertainment fields, which traditionally hire younger workers.

Six Flags Over Texas is the area's largest employer of youths. More than 2,200 seasonal staff members are hired to work full-time during the summer and on weekends during the spring and fall. The best time to apply is in January, when the theme park begins hiring for the new season. You can apply later in the year, too.

The secret is getting a jump on everyone else and not waiting until the last day of school to begin looking for a summer job. You want the odds to be in your favor, considering that applicants always outnumber the openings.

Special employment programs for youths include·

Employment and Training Program
Tarrant County
100 E. Weatherford
Fort Worth, TX 76196
(817) 334-1464
Several programs are available for youths from low-income families or those who are handicapped and live in Tarrant County outside of the Fort Worth city limits. The in-school program assists youths in finding after-school work. The summer program helps youths from the ages of 14 to 21 find work in the public and private sector. In the Try-Out program, participants receive training while the government pays a salary for a maximum of 250 hours of

work. The drop-out program prepares youths in a computerized learning center to take the GED exam.

Girls Club of Dallas, Inc.
5415 Maple Ave., Suite 222
Dallas, TX 75235
(214) 638-3641
Sponsors a year-round employment program for economically disadvantaged youths (male and female) between the ages of 16 and 21 who can work at least 35 hours a week. Participants receive a job orientation and take tests to determine skill levels. Classroom instruction is available to those who want to improve skills. Youths prepare for the job hunt by being videotaped in mock job interviews and then are given help in finding job openings. Extra assistance is provided, such as finding daycare facilities and transportation to job interviews.

Job Opportunities for Youths (JOY)
Call the Dallas Alliance of Business at (214) 528-6130 for the address and phone number of the office that is open only during the summer. Residents of Dallas County, ranging from 16-year-olds through college students in their mid-20s, are eligible for the service. Extra help is provided to individuals from disadvantaged neighborhoods, who can borrow clothes to wear to job interviews.

Summer Youth Employment Program
2601 Live Oak St.
Dallas, TX 75204
(214) 670-7343
Helps teenagers from the ages of 14 to 21 who live in the Dallas city limits. Call to find out when the office opens for the summer.

Texas Employment Commission

Check with any TEC offices in Tarrant or Dallas County. For information, call (817) 335-5111 or (214) 631-6050. Offers free assistance to anyone over the age of 16. Jobs are listed in the computerized job bank at TEC offices throughout the metro area. Part-time or full-time positions range from fast-food restaurant workers to camp counselors and life guards. The pay usually starts at minimum wage.

Try-Out Employment (year-round)

The Summer Youth Program (summer only)
Dallas County Department of Human Services
4917 Harry Hines Blvd.
Dallas, TX 75235
(214) 920-7843

Those who live in Dallas County but outside of the Dallas City limits are eligible for employment and training programs. A year-round program called Try-Out Employment helps place students from the ages of 16 to 21 in private-sector jobs, where they can work up to 20 hours per week. The Summer Youth Program places youths from the ages of 14 to 21 in public-sector jobs. Some combine remedial education and half-day work programs. Applicants can apply for these programs at the Department of Human Services field offices located in Garland, Grand Prairie, Irving, Mesquite, and Lancaster.■

Jack-In-The-Box Drive-Thru
Administrative Office
2711 LBJ Frwy., Suite 456
Dallas, TX 75234
(214) 247-8622
Personnel Director: Mary Dixon

Kentucky Fried Chicken
District Office
2845 W. Airport Frwy., Suite 144
Irving, TX 75062
(214) 570-1425
Personnel Director: Terry Stringer

Long John Silver's Seafood Shoppes
Regional Office
2964 LBJ Frwy., Suite 405
Dallas, TX 75234
(214) 247-9801
Personnel Director: Jane Rohrig

Mariano's Mexican Restaurants
1200 Executive Dr. East, Suite 129
Richardson, TX 75081
(214) 644-5287
Personnel Director: Wanda Martinez

McDonald's
Regional Office
511 E. John W. Carpenter Frwy., Suite 375
Dallas, TX 75062
(214) 869-1888
Personnel Manager: Dave Daniels

Pancho's Mexican Buffet, Inc.
3500 Noble St.
Fort Worth, TX 76111
(817) 831-0081
Personnel Director: David Dixon

Pizza Hut
Regional Personnel
14500 Trinity Blvd., Suite 118
Fort Worth, TX 76155
(817) 267-9274
Personnel: Maurice Ambler

Pizza Inn, Inc.
International Headquarters
2930 N. Stemmons Frwy.
Dallas, TX 75222
(214) 638-7250
Human Resources Department: Bob McComas

Pulido Associates
4924 Old Benbrook Rd.
Fort Worth, TX 76116
(817) 731-4241
Office Manager: Meri Lou Rendon

Prufrock Management Company, Inc.
2811 McKinney Ave.
Dallas, TX 75204
(214) 871-1985
Vice President of Human Resources: Sherry Snyder

Red Lobster Inns of America
Regional Office
1500 Norwood Dr., Bldg. C, Suite 300
Hurst, TX 76054
(817) 268-6895
Employment Manager: Al Spagnublo

S&A Restaurant Corp.
6606 LBJ Frwy.
Dallas, TX 75240
(214) 960-5000
Vice President of Human Resources: Levy Curry

Sandwich Chef
Corporate Office
4356 Spring Valley Rd.
Dallas, TX 75244
(214) 233-8287
Contact: Personnel

Sky Chefs
601 Ryan Plaza Dr., Bldg. B
Arlington, TX 76011
(214) 355-1776
Personnel Director: Pepe Pinto

Sybra, Inc.
701 E. Plano Pkwy., Suite 505
Plano, TX 75074
(214) 578-0560
Personnel Director: Saul Green

TGI Friday's, Inc.
14665 Midway Rd.
Dallas, TX 75380
(214) 450-5400
Personnel Director: Mike Waldron

Wendy's Old Fashioned Hamburgers, Inc.
1001 W. Euless Blvd., Suite 345
Euless, TX 76040
Metro (817) 540-0371
Area Human Resources Representative: Craig Widgreen

Whataburger Restaurants
Regional Office
305 Loop 820 NE, Suite 409
Hurst, TX 76053
(817) 284-1500
Personnel Director: Lorraine Hale

Wyatt Cafeterias
10726 Plano Rd.
Dallas, TX 75238
(214) 349-0060
Vice President of Personnel: Keith Morrow

▶Retailers and other merchandisers

To help you learn more about **merchandising,** check out the following professional organizations listed in Chapter 5:

Association of Executive Saleswomen
Dallas Business League
New Car Dealers of Metropolitan Dallas
Retail Marketing Professionals of Tarrant County
Sales and Marketing Executives of Fort Worth

For more information, you can write to:

General Merchandise Distributors Council
5250 Far Hills Ave.
Dayton, OH 45429

Manufacturers' Agents National Association
P.O. Box 16878
Irvine, CA 92713

National Association of Wholesaler Distributors
1725 K St., NW
Washington, DC 20006

National Retail Merchants Association
100 W. 31st St.
New York, NY 10036

Warehouse Distributors Association
P.O. Box 1128
Waukegan, IL 60085

Trade Publications:
American Import/Export Management
Catalog Showroom Business
Chain Store Age
College Store Executive
Fabricnews
Fashion Newsletter
Gift Digest
Greenhouse Manager
Home Furnishings Daily
Journal of Retailing
Merchandising
New York Apparel News
SAF–Society of American Florists
Store Planning
Stores
Women's Wear Daily

Directories:
Fairchild's Financial Manual of Retail Stores (Fairchild Books, New York, NY)
Nationwide Directory–Mass Market Merchandisers (Salesman's Guide, Inc., New York, NY)
Sheldon's Retail Directory of the U.S. and Canada (PS&M, Inc., New York, NY)

Ace Hardware Stores
Southwest Distribution Center
2257 Commerce Dr.
Arlington, TX 76011
(817) 649-5118
Contact: Personnel
Dealer-owned hardware cooperative.

Ambercrombie & Fitch
9100 N. Central Expwy.
Dallas, TX 75231
(214) 696-1116
Personnel Director: Jack Seligson
Retail sporting goods store.

Ted Arendale Ford
201 E. Division St.
Arlington, TX 76010
(817) 261-4261
Personnel Director: Ray Hanna
Automobile dealership.

Army Air Force Exchange Service
3911 S. Walton Walker Blvd.
Dallas, TX 75236
(214) 780-2345
Contact: Personnel
Headquarters for retail and food services located in army and air force bases throughout the world.

W. O. Bankston Ford
3333 Inwood Rd.
Dallas, TX 75235
(214) 358-8800
Personnel Director: Gayle Burrage
Automobile dealership.

Barber's Book Stores
215 W. 8th St.
Fort Worth, TX 76102
(817) 335-5469
Owner: Brian Perkins
Fort Worth's oldest bookstore.

Bedroom Shop
2012 W. Pioneer Pkwy.
Arlington, TX 76013
(214) 261-2244
Vice President of Sales: Stan McCants
Retailer of mattresses, box springs, and bedding accessories.

Best Products Company, Inc.
1102 West Frwy.
Grand Prairie, TX 75051
(214) 263-2731
Contact: Texas Employment Commission
Discount department store with seven area locations.

Bloomingdale's
13320 Montfort Dr.
Dallas, TX 75240
(214) 450-2212
Personnel Director: Lisa Shafran
Full-line specialty department store.

Bookstop, Inc.
5400 E. Mockingbird Ln.
Dallas, TX 75206
(214) 821-6520
Manager: Ned Bateman
Discount bookstore.

Henry Butts Oldsmobile-Isuzu
19800 N. Midway Rd.
Dallas, TX 75380
(214) 733-5400
Personnel Director: Mary Ann Butts
Automobile dealership.

Century Book Stores
3032 Mockingbird Ln.
Dallas, TX 75205
(214) 691-8157
Manager: David Whidmer
Retail books and magazines.

Century Chevrolet Co.
1201 W. 7th St.
Fort Worth, TX 76102
(817) 335-4611
Contact: Chris Hendrickson
Automobile dealership.

Cokesbury
6155 Samuel Blvd.
Dallas, TX 75228
(214) 328-8850
Manager: Paul Morales
Total service Christian bookstore.

Color Tile
3621 Marvin D. Love Frwy.
Dallas, TX 75224
(214) 371-2348
Manager: Ed Kuiper
Home improvement center with floor coverings, wallpaper, and paint.

Corrigan's Jewelers
4800 Hulen Mall
Fort Worth, TX 76132
(817) 572-1872
Manager: Mitch Lambert
Fine jewelry sold at 15 area stores.

B. Dalton Bookseller
1526 Main St.
Dallas, TX 75201
(214) 742-7232
Manager: Victoria Kemp
National chain of bookstores.

Don Davis Oldsmobile, Inc.
1901 N. Collins St.
Arlington, TX 76010
(817) 461-1000
Personnel Director: Renee Bortle
Automobile dealership.

Dillard's Department Stores
4501 N. Beach St.
Fort Worth, TX 76111
(817) 831-5111
Personnel Director: Melony Arnwine
Retail department store.

Dunlap Company
200 Greenleaf St.
Fort Worth, TX 76107
(817) 336-4985
Personnel Director: Vester Patterson
Retail department store.

Eagle Lincoln Mercury
6116 Lemmon Ave.
Dallas, TX 75209
(214) 357-0461
Personnel Director: Ellie Calt
Automobile dealership.

Eckerd Drugs
4409 Action St.
Garland, TX 75046
(214) 272-0411
Personnel Director: Bill Gilbreath
Large specialty store with pharmacy and photo finish services, cosmetics, drugs, and general merchandise.

Edison's Jewelers & Distributors
401 Throckmorton St.
Fort Worth, TX 76102
(817) 335-5503
Personnel Director: Laura McGee
Wholesale and retail jewelry and specialty items.

Federated Group
2161 Hutton Dr., Suite 200
Carrollton, TX 75006
(214) 788-2971
Personnel Director: Barbara Newland
Home electronic items.

Florsheim Shoe Shops
635 NorthPark Center
Dallas, TX 75225
(214) 361-4207
Manager: Susan Davis
Shoe chain.

Foley's
303 N. Akard St.
Dallas, TX 75201
(214) 749-2020
Sr. Vice President of Human Resources: George Wilson
Retail department store with several area locations.

Fox Photo
7300 Ambassador Row
Dallas, TX 75247
(214) 631-6700
Contact: Personnel
Photo and film processing chain.

Foxworth-Galbraith Lumber Co.
17111 Waterview Pkwy.
Dallas, TX 75252
(214) 437-6100
Personnel Manager: Howard Mayer
Lumber and building materials.

Freed Furniture Showcase
4355 LBJ Frwy.
Dallas, TX 75234
(214) 233-6871
Personnel Director: Howard Freed
Large furniture retailer.

Freeman Olds/Mazda
1800 E. Airport Frwy
Irving, TX 75062
(214) 438-2121
Contact: Department Heads
Automobile dealership.

Friendly Chevrolet
5601 Lemmon Ave.
Dallas, TX 75209
(214) 526-8811
Controller: Mitch Buckovich
Automobile dealership.

Gordon's Jewelry Corp.
1609 Main St.
Dallas, TX 75201
(214) 742-8791
Manager: Ron Harding
Retailer for jewelry, gift items, and other specialty merchandise.

Half-Price Books
5915 E. Northwest Hwy.
Dallas, TX 75231
(214) 363-8374
Manager: Jan Cornelius or Sharon Anderson
New and used bookstore that also sells records, tapes, and collectibles.

Handy Dan Do-It-Yourself Home Center
15765 Hillcrest Rd.
Dallas, TX 75248
(214) 233-8454
Store Manager: Linda Cunningham
Retail hardware chain with housewares, paint, building materials, electrical and plumbing supplies, and garden center.

Haverty's Furniture
4552 Simonton Rd.
Dallas, TX 75234
(214) 661-9898
Contact: Department Head
Furniture store operating in the Dallas area since 1885.

Highland Appliance Co.
5101 Highland Place
Dallas, TX 75236
(214) 780-5300
Human Resources Manager: Mark Groeneman
Discount household appliances.

Charlie Hillard, Inc.
1400 S. University Dr.
Fort Worth, TX 76107
(817) 336-9811
Contact: Ray Brown for office positions or Bob Brazil for sales positions.
Automobile dealership.

Home Interiors & Gifts, Inc.
4550 Spring Valley Rd.
Dallas, TX 75244
(214) 386-1000
Personnel Director: James Johnson
Decorative accessories sold through home demonstrations.

Horchow Collections
13800 Diplomat Rd.
Dallas, TX 75234
(214) 888-9700
Personnel: Winnie Magoba
Home furnishings, gifts, clothing, and mail order company.

Jim Johnson Chevyland
800 N. Central Expwy.
Richardson, TX 75083
(214) 234-8811
Personnel Director: Eva Thomas
Automobile dealership.

Jones-Blair Co.
2728 Empire Central Dr.
Dallas, TX 75235
(214) 353-1600
Sales Manager: Bob Asbill
Paints and home improvements.

Joske's of Dallas
1901 Main St.
Dallas, TX 75201
(214) 749-1029
Personnel Director: Jerry Hall
Major department store with more than a dozen branches.

K Mart Discount Stores
703 S. Industrial Blvd.
Euless, TX 76040
(817) 354-3700
Personnel Director: J. P. Daley
Discount store with several area locations.

Frank Kent Cadillac, Inc.
3800 Southwest Blvd.
Fort Worth, TX 76116
(817) 763-5000
Personnel Director: Robert Warren
Automobile dealership.

Levine's
511 W. Jefferson Blvd.
Dallas, TX 75208
(214) 948-7396
Store Manager: J. C. Nichols
Retail clothing.

Lord & Taylor
450 NorthPark Shopping Center
Dallas, TX 75225
(214) 691-6600
Personnel Director: Beverly Amaker
Specialty department store.

Marshall Fields
13550 N. Dallas Pkwy.
Dallas, TX 75240
(214) 851-1000
Personnel Director: Bea Vercammen
Retail department store.

Mary Kay Cosmetics
8787 Stemmons Frwy.
Dallas, TX 75247
(214) 630-8787
Personnel: Betty Bessler
International headquarters for cosmetics sold through home demonstrations.

David McDavid Pontiac, Inc.
3700 W. Airport Frwy.
Irving, TX 75062
(214) 790-6000
Business Manager: Paul Tyson
Automobile dealership.

Mervyns Department Stores
1600 E. Plano Pkwy.
Plano, TX 75074
(214) 578-9536
Personnel Director: Sandi Harmon
Softgoods department store.

Michaels Stores, Inc.
9015 Sterling St.
Irving, TX 75063
(214) 929-8595
District Manager: Vernon Lacour
Arts, crafts, and framing store.

Miller Business Systems, Inc.
912 113th St.
Arlington, TX 76011
(817) 649-1313
Human Resources Director: John Andrews
Office supplies and furniture.

Mitchells/Myers Department Stores
318 E. Long St.
Fort Worth, TX 76106
(817) 626-3726
Personnel Director: Linda Hardy
Corporate headquarters for retail clothing and housewares chain.

Monnig's Department Stores
500 Houston St.
Fort Worth, TX 76102
(817) 332-7211
Personnel Director: Barbara Glover
Retail department store with several Fort Worth branches.

Montgomery Ward & Co.
2600 W. 7th St.
Fort Worth, TX 76107
(817) 336-1170
Personnel Manager: Georgia Lewis
National mass market retail chain.

M.E. Moses
2919 Hansboro Ave.
Dallas, TX 75233
(214) 331-6501
Personnel Manager: Jerry Daniels
Variety store chain.

Neiman-Marcus
1618 Main St.
Dallas, TX 75201
(214) 741-6911
Executive Personnel Department: Rudd Johnson
Major national specialty store with several area locations.

Oshman's Sporting Goods, Inc.
4554 McEwen Rd.
Dallas, TX 75234
(214) 458-2940
Personnel: Keith Reed
Retail sporting goods chain.

Page Drug
General Offices
14303 Inwood Rd.
Dallas, TX 75244
(214) 661-9700
Vice President of Personnel: Mike Kissner
Drug store and pharmacy chain.

Frank Parra Chevrolet
1000 E. Airport Frwy.
Irving, TX 75062
(214) 579-1111
Contact: Sales Manager
Automobile dealership.

Payless Cashways Building Materials
4803 Belt Line Rd.
Addison, TX 75001
(214) 233-1096
Contact: Personnel
Discount home building materials and lumber.

Pearle Health Services
2534 Royal Ln.
Dallas, TX 75229
(214) 241-3381
Contact: Personnel
Retail eyewear.

J. C. Penney Company, Inc.
12700 Park Central Dr.
Dallas, TX 75251
(214) 387-6093
Personnel Director: Frances Tackett
National retail merchandise sales and service stores with several area locations.

Pier 1 Imports
301 Commerce St., Suite 600
Fort Worth, TX 76102
(817) 878-8000
Vice President of Human Resources: Mitch Weatherly
Imported merchandise with several area stores.

Radio Shack
500 One Tandy Ctr.
Fort Worth, TX 76102
(817) 390-3011
Personnel Director: George Berger
National headquarters for retailer of electronic equipment and computers.

Working for one of America's largest retailers

Here's an opportunity to see the world and work for one of America's largest retailers—the Army Air Force Exchange Service.

AAFES's international headquarters is located in Dallas, where more than 2,000 civilian employees work. Staff members have the option of remaining on U.S. military bases or transferring to any of AAFES's Army or Air Force units throughout the world—from Germany to Japan.

One advantage of working for AAFES is an opportunity for young people to move up quickly and assume greater responsibility, says Jeri Session, personnel clerk and recruiter. There are more than 70,000 positions worldwide that include working in retail stores, restaurants, and movie theaters.

When Session selects an employee, she says, "I look for someone who is outgoing, able to work under pressure, and enthusiastic about work. It helps to be career-oriented."

Session says competition for the jobs is stiff. She keeps clerical applications on file for three months and manager candidates are considered for six months.

Those applying for managerial, clerical, and warehouse work should go to the headquarter's Application Center located at 3911 S. Walton Walker Blvd.■

Regency Lincoln Mercury
11810 E. Northwest Hwy.
Dallas, TX 75218
(214) 328-4371
Personnel: Lydia Kiefer
Automobile dealership.

Revco Discount Drug Center
Regional Office
125 Plymouth Park Shopping Cntr.
Irving, TX 75061
(214) 923-1100
Contact: Personnel
Discount drug store and pharmacy chain.

Royal International
2760 Irving Blvd.
Dallas, TX 75207
(214) 638-1397
Assistant Corporate Secretary: Ann Houchin
Retail eyewear.

Saks Fifth Avenue
13250 Dallas Pkwy.
Dallas, TX 75240
(214) 458-7000
Personnel Director: Kris Phenson
Specialty department store.

Sears, Roebuck & Co.
5334 Ross Ave.
Dallas, TX 75206
(214) 841-2301
Personnel Director: Craig Hibbison
One of world's largest retailers and catalog services with subsidiaries in insurance and real estate. Several area locations.

Service Merchandise
Prestonwood Junction Center
5294 Belt Line Rd.
Dallas, TX 75240
(214) 233-7040
Manager: Steve Rish
Discount jewelry and variety store with catalog service.

Sewell Village Cadillac, Inc.
7310 Lemmon Ave.
Dallas, TX 75209
(214) 350-2000
Controller: Paul Morgan
Automobile dealership.

Sherwin-Williams Co.
10440 E. Northwest Hwy.
Dallas, TX 75238
(214) 349-9063
Personnel Director: Tom Hopkins
Retail and wholesale paint, wallpaper, and floor covering.

Sound Warehouse
5425 Greenville Ave.
Dallas, TX 75206
(214) 692-9750
Contact: Store Manager
One of area's largest record and tape chains.

Stephenson Motor Co.
4023 Oak Lawn Ave.
Dallas, TX 75219
(214) 526-8701
Personnel Director: Lynn Killam
Automobile dealership.

Sterling Jewelry & Distributing Co.
5801 E. Northwest Hwy.
Dallas, TX 75231
(214) 363-4551
Personnel: Mervin Isaacson
Discount jewelry and department store.

Stewart Office Supply Co.
400 S. Austin St.
Dallas, TX 75202
(214) 747-8581
Contact: Personnel
Office supplies and furniture.

Stripling & Cox
6370 Camp Bowie Blvd.
Fort Worth, TX 76116
(817) 738-7361
Contact: Store Manager
Department store with seven area locations.

Sunbelt Nursery Group
500 Terminal Rd.
Fort Worth, TX 76106
(817) 624-7253
Personnel Management Director: Steve Rushton
Retail garden centers and nurseries.

Suzanne's Shops, Inc.
8811 John W. Carpenter Frwy.
Dallas, TX 75247
(214) 637-5041
Personnel Director: Jill Womack
Women's discount dress shop chain.

Tandy Leather
3250 W. Seminary Dr.
Fort Worth, TX 76133
(817) 927-7519
Vice President: Jerry Roy
Home office for leather and leather-working tools.

Taylors, Inc.
5455 Belt Line Rd.
Dallas, TX 75240
Metro (214) 988-1500
Contact: Individual store managers
Large bookstore with several area locations.

True Value Hardware
4121 W. Jefferson Blvd.
Dallas, TX 75211
(214) 337-6213
Manager: Dave Allen
One of the nation's largest hardware chains.

Tuesday Morning, Inc.
14621 Inwood Rd.
Dallas, TX 75244
(214) 387-3562
Personnel: Debra Steerod
Discount linens, towels, and other household merchandise.

Vandergriff Chevrolet Co.
901 E. Division St.
Arlington, TX 76010
(817) 265-8231
Personnel Manager: Warren Leake
Automobile dealership.

Waldenbooks, Inc.
1084 Prestonwood Town Center
5301 Belt Line Rd.
Dallas, TX 75240
(817) 640-3142
Contact: Jim Crockett in Dallas (214) 385-8451 or Lisa Horlbeck in Fort Worth (817) 589-0569
National retail bookstore chain.

Westgate Fabrics
1000 Fountain Pkwy.
Grand Prairie, TX 75050
(817) 647-2323
Personnel Manager: Phyllis Isbell
Wholesale distributor of drapery and upholstery.

Jack Williams Automall
9101 Hwy. 80 West
Fort Worth, TX 76116
Metro (817) 429-0297
Personnel: Sue Santos
Automobile dealership.

James K. Wilson
Service Center
2503 Butler St.
Dallas, TX 75235
(214) 638-6350
Human Resources Director: Ron Chally, 6525 Jimmy Carter Blvd., Northcross, GA 30071
Men's and women's clothing store chain.

Zale Corporation
Employment Center: 901 W. Walnut Hill Ln.
Irving, TX 75038-1003
(214) 580-4161
Staffing Director: Mark Wichern
Home office for retail jewelry stores with some 1,350 outlets in 49 states.

▶Sports, recreation, and fitness

Three top trade publications covering the **leisure** industry are:

Parks and Recreation
Sporting Goods Dealer
Sporting Goods Trade

For additional information, you can write to:

National Recreation & Parks Association
3101 Park Center Dr.
Alexandria, VA 22302

National Sporting Goods Association
1699 Wall St.
Mt. Prospect, IL 60096

World Leisure and Recreation Association
345 E. 46th St.
New York, NY 10017

Directories:
Directory of Human Resources in Health, Physical Education and Recreation (ERIC Clearing House on Teacher Education, Washington, DC)
Sports Administration Guide and Directory (National Sports Marketing Bureau, New York, NY)

Bent Tree Country Club
5201 Westgrove Dr.
Dallas, TX 75248
(214) 931-7326
Contact: Personnel
Private country club.

Brookhaven Country Club
3333 Golfing Green Dr.
Dallas, TX 75234
(214) 243-6151
Personnel Director: Deborah Seay
Private country club.

The Charlie Club
117 S. Watson Rd.
Arlington, TX 76010
Metro (817) 633-4000
Personnel Director: Shirley Snider
Fitness center.

Colonial Country Club
3735 Country Club Cir.
Fort Worth, TX 76109
(817) 927-4200
Personnel Director: Colleen McGrath
Private country club.

The Cooper Clinic Aerobics Center
12100 Preston Rd.
Dallas, TX 75230
(214) 239-7223
Personnel Director: Windy Buechlee
Fitness center.

Cosmopolitan Lady
16801 Addison Rd., Suite 150
Dallas, TX 75248
(214) 654-1201
Personnel Director: Rita Grether
Fitness center.

Dallas Country Club
4100 Beverly Dr.
Dallas, TX 75205
(214) 521-2151
Controller: Paul Ditto
Private country club.

Dallas Cowboys
One Cowboy Pkwy.
Irving, TX 75063
(214) 556-9900
Business Manager: Dan Werner
Headquarters for professional football team.

Dallas Mavericks
777 Sports St.
Dallas, TX 75207
(214) 748-1808
Controller: Jim Livingston
Headquarters for professional basketball team.

Dallas Sidekicks
6116 N. Central Expwy., Suite 1212
Dallas, TX 75206
(214) 691-3676
Assistant General Manager: Bill Walker
Headquarters for professional soccer team.

Exchange Athletic Club
700 N. Harwood St., Lock Box 11
Dallas, TX 75201
(214) 698-1091
Assistant Manager: Scott Lacroix
Fitness center.

Fitness Unlimited
2227 Hollandale St.
Farmers Branch, TX 75234
(214) 484-6629
Personnel Director: Sabrina Smith
Corporate headquarters for fitness center.

International Athletic Club of North Dallas
13701 Dallas Pkwy.
Dallas, TX 75240
(214) 458-2582
Personnel Director: Tom Todd
Fitness center.

Las Colinas Country Club
4900 N. O'Connor Rd.
Irving, TX 75062
(214) 255-1141
Manager: Ed Schweykowski
Private country club.

Mademoiselle Figure & Fitness Center
1701 N. Greenville Ave., Suite 400
Richardson, TX 75081
(214) 234-5901
Area Manager: Bryan Hacay
Fitness center.

President's Health and Racquetball Clubs
13714 Gamma Rd.
Dallas, TX 75224
(214) 239-7190
Personnel Director: Rena Reser
Fitness center.

Prestonwood Country Club
15909 Preston Rd.
Dallas, TX 75248
(214) 239-7111
General Manager: Bob Huffman
Private country club.

Racquetball Health Resort International
2711 LBJ Frwy.
Dallas, TX 75234
Metro (214) 498-4417
Personnel Director: Debbie Spath
Fitness center.

Ridglea Country Club
3700 Bernie Anderson Ave.
Fort Worth, TX 76116
(817) 732-8111
Manager: Felix Pastore
Private country club.

Riverbend Athletic Club
2201 E. Loop 820 North
Fort Worth, TX 76118
(817) 284-3353
General Manager: Ed Ghanami
Fitness center.

Texas Rangers
1250 Copeland Rd., Suite 1100
Arlington, TX 76011
(817) 273-5222
Contact: Department Head
Headquarters for professional baseball team.

University Club of Dallas/Galleria
13350 Dallas Pkwy., Suite 4000
Dallas, TX 75240
(214) 239-0050
Contact: Department Heads
Private club with restaurant and fitness center.

Willow Bend Polo & Hunt Club
Farm Rd. 544
Plano, TX 75074
(214) 248-6298
Public Relations: Cindy Brinker
Private country club.

Woodhaven Country Club
913 Country Club Ln.
Fort Worth, TX 76112
(817) 457-5150
Personnel Administrator: Renay Roark
Private country club.

YMCA/Metropolitan Branch
Dallas Headquarters
601 N. Akard St.
Dallas, TX 75201
(214) 954-0500
Personnel Director: Zera Mackie
Fitness center and special programs.

YMCA/Metropolitan Branch
Fort Worth Headquarters
540 Lamar St.
Fort Worth, TX 76102
(817) 335-6147
Personnel Director: Patsy Green
Fitness center and special programs.

▶Travel and shipping

To learn more about **travel and shipping,** check out the following professional organizations listed in Chapter 5:

Women's Traffic Club of Fort Worth
Women's Transportation Club of Dallas

For more information, you can write to:

Airline Pilots Association
1625 Massachusetts Ave., NW
Washington, DC 20036

Airline Services Association, and **Regional Airline Association**
1101 Connecticut Ave., NW, Suite 700
Washington, DC 20036

American Trucking Association
1616 P St., NW
Washington, DC 20036

Aviation Distributors & Manufacturers Association
1900 Arch St.
Philadelphia, PA 19103

Institute of Transportation Engineers
525 School St., SW
Washington, DC 20024

National Air Transport Association
1010 Wisconsin Ave., NW, Suite 405
Washington, DC 20007

Trade Publications:
AOPA Pilot
ASTA Travel News
Air Transport World
Aviation Week and Space Technology
Business and Commercial Aviation
Commercial Car Journal
Distribution
Fleet Owner
Frequent Flyer
Heavy Duty Trucking
Mass Transit
Railway Age
Traffic Management
Transportation Journal
Travel Agent

Directories:
Aviation Directory (E. A. Brennan Co., Garden Grove, CA)
Membership Directory, Aviation Distributors & Manufacturers Association (Philadelphia, PA)
Moody's Transportation Manual (Moody's Investor Services, Inc., New York, NY)
Travel Industry Personnel Directory (American Traveler, Inc., New York, NY)

ABF Freight Systems, Inc.
6814 Harry Hines Blvd.
Dallas, TX 75235
(214) 350-8901
Contact: Personnel
Common freight carrier.

Addison Airport
4505 Claire Chennault St.
Dallas, TX 75248
(214) 248-7733
Contact: Personnel
General aviation airport.

Airborne Express
Cargo Building B
Dallas/Fort Worth Airport, TX 75261
Metro (817) 574-5900
Contact: Personnel
Air freight company.

American Airlines, Inc.
4200 American Blvd.
Fort Worth, TX 76155
(817) 355-1234
Personnel: Barbara Landers
Passenger and air freight services.

American Mayflower Moving & Storage
2605 LBJ Frwy.
Dallas, TX 75234
(214) 241-3581
Office Manager: Donna Meeks
Moving and storage company.

Amtrak, National Railway Passenger Corp.
400 S. Houston St.
Dallas, TX 75202
(214) 653-1101
Contact: Texas Employment Commission
Passenger rail service.

Atchison, Topeka & Santa Fe Railway
1401 Jones St.
Fort Worth, TX 76102
(817) 878-1300
Write: Barbara Akins, 9th & Polk St., Amarillo, TX 79171
Freight-handling railway.

Avis Rent A Car
1 W. N. International Pkwy.
Dallas/Fort Worth Airport, TX 75261
(214) 574-4110
Personnel: Diane Everly
Automobile rentals.

Big State Freight Line, Inc.
2355 Stemmons Frwy., Suite 700
Dallas, TX 75207
(214) 630-6663
Personnel Manager: Stacia Bishop
Common freight carrier.

Braniff, Inc.
7701 Lemmon Ave.
Dallas, TX 75209
(214) 358-6011
Employment Manager: Jona Mills
Passenger airline service.

Budget Rent-A-Car Systems, Inc.
Parkway Plaza Building, Level 1
Dallas/Fort Worth Airport, TX 75261
Grapevine, TX 76051
Metro (817) 574-3300
Personnel: Chauncie LaRoe
Automobile and truck rentals.

Burlington Northern Railroad Co.
777 Main St.
Fort Worth, TX 76102
(817) 878-3031
Professional Recruiting Manager: Steve Klug
Freight transporter.

Central Freight Lines, Inc.
5200 E. Loop 820
Fort Worth, TX 76119
(817) 478-8211
Office Manager: Helen Holmes
Common freight carrier.

Jack Cooper Company
2909 E. Abram St.
Arlington, TX 76010
Metro (817) 640-0829
Terminal Manager: Jack Watkins
Automobile transporter.

Dallas/Fort Worth International Airport
Dallas/Fort Worth Airport, TX 75261
(214) 574-6720
Personnel Director: Bill Chiabotta
Major international airport.

Dallas Love Field
8008 Cedar Springs Rd., Rm. 210
Dallas, TX 75235
(214) 352-2663
Personnel Administrative Assistant: Cathy Wilkins
Public airport for commercial and private carriers.

Dallas Transit System
101 N. Peak St.
Dallas, TX 75226
(214) 828-6700
Contact: Personnel
Dallas public transportation system.

Delta Air Lines, Inc.
8700 N. Stemmons Frwy., Suite 212
Dallas, TX 75247
(214) 920-3211
Reservations and Sales Assistant Manager: Marilyn Holmes
Passenger and air freight services.

Frozen Food Express Industries, Inc.
318 Cadiz St.
Dallas, TX 75207
(214) 428-7661
Personnel Manager: Florence Ward
Transporter of general commodities sold in grocery, discount, and department stores.

Gelco Travel Service
1112 E. Copeland Rd., Suite 200
Arlington, TX 76011
(817) 461-9551
Contact: Personnel
Corporate travel services.

The Hertz Corp.
275 W. Campbell Rd.
Dallas, TX 75080
(214) 783-0943
Employee Relations Manager: Robert Salmon
Automobile renting and leasing.

Working in the wild blue yonder

Tens of thousands of men and women apply each year for flight attendant positions at American Airlines. So what are your chances of landing one of these plums?

They're good if you possess the qualities Recruitment Manager Kathy Blair looks for in applicants.

"The airline industry has changed so much that this job isn't for everyone," Blair says. "It's very fast-paced and flight attendants are required to deal with a variety of people. These customers expect a lot and we promise it. You need to be very flexible, must cope with a varied work schedule, and you might wake up in a different city each day."

As for looks, Blair says, "You must be well groomed, but we aren't for cookie-cutter people. We are looking inwardly for individuals who truly care about giving service and selling the company. More and more, our flight attendants are becoming in-flight salespeople. They spend more time with the customer than anyone else."

American Airlines can be selective in who is hired because of its low turnover. "We see lots of wonderful people, but the number of positions we have open is very limited," Blair says.

As for basic requirements, applicants must be at least 20 years old and have a high school education or GED. Two years of work experience, preferably in positions that require contact with the public, or the same amount of time in college, is a plus, Blair says. She says people often ask what type of education is most helpful, and she believes a liberal arts background is one of the best because of the exposure to a broad range of subjects.

Finalists are carefully screened. They are required to write an essay to determine their writing skills. And they are evaluated during group interviews on how well they interact with strangers, to determine their poise, sensitivity, maturity, and warmth, Blair says.

Their weight and height are checked to make sure they fulfill safety requirements of being between 5-feet-2 and 6-feet tall. Weight must be proportionate to height. Candidates must also take a company physical, and pass an eye exam to make sure their vision is at least 20-50 in both eyes.

Those who are accepted for the program attend a 5½-week training course at the American Airlines Learning Center, located several miles south of Dallas/Fort Worth International Airport on Highway 360.

To apply for a position, write American Airlines Flight Service Recruitment, P.O. Box 619410, Mail Drop 908, Dallas/Fort Worth Airport, TX 75261-9410.■

IVI Travel, Inc.
7800 Stemmons Frwy., Suite 800
Dallas, TX 75247
(214) 688-0974
Personnel and Training Director: Tina Oller
Travel service.

Intertrans Corporation
1930 W. Airfield Dr., Cargo Bldg. D
Dallas/Fort Worth Airport, TX 75261
(214) 574-6750
District Manager: Sam Kuykendall
International transportation.

Metro Airlines, Inc.
8505 Freeport Pkwy.
Irving, TX 75063-2548
(214) 929-3400
Personnel: Lisa Grover
Airline passenger and cargo service.

Missouri-Kansas-Texas Railroad Co.
701 Commerce St.
Dallas, TX 75202
(214) 651-6700
Personnel Director: H. M. Hacker
Headquarters for freight railroad operating in a four-state area.

North Texas Lines, Inc.
710 E. Davis St.
Grand Prairie, TX 75050
(214) 263-0294
Vice President: Bob Prince
College and university transportation.

Southern Greyhound Bus Lines, Inc.
205 S. Lamar St.
Dallas, TX 75202
(214) 747-8093
Manager: Jim Smith
Regional division of a national bus line.

Southwest Airlines
8008 Aviation Place
Dallas, TX 75235
(214) 353-6100
Personnel Manager: David Carroll
Headquarters for interstate airline.

State Taxicab Co.
1231 E. Illinois Ave.
Dallas, TX 75216
(214) 823-2161
Supervisor: Essie Williams
Taxi company.

Sunbelt Motivation & Travel, Inc.
104 Decker Dr., Suite 300
Dallas, TX 75062
(214) 258-0317
Personnel Manager: D'ann Hardy
Travel service.

The T–Fort Worth Transportation Authority
2304 Pine St.
Fort Worth, TX 76102
(817) 870-6200
Personnel Supervisor: Ruth Lyon
Fort Worth's public transportation service.

Terminal Cab Co.
6303 Cedar Springs Rd.
Dallas, TX 75235
(214) 352-8421
Personnel Director: Ken Lott
Taxi company.

Trailways Lines, Inc.
13760 Noel Rd., Suite 620
Dallas, TX 75240
(214) 770-8500
Human Resources Senior Director: Rick Lesko
Bus lines.

Union Pacific Railroad Co.
505 N. Industrial Blvd.
Dallas, TX 75207
(214) 760-2050
Contact: R. H. Rockwell, Drawer M, Spring, TX 77383, (713) 350-4100
Freight-handling railroad.

Yellow Cab of Dallas, Inc.
1610 S. Ervay St.
Dallas, TX 75215
(214) 565-9132
Treasurer and Office Manager: Bob Hutto
Taxi company.

Utilities

For more information about public **utilities,** you can write to:

American Public Power Association
2301 M St., NW
Washington, DC 20037

Institute of Public Utilities
113 Olds Hall
Michigan State University
East Lansing, MI 48824

National Utility Contractor's Association
1235 Jefferson Davis Hwy.
Arlington, VA 22202

Utilities Telecommunications Council
1150 17th St., NW, Suite 1000
Washington, DC 20036

Trade publications
Electric Light and Power
Electrical World
Public Utilities
Public Utilities Fortnightly
Telecommunications Retailer

Directories:
Directory of Communications Management (Applied Computer Research, Phoenix, AZ)
Moody's Public Utility Manual (Moody's Investor Service, Inc., New York, NY)
Telephone Association Telecommunications Sourcebook (North American Telephone Association, Washington, DC)

AT&T Corporation
2777 Stemmons Frwy., Suite 1425
Dallas, TX 75207
(214) 879-1800
Personnel Manager: Paul Cadmus
Supplier of communication services and equipment.

Central and South West Corporation
2121 San Jacinto St., Suite 2500
Dallas, TX 75201
(214) 754-1000
Vice President of Employee Relations: Wayne Stice
Public utility holding company with four electric subsidiary companies.

Continental Telephone Company of Texas
10300 N. Central Expwy.
Dallas, TX 75231
(214) 369-1121
Contact: Personnel
Regional office for telephone company.

Dallas Power & Light Co.
1506 Commerce St.
Dallas, TX 75201
(214) 698-7000
Personnel Manager: Roy Bench
Public electric utility that serves Dallas.

General Telephone Co. of the Southwest
3500 N. Belt Line Rd.
Irving, TX 75062
(214) 256-7616
Human Resources Manager: Bill Eller
Telephone company that serves Irving, Grapevine, Keller, Carrollton, Garland, Azle, and the Dallas/Fort Worth Airport.

Lone Star Gas Co.
Dallas Office
301 S. Harwood St.
Dallas, TX 75201
(214) 741-3711
Personnel Manager: Robert Parish
Headquarters for one of the largest natural gas transmission and distribution companies. Serves Texas and a portion of Oklahoma.

Lone Star Gas Co.
Fort Worth Office
908 Monroe St.
Fort Worth, TX 76102
(817) 336-8381
Personnel Manager: A. Z. Drone
Natural gas transmission and distribution company.

Southern Union Co.
1800 Renaissance Tower
Dallas, TX 75270
(214) 748-8511
Contact: Personnel
Natural gas exploration, production, and distribution.

Southwestern Bell Telephone Co.
Dallas Office
308 S. Akard St., Three Bell Plaza, Rm. 101
Dallas, TX 75202
(214) 464-3171
Contact: Personnel
Telephone service.

Southwestern Bell Telephone Co.
Fort Worth Office
1116 Houston St., Rm. 105
Fort Worth, TX 76102
(817) 338-6411
Employment Office Manager: Janita Jennings

Southwestern Electric Service Co.
1310 MBank Bldg.
Dallas, TX 75201
(214) 741-3125
Office Manager: Glenn Hibbs
Purchase, transmission, distribution, and sale of electric energy.

TNP Enterprises, Inc.
4100 International Plaza
Fort Worth, TX 76109
(817) 731-0099
Employment and Training Coordinator: Vikki Teague
Holding company for utility and diversified operations.

Texas Electric Service Co.
115 W. 7th St.
Fort Worth, TX 76102
(817) 336-9411
Personnel Director: Don Hampton
Texas Utilities Co. subsidiary that generates and sells electricity in Texas.

Texas Power & Light Co.
1511 Bryan St.
Dallas, TX 75201
(214) 954-5000
Personnel Director: John Prickette
Headquarters for electric utility company that provides service in 51 Texas counties.

Texas Utilities Co.
2001 Bryan Tower, Suite 1600
Dallas, TX 75201
(214) 653-4600
Employment Supervisor: Bob Corley
Headquarters for holding company whose utility subsidiaries include Dallas Power & Light, Texas Electric Service Co., and Texas Power & Light.

Tri-County Electric Cooperative, Inc.
600 Northwest Pkwy.
Azle, TX 76020
(817) 444-3201
Contact: Department Head
Headquarters for electric co-op that serves cities in seven North Central Texas counties.

INDEX

D

E

U

V

W

Y